RACE WOMAN

GERALD HORNE

RACE WOMAN

The Lives of Shirley Graham Du Bois

New York University Press • *New York and London*

NEW YORK UNIVERSITY PRESS
New York and London

Library of Congress Cataloging-in-Publication Data
Horne, Gerald.
Race woman : the lives of Shirley Graham Du Bois / Gerald Horne.
p.   cm.
Includes bibliographical references (p.   ) and index.
ISBN 0-8147-3615-7 (alk. paper)
1. Du Bois, Shirley Graham, 1906–1977. 2. Afro-American
women—Biography. 3. Afro-Americans—Biography. 4. Afro-American
women political activists—Biography. 5. Afro-American women authors—
Biography. 6. Du Bois, W. E. B. (William Edward Burghardt), 1868–1963.
7. Afro-Americans—Politics and government—20th century. 8. Afro-Americans—
Intellectual life—20th century.   I. Title.
E185.97.D69 H67 2000
305.48'896073'0092—dc21   00-008809

Contents

All illustrations appear in two groups following p. 112 and p. 208.

Acknowledgments

This book had its origins in a chance encounter on a mid-Manhattan street in the late summer of 1993. I had just left the offices of the radio station WBAI when I bumped into David Du Bois, whom I had known as a result of my earlier research on the life of W. E. B. Du Bois. As we were chatting he mentioned casually that the papers of his mother, Shirley Graham Du Bois, were in his apartment in Cairo. I asked how large the collection was and he indicated that it was substantial. Immediately, I made plans to visit there in December 1993, which I did, laptop in tow. Throughout this project David has been extremely generous in providing me with insight, counsel, and hospitality. Thanks to David, his mother's papers will soon be housed in an archive in the United States.

Traveling to Cairo was the beginning of a journey that eventually took me to libraries at Georgetown, Howard, Oberlin, Stanford, Columbia, Fisk, Tulane, the University of Michigan, Wayne State University, New York University, and the University of Texas. Librarians and archivists there and at the Library of Congress, National Archives, Schomburg Center for Research in Black Culture, Hoover Institute, Indiana Historical Society, National Archives of Ghana, Niebyl-Procter Library, and the Reference Center for Marxist Studies all proved to be exceedingly helpful. I thank them all.

My original visit to Egypt was subsidized by the Center for Black Studies at the University of California–Santa Barbara, and part of my research was also supported by the Institute of African-American Research at the University of North Carolina–Chapel Hill. Librarians at both of these institutions provided enormous assistance in retrieving books and articles through interlibrary loan and other means.

I profited immensely from exchanges with a number of scholars and intellectuals, including Ernest Allen, Martha Biondi, Carole Boyce-Davies, John Bracey, Annie Chamberlin, Barbara Foley, Kevin Gaines, Paula Giddings, James Hatch, Mae Henderson, Savi Horne, Tera

Hunter, Bernard Jaffe, James and Esther Jackson, Oliver Jones, Chana Kai Lee, D. Sonyini Madison, Louis Massiah, Henry and Roselyn Richardson, Abbott Simon, Ula Taylor, Penny von Eschen, Alan Wald, Michael West, and Mary and Chris Young.

From infancy the strongest influences on me have been my mother and my three sisters. They merit my most profound thanks for helping me shape this book and, indeed, accomplish virtually everything I have done in life.

Preface

Shirley Graham Du Bois was born in the United States in 1896 and died in China in 1977. During her event-filled life, this diminutive, light brown–skinned woman with a broad gray streak in her hair was variously a composer, playwright, actress, drummer, biographer, editor, novelist, and political activist. However, the zenith of her life may have been the time she spent in the 1960s—after the death of her spouse, W. E. B. Du Bois—as a pivotal advisor and official in the government of Kwame Nkrumah's Ghana. Despite this shining list of accomplishments, for which she should be considered one of the leading black women intellectual activists of this or any other century, the life of Shirley Graham Du Bois has been cloaked in obscurity, at least since her death. An examination of her life not only brings back from oblivion an intriguing figure, it also sheds light on the ever important questions of blacks and cultural production, blacks and the Left, Pan-Africanism, blacks and U.S. foreign policy, blacks and feminism, and, not least, W. E. B. Du Bois himself.

She was a mercurial and creative person, who played fast and loose in recounting the details of her own life[1] and in writing her popular biographies. She was a protean personality who also happened to be prodigiously productive, often darting from one project to the next; this did not leave much time for ruminations about her life. She was not terribly self-reflective, and even when she engaged in introspection, she was as likely as not to manufacture this or that detail in order to conform to a societal expectation or other predilection. These swirling, ever changing facets of her life often make it difficult to get a firm handle on basic questions for the biographer: Who was she? How did she come to be who she was?[2]

Not least because she occasionally fudged the details of her life and was averse to introspection, reconstructing the life of Shirley Graham Du Bois provides a real challenge to a biographer. Her peremptory dismissal of the virtues of the self-examined life was

I

even more evident when she returned to the United States in the early 1970s after a decade of exile in Africa. She noted with disdain a "cult of psychoanalysis" that she associated with "white people." With disgust she linked this tendency toward private introspection with what she saw as a flight from public responsibility, for example, the responsibility to aggressively confront U.S. foreign policy in Vietnam and elsewhere.[3] Not surprisingly, it is easier for the biographer to uncover evidence of her public stances and maddeningly difficult to reconstruct her private self.

This may be true of many biographical subjects, but the problem has been complicated further here because of her deliberate obfuscation of the simplest details of her life. For example, she claimed that her first husband, whom she left in the 1920s after bearing two children, died. This was not accurate: he lived on after their breakup. Why she divorced—or, for that matter, why she married—remains unclear. This is one of many examples that could easily lead to the conclusion that she was as creative in devising her own character as she was in devising the characters in her plays and stories.

On the other hand, there were understandable reasons for her parsimony with the truth. At the time, not only was divorce frowned on, but marriage itself was seen as questionable for those women like Graham who opted to pursue careers. In the state of her birth, Indiana, "one black schoolteacher . . . confided that she never married, although she had been asked, because in the 1930s and 1940s"—and even more so in the 1920s—"to have done so would have cost her the position." The prevailing ideology of "racial uplift," which suggested that an educated and talented woman like Graham[4] was responsible through the force of personal example for the "advancement of the race and the uplift of black womanhood," at times imposed a corresponding standard of "morality" that was difficult to meet. Divorce and single motherhood, for example, were not viewed as exemplary.[5] Hence, is it fairer to say that Graham was frugal with the facts or that societal norms pushed her in this direction?

Or consider her sojourn in Ghana, where many—notably non-Ghanaians—considered her imperious and officious. Strikingly, these descriptions of her did not arise so forcefully and consistently until she arrived in Africa. Was officiousness an organic aspect of her personality, or was this perception of her grounded in the reality that many—male and female alike—had difficulty accepting and dealing with a woman who wielded real power in a West African society that had not rejected male supremacy altogether? Or did societal norms compel her to assume that her marriage to a renowned figure like Du Bois necessitated a shift in how she presented herself?

Or consider her list of accomplishments. When white-owned stores in Harlem during the Great Depression were forced to hire African American women, a controversy arose immediately when these establishments hired "only light skinned women."[6] When the sardonic black novelist George Schuyler penned his insightful volume *Black No More,* he included a character reputedly based on W. E. B. Du Bois—"Dr. Shakespeare Agamemnon Beard"—who "bitterly denounced the Nordics for debauching Negro women while taking care to hire comely yellow stenographers with weak resistance."[7] In retrospect, it is difficult to reconstruct to what extent Graham's rise was based not only on her considerable talents but also on the detritus of "white supremacy," that is, certain privileges that were extended intermittently on the basis of color. At this late date, who is to say that the vast confidence she displayed was buoyed by a secure childhood or a doting parent's influence or something more difficult to determine, like color privilege? Interestingly, through most of her life she continued to search far and wide for "Inecto Colour Crème," which she used to maintain her skin tone. In short, responding to the rudimentary question, "Who was she and how did she come to be who she was?" is difficult to do absent some consideration of the even more basic question, "What kind of society was she living in?"

Graham Du Bois, in any case, can be said to reflect a kind of "standpoint epistemology"; the identity she assumed and the positions that accompanied it were often shaped or determined by the situation she was in; her identity and, at times, her politics often were mediated by her location at a particular moment. It has not been unusual, according to some analysts, for African American women particularly to assume various identities serially, even simultaneously, in the interests of survival—their own and their families'.[8] "Inventing" or "reinventing" identity was not something peculiar to Graham Du Bois.[9]

Consider the various stages of her life: dutiful daughter, unhappy spouse, hardworking student at Oberlin College, struggling artist, accomplished writer, dutiful spouse (to Du Bois), powerful politico, political exile. Each of these stages, which at certain points overlapped, required her to display a rich palette of personality traits; each could be deemed a discrete identity, though there were traits that were hardly exclusive to one and not others. For example, the steely dedication she needed to get through Oberlin was similar to the dedication required to be an artist or to survive as a hardworking official in a tormented Accra government.

Graham Du Bois was a talented performer, and this skill too was fungible. "Putting on massa," "wearing a mask," or adopting a personality that was seen as necessary to avoid being brutalized or murdered in a society suffused with white supremacy was a trait developed over the centuries by Africans in North America.[10] What may have distinguished Graham Du Bois in this regard from her black contemporaries was that she studied performance and, as a partial result, was no bumbling amateur. The inevitable problem with assuming various identities, however, is that not only is it sometimes difficult for the biographer to pinpoint who the subject is, it is at times a problem for the subject herself.

When Nkrumah's government in Ghana was overthrown in 1966, her prized identity as a powerful politico was shattered. This, along with the harassment she suffered at the hands of the incoming military junta in Accra, fomented an existential crisis: so much of her psychological capital was invested in this now shattered identity that she was on the verge of a breakdown.

There are other problems involved in the biographer's attempt to reconstruct the interiors of her life. Because she obscured various details and disdained the virtues of the self-examined life, the attempt to comprehend her character often rests on the opinions of others who might not be disinterested parties. She was a controversial figure, given her pro-socialist, pro-Moscow, then pro-Beijing stances, and her notoriety attracted no small amount of envy. Ollie Harrington, Richard Wright's best friend during their exile in France, recalled that there was a "tight band of Americans who never tried to cloak their outright hatred of the great Negro writer. They would often attack Wright in the most insulting manner, referring to his books and his opinions with contempt . . . for the most part Americans [in Paris] viewed Wright with distaste." Harrington had difficulty understanding this raw venom, though arguably it was driven by a form of covetousness. Graham Du Bois, particularly in exile in Africa, was also subjected to bitter assaults that in retrospect seem motivated in no small part by rank jealousy colored by opposition to her politics.[11]

Nevertheless, there are fascinating clues that may provide further insight into her character. By her own admission her father, an abstemious pastor, was the defining influence on her life; she acted as a "mother" toward her own mother, who was frail and sickly. In the early stages of her life she identified closely with her accomplished father and had reason to resent her mother; for much of her life she frequently succumbed to the blandishments of powerful men and had few close women friends.

Yet with her early marriage and divorce and her choice of the bohemian career of creative artist, she defined herself in opposition to her father. Her relationship with her father, in sum, was qualitatively different from that with her mother and, in some ways, more complicated.[12] The point is—and this too is not unusual—he was an indelible, lifelong influence on her.

Three years before her death she confided that "he instilled in me at a very early age, a veneration of the Word, a kind of reverence for that which was recorded." He frequently read to her when she was a child; those times "shine as the happiest moments of my childhood days."[13] Her father "instilled" in her his own "inquiring and imaginative mind."[14] He impressed on her the strength of "the Word"; she learned early on that powerful words were like loaded pistols.

Her life reverberates with the profound influence of this man: she was a voracious reader and a prolific writer; she possessed a creative imagination that was manifested both in her writing and in the stories she wove about her own life. Her own brother termed her a "skillful liar"; certainly she was no slave to the truth.[15] This "skill" was a response to her father's strictness. She contrived ever more fanciful stories in order to escape his questioning grasp—and his wrath. This same "skill" also was fungible, and no doubt played a role in her talent for creating dialogue and other fictions.

Like many pastors, her father was also a humanitarian, and this too did not leave her unaffected; decades later she still had a vivid recollection of his bringing "every itinerant, shabby preacher to [the] house for dinner."[16] Just as she contributed her talents to Ghana, he did the same in Liberia. He faced down racists in the Deep South, while political activism consumed a great deal of her life.

Even her ability to make friends easily and readily may have been influenced by her father. He was something of an itinerant preacher, residing variously in Indiana, Louisiana, Colorado, and the Pacific

Northwest, not to mention West Africa. Moving from place to place meant that at an early age Shirley Graham had to learn how to adapt to new situations and new people regularly. Indeed, her own life, once again, mimicked his as she too was something of a roustabout, journeying from Paris to New York to Washington, D.C., to Tennessee to Illinois to Connecticut to Indiana to Arizona to Ghana to Egypt to China—and points in between.

This *movement,* which she inherited from her father, is also a useful metaphor for understanding her. Not only did she move geographically, she also moved quite a bit creatively, from operas to plays to biographies to novels. She also moved quite a bit politically, from a simple concern with racial uplift to the Communist Party-USA, not to mention Pan-Africanism and Maoism. This creative and ideological *search* was a reflection of her peripatetic youth and, likewise, a reflection of her various residences.

This movement, this search, placed her in a category apart from many of her contemporaries, in both the artistic and political realms. She was engaged not just with domestic politics and concerns but also global politics and concerns. Jim Crow in the United States was an insular, all-consuming reality; it was so oppressive and suffocating that by its very nature those who were ensnared by it often had neither the time nor the inclination to peer across the oceans. This was not unintentional, for seeking allies abroad was precisely what the Jim Crow rulers sought to deny African Americans.[17] Her ability to violate this basic norm not only differentiated her from many of her contemporaries but also made her more dangerous in the eyes of some. Similarly, while many of her peers were consumed with familial and other private matters, she was consumed with politics, the arts, and other public matters.

She knew well heads of state in Africa, Asia, and Eastern Europe—but not North America. Her socialist principles were transnational and, she felt, were equally applicable in the United States and elsewhere; of course, authorities in the United States vehemently disagreed, which is one of the many reasons she felt more comfortable abroad.

There was an intersection of the personal and political in her life. Her upbringing meant that abandoning home—actually or politically—held little terror for her; thus she was able to leave Brooklyn Heights for Accra, Ghana, in 1961 and West Africa for Cairo, Egypt, in 1966. Similarly, her move to New York City, the headquarters of the Communist Party, in the midst of World War II facilitated her decision to join this organization, which was enjoying a rare bout of popularity due to the wartime alliance between Moscow and Washington.[18] In the same sense, her move to Ghana facilitated the flowering of her Pan-Africanism, just as her frequent trips to and residences in China facilitated her attraction to Maoism. This fondness for movement, both physical and ideological, was in no small part a function of the household in which she was raised.

The influence of her father does not stop there. Throughout her life, she had a remarkable tendency to serve—even "mother"—powerful men even if this seemed to mean a decline in her own productivity and accomplishments. It would be easy to ascribe this to her relationship with her father. After all, she was the only daughter in her family; as such, she was compelled to play a role in rearing her younger brothers and in performing various household chores. Her desire to escape this domestic drudgery may have been a factor that pushed her toward marriage. On the other hand, we are back to the same question: to what extent is this trait of attaching herself to powerful men a reflection of her character or a reflection of a society in which men like W. E. B. Du Bois and Kwame Nkrumah held a disproportionate amount of influence and power, connection to which would allow her to advance aspects of her own agenda?

Even her fierce opposition to Jim Crow was colored by her domestic experiences. In 1910 the teenaged Shirley Graham was living with her family in Nashville. One day as she and her brother Lorenz were walking home from school, a white eighteen-year-old named Tom Bennett—a ruffian who despised blacks—hurled a rock at Lorenz that hit him in the head and drew blood from a deep gash. A stunned Shirley Graham did not flee but frantically carried her brother to a nearby house where she surmised she could get assistance. Her surmise proved to be incorrect. A white woman rushed to the door and screamed, "Don't bring him here, I don't want nigger blood in my yard!" Brusquely turned away, Graham sought to stanch the gush of blood with a piece of cloth as Lorenz noticeably weakened. By the time they arrived home, he was barely conscious. With her mother she attended to a now gaping wound as they awaited the arrival of a physician. When her father arrived, he was outraged. He sought to file charges against the assailant with the local police, but this proved unavailing in Jim Crow Tennessee, not least because Bennett was the scion of a well-known family.[19]

This episode sheds light on Shirley Graham's future trajectory: enduring a brutal encounter with racism, taking care of a male in need of assistance, being rejected by a "sister" wedded to the color line, being rebuffed by hostile authorities.

Thus, by the time she approached the prominent playwright Paul Green in 1940, she had learned quite well the conventions of race in the United States, which involved a Kabuki-like choreographed deference by African Americans. He was not a close friend, but he was an influential figure in the world of theater in which she was then enmeshed. Although she was in her mid-forties at the time, she introduced herself as a "colored girl." Green, though a liberal of sorts, was a resident of North Carolina, and Graham may have understandably felt that prevailing Jim Crow etiquette dictated such a posture.[20]

She told Green that she had "been in school"—at Yale—"earning nothing for these two years" while she perfected her skill in writing plays. She was all too aware "of the difficulties of getting a Negro play produced."[21] Perhaps he could help her, she asked. Obviously, Graham had reason to believe that there was not only an etiquette of Jim Crow but a protocol of male supremacy as well that dictated how men in Green's position should be approached when she needed assistance. Perhaps she felt that if she were to receive aid in getting her play produced, it would not be sensible to risk violating existing rules of protocol and etiquette. The larger point is that Graham was sailing in uncharted waters; there were few women of her race then—or sadly, now—who were writing and producing plays that aspired to Broadway. Those in a position to help her were almost all men. Thus, was her studied deference to Green a mere personality trait or the result of harsh experience with Jim Crow's codes of behavior? Were her attachments to potent men a personality trait or a function of the society in which she lived—or both? Was it an expression of a personality trait or a function of society that she chose to "mother" younger men, for example, the activist once known as Stokeley Carmichael or the young men at the military base in Arizona where she worked in the early stages of World War II?

Actually, her tendency to "mother" can be located both in her background and in the society in which she lived. After leaving her husband in the 1920s, she left her children with others and went off to make her mark in the world. Her grave concern about leaving her sons with others and keeping them away from their father was both intensely personal and a reflection of the societal opprobrium that attached to women who broke the traditional maternal mold.[22] Assuredly, her own immense productivity was a direct product of this concern about how her divorce impacted her two young sons: "everything I did," she explained, "everything I planned, everything I tried to do was motivated by my passionate desire to make a good life for my sons."[23]

She was marked irrevocably by this parental relationship; she walked with a slight limp that reputedly stemmed from an injury she suffered while giving birth to her first son, Robert. Ironically, the ideology of the private sphere—"maternalism"—drove her toward guilt about her inattention to her children, attentiveness to the needs of younger and older men alike, and immense productivity in the public sphere.

"Nurture" may be a more appropriate term to use in this context than "mother"; however, her relationships with these younger men were not matched by similar sustenance provided to younger women. Was this an outgrowth of her relationship with her mother?

Her marriage to Du Bois could also be viewed through a familial lens. The twenty-eight-year age gap between them, the political affinities he shared with her father, and related factors prompt the thought that her marriage was a reflection of her relationship with the Reverend David Graham. Her relationships with men later in life, in other words, were influenced by her earlier status as a daughter, then a parent.

It would be simplistic to view her life in some sort of teleological manner, whereby once one ascertains her relationship to her father or her sons or other men one can predict her every move from that point. Such an approach would not account altogether for the fact that she did not follow the route trod by many men as she moved steadily to the left as she grew older. Also, her leftward movement occurred as her economic fortunes improved, again in contrast to the experience of others. In addition, most blacks who joined the Communist Party either stayed with it as its numbers shrank or left Communism altogether; but few emulated her when she moved toward Maoism, an ideology born in China that became increasingly hostile to Moscow. On the other hand, it would be purblind to ignore the reality that her early years with her father and her ongoing relationship with her children were the crucible in which her persona was forged.

When she threw tact and diplomacy to the winds and chose to become friendly with the U.S. ambassador to Ghana at a time when this government was hostile to Nkrumah, was this a personality flaw or yet another reflection of her complicated relationship with men generally? This unfortunate dalliance is more difficult to rationalize. Since she was a high-level Ghanaian official, it was understandable why she would seek to use her preexisting U.S. ties to bond with him. This could have been a useful "back channel" relationship for the Nkrumah government to communicate with Washington, helping to smooth the rough edges of a contentious diplomatic arrangement.[24] However, this point does little to explain why she would visit him at his home in Arizona after the coup, when she was simultaneously proclaiming far and wide that his government had played a leading role in dispatching the government of her adopted homeland. This relationship may have derived from her unalloyed tendency to succumb to the cajolery of strategically placed men. Certainly it is hard to say that she simply attached herself to him for personal gain, for it is difficult to say what material benefit she expected to obtain from this ambassador after he had left office and she no longer resided in Ghana.

Even the most generous observer is left to conclude that Graham Du Bois was more resolute in resisting the snares of white supremacy and less successful in resisting male supremacy. Yet even this trait has societal as well as personal causes: during much of her life, the movement against white supremacy was much more developed and much more willing to include her than the movement against male supremacy; this may help explain why her antiracism was more consistent than her antisexism. Indeed, given the alleged "racial origins" of feminism in the United States, it is unsurprising that the women's movement would be relatively weak—compared to its counterpart in New Zealand, to cite one example—and that a woman of African descent like Graham would not necessarily be attracted to it.[25]

In sum, Shirley Graham Du Bois was a woman of many dimensions and talents, a woman marked indelibly by an era that she resisted staunchly. Chameleon-like, she adapted to the location in which she found herself, often appearing imperious or eager to yield to the inducements of alpha men, depending on the circumstances.

Roselyn Richardson, the person today who, arguably, knew her longest, has provided the best insight into her personality. They met in the early 1940s when Graham was working with the Young Women's

Christian Association in Richardson's home state, Indiana. Graham was "in and out" of her house during those times, and they corresponded frequently over the years. Richardson describes Graham as "outgoing." In fact, Graham was effervescent, witty, loquacious, and a raconteur of rare skill; these talents were reflected in her plays. She was a hard worker, completing one project after another with frenetic urgency. Her quick mind seemed constantly to be running.

She was "very talkative," according to Richardson, and used "similes" frequently in everyday conversation; she was "never at a loss for words" and was not above "embroidering experiences." She would not "deliberately mislead," though she had an endearing habit of telling "stories that [could] go on and on," which often included details that stretched credulity. She "knew something about most things" or "thought she did," concluded Richardson ruefully.

She was also a woman of "strong opinions," particularly after joining the Communist Party; she was "forever contrasting" the USSR and United States to the detriment of the latter. However, despite these fiercely held opinions, she and Richardson "didn't fall out," for Graham had the ability to engage in ferocious debate with an adversary, then engage in light banter about it afterwards. But these passions were not limited to opinions about socialism versus capitalism. "Whatever she was engaged in at the moment was with a great deal of enthusiasm and exaggeration." This could include writing plays or courting her future husband, Du Bois, or defending Nkrumah. Perhaps befitting one of the Left, she was hardly religious, though—perhaps because of her father— she was not combative about this subject.[26]

Because of this personality, she could become a Communist and doggedly maintain her membership even after her party became wildly unpopular. Because of her confidence in herself and her opinions, she could embark on new career paths without the anxiety that would afflict most mortals. Because of her adroit way with words, she could churn out a river of typed pages in various genres or give a well-received keynote speech at the Progressive Party convention of 1948 or convince the doubting to support her newlywed, Du Bois, as he went on trial in 1951. Because of her feistiness, she could flail away at her coeditors of the publication she helped to initiate, *Freedomways,* while remaining on cordial terms with them throughout. Shirley Graham Du Bois was a woman of many facets who lived many lives.

∎

In the following pages I will seek to provide a portrait of Shirley Graham Du Bois that will help to explicate who she was and how she evolved.

The introduction provides a broad overview of her life, focusing on why her star has faded despite her manifest accomplishments. Also examined are her relationship to the Communist Party, the Left, and Africa, along with the similarities she shares with other well-known women.

Chapter 1 examines her childhood, the influence of her father particularly, her abortive marriage, and the birth of her two sons. Chapter 2 looks at her life after she left her sons in the care of others and moved to France in December 1926, where she lived intermittently until 1930; her friendship with the writer Eric Walrond; the spectacular success of her Africa-tinged opera *Tom-Tom*; and her education at Oberlin College, which she left in the mid-1930s with both a B.A. and an M.A. This chapter also touches on her unorthodox relationship with one of her Oberlin professors, who wrote her intensely personal and passionate letters. Her relationship with one of the few powerful women who assisted her, Mary White Ovington, is also touched on.

Chapter 3 assesses her life after Oberlin, beginning with her college teaching experience in Nashville. From there she moved to Chicago, where she briefly operated a business with one of her brothers before initiating a rich phase of her life as a playwright and administrator of the Federal Theater Project. Her productions there were all too successful in that they sparked the enmity of commercial producers, who considered government-sponsored theater to be terribly unfair competition. A premature Red Scare drove her away from this project to the Yale School of Drama. Despite the fact that by the late 1930s she was already occupying the highest ranks among Negro dramatists, her standard of living was not very high and she continued to scrimp and scramble to take care of her sons, who for the most part grew to maturity in her absence.

Chapter 4 concerns the central turning point of her life: World War II. She finally abandoned the theater and moved to Arizona to work with Negro soldiers. The wilting racism she experienced there did not enfeeble her but instead revitalized her political consciousness; this, along with the tragic death of her first son, drove her further to the left. After she moved to Manhattan, a borough that at that moment was in the process of electing an African American Communist—Ben Davis—

to office, she too joined the party. Her decision is not as odd as it may appear to some in retrospect. Not only did leading figures like Paul Robeson, Lena Horne, Teddy Wilson, Billie Holliday, and many others lend support to the party, but at that moment anticommunism was muted as a result of the antifascist alliance between Moscow and Washington. She also worked alongside the legendary Ella Baker as an organizer for the NAACP at a moment when it experienced a remarkable membership boom. However, she abandoned the association to assume a life as a writer and quickly found increased fame and, decidedly, a greater fortune. This was occurring as the Red Scare was dawning. When W. E. B. Du Bois, an early casualty of this trend, was ousted from the NAACP in 1948, she played a leading role in rallying masses to his defense.

Chapter 5 tells of her developing relationship with the organized Left in the late 1940s and early 1950s; this happened as she was becoming ever closer to Du Bois. This was an escalation of a relationship that had become quite friendly in the 1930s and, most likely, became adulterously intimate at least by the mid-1940s. Though she was an uncommonly strong and determined woman, when approaching Du Bois she often appeared vulnerable and in need of assistance. He, on the other hand, described himself as her "father confessor."

Chapter 6 extends the examination of their relationship. They were married in 1951, as he was about to be tried as the agent of an unnamed foreign power, believed to be Moscow. Again, she rallied opposition to this indictment and in a rare victory during the Red Scare, her eighty-three-year-old spouse was able to escape imprisonment. Though she had contemplated living abroad, the government's failure to renew her passport complicated this idea; thus, the elderly couple settled down to a life of domesticity in Brooklyn Heights, in a home bought from the playwright Arthur Miller.

Chapter 7 picks up her life in 1958, when their passports were renewed and they quickly decamped for an extended trip to Europe and Asia. She also visited Africa during this extended journey, and they were both outside the United States for a good deal of 1958 and 1959. Her trip to China made a deep impression on her. She was particularly moved by the role of women there and, suitably inspired, returned to the United States and played a leading role in initiating the journal *Freedomways*, which became essential reading for a number of progressives involved in the nascent civil rights movement. She and her spouse decided to move to Ghana in 1961, where their friend Kwame Nkrumah had assumed power in 1957. They became Ghanaian citizens.

Her years with Du Bois, 1951 to 1963, were in some ways the least productive of her life as she spent a considerable amount of time as his caretaker. When he passed away in 1963, she entered what may have been the most significant phase of her many lives, as she became the director of television in Ghana and an influential advisor to Nkrumah. This is the central focus of chapter 8. A number of acquaintances began to describe her as overbearing, even domineering, as a result of her acute awareness of the magic of the surname Du Bois and the fact that she had the ear of Nkrumah. These criticisms became even more insistent when Malcolm X arrived in Accra and she adopted yet another "son." His experience there, where he saw Africans, Europeans, and Asians working side by side on behalf of a common socialist goal, evidently influenced him to move away from his view of whites as "devils."

Chapter 9 deals with another major trauma and turning point in Graham Du Bois's life. The Nkrumah regime was overthrown in February 1966; she barely escaped Accra intact and became something of a "Flying Dutchwoman," meandering from port to port in search of a home. Finally she settled in Cairo, where her son David had moved a few years earlier. There she studied Arabic and espoused "Egypt-centric" ideas that bloomed years later as "Afrocentrism."[27] However, her previous status as one of the most influential women in the world evaporated.

Chapter 10 looks at her experience in China, where she was drawn to the regime of Mao Zedong. His anti-Sovietism complicated her relationships with erstwhile Communist comrades in the United States who remained pro-Moscow and led to conflicts with the editors of *Freedomways*. Similarly, her unflinching support for Nkrumah—whom she supported during his post-coup distress in a manner not unlike her support for Du Bois after his indictment—complicated relationships with those who were more critical of his rule. Moreover, her move to Egypt also influenced this ideological turn, as Gamal Abdel Nasser, despite the formidable aid he received from Moscow, was hostile to Communists in his own land.

Chapter 11 scrutinizes her attempts to obtain a visa to return to the United States during the Nixon administration; after initial reluctance, her visa was granted and she returned to a rapturous welcome. It appears that as she grew older, she mellowed and became more ecumenical, though she did not retreat from her fervent admiration for China, where she passed away in 1977.

·

Shirley Graham Du Bois's many lives present us with many lessons, not least concerning the Jim Crow that hampered her career in the theater and helped push her to the left in Arizona during World War II. Her relationships to men remind us of the potency of patriarchy. Her constant movement—not only geographically but also ideologically—reminds us that she and the people from which she sprang, African Americans, remain in flux and continue to search for a true and redemptive home.

Introduction

Perspectives

IT WAS THE first Saturday of April 1977 in Beijing, China. The auditorium at the Paposhan Cemetery for Revolutionaries was full. The vice-premier, Chen Yung-kuei, and the widow of former premier Zhou En-lai were among the dignitaries present. The Communist Party chairman, Hua Kuo-feng, sent a wreath to this "memorial meeting," as did the embassies of Tanzania, Ghana, and Zambia.[1]

These leaders and ordinary citizens had come to mourn the passing of a woman, born an African American, who died in China as a citizen of Tanzania. Shirley Graham Du Bois—the name that most knew her by—was eighty years old and had come to the Chinese capital for medical treatment. This was not her first visit. Though some in the United States still considered China a close cousin of the "evil empire," Wang Ping-nan, the president of China's Association for Friendship with Foreign Countries, called her a "close friend" who "did a lot [of] work in enhancing the friendship and understanding between the Chinese people . . . and the Third World."[2]

She had been visiting China since the late 1950s, initially with her husband, W. E. B. Du Bois, and had lived there intermittently since then. The presence at this memorial meeting of Zhou En-lai's widow was emblematic of the close relationship Shirley Graham Du Bois had developed with many of the leaders of the Chinese Communist Party. In 1967, almost four years to the day after her famed spouse had died in Ghana, she had a frantic and lengthy meeting with Zhou En-lai; this was during the Cultural Revolution, just after he had been besieged for eighteen hours by Red Guards. There, according to one informant, Zhou confided to her matters about the nature and fate of the Chinese revolution that he would have been reluctant to share with others in

China and elsewhere, thus confirming her stature as a trusted comrade and important dignitary.[3]

■

Shirley Graham Du Bois was one of the most versatile and creative artists and activists that this nation has produced. She was familiar with German, Italian, and French, and evidently knew Russian sufficiently well "to read *War and Peace* in the original." She also said that she "read Homer in the original." She knew some Chinese, and as a result of spending most of the last ten years of her life in Cairo, also could speak some Arabic.[4]

Her opera *Tom-Tom*, produced in Cleveland in 1932, was "the first all-black opera to be produced on a large scale, with a professional cast of approximately 500 actors. It was also the first opera by an African-American woman to be produced."[5] Her play *It's Morning* was termed by one critic "a major breakthrough in African-American drama" that "innovative[ly] embed[s] African rhythms and oral culture within a traditional Aristotelian structure."[6] Carl Van Vechten was "astonished" by her biography of Frederick Douglass and added with gratitude, "four orchids to you, a diamond tiara, and seven magnums of champagne!"[7]

She was not only a musician and writer but an activist as well. She worked as an organizer for the NAACP during World War II at the time of its largest spurt in membership and served as the director of television and a key advisor to the Nkrumah government in Ghana until its overthrow in 1966. During that latter period, the writer Julian Mayfield—also in exile in Accra—called her a true "socialist and a revolutionary," which in those days in that place was high praise indeed.[8]

Her accomplishments have been shrouded in part because of her controversial political positions and in part because of the towering achievements of her spouse; yet she was well known during her lifetime and was associated with many who were prominent. She was in close touch with a small coterie of talented African American women, but her busy schedule and her concern about her children did not leave much time for these colleagues. In any event, she was much more likely to gravitate toward men who could assist her with her life and career.

Still, she had a "close and personal" relationship with the chanteuse Josephine Baker, whose activism mirrored her own.[9] She was friendly with the dancer and choreographer Katherine Dunham. The singer and actress Ethel Waters advised her about a film script she was writing.[10]

The musician and folklorist Maud Cuney-Hare provided counsel to her concerning "'musical idioms, figures and rhythms' in modern music."[11] Graham worked alongside Ella Baker, a founder of the Southern Christian Leadership Conference and the Student Non-Violent Coordinating Committee, when both were working as NAACP organizers.[12] Though her spouse was closer to Lorraine Hansberry—she "had been [his] favorite pupil" and "he was exceedingly fond and proud of her"—as a fellow playwright, Graham Du Bois also knew and admired her work.[13]

Befitting the spouse of W. E. B. Du Bois, Graham also was friendly with and influenced numerous male luminaries. In the 1930s she was baptized by Adam Clayton Powell, Sr., of Harlem's famed Abyssinian Baptist Church; later he counseled her about her work.[14] Even before she worked with him in the 1940s, she was in touch a decade earlier with a fellow writer and activist, the NAACP leader Walter White, who encouraged her as *Tom-Tom* was facing its debut.[15] In turn she provided encouragement—and occasional loans—to the Harlem Renaissance writer Eric Walrond, particularly during his sojourn in Paris.[16] She admired Paul Robeson and wrote a well-received book about him.[17]

She occasionally enjoyed a "long, quiet chat" with Richard and Ellen Wright in New York City during the 1940s. At the time both he and Graham were of the political Left and contemplating the process of moving the nation in the same direction. As Graham recounted, "Just the other day he said to me, 'Labor organizations are the natural channels through which Negroes with ideas should work.' Then he shook his head, 'But labor organizations . . .' He made a helpless gesture."[18] Thus did Graham and Wright confront a recurring dilemma of the African American leftist: how to build an alliance with a Euro-American working class that was influenced profoundly by the doctrines of white supremacy. This dilemma helped drive Wright to France and Graham to Africa.

Her relationship with Wright was sufficiently close that he shared the galleys of *Black Boy* with her, which she then passed on to the scholar Alain Locke.[19] But unlike Locke, Graham was not just a devotee of the arts and matters intellectual. She was an activist and also in close touch with those in the political arena. She had known Hastings Banda, the first leader of independent Malawi, since the 1930s.[20] Her tenure with the Nkrumah government brought her into contact with world leaders—notorious and otherwise—including one memorable encounter in Tirana with Enver Hoxha, the leader of Albania during its most reclusive period.[21] And, of course, she was particularly close to African Americans who were progressive artists and activists like herself, for example, Ossie Davis and Ruby Dee, who often expressed their love for her.[22]

Given her notoriety and attainments, why is Shirley Graham Du Bois routinely ignored by contemporary critics and scholars?[23] And why is it that those who have not ignored her have instead criticized her, at times harshly? Maya Angelou, who knew her during their tenure in Ghana, has provided a sour description of what she considered Graham Du Bois's officious nature there.[24] When Malcolm X visited Accra and queried her about her opinion of Graham Du Bois, Angelou "let loose. I spoke of her lack of faith, her lack of identity with Black American struggle, her isolation from her people, her pride at sitting in the catbird seat in Ghana." Angelou's claim that Graham Du Bois lacked an "identity with Black American struggle" was misguided, though her point about Graham's alleged arrogance was confirmed by others.

Alice Walker berated her affecting memoir of her life with W. E. B. Du Bois, *His Day Is Marching On,* asserting that Graham Du Bois's "recollections, unfortunately, are a cloying intrusion into any serious effort to understand Du Bois."[25] Dorothy Hunton, whose husband, the progressive activist W. Alphaeus Hunton, worked with W. E. B. Du Bois in the Council on African Affairs, has echoed Angelou's description of Graham Du Bois's alleged insolence, particularly during the Ghana years.[26]

On the other hand James Jackson, who recruited W. E. B. Du Bois to the Communist Party in 1961, has taken a different tack. He has spoken vividly—and, I believe, accurately—of her fertile imagination and creativity, her raffish, unconventional, and idiosyncratic nature, which not only allowed her to write significant fiction but also helped her invent and reinvent the details and substance of her life.[27]

Actually, the portraits by Angelou and Jackson can be reconciled. While in Ghana, as the spouse, then widow, of an esteemed man and then as the trusted advisor of Kwame Nkrumah, Graham Du Bois did strike some as a bit snooty, all too aware of her own importance; she quickly assumed the presumed trappings of her lofty position. On the other hand, she *was* different from many of her Afro-American colleagues in Ghana; she was an official of a government that the United States did not consider friendly. Her *position,* her standpoint, was different. She was a close advisor to a man who was being spied on and subjected to assassination plots. She could not be as open as other expatriates in Ghana; she had to be more guarded. This may have bred resentment. For the full measure of her life, Jackson's analysis is closer to the mark in that he knew her during her U.S. sojourn, when her position was closer to that of her peers. Her perhaps overbearing manner in Ghana was just an aspect of one of the many lives that she lived, but it was far from being the essence of her life.

Moreover, often there are expectations that the well-known will be haughty, and this prophecy becomes self-fulfilling. Du Bois himself was viewed by some as aloof, whereas the journalist Marvel Cooke, who worked with him and knew him well, disputed the accuracy of this description and suggested that his shyness was misinterpreted as haughtiness.[28]

In addition, Graham Du Bois felt justifiably that she did not receive the credit—and perhaps the respect—that was due one of her stature; all too often she was viewed simply as the faint extension of the lengthened shadow of her well-known spouse. This may have generated what was perceived as haughtiness. In 1974 she confessed increasing disgust with the inattention to her writings in the United States.[29] She was generally better received abroad than at home, and this may have influenced her attitude abroad toward her U.S. compatriots.

In a similar vein, she told the scholar Nathan Hare that she was "unhappy" with how his journal, the *Black Scholar,* had treated her:

> Forgive me if this sounds like a personal peeve. . . . The Association of Negro Life and History [*sic*] has never listed any of my work nor have they ever so much as invited me to any of their sessions. But, I was certainly among the pioneers in the States in lifting black men and women out of obscurity.

Her works had been translated in China and Eastern Europe and she had received numerous awards—"and all this occurred before I married W. E. B. (You'll now see this as a women's lib complaint!)"[30]

It is possible that if she had been a man she would have been viewed differently: her supposed arrogance might have been seen then as the understandable manner of a busy, authoritative figure. As her comments about her pre–Du Bois accomplishments suggest, Graham Du Bois was then wrestling—not always successfully—with the new realities introduced by a stirring women's movement. However, her larger point was accurate: for whatever reason she received short shrift from far too many—before and after her death.

This point was reinforced when a nationally syndicated cartoon strip in 1996 lampooned Graham Du Bois's dilemma. A female character asked, "What does the name Du Bois mean to you?" The young male character answered, "This is one of your black history month quizzes, isn't it? Well, I'm ready for you this time Marcy! W. E. B. Du Bois was a civil rights leader and author! Ha!" She responded with satisfaction, "Actually, I was thinking of Shirley Du Bois, his wife . . . famous playwright, musicologist and activist." He answered sheepishly, "I'm going to need more time if you're going to include the wives!" All the while, another young girl looked on knowingly.[31] Of late, time has not been found for the wife—Shirley Graham Du Bois—who often has been forgotten when she has not been castigated.

■

There has been a tendency in biographies of prominent U.S. figures to portray them in a harsh and negative light. Joyce Carol Oates has termed this trend "pathography," while Edmund White has referred to it as the revenge of the little people on the big people.[32] Some celebrities in the United States have referred bitterly to the process whereby they are built up only to be torn down. The process serves the social function of morality plays: the high and mighty are brought down a peg, which reminds us that it is dangerous to fly too high. As with most processes in a patriarchal society, this one too has had a disproportionately negative impact on women, in that the existence of powerful, influential women has not been consistent with the theory and practice of male supremacy. All the more, women of African descent have experienced this negative impact.[33]

Though Graham Du Bois occasionally mocked "women's lib," she was well aware of patriarchy and its manifestations, particularly as it pertained to women with reputations to protect. In 1947 she told the *Daily Worker*, "I came to feel that not only as a Negro must I do outstanding work but especially as a Negro woman." She acknowledged that although African American women then were often more aware than their men of the struggle and their responsibility, "We lack the grit of Sojourner Truth and the courage of Harriet Tubman."[34] Though most of her biographies concerned male figures like Paul Robeson and Gamal Abdel Nasser, she also wrote at length about Pocahontas and Phillis Wheatley. One of her most noteworthy unpublished works concerns a personality from colonial North America, Anne Royall, who she argued was subjected to male supremacy. Her lament for Royall could be applied to Graham Du Bois herself: "Anne Royall made her way from frontier obscurity to places unheard of for a 'female' in her day, yet now has no place at all in American literary history."[35]

Indeed, her skeptical remarks about "women's lib" notwithstanding, it would be a mistake to fail to view Graham Du Bois as a feminist. She exemplified the struggle for women's equality even when she was not proclaiming this principle from the barricades. One scholar has coined the term "de facto feminist" to characterize those whose lives embody feminism yet who may occasionally scoff at the term. Graham Du Bois is an example of this tendency.[36] On the other hand, one must hesitate in holding Graham Du Bois to the standards of twenty-first century feminism when during most of her life, even the mainstream feminist movement was marginalized by powerful elites and, in any event, not necessarily forthcoming to women of color. Asking why Graham Du Bois was not more of an articulated feminist may be like posing the fatuous question of why Nat Turner did not opt for utopian socialism rather than massacring Euro-Americans.[37]

Faith Davis Ruffins has wondered why "famous African-American men have been memorialized and famous African-American women have not." She suggests that it is because the former had wives and the latter did not:

> many well known Afro-American men were survived by their wives. Before 1950, a large minority of Afro-American professional women did not marry because of strictures within the teaching and nursing professions, and those who did often survived their spouses. Widows of prominent men have spent the rest of their lives ensuring that their husbands' names would not be forgotten.

Ruffins lists Shirley Graham Du Bois as an example, in addition to Amy Jacques Garvey, Coretta Scott King, Betty Shabazz, and Margaret Murray Washington.[38] When W. E. B. Du Bois died, Shirley Graham Du Bois moved to insure his legacy by preserving his papers and manuscripts, writing a memoir about his life, and the like; when she died, there was no widower—or widow—to perform a similar task.

Shirley Graham Du Bois had the added liability of being, in Julius

Mayfield's terms, a "socialist and a revolutionary" in a nation that, of late, has not celebrated either. The feminist theorist Betty Friedan, to cite one example, found that she had to obscure her ties to the organized Left and working-class radicalism in order to avoid being marginalized when she discussed patriarchy. This caused her to overemphasize the middle-class origins of feminism, which has handicapped the movement in its attempt to reach out beyond this class.[39] Graham Du Bois was not willing to make this compromise.

Moreover, Graham Du Bois abandoned the land of her birth and became a citizen of another country. She was part of a long though frequently ignored tradition of expatriation among African Americans. Ghana, to cite one example, attracted scores of black expatriates during the Nkrumah years. However, she was not just an expatriate but one who allied with real and imagined enemies of the United States; historically, those who have done so have been denounced when they have not been forgotten.[40] This trend, too, has impeded the formation of an objective retrospective—or any recollection—of her life and career.

Still, Graham's own behavior has not improved her chances of being reclaimed by a later generation of feminists and scholars. Though her point was not altogether accurate, she proclaimed that after she married W. E. B. Du Bois in 1951,

> I gave up all my own work: whatever I was doing seemed so insignificant compared to what he was doing that I let it all go so I could devote myself to him and his needs. He'd want a cup of coffee; I'd be there with the coffee. He'd need a special book; off I'd go and find it for him. Some people said I'd become his slave woman! Needless to say, Women's Lib hadn't even been heard of in those days.[41]

Her self-conscious reference to "women's lib" suggested that Graham Du Bois was not unaware of how her recollections represented a concession to patriarchy. An accomplished woman like Graham Du Bois was unable to escape the bonds and manacles of male supremacy: the prescribed roles of "caretaker" and "mother" were dominant motifs in her life. This was a partial outgrowth of her relationship with her father and the fact that as the only and oldest daughter in a family of sons, she became a virtual "junior mother" at an early age. This youthful experience influenced her throughout her tumultuous life.

To be sure, her failings in the arena of gender relations were not hers alone. Doris Lessing has bemoaned the fact that "there is not one woman writer, ever, at any time in the world's history who has not heard these words—'you don't love me; you only care about your writing'—from her man."[42] Many women were not able to escape the magnetism of this patriarchy. To his credit, Du Bois was never accused of making statements akin to those of Lessing's putative lover. On the other hand, the power of patriarchy was such that every man did not have to make such a statement to prompt a woman writer to forgo her work and become a caretaker to a man, Lessing's admonition notwithstanding.

Graham Du Bois faced a unique situation in that she married an elderly man whose life expectancy already had exceeded the norm; when they wed, Du Bois was in his eighties and she was almost thirty years younger. Thus, a concern about age as much as gender may have motivated the caretaker role she assumed with him. John Henrik Clarke is not alone in suggesting that "in many ways she extended his life." Still, her loving attention to her spouse exceeded the call of duty, in his opinion: "she worshipped him and she served him. . . . She showed him how to manage money . . . she made a whole [lot] of people pay him." She was a "devoted companion."[43] Clarke was not alone in sensing that in many ways, she was a custodian of his body and spirit.

But the age factor hardly figures in comprehending her relationship to another powerful man, Kwame Nkrumah, who was closer to her in age than Du Bois. Maya Angelou wrote that "she and the president were family close. It was said that Nkrumah called her 'little-mother' and that she telephoned him each night at bedtime."[44] It seemed that Graham Du Bois's relationship with Nkrumah was similar to her relationship with her spouse. After his overthrow in 1966 this became evident; he asked her to provide him with a "regime . . . what to drink as soon as I wake up in the morning to race me up, what to have for breakfast." In a final flourish he added, "How I wish you could be in my kitchen!"[45] Dutifully, Graham replied, "I recommend a small glass of port wine before you go to bed" and a diet of nuts, cheese, garlic, and the like.[46]

The spread of a conservative antifeminist domestic ideology was an essential component of Cold War policies that sought to contain not only the spread of communism and the unleashed atomic bomb but also the potential power of women.[47] This ideology was so pervasive that even self-proclaimed revolutionaries like Nkrumah and Graham

Du Bois found it difficult to escape. What is even more fascinating about Graham Du Bois is how she was able to resist anticommunism more successfully than she resisted male supremacy, which serves to underline once more the persistence and power of patriarchy and the inadequacy of the middle-class orientation that was forced on post-1940s feminism. Though early in life she refused to adhere to primary norms concerning marriage and motherhood in a manner that signaled a protofeminism, she resisted identification with the feminist movement for a good deal of her life. Certainly aspects of her relationship with figures like Nkrumah did not exemplify the finest traditions of feminism.

In a sense, Graham's political activism corresponded with what has almost become a cliché in describing women's frequent role in the movement. As one writer put it, women in politics "tend to emphasize connectedness to others and to devote more energy toward nurturing personal relationships and building networks of support, whereas men are more comfortable emphasizing their separateness."[48] Without descending into "essentialism," we can safely assert that patriarchy has shaped the activism of women. Hence Graham could acquiesce, at least subconsciously, to being a caretaker and attending to the needs of powerful men like Du Bois and Nkrumah, seeing this as part of her duties and therefore useful to the movement. This was part of the price she paid for growing to maturity in a nation where patriarchy and conservatism were strong and durable.[49]

Still, it is conspicuous how often male activists like Nkrumah referred to Graham Du Bois as "mother." John Bracey, who was her colleague when they taught at the University of Massachusetts–Amherst, said she was "like a mother" to everyone and often played a conciliatory role in resolving disputes among students and faculty.[50] She spoke of Malcolm X as a "son." The activist then known as Stokeley Carmichael called her "grandma." This maternal, reconciling role also contrasts with Angelou's portrayal of Graham as aloof. In fact, Joanne Braxton's description of "mother" could easily dovetail with Graham's sociopolitical role:

> The archetypal outraged mother travels alone through the darkness to impart a sense of identity and "belongingness" to her child. She sacrifices and improvises to create the vehicles necessary for the survival of flesh and spirit. Implied in all her actions and fueling her heroic ones is abuse of her people and her person.[51]

In her relationships with Carmichael and Malcolm, Graham Du Bois may not have been providing these eminent men with "a sense of identity," but she did sense that her maternal approach to them might be useful in repelling "abuse of her people."

Indeed, what fueled Graham's activism was the necessity to redress "abuse of her people." The most egregious horrors of U.S. apartheid have faded, but it was a reality that she lived with for most of her life. Even the relatively conservative black businessman John Johnson, the founder of the popular magazines *Ebony* and *Jet* and one of the wealthiest African Americans of this or any era, was so offended by Jim Crow that he once was reported to have exclaimed, "Sometimes I wish they'd drop an H-bomb on this country and wipe out every white man! Sure, they'd kill all us Negroes but it would be worth it!"[52]

The ravages of Jim Crow were sufficient to push her toward political activism—and away from futile thoughts about violence. This activism was shaped by her experience as a mother. She bore two sons before she married Du Bois and once confessed, "Frankly, I think I am a writer today because I was a mother and teacher."[53] An early turning point in her life was her decision to leave her children in the care of others and embark on a career. Although the involvement of the extended family in child rearing was not unknown among African Americans, this decision bothered her throughout her life. The death in the early 1940s of her firstborn, Robert, was another turning point in her life and drove her deeper into political activism and, possibly, into membership in the Communist Party: "His loss," she recalled, "was the greatest tragedy of my life." It was only

> after I found a way to involve myself in work which would eliminate the basic causes of his death and would save other mothers from the suffering which engulfed me, that I was able to sustain that loss. His death gave me impetus and determination to change many things in our society.[54]

For Shirley Graham Du Bois, the role of mother was a significant force in her life and was manifested in her work as an activist, in league with Nkrumah, Malcolm, and others.[55]

■

Many of her duties as an activist and a writer concerned her "motherland," Africa. At a time when many African Americans shunned the continent in embarrassment because of its underdevelopment, she was presenting an alternative vision in her opera *Tom-Tom*. She wrote biographies of leading African personalities, worked at the shoulder of Nkrumah when he was seeking to build a "United States of Africa," and became a citizen of Ghana, then Tanzania. In turn, the continent itself had a dynamic impact on her, particularly during her days in Ghana; in 1964 she told John Henrik Clarke, "having 'found Africa' my life has become wholly absorbed!"[56]

Her experience in Ghana reflects an important element of the ongoing relationship between Africans and African Americans. At various times Africans had looked to blacks across the Atlantic for inspiration and support; as a key advisor to Nkrumah she was a living embodiment of this alliance. However, the former Gold Coast, Ghana, had been a regional headquarters for a school of thought that looked askance at African Americans as deracinated—perhaps lackeys of Euro-American elites.[57] Many Africans had legitimate reason to believe that many of those African Americans who were engaged with Africa were procolonialist.[58] Graham Du Bois worked tirelessly to dispel this notion. However, as African Americans were being "integrated" into the highest levels of U.S. government and business, they naturally had to observe the mandate of powerful elites—who often were hostile to the Nkrumah regime—thus accelerating this historic suspicion of the people Ghanaians came to refer to as "Afro-Americans." Some of those Ghanaians who were suspicious of Afro-Americans were influenced by a long British tradition of suspicion of Afro-Americans as vectors of militance or stalking horses for Washington.

After her move to Cairo in the aftermath of the 1966 coup that dislodged Nkrumah, Graham Du Bois was essential in helping to popularize "Egypt-centric" views of black history that came to be characterized as "Afrocentric."[59] However, her brand of nationalism was hardly xenophobic, colored as it was by her experience with the multiracial Left. Indeed, as will be suggested below, Malcolm X's experience with her in Ghana (not his experience in Saudi Arabia, as has been asserted) may have been the crucial factor that led him to move away from his belief that whites were "devils." Strikingly, the rise of this black nationalism in the 1960s and 1970s, a development that she helped to propel, also buoyed an antifeminist ideology that pushed her further in a "maternalist" direction.[60]

She evolved toward a brand of "left nationalism" that simultaneously proclaimed a form of socialism while remaining deeply apprehensive about the intentions of those defined as "white," be they socialist or capitalist.[61] It was difficult for many African Americans to maintain a leftism untouched by nationalism when many of their Euro-American counterparts were moving, likewise, from the left to various forms of white chauvinism that consciously excluded blacks.[62]

Graham, as one of the better-known advocates for the People's Republic of China, was also essential in influencing the small but influential group of "Maoists" or pro-Beijing devotees in the United States. A popular photograph of the era that appeared in *Muhammad Speaks,* the organ of the Nation of Islam, showed her costumed in a quasi-military "Mao" outfit, replete with a cap bearing a red star; in this photograph, captured in Guinea-Conakry, she is accompanied by Nkrumah and the activist then known as Stokeley Carmichael.[63]

Though much has been made of Moscow's attraction for African Americans, less has been said about Beijing's. But the fact is that Graham Du Bois was just one of a number of leading African American personalities who spoke glowingly of China and subscribed, in varying degrees, to Mao Zedong's ultraleftism, "great leaps forward," and critique of the Soviet Union. Huey P. Newton and other Black Panthers could often be found in Beijing and Shanghai.[64] The writer Amiri Baraka (Le Roi Jones) was an avowed devotee of "Mao Zedong Thought."[65] Robert F. Williams, who fled North Carolina after a run-in with both the national NAACP leadership and conservative Euro-Americans, wound up in China, where he was embraced warmly.[66]

There was a connection between nationalism and Maoism: at times those African Americans who were fiercely opposed to the domestic and foreign policies of the United States but would not ally with "white" Moscow bonded with Beijing. The fact that China often collaborated with the United States and apartheid South Africa in Angola in the mid-1970s and elsewhere was somehow forgotten.[67] Ironically, though some African Americans aligned with Beijing because of hostility to their own country, apparently they did not fully recognize that at the same time China itself was allying with the United States.[68]

Still, it is not difficult to see why so many were taken by the idea that China had supplanted Japan as the "champion of the darker races."[69] Africans fighting colonialism in the nation that was to become Zimbabwe reported that "the Chinese always identified themselves as a coloured people and therefore sharing a common cause with the African people."[70] China was also quite close to Graham Du Bois's eventual adopted home, Tanzania; according to one analyst, Dar es Salaam by the early 1970s "had probably developed more extensive ties with that country than with any other non-African state."[71]

Hopes for a united "colored" front against white supremacy received a boost in 1963 when Mao Zedong made a widely publicized statement in solidarity with the struggles of African Americans. Though there was concern expressed in the *New York Times* that an "antiwhite drive by Peking" was in motion, the journalist Tad Szulc correctly predicted that this drive would ultimately be directed more at Moscow than Washington: at a recent meeting in the country that was to become Tanzania, China sought to expel a Soviet delegation because it was "noncolored." Nevertheless, when a rally of ten thousand in Beijing was addressed by the trade union leader Liu Ning-yi, who observed that African Americans "would one day become the masters of the United States," these words resonated in a nation that less than a century earlier had fought a bloody war that led to the abolition of enslavement of Africans.[72]

Washington had reason to be apprehensive about this "rising tide of color" in the 1960s. After the murder of the Congolese leader Patrice Lumumba in 1961 with the reputed assistance of the Central Intelligence Agency, "Negro demonstrations" in the United States, "many of them violent, continued." The *New York Times* columnist James Reston was not alone when he concluded, "We are beginning to see a confluence of the world struggle for freedom in Black Africa and the struggle for equal rights in the Negro communities."[73] Beijing was widely perceived as being allied with these "colored" struggles in confrontation with Washington, capital of the Pan-European world.[74] In some respects, a "Black Scare" or "Colored Scare" had come to loom larger than the obligatory "Red Scare." This in turn buoyed the nationalism that Graham Du Bois was rapidly adopting.

These international struggles helped to weaken Jim Crow. As one writer has put it, "the international community"—of which the Soviet Union and China were important elements—"exerted enough pressure on the United States to contribute significantly to ending legalized discrimination against, and segregation of, African Americans."

Desegregation was a Cold War imperative; decolonization was similarly driven by this global context.[75] Washington feared that if the more egregious aspects of Jim Crow and colonialism were not eliminated, more African Americans and Africans could be enticed by the appeals of Moscow—and, for a while, Beijing—thus jeopardizing national security. In turn, as African nations gained independence they could become more effective advocates for desegregation of the United States, and the fear that these nations might turn to the left was useful in prodding Washington to move more aggressively against Jim Crow.[76] Thus, Graham Du Bois's intervention on the global scene, her alliances with Moscow and then Beijing, were part of the process that caused Jim Crow to crumble.

Certainly the abuse suffered by Africans and African Americans helped convince Shirley Graham Du Bois that capitalism could not be depended on to deliver justice, economic or otherwise. And though her passion for Stalin's Soviet Union, then Mao's China, has been questioned and pilloried, on balance her devotion to the Left was not a liability—but an asset to the movement of Africans worldwide for freedom.[77]

Her devotion to the Left led Shirley Graham Du Bois to join the Communist Party shortly after the death of her son Robert. Like many others, she was not forthcoming and expansive about her membership, assuming—perhaps correctly—that volubility about her Red ties would only lead to further persecution.[78] Indeed, her son David, who was in a position to know, is himself not certain beyond a shadow of a doubt that she was a card-carrying Red.[79]

David also suggests that if she was a Red, the popular writer Howard Fast recruited her. Fast, in response, states unequivocally that Graham was "proud and open" about her party membership.[80] There is evidence to substantiate Fast's assertion. In the spring of 1945 the Communist city councilman from Brooklyn, Peter V. Cacchione, wrote to the Communist leader Earl Browder about "Shirley Graham . . . [who] joined our movement about two years ago."[81] In her accompanying letter to Browder, Graham acknowledged that "two years [ago] I came to New York and had the good fortune of becoming a member of the Communist Party."[82]

The overriding point is that powerful elites treated her as if she were a Communist, even if they or others may not have been sure about her party membership. The professional stool pigeon and former Communist Louis Budenz said she was a dangerous Red and should be handled accordingly.[83] The Senate Internal Security Subcommittee had information that listed her as "one of the foremost propagandists of the Communist cause in the USA and a leader of Communist agit-prop work among Negro Americans."[84] In any case, Graham was an open member of organizations perceived by many as "communist fronts" and worked closely over the years with numerous Communists; in the United States that alone has been sufficient "proof" to be deemed a Red, with all the untoward consequences attendant.[85]

For some, worse than Graham's own party membership was the alleged radicalizing influence she had on W. E. B. Du Bois, whom she supposedly inveigled into joining the party as well. It is true that as Du Bois got closer to Graham, simultaneously he did seem to be moving closer to the organized Left, though too much can be made of this given his well-established taste for radicalism.[86] However, such an analysis is a far cry from arguments that have portrayed Graham as a veritable ideological seductress, a courtesan with a radical mission. Ironically, some have leveled a similar allegation at Eslanda Robeson, charging that she was responsible for the pro-Soviet stances of her husband, Paul.[87]

Harold Cruse, whose work indicting the black Left has not spared the Robesons or the Du Boises, feels that Graham "had a lot to do" with her spouse's joining the party: "I knew her pretty well, and I know what kind of woman she was. She was always on the left . . . always, since the 20's. I think she helped bring him closer and closer and closer until, you know, he actually joined the party."[88] John Henrik Clarke, Graham's colleague from her days with the journal *Freedomways*, goes further. His "considered opinion" was that W. E. B. Du Bois's liaison with Shirley Graham was a "communist arranged marriage."[89]

The fact remains, however, that in the spring of 1945 she wrote a letter to the party leadership on the specific issue of "recruiting Dr. W. E. B. Du Bois" to the party. The "salvaging, guiding and shaping of this one man will be reflected in the lives and actions of thousands of other people," she suggested. After she became a Communist she began "discussing with him this wonderful thing. He listened and asked questions." She began bringing him into closer contact with Howard Fast, Howard Selsam, Samuel Sillen, and other Reds and "fellow-travellers." In a somewhat paternalistic fashion, she informed party chief Earl Browder that this consummate intellectual "must be reached and helped." She—not leading Communists like "Ben Davis or Dr. [Max] Yergan"—was in a position to do so, and she requested Browder's aid in recruiting him.[90]

Weeks later Browder himself had been ousted from the party and Du Bois did not officially join until sixteen years later as he was departing for exile in Ghana. It is possible that Graham may have been inflating her own influence on Du Bois in order to appear more powerful than she actually was. Yet she had a point when she suggested that her close and intimate relationship with the elderly Du Bois was probably the best vehicle to recruit him, as opposed to the efforts of Davis and Yergan.

In any case, the idea that a weak-minded Du Bois was seduced into joining the party does not do justice to him and, perhaps, overstates Graham's powers of political persuasion. On the other hand, it would be naive to underestimate her dynamic influence on him, particularly her ability to bring him into radical circles that he otherwise avoided. For when Du Bois was ousted from the NAACP in 1948 he lost his base among black centrists and liberals, and it was the black radical Left—of which Graham had become an essential element—that embraced him.

■

Though the image of the vivacious Graham leading the trusting Du Bois astray is titillating and perhaps both "sexist" and "ageist," it is reflective of larger questions; the image of Graham manipulating Du Bois is mirrored by the image of Communists manipulating African Americans. The role of Communists in the struggle for black liberation in light of the dissolution of the Soviet Union and the role of women Communists, more specifically, remain a subject of debate.

Adam Fairclough enunciates a gathering historical consensus when he suggests that "on balance . . . the anticommunism of the early Cold War damaged the cause of racial equality far more than it helped it . . . the most profound effect of the anti-Communist fever, and also the one most difficult to measure, was the divorcing of the civil rights agenda from the labor-left agenda."[91] African Americans, a mostly working-class population, suffered grievously when labor unions were weakened as a result of the anticommunist upsurge. As the adage went, they had the right to eat at a lunch counter but not enough money to buy a hamburger; they gained the right to check into a hotel but did not have the funds necessary to check out.

Howard Fast allegedly recruited Graham to the party. He left in the wake of the revelations in 1956 about Stalin's rule but maintains still that

> one of the fine glories of the Communist Party of the United States was that we fought and often enough died for black freedom, and the truth that nobody much remembers is that in the very early years of the struggle for civil rights, we were at the side of the blacks, and precious few others who were not black were there with us.[92]

Recent scholarship backs this latter point. Indeed, a section of the black middle class had such a deeply vested interest, economically and socially, in Jim Crow laws, which provided them with a captive market, that they were reluctant to dismantle the status quo; this was also true for a sector of the Euro-American community.[93] And likewise, too many Euro-Americans were so busily—often blindly—enjoying the actual and perceived fruits of white supremacy that they did not bother to protest the atrocity that was Jim Crow. Hence, the brio and energy that a small band of Reds brought to the black freedom struggle were even more important.

Other scholars also have buttressed Fast's overall analysis, particularly as it pertains to the literary circles that occupied so much of Graham's early career.

> The would-be writer Richard Wright found himself sympathizing with the Party alongside William Attaway, Gwendolyn Bennett, Arna Bontemps, Countee Cullen, Frank Marshall Davis, Ralph Ellison, Chester Himes, Langston Hughes, Louise Thompson, Margaret Walker and Dorothy West—with the exception of [Zora Neale] Hurston, a pretty fair "Who's Who" of black writing in the thirties.[94]

Even in the case of Wright—the most notable defector from party ranks—his membership probably helped his important voice to be heard by a wider audience. In short, when Graham joined the party this was neither a bizarre nor an isolated gesture. At a time when Jim Crow drastically limited the opportunities of black intellectuals, the radical Left consciously moved in an opposing direction; as a consequence, a number of leading black writers like Graham were attracted to the Communist Party.

That the party once embraced Stalin cannot be ignored, and this certainly harmed its image in the eyes of many, but then again, African Americans could and did argue that the Democratic Party once endorsed slavery, then Jim Crow, but this was insufficient to discredit this party.[95]

Moreover, Communists in the United States were facing a situation that in many ways was more extreme than that faced by their counterparts elsewhere. Doris Lessing, who for a while in the 1950s was a member of the Communist Party in Great Britain, has observed that "even the worst time of the Cold War" in her country was "mild compared to the United States. . . . No British Communist was ever treated with the harshness the American government used towards Paul Robeson and some other American communists."[96] Such extreme situations often elicit the kind of misjudgments that Graham Du Bois was accused of making. Nevertheless, Communists like Graham Du Bois were in a bind, particularly after publication in 1956 of the damning reports about Stalin's rule. How, it was asked, could she continue supporting a regime that had engaged in such gross violations of human rights?[97] How, it was asked, could she continue membership in a party that was tied to Moscow?

Nonetheless, the Catholic Church in the United States cannot be fully or exclusively comprehended as an appendage of Rome, although certainly it is that. Catholics here try to follow papal decrees, but even cardinals and archbishops find that cultural, political, economic, and other realities mediate their ability to adhere to the wishes of the Vatican. Likewise, it would be misleading to understand Graham's party—least of all Graham herself—as solely a Soviet tool.[98]

Other questions remain. As has been suggested about party members in the unions, their militancy "led to success"; however, because party members like Graham often were covert about their membership—in part because of fear of persecution—this hampered the process of "ideological conversion of the rank-and-file" to the Left. This "was a maze with no exit. No other Marxists in the western world faced this dilemma."[99] Black Communists faced the added problem that their appeals to African Americans carried less resonance when Jim Crow began to crumble while Reds themselves were being persecuted: in this context, what would be the incentive to join the party?

Furthermore, for the longest time Graham had difficulty convincing many of her fellow African Americans that fighting for decolonization in Africa was in their self-interest, that a strong Africa could rally support for the struggle in the United States. Because of anticommunism, African Americans were often pushed to downplay anticolonialism, which could be perceived as yet another Red "plot." Thus "in 1948 the five national African-American newspapers devoted four times [more] space to world communism than to European colonialism" and "had little to say about the South African elections" of 1948 that inaugurated apartheid. Graham, on the other hand, did not dodge the issue of Africa's decolonization, and her party membership did not obstruct, and may have facilitated, this posture.[100] When Graham Du Bois and her spouse moved to Ghana and joined Nkrumah, they were demonstrating to U.S. elites that Jim Crow could be met with potentially powerful alliances with independent Africa and its socialist allies.[101]

Understandably, U.S. elites had good reason to believe that her alliance with Nkrumah had Communist overtones. He was "closely connected" with the British party; he and other Africans with London ties "regarded themselves as Communists and were viewed as such by the Colonial Office and the operatives of MI5."[102] As she and certain African leaders moved toward the Communists, African Americans were moving in an opposite direction; this made it inevitable that at some point she would abandon the United States and move to Africa itself.

But Graham was not just an African American on the left, she was also a woman of the Left, and in this role she was not alone.[103] She also was not alone in facing dilemmas often confronted by women sufficiently audacious to be part of organizations that challenged both imperialism and male supremacy. And just as the party has been criticized for its presumed negative impact on the civil rights movement, it similarly has been assailed for an alleged negative impact on the struggle for women's equality.

However, one perceptive analyst has cautioned that "Communist efforts on behalf of women in the 1940s and 50s were, in some ways, more advanced and more far-reaching than those of reformist organizations of the time." After all, "in the racist and sexist atmosphere of the 1950s Communists were probably the only white political [activists] who were thinking and writing so much about women's particular social, economic and political circumstances." Gerda Lerner and Eleanor Flexner were among the women involved with the Congress of American Women, an alleged "Communist front." Graham, the writer Alice Childress, and the actress Frances Williams were among the black women involved with Sojourners for Truth and Justice, yet another presumed "Communist front." As with the civil rights movement, Communist activism was no detriment to the movement for women's equality and, indeed, may have helped to lay the foundation for the flowering of feminism in the 1960s.[104]

Still, just as Graham was more effective fighting white chauvinism than male supremacy, so was the Communist Party, which may suggest that her perceived weaknesses were not hers alone and reflected more pervasive trends. Yet this weakness was no small matter since, according to some, it was patriarchy that stood as the major bulwark against radicalism and progressive reform generally.[105]

■

Other women had to adapt to the same problems Graham confronted. For example, Ella Reeve Bloor, like Graham, was a divorced woman of the Left who faced ceaseless gossip and errant speculation about her sex life. Like Bloor, Graham also encountered "the question women with children faced": "how could they leave their family responsibilities and go out into the larger world to fight for the care of other people?"[106] When Graham left her children in the care of others so that she could build a career and more effectively make a better world, she felt an apprehension that she shared with other like-minded parents, particularly women. It did seem that this vexing dilemma helped propel her insatiable appetite for hard work and, as well, shape her political activism. In so many ways she mirrored the experiences of her contemporaries; thus, despite her level of accomplishment, she was a prototype of accomplished women generally and accomplished African American women particularly.

Like Simone de Beauvoir, she reinvented the details of her life repeatedly.[107] Like Lena Horne, she sought to escape from her parents' grasp by making an ill-advised marriage, then left her children to embark on a career.[108] Like Mary Church Terrell and Anna Julia Cooper, she was an Oberlin graduate.[109] Like Amy Ashwood Garvey, she was an active Pan-Africanist, West African exile, and devotee of the theater.[110] Like the sculptor Augusta Savage and the writer Jesse Redmon Fauset, she benefitted from the counsel and advice of W. E. B. Du Bois at an important stage in her career.[111] Above all, like Claudia Jones, she was a committed woman of the Left.[112]

Alice Dunbar-Nelson had a "lifelong career as a widow," and this "auxiliary identity often eclipsed her own important accomplishments but it paradoxically gave her much needed income and visibility."[113] Dunbar-Nelson also resembles Shirley Graham Du Bois. Even the repeated references to her as "mother" by Nkrumah and others was not peculiar, in that Ma Rainey, Jackie "Moms" Mabley, Big Mama Blues, and her colleague Ethel Waters ("Sweet Mama Stringbean") also drew on the "power and associations of the maternal."[114]

In 1958, writing from Tashkent in Soviet Central Asia while attending a conference of African and Asian writers, Graham Du Bois rhapsodized about a delegate from her home to be, Ghana: "As she spoke, her eyes flashing in the deep-carved ebony of her face, this black woman was Africa, the Mother-Africa, of deep and mighty rivers, Africa, hailing the new dawn with joy and happiness."[115] This black woman, Shirley Graham Du Bois, lived many lives and in so doing she made significant contributions to art, politics, and "Mother Africa," while mirroring the lives of many of her sisters. Shirley Graham Du Bois, in short, was a "Race Woman."

I

Family

SHE WAS BORN Lola Shirley Graham on 11 November 1896, but at points in her life she shaved as much as ten years from her true age.[1] The place where she was born, Indianapolis, Indiana, at that time was not the most hospitable place for African Americans. Jim Crow was prevalent. The conditions that would allow Indianapolis to become "the unrivaled bastion of the Invisible Empire [Ku Klux Klan] in Mid-America" in the 1920s were already in force when Graham was born.[2]

Her family background was as varied as her life. She claimed French, Scotch-Irish, English, and Native American ancestry, in addition to African; her light brown skin was suggestive of this potpourri. Despite her multiracial background, she was explicit in stating, "I am a Negro. I say that first because here in America that fact is the most determining factor of my being. I cannot escape."[3]

This conclusion and her background were quintessentially those of the United States. She once recalled that "one of my forebears was with Washington at Valley Forge, another died in the Battle of Shiloh; a great-grandfather fought his way out of slavery; a town in Indiana is named for my grandmother."[4] This great-grandfather, Wash Clendon, "after buying his freedom in Virginia, had come to Indiana and settled. He was a blacksmith and could read and write. . . . After a while he acquired land. . . . His farm was one of the 'underground railway' stations."[5] Graham Du Bois also recollected a story that has been discounted, "that our great-aunt Eliza was the original 'Eliza' immortalized by Harriet Beecher Stowe."[6] The larger point, however, was accurate: her roots in this nation ran deep.

Her Native American ancestry came from her mother's side of the family. Etta Bell Graham was born on 30 April 1873 near Kidder, Missouri. Her father, "Big Bell . . . a Cheyenne . . . stole his bride Mary from a plantation" near the Missouri River. After their marriage he made a living as a saddle maker. The family wound up living in St. Paul, Minnesota, where Etta was the "first colored graduate" of Central High School there.[7]

More is known about Graham Du Bois's father. David A. Graham was born on 11 January 1861 in Princeton, Indiana.[8] Like his daughter, he was relatively small: she was five feet two inches tall, he was five feet four. Graham Du Bois's mother was his second wife, and while his first spouse "looked exactly like an Indian," Etta Bell Graham "looked more Jewish in some ways, her high nose and so forth, quite fair."[9] By the time he married Etta Bell, he had two children; then he had three more with her. Shirley was his only daughter.[10]

David Graham was a preacher in the African Methodist Episcopal (AME) church. His son Lorenz recalled him as a "well educated man; he had taught at Wilberforce for a while and then went into the ministry." He was a pastor in a number of churches, "first in the north, the largest AME church in Indianapolis, the largest one in Detroit, the largest one in Chicago." He seemed to be moving steadily higher in the ranks of the black petite bourgeoisie, but then, "because he offended the bishops . . . by his exposing of the rascality of some of them, they sent him away to the smallest parishes in the South they could find."[11]

Graham Du Bois recalled her father as "the last of the old-fashioned Negro preachers who was really the shepherd of his flock, who was totally devoted, who would give his last coat away." In a phrase she would later use for one of her better-known plays, she noted that his attitude was that "the ravens fed Elijah, so we don't have to worry and he didn't worry." Actually the Reverend Graham proved to be as prophetic as the original Elijah in that his insouciant approach toward taking care of himself and his family did not prove to be disastrous.[12] She too pointed to his "protest over the doings of a certain drunken and immoral Bishop" as a negative turning point in his career.[13] For his part, the feisty Reverend Graham said he was eager to "more effectively pursue an uncompromising warfare upon corruption in every rank of the church."[14]

His removal from the fast track of the AME church did not plunge the family into penury (Graham recalled, "I don't remember ever having been without food or being cold"), though it was harmful to their economic well-being. Their father was not visibly worried about this decline, according to Graham Du Bois: "In one of her infrequent moments of 'high tension' my mother said that father should have been a monk—that he would have been happiest in a perfectly bare monastery!"[15]

Graham Du Bois had a high opinion of her father's skill as a pastor: "he was a marvelous troubleshooter . . . in a community where there was racial trouble because he was . . . the kind of person who could both protect his flock and speak up to the white folks." This opinion may have flowed from a particularly tense situation when she was a child and the family was living in New Orleans at a time of racial tension. There had been a well-publicized killing of an African American; Graham, who was no more than seven, "experienced a feeling of resentment" at the "burning" of this man. This feeling became more personal after a letter came to her father instructing him that if he held a protest meeting that he had announced, "he too would be 'lynched.'" Then another letter arrived telling him, "We give you twelve hours" to leave town. In those racially charged times, "a white man would have called the police. But at that time a Negro in the South never thought of calling on the police to protect him."

He arranged to have handbills passed out announcing a mass meeting at his church. In response, those opposed to black self-assertion threatened to burn down this striking edifice. Shirley Graham was not too young to recognize the gravity of the matter.

> "Papa," she wailed, "they may burn our house down. What are you going to do?"
>
> "Never mind, dear," he responded. "If they come, we'll be ready for them," he assured her with confidence.

Providing her with the liberating idea that Jim Crow could be confronted, the unruffled family had an early supper that day, then left home and marched a few paces to the nearby church. Graham was surprised to see such a large turnout. As was his wont, her father began on time with a prayer, then read a verse from the Bible: "The Lord your God goes before you to fight against your enemies. The battle is not yours but the Lord's." A self-reliant sort, her father proceeded to place a loaded gun on top of his Bible. Graham also noticed that a number of men had pistols resting in their laps. Her father then demanded that women and children leave the church; twenty-one men with loaded guns remained behind.

Shirley Graham was too nervous to sleep. She and her mother stood at the top of the stairs peering from the front of the house, which faced the front of the church. They could hear the frightening sound of an approaching mob. In the doorway awaiting them her father stood alone. She could hear bullets from the enraged mob whizzing through the night air. Her "father fired one shot in the air. . . . They were afraid of one man who had a gun—and who was not afraid!" The mob dispersed.[16]

This gripping incident left a lasting impression on Shirley Graham. Growing up in a state where Jim Crow had only recently been sanctified in the landmark case of *Plessy v. Ferguson*, she was able to witness first-hand that racial bullies could be made to retreat if confronted with countervailing force. Yet the gender lessons were probably not lost on her either: it was left to the men to do this crucial labor, while the women were ordered to retreat to the lair of domesticity.

■

Perhaps because she was the only daughter, her father doted on her. "My brothers all said that my father spoiled me and that I bossed all of them. Now there might be a little truth in that. . . . Well, naturally, I had to look after them, didn't I, and tell them what to do."[17] Though she viewed it lightly in retrospect, this familial burden—being a de facto mother for her brothers—may have propelled Graham Du Bois into a premature marriage in an attempt to escape.

Her earliest memories of childhood were of her father reading to her. He would read to her from *Uncle Tom's Cabin*; she would "always get the book" for him, and as he read "from time to time father would stop to explain something to us. And so we learned all about slavery." "Every night" he would read to her, mostly novels, including *Les Misérables* and *Quo Vadis*.[18] Throughout her life she remained a voracious reader of fiction and nonfiction alike.

In her late seventies, these memories remained with her.

> "In the beginning was the Word, and the Word was with God." St. John I, verse I. This was a favorite text of my Preacher father. He instilled in me, at a very early age, a veneration of the Word, a kind of reverence for that which was recorded. Those "bedtime moments" of him sitting beside my bed at night . . . shine as the happiest moments of my childhood days. I quickly learned to read because I

wanted to make the Words my own. I handled all books gently. They were precious![19]

Fondly she remembered her father as a man with

an inquiring and imaginative mind and this kind of mind he instilled in me. . . . He enjoyed historical novels, travel books, descriptions of faraway places and peoples. And these were the kinds of things he read to me beginning when I was no more than four years old. So it was before I could read I made friends with the characters in Charles Dickens [and Victor Hugo] novels. . . . I particularly remember [the] vivid description of the three wise men following the star of Bethlehem as told in the novel *Quo Vadis*.[20]

She had finished all the novels of Dickens by the time she was twelve and eventually read her favorite novel, *Les Miserables*, in French. *The Huguenots* "opened up my imagination and my world." Years later in 1958, when she was traveling through the desert of Egypt, the first thing that came to her mind were scenes from *Quo Vadis* that had been burned into her brain as a child.[21]

Though her father's economic status may have plummeted from time to time, Graham Du Bois remained a privileged child. Her mother's sister was married to Bishop Samson Brooks of the AME church, and on his shelves she found all the novels of Dickens, plus the works of Balzac. Her close encounters with the printed word inexorably pushed her in the direction of being a writer: "all of these things influenced me tremendously." Though she "never thought about" herself as "a writer," she "always wrote things." Furthermore, though conscious of the various methods and styles that writers used to convey different points and moods, she "never tried to write like anybody else"; she just tried to say things in the "simplest possible terms so other people could get it."[22]

While her "mother worried about me a bit because I always had my nose 'stuck in a book,'" her father continued to encourage this passion.[23] On the other hand, her mother encouraged her early interest in music—"Wagner had been my favorite of the composers"—and she learned to play the piano at a relatively early age.[24] This, in turn, influenced her writing "a great deal," for she "learned what a symphony was and to project movement, theme, etc. and how to weave all together in allegro." Her biography of Paul Robeson, for example, was written "consciously" like a "symphony of life."[25]

While the family lived in Tennessee her skill as a musician flourished. Her father's church had acquired an organ, but her tiny legs were not long enough to pump the pedals, so she stood to conquer—her small fingers darted over the keys as her equally diminutive feet danced across the pedals.[26] As she was to do so often later in life, she adapted creatively and was not flummoxed by a situation that was not tailor-made for her. Then again, she would not have had the opportunity to adapt her creative skill as a musician if her father had not been in a position—not necessarily common for black pastors—to have an organ installed in his church. Her father influenced her in another way that was not immediately apparent. His nomad-like wandering from parish to parish—Indiana, New Orleans, Nashville, Colorado, the Pacific Northwest, and so on—frequently thrust her into unfamiliar settings where she was compelled to adapt by making friends easily; this helped to shape her outgoing personality. Her family experience provided other advantages. When she entered school in New Orleans, admittedly her early experience with books gave her a distinct advantage over many of her classmates. Her school was close to the St. Louis Cathedral near Orleans Street, and her teachers were part of an "order of Negro nuns." Graham and her fellow students, who were also "predominantly 'light,'" were privileged by the complex politics of color in New Orleans. This happened to be one of the better schools for Negroes in the city, which meant that her color and her father's concern for her provided her with a certain advantage early in life. Though she "decided at once" that she liked school, her life there was not without incident: early on she contracted "typhoid fever" from the water and all of her hair "came out." Her father decided to enroll her elsewhere.[27]

David Graham was decidedly a most significant influence on her early life, and not simply because of his encouragement of her literary skills. He was a humanitarian, who "brought every itinerant, shabby preacher to [the] house for dinner." He organized NAACP chapters; "enterprising boys sold copies of the *Crisis* after meetings at [his] church." Her father was a "Du Bois man," not a follower of Booker T. Washington. This influenced her directly, for she "first read articles by Clarence Darrow, Dantes Bellegarde, Norman Thomas, Maxim Litvinov and Unamdi Azikiwe" in the *Crisis*.[28] Early in life she developed a conception of "racial uplift" and "advancing the race."

David Graham was something of an intellectual, but he was also an unforgiving cleric who demanded a strict upbringing for his offspring. He felt that "family worship should be held at the pastor's house daily under all circumstances and all of the family, old and young should be called in and, if possible, participate." He insisted that "the pastor should be very careful in the religious instruction and training of his children."[29] Some of his viewpoints contrasted with those of his contemporaries: "No girls should marry under eighteen years of age," he proclaimed. Other opinions contrasted with viewpoints of today: "You are not prepared to marry until you have learned to keep house . . . be sure to have his meals ready when he returns home in the evening." He believed that "the law of God is that you should remain single as long as your companion lives" and was harshly critical of those who divorce:

> They may appear to be respectable in society! But in the law of God, they are written down among those whom He says shall not inherit eternal life . . . I warn all therefore to never think of separation from your companion, but if you have done so, remain single as long as the other lives.[30]

Such unforgiving opinions no doubt illuminate why Graham Du Bois not only abruptly left her first husband but then symbolically killed him by claiming that he died. Her father's rather traditional opinions concerning how women should relate to men no doubt left their imprint on her.

Graham Du Bois acknowledged that she "was brought up in a strict, Calvinistic home where one was expected to have a reasonable explanation of every act." Such an atmosphere may have fueled her creativity with language, for "my brothers often fell short of satisfying our clergyman father, but I, perhaps because I was the only daughter, usually came off very well. My brothers still declare that I was the more skillful liar."[31] The straight and narrow that the Reverend Graham demanded may have been the initial impetus for the fanciful way that she reinvented the details of her subsequent life.

He was also the inspiration for her writing career, which began when she was eight or nine and they were living in Nashville; the "first money" she "ever earned came from writing" for the local newspaper there.[32] When they were living in Colorado Springs she wrote another article, this time about her experience with Jim Crow when she was barred from a swimming class at the YWCA. She had a good friend then, a white girl named Mabel Osborne. Though they lunched together daily, neither visited the other's home. One day after lunch they made plans to swim at the YWCA on the forthcoming Saturday, late in the afternoon. This was a good time for Graham since it would allow her to finish her chores, which involved extensive cooking and cleaning. That Saturday after completing her domestic drudgery she bathed, then dressed for her outing. She donned her best blue print blouse and excitedly arrived ahead of time. She met Mabel and they proceeded to fill out registration cards being doled out by an otherwise affable woman who greeted the growing crowd of girls with the words, "Welcome to a summer of fun in our new pool!" As the queue moved forward Graham soon found herself face to face with this seemingly pleasant woman. But her visage shifted from a smile to a frown when she glimpsed Graham's light brown face.

"What do you want?" she growled. Graham was jarred by her words. Groping for a response, she stuttered, "I came to sign up for swimming lessons."

Noting that this incipient confrontation was causing unease among the other girls, the woman changed her tone but not her meaning.

"We don't have classes for . . . colored girls as yet," she purred. Graham was mortified, though she drew herself up and replied forcefully, "the lady said that all students could join." Mabel comforted her friend, giving her a warm embrace, but this was insufficient to stem Graham's anger. Tears rolled from her eyes as she turned away. As she walked the six blocks to her home she felt simultaneously confusion, anger, and sadness. What about Mabel, she thought, and her other "friends"; "suddenly, I was thinking of them as my white friends! Or, were they really friends?"

When she arrived home, it was her father she went to and it was he who comforted her. "You are now thirteen," he told her, "young but not too young to speak out in protest against this kind of evil by a so-called Christian organization."

Already she had developed an appreciation for the power of words, so she responded by writing an editorial that her influential father was able to place in a local newspaper. Though attempting to soothe the situation, the YWCA executive director roiled the waters further by explaining to the Grahams, "can't you understand the problem we have? Can't you see that we have to consider the feelings of all our citizens?

We can't insult people before we educate them to accept . . . your people!" After Graham's father finished rebuking her, the woman left his
office in tears.

This was another piercing experience with racism that helped to
shape Graham's consciousness. It was also another lesson in gender relations, in that her "sisters" across the color line disdained her while her
father rose to her defense.[33] Such incidents may also have had an ideological impact as she witnessed that the "Christianity" of the YWCA
was something less than all-encompassing. As a junior in the Colorado
Springs high school, already she was expressing the exasperation with
religion that would eventually lead her to Marxism:

> The white saloon keeper's daughter is invited and welcomed. Oh! she
> needs help and encouragement. Of course she does. But the colored
> minister's daughter is turned away. And why? . . . Christian associa-
> tion! Far better would it be to change their name and call themselves
> any kind of society or club except a Christian one.[34]

■

The constant moves of her peripatetic father meant that Graham was
forced to interact and become friendly with new people regularly; she
had to learn the skill of dealing effectively with relative strangers. This
constant movement also meant, in her words, that she was either "way
ahead of class" or "way behind." She attended racially "mixed schools"
and "separate schools." Her schooling was "checkered," but she
learned a great deal about the nation and "our people." This constant
movement and frequent interaction with strangers also gave her insight
into human personality, which was to prove useful in both her art and
her politics.[35]

In 1912 she was enrolled at the Tenth Street High School in
Clarksville, Tennessee. That year she graduated from the equivalent of
junior high school; "Lola Graham," the valedictorian, provided an ora-
tion at commencement on "The Ends of the Earth," and her remarks
were "frequently interrupted with applause." Her proud father also
spoke. She left with the "highest honors of her class."[36]

Shirley Graham had become a talented young woman. In 1915 her
family was living in Spokane, Washington, and she was distinguishing
herself by winning the "gold medal offered by the Remington Typewriter Co. for proficiency."[37] Regularly she was giving piano recitals;

one at the First AME Church in Seattle featured her playing the works of Chopin. She graduated from Lewis and Clark High School in Spokane with high honors. She had been recognized as the class poet and won an essay contest by writing about the subject of one of her later biographies, Booker T. Washington.[38]

The Pacific Northwest was not graced with a heavy concentration of African Americans, though it did have a substantial number of Native Americans and Asian Americans. This could lead to a contradictory effect: bigotry that in other regions would otherwise be absorbed by blacks was dispersed and diffused; yet the absence of bipolar racism could also foment a "compounded" racism that could appear worse than what other areas of the nation had to offer.[39]

Thus, despite Graham's manifest talents, opportunities were not widespread for African American women during the World War I era, even in the Pacific Northwest where they were few and far between. After leaving high school she entered a trade school, where she polished her typing skills and qualified as an office clerk. She moved further west to Seattle, where she worked at a naval yard and part-time at a movie house playing the organ and singing between the changing of the reels. There she met Shadrach T. McCants, whom she married in 1921.[40] It was a large wedding with her father presiding.

Not much is known about her first husband, with whom she gave birth to two sons, Robert in 1923 and David in 1925. He was from South Carolina but wound up in the Pacific Northwest, where he worked for a newspaper and as a tailor, not to mention owning a clothing store. The marriage was short-lived. Subsequently Graham claimed—falsely— that he died in the 1920s; still, the reasons for her divorce remain murky.

In her memoir, for example, she claims—inaccurately—that "within three years" of her marriage, "I was a widow with two small sons, the younger still a baby." However, she was definitely accurate when she stated, "for the years immediately following, everything I did, everything I planned, everything I tried to do was motivated by my passionate desire to make a good life for my sons—to be able to bring them up in security and dignity."[41] Her desire to provide for her sons—along with her concern for racial uplift and a not insubstantial ambition— fueled her enormous productivity.

Her divorce decree was rendered in Portland, Oregon, in 1927; her husband defaulted and, apparently, did not contest the divorce.[42] Why did she leave her first husband? The answer is unclear. Her surviving son, David, feels that she felt burdened with the responsibility of being a caretaker for her family, her younger brothers particularly; her mother, he says, was "physically weak" and perceived as "delicate," which resulted in Shirley Graham's being given "much greater responsibility" for household duties. Thus, her marriage was an escape. Moreover, Shirley Graham apparently was disgruntled with other aspects of her family life. Her mother's family were "very, very light skinned Black Americans" and resented her mother's marriage to David Graham, who was rather dark. And the fact that Shirley Graham was baptized a Baptist—not a member of the AME church of her father—suggests some alienation from family tradition, just as changing her name from McCants to McCanns after her divorce and referring to herself as Shirley, not Lola, were other examples of her desire to forge her own path and identity. Hence, her son does not feel that "she married out of love or desire to raise a family" but as a means of escape and defiance.[43] Late in life, Graham Du Bois felt guilty about her behavior toward her first husband, suggesting that he was more "sinned against than [sinning]."[44] Still, when her sons were growing up, she would become violently angry when his name was mentioned.[45] When David was twelve and she discovered he was trying to contact his father, "she nearly had a fit." "She ranted and raved," though she later manifested a "terrible, terrible sense of injustice" about how she had treated her spouse and feared that "the real nature of their separation" would be discovered. She raised them under the misimpression that their father was a "gambler," that he "sold his house and abandoned us," that "he threatened to kill us." Her son David says, "I doubt now that any of this was true."

Thus, David and his brother were raised by their maternal grandparents, a time filled with "happy memories"; however, being "sons" of a minister, they were "expected to behave in that way," and as a result their "very stern" grandfather "whipped [them] regularly."[46] Unfortunately, growing up without their father impacted her son David particularly in a negative way. He conceded,

> How I wish I had known him! . . . I know that the fact that I never knew my father, that I was raised in a variety of homes other than that of my mother and father, that I grew to manhood hardly knowing my mother . . . all these things have deeply affected my life and the person that I am today.

With a final note of bitterness he referred forlornly to his mother: "she does not know me, she has never known me—and possibly now it's too late."[47]

Ironically, though she was able to nurture and "mother" other men during her long life, she was accused of abdicating this responsibility as it pertained to her own sons. Perhaps there was a connection between the two: her "mothering" of others may have been a substitute and compensation for her perceived failings in providing it to her offspring.

Her son's aching rancor stems in part from the fact that after divorcing, Graham Du Bois left her sons with her parents and others and embarked on her career. Her children felt abandoned. Her responsibility as a caretaker had helped drive her into an unwise marriage, and fleeing the responsibility of caretaker to her sons helped drive her into her engagement with African art and politics. But like the daughter of Nelson Mandela, who flinched in his embrace because she felt he was more interested in being father to a nation than father to her, Graham Du Bois's son felt similar ambivalence about his mother.[48]

Graham Du Bois did learn from this wrenching experience. Subsequently, she became a pillar of strength for those women friends of hers who were experiencing the emotional turmoil of divorce, which was viewed much less benignly in the past than it is today.[49] Still, the scars left from starting her own family never completely healed.

■

As noted, David Graham, Shirley's father, was hostile to the idea of divorce; perhaps not coincidentally, she abandoned Shadrach McCants as her father was leaving to work in Africa, thus minimizing direct negative reaction from him. Liberia College was his destination. Graham Du Bois's sister-in law Ruth Morris Graham (who met her future spouse— Graham Du Bois's brother Lorenz there) recalled the city of Monrovia as "very shabby, not a restaurant, not a movie theater." The college itself was "really [a] shambles when we arrived . . . it was very poor." There were sociopolitical tensions too as an Americo-Liberian elite of ten thousand, descendants of African Americans, confronted "a million indigenous people and there was always a conflict there."[50]

Liberia College, also known as Monrovia College, was founded by Graham Du Bois's uncle, Bishop Samson Brooks. There were a few hundred students registered of all ages, from adults to children. They were taught gardening, carpentry, housekeeping, "self-care," and "sanitation." This model of education was definitely of the Washington—not the Du Bois—variety, which may help to account for the disgruntlement of the Reverend Graham. The government was an autocracy and slavery was tolerated; anticipating his daughter's political evolution, he was of the opinion that a "revolution" might be necessary there.[51]

Liberia College was "the first secular English-speaking institution of higher learning in tropical Africa." Despite this manifest accomplishment, it was easy to see why the Reverend Graham's mind turned to "revolution" upon arriving there. Hollis Lynch has observed that "social stratification based on color" with a mulatto elite at the top was an integral aspect of Liberia at that time.[52] "The faculty" of the college "were all biased in favor of European points of view"; they "assumed the inferiority of African languages, cultures and societies."[53]

Meanwhile, free of direct familial responsibilities, Graham Du Bois left to study at the Sorbonne in Paris, worked at Howard University and Morgan State University, then subsequently enrolled in Oberlin College. However, she was plagued by a solemn concern, expressed repeatedly, about leaving her two young sons in the hands of others.

Consequently, she sought to compensate for her absence by showering them with gifts, which was not easy since she frequently skirted the edges of poverty. Her son Robert, concerned about her frazzled appearance, once told her,

> grandma . . . told me something that I am worried [about]. She said that you were thin and looked tired from work . . . mother your life is not worth any Ph.d. Momma make plans this summer for at least two months worth of rest and joy . . . you have been working for the last four years very hard. . . . Rest mother so you can live a long time . . . even if it is us you [are] working for. Make it for us you are resting.[54]

However, earlier—and more typically—he had written, "Mama I hate to bring this up but Mrs. Barnes [his caretaker] wants me to [say] she told me that Graham and I need some shirts, pants, and socks, underwear."[55]

As an absent mother, she was no doubt concerned when Robert wrote from his boarding school in Virginia, recounting his experiences with racial segregation—"They have one show and Negroes sit in the balcony." How did she feel when he said that instead of traveling to see her, he preferred to use the money for clothes? "I think right now clothes are more important to me than travelling." He wanted "'dark' glasses . . . a pair of pants, some socks and underwear . . . maybe a few 'polo shirts,'" while a bicycle would be a "fine tonic" for his brother. Of course, he was concerned that his mother might not be "eating enough" and reminded her of a "McCanns famous saying, 'If you save money from life's necessities, what have you gained.'" Nonetheless, satisfying his material wants became her surrogate for satisfying his emotional needs, and Shirley Graham McCanns was forced to work even more and engender even more concern from her firstborn.[56]

Her young son David was equally supportive:

> you said something to me about Robert and I standing on your shoulders. Well I am sure if we didn't have your shoulders to stand on we would be in a pretty bad fix. Sometimes I think about the boys and girls who have no mother's shoulders to stand on and how they need them so much. I am proud of [you]. So now don't work too hard for you have two sons standing on your shoulders and if you work too hard the burden will be too much for you.

Still, these affecting words aside, she must have been moved when he mentioned experiences with his grandmother that he could have been sharing with his mother: "Mama you would be surprised if you could see Grandma some time after I had fixed her hair nice and put on a little touch of makeup, she is bee-oo-tee-full." Graham was so distant that at times the only time he heard her voice was when she was on the radio: "Gee!! Just think, listening to my own darling sweet mother broadcasting."[57]

Graham's journey from domesticity to a career was an untidy one, filled with difficulty; however, the pains and aches of that journey paled into insignificance compared with the concern she felt as a result of being an absent mother. Yet, as with so many other setbacks in her life, she converted this one too into an advance, for this hurt was converted into an almost heedless energy that led her to obtain two college degrees and churn out a torrent of operas, plays, and books.

2

On Her Journey Now

HER SON DAVID described Shirley Graham Du Bois as "demonstra-tive" and "vindictive" as well as "impulsive."[1] This last term best de-scribes her departure from New York City in December 1926 on a ship for Paris, leaving her children behind. Fortuitously, her strict father was in the process of departing for Liberia, so the possibility of facing his wrath had diminished. Symbolically, she had slain her spouse, describ-ing him as "deceased." Though her initial trip was not lengthy, until 1930 she would spend time intermittently in Paris.[2] This rich experience whetted her appetite for more knowledge, particularly about music and the arts, which she gained when she enrolled in Oberlin College in 1931.

Eventually her father reconciled himself to his daughter's decision to go to France, for he, her mother, and her brother Lorenz agreed to partially subsidize this venture. Lorenz Graham, who ultimately be-came a writer of note, felt that if her "jazz playing [were] passable," she could make a living as a pianist and avoid the "constant dread of an im-pending disaster." He suggested an idyll: "You can take an apartment, study your French and rester tranquille"; above all, he said, "don't let being out of work worry you."[3]

It did not. She enjoyed Paris immensely, once rhapsodizing,

> I am sitting here in my balcony window in the very center of the fa-mous Latin Quarter of Paris. When I raise my eyes I can see the tow-ers of Notre Dame. My hotel faces Le Rue De L'Ecole where stands the University of Paris. Le Boulevard Saint Michel passes in front of us and down that boulevard a couple of blocks are the Gardens of Lux-embourg, which is now the House of Senate.

It was June and she had just attended church; she "knelt . . . there on the stone floor, knelt and thanked God." According to the future Marxist, "We need not worry about the religion of Jesus Christ dying out in the world." She had enrolled in the Sorbonne and was providing articles for a black newspaper in the Pacific Northwest.[4]

Tyler Stovall has written that "blackness became the rage in Paris during the 1920s"; "the part played by Paris in the African-American rediscovery of Africa," he adds, "was both fascinating and deeply ironic." Standing near the confluence of these trends was Shirley Graham. As a black woman she felt embraced in France in a way she had not been in the United States. In Paris she encountered blacks who were not African American, and they introduced her to a part of her heritage with which she was unfamiliar.

Paris was an enchanting environment for such rediscoveries. Eslanda Robeson, an anthropologist and the wife of Paul Robeson, enthused about

> extravagantly wide sidewalks with splendid trees marching along the curbs; beautifully laid out boulevards, avenues and streets with fascinating names; lovely quiet shabby sections reeking with historical associations. Sacre Coeur in the sunlight, in the moonlight. Notre Dame. Bookstalls on the banks of the Seine. Marvellous food. . . . The Opera, American Express, Thomas Cook's. Rue de la Paix, Galeries Lafayette, Au Bon Marche. Montmartre and the cabarets; Montparnasse and the sidewalk cafes.

For "young black intellectuals," she concluded, "the French capital served as the gateway to Africa."[5] Certainly it played that role for Shirley Graham, for it was here that she encountered various forms of African music that she incorporated into her first opera.

She also encountered the small but growing colony of African Americans in Paris, which included the writer Eric Walrond.[6] Though often associated with his homeland (then known as British Guiana) and Harlem, he spent a considerable amount of time in Europe. He had worked as an editor with Marcus Garvey's *Negro World* and also with the Urban League's journal, *Opportunity*.[7] He and Graham became fast friends and frequent correspondents. Their mutual friend Ethel Ray Nance remembered him as a convivial sort who "had the knack of making friends easily. He was always bringing someone to Harlem or if people wanted to come they would say get in touch with Walrond and he'll see that you meet interesting people." He "may not have been six feet, he was slight[ly] built. He had flashing eyes, his face was very alert and very alive. . . . He was very pleasant and . . . as soon as he entered the room, you knew he was there. . . . He had quite a way of meeting strangers."[8] One of the "strangers" he admired was Graham, who, he said, was "the one person alive who really knows me inside and out. There may be something prophetic after all in our meeting." She provided him with companionship while she lived in Paris and sent him money after she returned to the United States. She also provided him— in his words—with "niggeratti gossip," as Graham was quickly becoming intimate with a select circle of Black Atlantic artists.[9]

This was not a one-sided relationship, as Walrond provided her with contacts valuable for her budding writing career; he counseled her to develop a "fame outside of the 'black belt.'" When she decided to apply for a fellowship from the Guggenheim Foundation, he suggested that she should not "go cramming your list of sponsors with niggers or negro uplift workers. Walter White, Rev. Powell, Mary Ovington," the well-known personalities she had come to rely on. No, he added, "the nature of [these] sponsors was enough to put the Foundation on its guard! Look for disinterested sponsors without personal or group axes to grind." She was interested in doing studies of African music, and he thought she should not "drag in Ras Tafari if you can help it." His questionable advice was unavailing, since she failed to win the award.[10]

Failing to gain fellowship support and not being independently wealthy, Graham was forced back into the labor market in the United States. There she gave recitals and lecture demonstrations on, for example, "The Negro's contribution to American music." One critic in 1929 described her presentation: "'singing expressively in a mood typical of a baptismal number, Mrs. McCanns struck immediately a responsive chord in her audience which clamored for more, and at least let [all] know they were listening to a true artist.'" She lectured on "The Philosophy of the Negro Spiritual" and punctuated her lecture with her lilting and mesmerizing soprano.[11] In one memorable recital in Baltimore at Grace Presbyterian Church she played Liszt and Brahms and "Ethiopia's Paean of Exaltation."[12]

In between traveling to France during the 1927–30 period, she worked as a music librarian at Howard University and a music teacher at Morgan State University in Baltimore, and she took classes at various schools during her summers, including Columbia University. She was barely scraping by. Howard, which sat on a hilltop in the middle of Washington, D.C., was regarded as the "capstone of Negro education."

Working there, for her, was akin to starting at the top. It was also a political hothouse, where student strikes and racial politics led to the appointment of Mordecai W. Johnson as its first Negro president in 1926. Such an environment was conducive to Graham's growth and development.[13] At Morgan she also taught drama and helped produce sprawling pageants, which served as a precursor for her opera *Tom-Tom*.[14] Her salary at Morgan—$1,600 per year—was meager, though it did allow her to stay directly involved in the arts.

By 1931 the thirty-five-year-old Graham was ready to take the next step in her blossoming career as an artist, as *Tom-Tom* received a full-scale production that was to bring her more directly into the public eye.

■

Shirley Graham had the skill of telling a gripping story. Her friend Abbott Simon recalls one occasion in a Manhattan restaurant when she was telling him about her latest novel in progress:

> Shirley was so dynamic in relating all the incidents that took place and relating all the intricate details and fitting them in. And, all the waitresses who had been scattered near their stations generally came near our table. And there were about 10 or 12 waitresses just hanging on every word as we were.

She had a panache that not only infused her fictional creations but was part of her everyday life. The famed sociologist Charles Johnson, one of the many powerful men who consented to lend her a hand, once observed, "your letters always give me the impression of throbbing and bouncing about from the force of your expression. This is probably the thing that gives vitality to your plays."[15]

In an ideal world, this talent—and her connections—would have meant that she could have spent the rest of her life turning out plays and film scripts. But unfortunately Graham's major works for the stage were launched in the 1930s during the Great Depression, when drama and opera were not the highest priorities for her audience, many of whom were simply trying to survive. During this time, "in Cleveland the black unemployment rate exceeded 50 percent. In Chicago and Detroit, over 40 percent of black men and 55 percent of black women were unemployed. In Harlem the unemployment rate approached 50 percent and in Philadelphia it surpassed 56 percent."[16]

Thus she quickly discovered that talent alone would be insufficient to support the two young sons she had left behind when she embarked on her new journey.[17]

Besides being African American, Graham was a woman—an additional handicap. Over time "black [women] novelists have received some degree of exposure," but "black women dramatists remain relatively unknown because their stories are considered too private for the male-dominated and public arena of the theater."[18] More pointedly, black dramatists generally have had difficulty in overcoming the social and economic difficulty involved in mounting major productions. During the 1930s, for example, "most Black theatre companies folded."[19]

That was not all. Theater generally has often attracted disreputable investors; black theater—sometimes called the "chitlin circuit"—has been no exception.[20] This often made payment of performers, playwrights, and crew unreliable. In the racially segregated world of the 1930s, "performers' salaries, like their dressing rooms, were small and shabby. A producer often absconded with the box office take, leaving the talent stranded without funds or union recourse." African American "talent" was often excluded from the unions and guilds that provided a level of protection for their Euro-American counterparts.[21] Not surprisingly, Graham faced persistent difficulties with producers and theaters.[22]

W. E. B. Du Bois had stated explicitly that he wanted to teach "the 'colored people' the meaning of their history and of their rich emotional" life and to use theater to "reveal the Negro to the white world as a 'human, feeling thing.'"[23] He wanted a theater by Negroes, for Negroes, about Negroes and near Negroes.[24] The pageants he devised—a form extended by Shirley Graham—were an essential part of this process.

Ironically, the economic and social dislocation induced by the Great Depression did provide fertile soil for the rise of an alternative theater similar to what Du Bois envisioned. The rampant radicalism of the era was largely responsible. Lionel Trilling is correct in suggesting that "in any view of the American cultural situation, the importance of the radical movement cannot be overestimated. It may be said to have created the American intellectual class as we now know it in its great size and influence."[25] However, there were limitations. The "symbolic systems of the Popular Front" of that era "drew on a traditional iconographic and rhetoric of manhood and womanhood that was at odds with the utopian and emancipatory hopes of the movement."[26] Consequently, "women remained in a marginal and subordinated position in that movement, excluded both from the arrangements of power and from the symbolic system of labor."[27] As a result, "American radicalism" in a fundamental sense "remained a guardian of male sexual authority."[28]

This analysis was applicable with added force to Graham, for the culture industry was known for its use of the "casting couch." As a single mother and divorcée at a time when both were viewed widely as a marker for loose morals, she was even more susceptible to being preyed on and not taken seriously as an artist.

However, the theater may have been a mite better than, for example, the film industry. On the stage, for decades, women had been an essential part of production; though "the theater remains curiously absent from larger considerations of women's history and from histories of feminism," the fact is that "the history of the suffragette movement," for example, "is thus a history of carefully produced pageants and processions, dramatic scenes and elaborate disguises"—that is, the kind of drama that had become Graham's early specialty.[29]

■

Over the course of her life Graham moved from operas to plays to biographies to novels, as if seeking a form that would allow her to express her creativity and earn a secure income. She quickly discovered that writing operas during the Great Depression was not the soundest method by which an African American woman could escape privation.

Black women composers had been active in the United States only since the late nineteenth century; thus Graham was in some sense a pioneer.[30] In the spring of 1929 while at Morgan State she produced an early version of her opera Tom-Tom. Randolph Edmonds directed; the pioneer African American filmmaker Carlton Moss was also involved.[31] Her early work in this realm was inspired by the great African American performer Roland Hayes, who was "so helpful, so anxious to encourage any young person of the race who sought his advice and counsel," though when she bumped into him in Europe she "found him quite different . . . more reticent, more aloof" (as she herself would be described later).[32] Nevertheless, Hayes—yet another powerful man who sparked her creativity—was an inspiration as she began to craft her major work.

After its preliminary production in 1929, *Tom-Tom* did not receive a full-scale production until 1932. In the meantime she was scrambling for fellowship money, working at Morgan State, applying to and being admitted to Oberlin College, and seeking vainly to maintain close ties to her two children. By mid-1931 her brother Lorenz was commiserating with her about her "suffering a breakdown," though he was "by no means surprised."[33] She claimed that her "greatest ambition" at that point was simply to "go fishing."[34] Yet somehow she managed the energy to put together what one critic has called "the first all-black opera to be produced on a large [scale]," with "a professional cast of approximately 500 actors," and the "first opera by an African-American woman to be produced."[35] Filled with pride, her brother Lorenz termed it "the biggest Negro work of many a year and the most important musical work of America."[36] With *Tom-Tom,* though her financial situation did not improve markedly, Graham was catapulted into the front ranks of black America and established herself as a major artistic force.

Tom-Tom was an ambitious effort in music, dance, and drama that sought to map the journey of Africans in North America from slavery to freedom. One catalyst for this ambitious work was her father, who "instilled" in her a "deep love and reverence for the spirituals. . . . Long before the spirituals became popular it was his custom to use them as text for his sermons and as subjects for lectures when invited to speak at other churches." While residing in Paris she "listened to the even more primitive music of the French Negroes"; she found it "strange that I could remember that harmony so much more easily than I could the harmony of my conservatory class." Then when her brother Lorenz returned from Liberia he brought melodies he had heard "which seemed far more familiar than did the popular songs which I heard all around me." Combining with these influences was her innate musical sense: "to this day my personal friends knew my secret 'knock' which for them is even more certain than my signature." While teaching at Morgan she "dramatized music with my pupils. That really was the beginning of *Tom-Tom.*" This sweeping opera was designed to show the ties between the "blues" in "Harlem cabarets" and the rhythms of Africa. It was the "beating heart of a people."[37] This massive work, produced at a time when some Africans who had been slaves in the U.S. South were still living, had as its signature the persistent percussion of the drum— a pervasive sound that punctuated plantation life and the postslavery experience of African Americans.[38]

Tom-Tom, she said later, was "an attempt to show the development of music from the most primitive drum beats to the highly complicated tonalities of today. This thread is traced through . . . the particular medium of the Negro."[39] This exhaustive work was conceived by a woman without the formal training of many of her peers. While working at Howard she had also taken classes in music and had studied music in New York City in the summer of 1929 at the Institute of Musical Arts.[40] But this was a far cry from the finished conservatory training of many with whom she was competing for funding and attention.

However, what she lacked in formal training she made up for in ideas: her gravitation to things African was inspired and provocative. Deftly she "took three pairs of timpani and wrote the overture just for the timpani"; this, she recalled later, "had never been done before so I understand." She continued, "if you take three pairs—that is actually six drums—and pitch them and you just pitch them by the chain that is purely the timpani, it is a copy of the African drum."[41]

This creativity was in the service of a theme of "premature Afrocentrism," for she described her opera as "the voice of Africa calling her children to a better understanding and a deeper appreciation for the gifts which she has showered upon them."[42] Thus, this work placed her decisively on one side of a looming divide about the role of Africa in African American life. The philosopher Alain Locke had counseled African Americans to look to Africa for inspiration, while other, more powerful forces sought to deny this tie.[43] The *New York Times,* for example, boldly proclaimed, "American Jazz Is Not African."[44] Graham's contemporary, the black painter Allan Randall Freelon, agreed with the paper of record and worried that African American artists would be "misled into attempting to create an African art in America. The American Negro," he asserted, "has no more actual knowledge of his 'tribal background' and 'jungle ways' than has the Anglo-American of ancient Druidic Rites."[45] Graham dissented, feeling that her work would help to reestablish trans-Atlantic ties long frayed, while reflecting ties that had not disappeared. Still, a dismissive, if not negative, attitude toward Africa was all too common at that time, particularly in the theater;[46] Graham's work countered this trend.

What was even more stunning about this work were the conditions under which it was written. Graham had just been accepted by Oberlin College in 1931 and had sent her earlier version of the opera to Cleveland's renowned Karamu Theater for consideration. The producers were suitably impressed, but wanted her to rework it for the Cleveland Opera. So she took a leave of absence, got a hotel room with a piano, and in three months expanded this work into a three-act, sixteen-scene opera for which she wrote both the libretto and music.[47]

The main characters, Voodoo Man, Preacher, and others, were meant to signify the profound figures that had driven African history in this hemisphere. Scenes involved Africans' being brought as slaves to the Americas in darkness, then "the light of Christianity appears."[48] The premiere in the summer of 1932 at Cleveland Stadium drew a crowd of ten thousand; the second performance, fifteen thousand. The prominent Washington figure Newton Baker, the governor of Ohio, and other notables attended.[49]

She received instant critical acclaim. The NAACP organ, the *Crisis*, was enraptured, marveling at how she

> used as a background for her melodic structures weird, unpublished, rarely heard Negro folk songs of the Southern swamps. . . . The first act opens in an African jungle before 1619, the second indicates the African in America, the third and last act takes the Negro to Harlem. Running through and underlying all the action from jungle to Harlem is the steady beat of the tom-tom, reminiscent of a similar practice in the "Emperor Jones." To secure realism for its jungle reproductions, producers have imported from Africa, Indoxiz Chiakazia, native voodoo-man. Elaborate staging plans call for elevated trains, subways, automobiles, cabarets, sailing vessels which explode, hundreds of dancers, pantomimists, warriors, headhunters. . . . If successful, the entire production will be moved to New York for a series of presentations at Madison Square Garden this winter.[50]

One critic corrected the *Crisis* by disputing the notion that there were elevated subways on stage; however, apparently, there were live elephants. Whatever the case, it could not be denied that this was a major and significant production.[51]

One critic, John Gruesser, years later was similarly kind to this work: "Although a significant number of the African-American dramatic works of the period concerned the continent, only Shirley Graham's opera *Tom-Tom* possesses the length, complexity, and power to be called major." George Walker and Bert Williams in earlier works like *In*

Dahomey and *In Abyssinia* fundamentally had lampooned the continent, displayed contempt, and bowed to reigning racial stereotypes. W. E. B. Du Bois's pageant *The Star of Ethiopia* was comparable to her work but not as ambitious. Graham's work, in contrast, had "modernist ambiguity and heartfelt sensitivity" and, ironically, surpassed the work of her future spouse with an early example of "double-consciousness." In this opera Graham "continually presents theses and antitheses." In the first act the Voodoo Man selects a Girl to be sacrificed to the gods in order to halt slave traders, while the Boy encourages her to escape. In the second act Voodoo Man clings to his African religion and rejects Christianity. In the third act the Boy, now a minister in Harlem, condemns Voodoo Man's plan to transport African Americans back to Africa. A "recurrent theme in the opera is the prospect of separation that confronts the Girl and her Mother . . . in the final act . . . the Mother decides to go to Africa and leave her daughter behind because of the crass materialism and immorality she sees in the United States." Though Graham did not provide an unqualified endorsement for then popular "back-to-Africa" themes, she warily suggested that Africans could live in North America without "sacrificing their African heritage." *Tom-Tom*, Gruesser concludes, "epitomizes 'twoness,'" the duality felt by many Africans in this hemisphere.[52]

That summer the Cleveland Opera also presented *Carmen, Die Valkyrie,* and *Aida,* but *Tom-Tom* was the hit of the season. It was broadcast over NBC radio and "received great media attention and the reviews, apart from some complaints about technical problems, were generally quite favorable."[53] These favorable opinions were a reflection of a high-powered cast that included Jules Bledsoe, Charlotte Murray, and Luther King.[54]

The *Cleveland News* was enthusiastic. "In the second act, Miss Graham proves herself a folk-poet. . . . In the third act, Miss Graham exhibits a robust talent for humor and . . . irony."[55] The *Cleveland Press* felt likewise, noting that the opera

> drew the two largest audiences of the season . . . Miss Graham can talk—they call her "the little minister." She can play the piano. She had made a wide study of the development of the Negro from the jungle to his present in America, particularly his music, from jungle rhythm to spirituals and to modern jazz.[56]

Shirley Graham had heeded the call of Alain Locke. Still, modern eyes might look askance at her evocation of Africa. One critic has suggested that this opera "was acceptable to whites and . . . reinforced their belief that Blacks were 'exotic' and 'primitive.'"[57] At the final dress rehearsal some of the women dancers held up the performance by going on strike. Why? There was an "attempt to have them dance with just loin cloths and exposed breasts and the girls refused."[58] Nevertheless, compared with the images of Africans that then reigned, *Tom-Tom* was a great leap forward.[59]

Ironically, some of Graham's toughest critics were Euro-American liberals. Her friend Mary White Ovington wondered why she did not have more whites in the orchestra: "you could get a French horn or other instruments among the whites. Of course, it's fine to help the race, but . . . It would help to have some whites."[60] Taking note of Graham's fascination with Wagner, Herbert Miller of Bryn Mawr College pointed out that this composer

> is more responsible for this racial monstrosity that has come into Germany than any other person. He did it exactly with the same animus that has underlain much of your frantic struggle to prove the greatness of the Negro in Music. It would be a dreadful thing, if, a century hence, it could be shown that you were to blame for precipitating race suppression and cruelty.

Irate with her presumed ethnocentrism, he concluded with a final thrust, "Much of the Jewish reaction to Hitler is taking his own argument in reverse, and is therefore equally bad."[61] It was true that racism helped to generate nationalism, but was the nationalism of an oppressed group comparable to that of the oppressor?

Niggling criticisms aside, the opera burnished Graham's reputation, but it did not substantially alter her bank balance. She was "negotiating for a New York production when the final bank crash came. The company still owes me money."[62] Still, her tireless labors were not without effect: *Tom-Tom* had helped to beat her name into the consciousness of black America.

■

Graham continued to face the problem of how to construct a livelihood that would allow her to support herself and her two sons. Attending college was yet another way to address this nagging question. In 1931 she entered Oberlin College and eventually left with both a B.A. and an M.A. From there she taught at a college in Tennessee before joining the Federal Theater Project in Chicago, for whom she helped to adapt the Gilbert and Sullivan play *The Mikado,* a work that won numerous accolades—and imitations. This led to a two-year Rosenwald Fellowship that took her to the Yale School of Drama. All the while she was creating a stream of plays, *Dust to Earth* and *Elijah's Ravens* among them. This was a formidable litany of achievement by any measure. Yet surviving as an artist—particularly an African American woman artist—at this time remained difficult.[63]

She entered Oberlin—a school noted for both its willingness to educate African Americans and its music conservatory—with high hopes and ambition. With a stern determination typical of those W. E. B. Du Bois had called the "Talented Tenth" of Negroes, Graham argued that "we do not have in our race a thoroughly trained musicologist, one who speaks with authority, whose word must be received. If the Negro is to attain his place in music we must have such leaders."[64] One of her professors there, impressed by her tenacity, felt that the "dominant purpose of her life is to contribute something in her power to the educational purposes of her people." Graham, he continued, was "not like some colored people of exceptional abilities who seem anxious to get away from contact with the rank and file of their race but precisely the opposite."[65] No, she was a "race woman" imbued with the ideology of racial uplift and determined to make a contribution to her people. Music, the talent encouraged by her mother, was her vehicle for this project; music could not only soothe the savage breast but also, as her opera demonstrated, spark interest in the roots and realities of African Americans.

Graham possessed a firm belief in the creative impulses of her people, which she hoped to redeem at Oberlin. She believed in the "innate artistic soul of the Negro." This belief was not metaphysical but grounded in "age-old wisdom." For Negroes, she thought, "beaten down by suffering, pain and hurt to which we are constantly exposed, whimsical fancy, soaring high hopes, all these and more like smothering coals lie planted in our beings." These harsh conditions dialectically could spur the creation of moving art. The power of this impulse led her to the conclusion that "Negro music has become American music."[66]

Oberlin was "wonderful" for Graham "in every way. I have never been so happy. My life has never been so full."[67] Still, this idyllic description could not mask the past that accompanied her to Ohio. When she applied to Oberlin in the spring of 1931 she was almost thirty-five, substantially older than her classmates; this may help to explain why she shaved years off her age in her application, alleging that she was thirty.[68] Once more, this falsification can be seen not only as reflective of a personal flaw but, perhaps more so, reflective of a society where age and gender discrimination were far from absent.

Nor did her tenure at Oberlin reduce the "responsibility which I owe my two little sons . . . I have had to sacrifice them greatly in order to get this training." Robert and David had to relinquish "so many things, good schooling, music lessons . . . their grandparents have given them a good home, but all the kind of training which I wanted them to have has of necessity been neglected."[69] Her anxiety about how her drive to establish herself as an artist affected her children fueled even more her already frantic pace. She did "sacrifice them," but she also sacrificed in other ways to obtain a higher education during the midst of the Depression. Fortunately, her engaging personality made it easier for those she encountered—particularly powerful men—to assist her.

Still, Graham entered Oberlin with sound qualifications. She had matriculated at the Sorbonne and Columbia and had studied Latin, French, Spanish, ancient and medieval history, and physics. She had won prizes in high school in "composition and public speaking." She entered with a "definite plan for research work in Africa." Why did she apply to this college? Because "Oberlin has produced more Negroes who are giving valued service to humanity than any other college." Why had there been an interregnum between her high school graduation and college application? "Because it was necessary for me to work" was her simple reply.[70]

While studying at Oberlin she worked at a laundry to support herself and her sons. This kind of labor was one of the few jobs that African American women could obtain at the time.[71] Though some have viewed her as part of an affluent Negro elite, she continued to share the lot of the black working class, which made her effort to portray this life in her plays even more heartfelt. This labor did not allow her to escape debt, however, as she remained dependent on the college and the kindness of virtual strangers to help her make ends meet.[72]

Though Oberlin had a merited reputation for being more accepting of black students when other colleges were shunning them, it was far from being a pristine refuge. Graham noted at the time that "fully eighty-five per cent of those on the town relief" in the area surrounding the campus were Negroes.[73] It was easier for her to keep the faith with the downtrodden when she herself was not far from this status.

She maintained a full load of courses. While conceding, "I'm intimately interested in all of this," she complained that for "the last three weeks I worked in a kind of blind stagger . . . this semester I'm taking courses in 'Opera,' other than Wagner, 'Beethoven,' 'Renaissance Painting', 'Essay Writing', and 'Piano.'"[74] Working in a laundry while studying constantly did little to offset a financial—and perhaps emotional—deficit for her. In one fell swoop she made a combined effort to meet both deficits; in an unorthodox arrangement she borrowed funds from one of her professors, Edward Dickinson, with whom the attractive divorcée apparently had more than a casual relationship. He taught history and music criticism and besides giving her grades occasionally provided her with a loan. In return he noted, "there is one thing you may give me in its stead, and that is your love."[75] Once he confided frankly, "From me you have love. Oh, if love could be turned into shekels you would be a millionaire!" This professor of desire also provided emotional sustenance, telling her, "I think of your hard life and I admire and love your courage and faith."[76]

Actually, it is unclear what the exact dimensions of the Dickinson-Graham relationship were, although it is safe to say that it would not meet current standards in the academy. Nevertheless, it is entirely possible that this relationship was an example of unrequited affection, with her viewing him as a mere confidante—or a source of funds occasionally—and the lusty professor viewing her as something more. Evidently she had disclosed to him details of her affections for another man or men. In response he wrote her a fourteen-page missive—somewhat akin to a term paper—waxing poetic about sex and sin, virginity and women's liberation; but for whatever reason she apparently did not open it. I did.[77]

Presumably, Dickinson was a kind of voyeur, since by his own count eleven women were writing him about their "love 'affairs.'" Apparently Graham was among them. As he once told her, "And when you, dear, spend a night in a hotel bedroom with an old friend, and you say, in a phrase that made me smile: 'We did come very close that night, as close as two human beings can come.'" From there he launched another disquisition, citing Swinburne, Casanova, and *Anthony Adverse*. Posing a query that was intuitively obvious, he continued, "Perhaps you wonder why a man like me with the most sensitive and enthusiastic appreciation of the most delicate and the most imposing aesthetic values in literature and art should be fond of risque stories."[78]

As an unmarried woman in a society where women's sexuality was both hard to discuss and hard to fulfill, Graham may have viewed this relationship as a form of therapy. She was, after all, a human being with human desires, despite the stultifying nature of the society in which she found herself. On the other hand, Dickinson may have been an eccentric taking literary liberties, since it is unclear if her own letters were sufficiently provocative to elicit such sexually suggestive responses from him. At one point he described her as "one of my wisest friends" who had "spoken of 'beauty' in connection with sexual pleasure." It seemed that she was considering submitting an article on sexuality to the *Forum*, while confessing intimate details to him. He responded, "your 'playboy' as you call him, is a mystery to me. Is he still in love with you, and wants to marry you?"[79] Later he added, "Be sure that I consider your risque indulgences in former times perfectly legitimate for they never did any harm to yourself or to anyone else."[80] But soon Dickinson was complaining, "I am clamoring for another of your brilliant and affectionate letters. I have not had one for two weeks, which is a long and desolate period of deprivation." Yet despite this vacuum, he added, "you have brought this exaction of mine upon yourself because you love me and have made me love you."[81]

Other than saying that this was a fascinating professor-student relationship, it is difficult to arrive at firm conclusions about this liaison. She had bolted from her father's home to that of her husband and now she was by herself and in college, far away from family and close friends. Was she hungry for an emotional life beyond the mundane or was Professor Dickinson simply exceeding the bounds of propriety?

It did appear that Graham was involved intimately with Joseph Himes, who taught at Shorter College in North Little Rock, Arkansas. Like Dickinson, he supplied her with funds from time to time, though he too was far from being affluent. On one occasion he sent her seven dollars from his monthly salary of seventy-five dollars: "two dollars are for the children. Take them to a show or something, make them happy, you know dearest." He was "afraid that you wouldn't want me to send you any money" and professed love.[82] Writing love poems was part of his arsenal too, though he was concerned about a "load of gossip circulating in Oberlin, about me and you and about you and me and the small-town tongues are darting out deliciously in wicked little blue-forks and having a glorious time of wagging."[83] That society might have frowned on their relationship helps to explain why she may have been reticent about it, and why today it is difficult to ascertain its exact contours.

Himes, according to his own description, was a handsome African American man; he had light eyes and light skin and was fashionably thin. His words to her were often overwrought, sometimes lyrical, often blunt. He once asked her, "Did you or did you not try to make me fall in love with you. The circumstantial evidence, as I see it . . . seems to point to 'did.' You thought me interesting and attractive, more so in-deed than any other man you had met (I quote you here)."[84] Himes was trying to remind her why she had found him attractive because Graham was tiring of him; his presence in Arkansas, then Austin, Texas, did not appear to make her heart grow fonder. She moved around quite a bit but apparently was not taken with the idea of long-distance romance. Concerned that she was contemplating ending what he described as their "engagement," he said plaintively, "you must never say such a thing."[85] But she did. Himes might be described today as a "mama's boy," and at this stage in life she was fleeing the caretaker role that she adopted later when she married W. E. B. Du Bois.

During this period Graham was not neglectful of the emotional side of her life. During the Depression decade she struck up a close friend-ship with Thomas Poston; he was flattered by her attention, adding that "I didn't feel [that] . . . a mail-carrier could retain the interest of so fine and aggressive a person" as herself. Now that she had moved he wanted her to come visit, helpfully adding, "of course if you come here as my guest arrangements will have to be made accordingly."[86]

As an ambitious woman with two young sons to support, Shirley Graham needed to establish contact with powerful individuals—who in a patriarchal society were mostly men—that could help her succeed. Thus, when she applied again for a fellowship from the Guggenheim Foundation, James Weldon Johnson was one of her references.[87] She corresponded with the president of Birmingham Southern College, who promised that if he were in her "vicinity . . . at any time during the year I shall certainly get in touch with you."[88] The Reverend Adam Clayton Powell, Sr.—father of the future powerful congressman—bap-tized her and added, "if I should see an opening of any kind" for work "I will be glad to write or wire you."[89] Her initial contacts with W. E. B.

Du Bois during the 1930s probably stemmed from a genuine desire to make contact with someone who might be helpful to her career. For as the economy collapsed during the Depression decade, like so many others, Shirley Graham found that she needed help; both professors Dickinson and Himes provided her with funds, not just sensual words.

Moreover, one of her friends once told her, "I'm doing fine just being a house-wife but truly I get awfully restless sometimes."[90] Graham, who had escaped the bonds of domesticity by fleeing to Paris, knew what it meant to be "restless" and at this moment felt that being a "housewife" alone could detract from her fervent wish to uplift the race, the goal of her tenure in Oberlin.

Besides, Graham was buoyantly spirited, intelligent, and a boon companion. The candid Professor Dickinson once confessed to her, "from grave to gay, from lively to severe, reflective, observant, serious, emotional, intellectual—I find in you everything that a man of my sort can desire in a friend and correspondent."[91] Dickinson was effusive but not inaccurate in describing her; he captured the qualities—and multiple identities—that made her so appealing to so many: "How many different personalities are you? Student, writer, dancer, actor, director, visitor, and not least, an ardent friend and tireless correspondent."[92] These attractive qualities made it easier for the influential to respond to her entreaties.

And simple economic necessity often motivated her contacts with these powerful men. But when she reached out to the Reverend Powell for help in finding work, he reminded her that

> without exaggeration there are more than 10,000 people in New York belonging to the white collar class of which you are a member, that find it impossible to get anything to do. There are 5000 teachers here now on the waiting list. Many of them have gone into private families and are doing the work of maids.[93]

Mary White Ovington, the writer and NAACP founder with whom Graham was friendly, confirmed that "everyone wants to come to New York and of course we have nothing like enough work for the people already here."[94] In order to become a maid, Shirley Graham did not need to sacrifice for an Oberlin education.

Headlines were replete with stories of breadlines and homelessness. This was sufficient by itself to motivate her to work ever harder.

An amazed Professor Dickinson once asked her, "when you speak of working from 7:30 a.m. to midnight or after, you don't mean 7:30 a.m. You can't mean that."[95] She did mean that. Dickinson thought "an ordinary person would be exhausted by the work you are doing." She was not ordinary, but she was often exhausted.[96] Thus Dickinson was forced to accept that "in a recent letter you say you are so crowded with work that you have no time for romance—'refusing all plans of a romantic nature.'"[97]

Her tireless labor was so stunning that her friend Mary White Ovington, who circulated in the same elevated circles as Graham herself, also advised her to take it easy.[98] But economic necessity, the desire to avoid the monotony of the "mad housewife," and her wish to make a contribution to her people all impelled Graham to work relentlessly.

Consequently, she left Oberlin in 1935 with two degrees. Her M.A. thesis on African music, part of which was published, was described by one editor as a "splendid piece of research" that "presented the achievements of your race . . . in a very dignified and thorough manner."[99] Despite having to hold down a regular job, she was an active student, having organized a "Caravanzia" at Oberlin that featured the cultural contributions of fourteen nations; this harbinger of "multiculturalism" and precursor of her own internationalism included a tango, a Hindu worship ceremony, Seppaku ("an ancient Japanese suicide ceremony"), and Korean folk music. All the while she was giving recitals and performances in the immediate region for extra income.[100]

Graham cherished her years at Oberlin and was not averse to coming to the defense of her alma mater. After Gustavus Adolphus Steward wrote an article containing a "general criticism of Oberlin," she sprang into action. She collected information surreptitiously from the school's administration for a counterattack. "Somehow or in some way alumni groups must reach such people," she acknowledged. She felt "very strongly about this." "I promise to be careful," she conceded, in seeking to undermine this writer, if not his stinging points about her alma mater.[101]

A grateful alumna, she contributed financially to her alma mater over the years. Years later she was conducting research in the archives of her adopted homeland, Tanzania, when a woman approached her for an interview. Graham was trying to shoo her away. However, she recalled, "she clinched her argument with, 'But I'm from Oberlin, too!' I gave her an interview. We Oberlinites have to stick together!"[102] She remained grateful for her education there, staying in contact over the years with Professor Frederick Artz, who "opened up history to me and made it live."[103]

Now Graham had the formal education necessary to fulfill her wish to speak with "authority" in a field—music—to which Africans had made contributions of global significance.[104] But the Depression still lingered and she was still an African American woman in a society dominated by Jim Crow, so her prospects for fulfilling her desire were not bright.

3

The Middle of Her Journey

BY THE MID-1930s Shirley Graham was in a sense part of the highest echelon among African Americans: she held two degrees from Oberlin and was rapidly gaining a sterling reputation as a creative artist. This high standing was to bring her a preeminent role in the newly formed Federal Theater Project, a New Deal enterprise designed to give work to unemployed artists while spreading widely the bounty of culture. However, she was quickly discovering that devising operas and plays was not the optimal way to secure an adequate standard of living. Mere mercantile considerations could not drive her away from the theater at this juncture so she decided to enroll in the Yale School of Drama in order to gain enhanced credentials. But even this advanced training could not overcome the triple jeopardy of Jim Crow, male supremacy, and general economic distress nationwide and globally.

•

After Oberlin, Graham had an offer to travel to Vienna; though she was tempted, she decided instead to pursue her dream of advancing the race by teaching at a historically black college now known as Tennessee State University in Nashville.[1] This was not an easy assignment. Like so many other historically black colleges, the school was not funded adequately: teaching loads were crushing, supplies were sparse, salaries were small. As a result, unrest among students at such campuses was ever present.[2] The beleaguered Graham was teaching fine arts, music history, music theory, and French, while conducting the school orchestra on the side.[3] Her "insanely busy" schedule should not have come as a surprise since the school's president had promised she would "have all the work you can do and some more. We major here in small checks and large amounts of work."[4] This proved to be an understatement.

Frederick Artz, a former professor at Oberlin, was astounded by her list of duties and appalled by the "petty jealousies" she faced among her colleagues. Though he felt that the job was beneath her capabilities, he reminded her that "it's far better for people to wonder why [you] haven't a better job than for them to wonder how in the world you got so far up."[5] So advised, she soldiered on.

Besides envious colleagues, she also had to contend with an authoritarian college president, whom Artz referred to as "Mussolini."[6] Her friend Mary White Ovington denounced President W. J. Hale as "filled with his own ego and not a really educated man"; "despot" was one of the milder epithets she used to describe him.[7] She knew there was "no good in my telling you not to work so hard," but still worried that Hale was trying to make Graham a "mere teaching machine."[8] Displaying a characteristic creativity, Graham persevered. Stymied in her fine arts class by a lack of resources, she interested her students in carving soap; from that class emerged Inge Hardson, who later established a major reputation as a sculptor.[9]

But despite such successes, Graham quickly tired of Nashville and would not return to the professorate until coming to the University of Massachusetts–Amherst in the twilight of her life. By 1936 she had decided to move on. She contemplated a move to Talledega College in Alabama but instead chose to move to Chicago. It was understandable why she decided to reject this historically black school in the wilds of the Deep South. The school may have made Nashville seem like a vacation in comparison.[10]

In Chicago she opened a business with her brother Bill booking and managing artists, but "in spite of all we could do, money just wouldn't turn . . . ours was one of those 'glorious failures.'"[11]

It was at this point that another "life" opened up for her: she moved from writing operas to writing a series of well-received plays, while directing and adapting others for the government-sponsored Federal Theater Project. This brought her more headlines and more notoriety, but it did not bring the income that she felt she needed to support herself and her two sons.

Chicago at that time was a center of black cultural production, featuring blues, jazz, theater, and dance. It was also a magnet of activity for the political Left. The Communist Party was growing in numbers and influence. It published a paper, the *Midwest Daily Record*, that was edited for a while by the fiery African American lawyer and activist William Patterson, who had led the campaign to free the Scottsboro defendants. Contributors included the anthropologist St. Clair Drake, the actor John Garfield, the writer Jack Conroy, and the critic Bosley Crowther.[12]

Richard Wright, with whom Graham later became friendly, was in Chicago at that time and firmly within the embrace of the Left. He was doing publicity for the same Federal Theater with which she was to work. His negative opinion of this venture sheds light on some of the difficulties she encountered there. Graham's jazz version of the Japanese-themed *Mikado* won rave reviews, but Wright was not impressed with the precursor of today's "nontraditional casting." He was dismissive of taking "ordinary plays, all of which had been revamped to 'Negro style,' with jungle scenes, spirituals and all. For example, the skinny white woman who directed it, an elderly missionary type, would take a play whose characters were white, whose theme dealt with the Middle Ages, and recast it in terms of Southern Negro life with overtones of African backgrounds." He was outraged by the "waste of talent": "there were about forty Negro actors and actresses in the theater, lolling about, yearning, disgruntled." Wright, who was "doing publicity" for the project, forcefully "asked" for the replacement of the "white woman—including her quaint aesthetic notions" with "someone who knew the Negro and the theater." He was not successful in this campaign and was soon to be found in Harlem.

This was a typical Wright tirade, one-sided in his analysis of his fellow Negroes, most of whom he said "had spent their lives playing cheap vaudeville."[13] This description did not embrace Shirley Graham, and the audiences that jammed the productions she was involved with would not have agreed totally with Wright's aesthetic assessments either. The FBI, however, took note of his distaste for the Federal Theater Project, which was viewed by some as little more than a "communist front."

The FTP did emerge from a maelstrom of cultural and political ferment in the theater. Even before its initiation, there had been a thriving theater in the United States featuring Yiddish, Hungarian, Ukrainian, and other "minority" languages; this was an era when the idea of "theater as a weapon" of struggle was not an alien concept.[14]

It was true that the FTP had a complement of Reds—they issued a periodic newsletter, for example—though the extent of their influence is not ascertainable.[15] Yet, though the Red impact is difficult to measure, the same cannot be said for the project's impact on blacks. By the time Graham joined the FTP there were sixteen "Negro theatrical units," employing 235 of the more than 800 "colored theatrical workers on the project's total payroll." There were "marionette groups now working in Buffalo, New York and San Francisco" and "the only all-Negro puppet troupes in the world" were part of the FTP. There were "all colored vaudeville units" and "musical comedies," but there were also African Americans integrated throughout the ranks. The FTP was prematurely sensitive to affirmative action, partly as a result of an extraordinary militance shown by African Americans and their allies in the cultural realm, some of whom were Communists.[16]

The project was one of the many New Deal responses to the blight of unemployment and Depression. Like much government spending, it had a disproportionately positive impact on African Americans, who had more to gain because of their declining status. There were 851 African American actors employed—out of a total of 12,000—at the rate of $23.86 per week; this may not seem like much, but since many of these actors previously were unemployed, the FTP was a great boon.[17] Warren Cochrane of the Harlem YMCA was probably correct when he told Graham that "until the coming of the Federal Theater, Negro drama was at a complete stand-still." Sadder still, he was certainly correct when he said that since its "collapse," as a result of an early Red Scare, "little, if anything, has taken place" in Negro drama.[18] Before the FTP, according to one analyst, African Americans "had found acting a hazardous profession . . . audiences were poor and theatres never able to support the most talented group for more than a short time."[19] After the FTP collapsed, theaters and actors were again at risk. The rise and fall of the FTP had impact, above all, on the life of one of the few Negro dramatists, Shirley Graham.

The year she joined the project was a difficult one for her. Her beloved father died in April 1936.[20] Her sons still were not living with her. Besides, she found Chicago to be the "hardest place for an 'outsider' to attempt anything which involves a group of Negroes." With bitterness unveiled, she concluded, "Negroes here care only for one thing—money. The city as a whole is utterly devoid of cultural interests." "Standards" there were "set by Joe Louis and Al Capone." What had soured her was her difficult experience with her business, managing artists. It was her "bitterest experience"; she "lost every cent" and was "still paying debts." She was feeling that the years spent away from her children were for naught and that it had become "impossible to capitalize on all my efforts and sacrifices." Objectively, she recognized that this was largely due to a general "state of depression" and the "general economic condition" of the nation, but this was small solace as she contemplated her immediate future.[21] For a while she made do "conducting musical classes there in her apartment . . . piano lessons."[22]

She was wary and excited about the prospect of working with the Federal Theater Project: wary, because initially she was "thrilled" then disappointed with teaching in Tennessee and was conscious of repeating this cycle in Chicago; excited, because the steady income and the proximity to her sons allowed them to spend more time with her.

These were "difficult and trying years" for her. Though she now was "combining housekeeping with a very heavy schedule," she had "wanted to have the boys with me so long that this has been a great satisfaction."[23] Directing the Negro Unit of the Chicago Federal Theater made this possible.

Quickly she established a reputation within the Federal Theater Project as a creative writer, expert director, and deft administrator. Hallie Flanagan, the project's overall director, called her "one of the most brilliant students I have had in [the] Theatre."[24] Because of her glowing performance she was invited to Vassar College during the summer of 1937 for a special program for actors, directors, playwrights, and the like. There she learned more about lighting, costumes, and other aspects of the theater. She perfected a "Jewish dialect" in order to play on stage "'Rebecca,' the Jewish mama with a Maxwell Street brogue."[25]

She kept up her usual packed schedule, beginning at "nine in the morning" and continuing "until ten-thirty or eleven at night." She was the "only Negro on campus," which at this point in her life she did not lament but viewed as a "responsibility." Yes, Graham concluded, "we are a race of artists"; "these doors are open to us, not through force and effort, but because the world believes we have something definite and valuable to offer."[26] At this point in her life—contrary to Harold Cruse's subsequent recollections—Graham was more liberal than radical.

These remarks also suggest that Graham at this juncture possessed what might be called "essentialized" conceptions of the Negro. Though she no doubt felt that terming Negroes a "race of artists" was complimentary, such remarks could be distorted to suggest that Negroes were not, say, a "race of intellectuals." Her implicit disdain for "force and effort," like these essentialized conceptions, were to fall by the wayside as time passed and her attention moved from purely artistic endeavors to more overtly political crusades.

Such remarks also suggest why Richard Wright was not alone in his negative opinion of the project's Chicago productions. Graham directed and provided the music for a wildly popular production of *Little Black Sambo*, where "puppets with black faces" had "thick red lips." In a thinly veiled stab at Graham, one critic complained that "quite clearly, some people working within Negro units had no qualms about producing such entertainment."[27]

Graham's attitude was more benign. She described the production, based on a work by Charlotte Chorpenning, as an

> attempt to catch the whimsical, poetic and colorful conception of the script itself. We wanted to project upon the stage the "never-never land" of children, a land in which monkeys and tigers spoke our language with ease and naturalness, a land where imagination did away with physical barriers and anything might happen. . . . We stressed the Negro character of the play by the play of brilliant colors, decided use of percussions, intensity [of] rhythm and in a definite minor melodic line of the music.[28]

Though some African Americans and progressives saw this production as a gigantic leap backward, Hallie Flanagan disagreed, remarking that "critics put it on the 'must' list for children," in part because of the "vivid jungle quality of sets and music."[29] Part of what Graham had inherited from her father was a deep appreciation for nonhuman life, and this came across in this production. Flanagan was moved by the production's "simplicity and directness," its "abandon and restraint"; its "affectionate understanding of both animals and people" was "savagely convincing"; "no person could leave the theater without a feeling of closeness to such great natural forces as rain and fire."[30]

She was right about the critics: they were enthusiastic. Said one Chicago paper, "It is the 'Wizard of Oz' of today . . . directed with rare skill and grand imagination by Shirley Graham."[31] Writing from Cincinnati, Anna Maria Shawbaker of the Catholic Women's Association was thrilled, claiming that *Little Black Sambo* "was a great success theatrically as every one who [saw] the performances have acclaimed it as a perfect production. At the performance witnessed by five-hundred orphans I have never heard such enthusiasm from any audience as was expressed by them."[32] It played in Cincinnati for six weeks and in Chicago for months.[33]

Some critics may have raved about *Little Black Sambo*, but others were not as pleased with the Theodore Ward play Graham directed, *The Big White Fog*. This powerful but little-known drama, with its intertwined themes of Garveyism, the African American family, and the rise of the Left, stirred audiences and Chicago elites. Leaders of the University of Chicago wanted it canceled for fear it would "incite inter-racial hatred"—actually, class hatred was more like it.[34] Graham, caught in the middle, played a "mediating" role between the playwright and his opponents. When she previewed the play on the South Side at the YWCA she invited the National Urban League, the NAACP, religious leaders, and other opinion molders. The NAACP intensely disliked the play's "communist propaganda"—a description that Ward staunchly opposed. Evidently Graham panicked and in the words of one critic, assumed the role of "cultural commissar" when she turned against the production she directed. Though Langston Hughes called this work "the greatest encompassing play on Negro life that has ever been written," the production was sidelined and Graham's reputation among the left-wing suffered.[35] The message was clear: theater involving *Little Black Sambo* brought kudos, while a play that seriously sought to grapple with complex issues brought ferocious condemnation. Such messages did not bode well for her future career in the theater.

Graham was facing the dilemma of trying to produce significant work sponsored by a government sure to be buffeted by powerful gales from the Right. *Little Black Sambo* was acceptable but *The Big White Fog* was not. Her adaptation *Swing Mikado* was in another category altogether, compounding further her dilemma: it may have been ideologically acceptable to the right wing, but it proved to be all too popular and caused commercial producers to resent the stiff competition it provided.

The production of *Swing Mikado* was made more complicated by the rifts revealed in an earlier project, her effort to produce a Negro version of Eugene O'Neill's play *The Hairy Ape*. After returning from Vassar she found her "responsibilities doubled." She had a role in the FTP's three downtown theaters and the Negro unit. She was giving classes in "play acting and play reading," in addition to finding time for her own writing.[36] Adapting O'Neill was a challenging increase in her duties; she changed his "imagery and philosophy" and provided a "Negro setting." This drama, one of O'Neill's most significant works, was also suggestive of her effort to wrestle with class conflict and bring this question to African Americans well before she joined the Communist Party. O'Neill's work concerns a stoker, Yank Smith, and his vicissitudes as he is rebuffed by an aristocratic young woman; the psychology of radicalism is a major theme. In what O'Neill himself called his "unconscious autobiography," Smith dies in the arms of a gorilla in a zoo.[37] Graham

> dropped out long passages, in one case writing an entirely new scene. The play is a psychological study of one man in somewhat the same manner as is *Emperor Jones*. The result of my changes has produced a study of Negro psychology and the clash of Negro "classes" such as has never been placed on the stage.

This dramatization reflected the gradual process of her move toward the left during a decade, the 1930s, when the Communist Party was near the height of its popularity. One scholar has asked plaintively, "Why would the Soviet Union appeal to African-Americans in the 1930s? Why would African-Americans appeal to the Soviet Union in the 1930s?"[38] A partial answer can be found in the deteriorating economic and racial conditions that gripped the nation and spurred a search for radical remedies. Though Graham had found a temporary refuge in the Federal Theater, all she had to do was look about the streets of Chicago in order to realize that something in society was terribly wrong. Young men stood listlessly on street corners, occasionally starting huge fires in drums as a buffer against the biting Chicago winds that ricocheted through the streets. Police brutality was as common as the "Second City's" scorching hot summers and frigid winters that brought virtual paralysis.

Yet some of her colleagues apparently did not recognize that she was seeking to tussle with the serious dilemmas caused by this social and economic calamity. They did not appreciate her adaptation of *The Hairy Ape*—or any other project she was involved in, for that matter. The problem was the same one that had dogged her in Nashville: envy—or so it appeared to her. As Richard Wright had intimated, there may have been merit to the claim that the Euro-American bosses of the FTP preferred the "exoticized" images of peoples of color presented in *Little Black Sambo* and *Swing Mikado*, or they preferred adaptations like *The Hairy Ape* rather than original productions. This seemed to be the complaint of her latest critic: Why couldn't the FTP simply produce plays conceived with African Americans in mind rather than converting other plays that had not been written to encompass their experience? Would not the former approach increase the sparse stock of African American dramatists?[39] With anger hardly concealed, she disagreed with such criticism: An African American man in the Chicago FTP

> had represented me to my own people as having completely alienated myself from them . . . I had allied myself with the "white folks" . . . that I was seeking my own selfish ends; I was ruthlessly ambitious; *The Hairy Ape* was entirely a personal undertaking; I was adding my personal friends to the project; the play was an "insult" to the Negro.

She was "speechless. (Imagine that!)" Her antagonist "declared" her "incompetent" and "anti-social," having "no friends among the Negroes of Chicago holding myself aloft and disdainfully exploiting people . . . the white folks got mad and I found myself in the humiliating position of being pitied for what my own people were doing to me."[40] She was compelled to drop the O'Neill project. This did not augur well for her next venture, yet another adaptation, *Swing Mikado*.

Graham has been given credit for the innovation of taking the well-known Gilbert and Sullivan play *The Mikado* and adding jazz-tinged themes and African American actors in the kind of stew that had so irritated Wright. This light comic opera, with its intertwined themes of love and death, "pooh-bahs" and "Lord High Executioners," was a useful vehicle for the Federal Theater, which was seeking to dodge charges of "communist infiltration"; alas, the charges continued nonetheless.[41] Still, one critic has praised the "populist aesthetics" of the production in the "imaginative way . . . jazz music and dance" were incorporated.[42] Other critics compared it favorably with Orson Welles's similarly staged adaptation of *Macbeth*. Apparently Graham redeemed herself in the eyes of the Left, since the Communist *Midwest Daily Record* called it a "killer-diller."[43] The *St. Louis Post-Dispatch* provided a huge, full-page photo spread and noted that "African and Japanese motifs are evident" in the production; in an enormously positive review, the critic wrote of dances of "shag, big apple, truck and swing . . . the scene is transferred from Japan to an anonymous island in the Pacific."[44] Jane De Hart wrote that it "achieved a publicity record which any commercial producer might envy."[45] An administrator and her coworkers at the Rosenwald

Fund—an important entity that doled out funds to African American artists and scholars—saw the production, and "we are all going about the place this morning humming the tunes."[46] Hallie Flanagan felt that *Swing Mikado* was one of the "outstanding box office successes" of the entire Federal Theater.[47]

That was the problem. Traditional producers on Broadway felt that the government was subjecting them to unfair competition. They sought to produce their own version, *Hot Mikado,* in which Shirley Temple's former dance partner, Bill "Bojangles" Robinson, would star. In a sense, they mandated that the FTP could be successful only within narrow limits; that it should epitomize "lemon socialism," that is, it should produce only works that would not be successful. Otherwise it might let loose the seditious idea that private enterprise could be supplanted. Nor could the FTP produce thought-provoking plays, like *The Big White Fog.*[48] Ultimately *Hot Mikado* became an early hit for the impresario Mike Todd.[49]

As for Graham, she had difficulty obtaining credit for the adaptation, as her superiors within the project left the impression that they had been solely responsible for its success. Mary White Ovington told her, "don't feel you must be modest about publicity," but finally had to concede that "this seems to me a time when a woman is ignored partly because she isn't supposed to say anything, being a woman and a Negro."[50] Another friend recalled ruefully "opening night in New York" when he and his mate "were sitting there saying nasty words because your name wasn't in the program."[51] Graham was rapidly discovering—if she did not already recognize—that she was not immune from the double jeopardy of racism and sexism.

Soon not only Graham was in jeopardy. *Swing Mikado* disappeared. The Federal Theater Project itself was under the congressional microscope, inspected for evidence of a "Red" taint. Soon it was no more. The victims were many: audiences, the theater itself, actors, stagehands, and dramatists like Shirley Graham.[52]

Nevertheless, the experience had enhanced her name and celebrity. Few—male or female, black or otherwise, before or since—have excelled as writer, composer, and director, while conducting and acting as a sideline. Before and during the FTP, Graham had done just that.

She had begun to travel in increasingly distinguished circles and had become reacquainted with an elderly gentleman whom she had met as a girl: W. E. B. Du Bois. He had a penchant for cultivating young talent, as he was still harboring the illusion that a "Talented Tenth" would lead African Americans to the promised land. If anyone fit in this esteemed elite category, it was Shirley Graham.

Writing from Chicago in 1937, two weeks after his departure from there, she told him about her new "choral number which I am calling *Mississippi Rainbow*"; she was "making interesting contacts which might" lead her to "Broadway or out in Hollywood." A "flame of energy" had "been lit within" her and "all sorts of possibilities are opening." It seemed she was trying to impress him: she mentioned casually, "they tell me I'm going to Hollywood" and noted in passing, "my thesis is being used as reading material for students in one of the departments at Northwestern."[53]

The goal she had described in her application to Oberlin—her ambition to be sufficiently trained so that she could be deemed an "authority" in music—she now adapted for her letters to Du Bois, as if she were making another kind of application: "Believing that the theatre, particularly that combination of drama with music offers the most complete medium for the expression of the versatile talents of the Negro, I wish to train myself for leadership in this field."[54] She also provided critique of his own dramatic handiwork, suggesting that one of his works was "too short for a full evening", it required "characterization in dialogue and . . . transitional scenes." Another work was "beautiful and moving" but "won't work for the WPA audience."[55]

If he read the newspapers carefully, Du Bois would know that if anyone was in a position to say what worked with audiences, it was Shirley Graham. She now could approach the doyen not just as yet another pupil in search of edification but as a peer who could help him with his own work.

■

By late 1938 the FTP was under siege from the House Un-American Activities Committee and commercial producers incensed by the competition it created. It was evident that the FTP was coming to a screeching halt. Graham did not have to be a political seer to recognize that it was time to move on. This movement was to take her to Yale Drama School, a move not as decisive as her move to Chicago or to Nashville but a significant departure nonetheless. Her now established reputation, connections to influential personalities like Hallie Flanagan and W. E. B. Du Bois, and funding from the Rosenwald Fund facilitated her residence in

New Haven.[56] At Oberlin she had studied music; now, said Flanagan, Graham planned to write a dissertation on "the history of the Negro in the Federal Theatre—a record which she believes suggests what the Negro race might, given an opportunity, accomplish in the theatre of our country."[57] Graham's attempt at racial uplift had migrated from music to the allied realm of the stage.

Again she left her sons behind as she moved to Connecticut. Again she plunged into a cascade of activity, churning out term papers analyzing screenplays, studying Italian, performing in an occasional recital, while penning a number of original plays.[58] She conducted research on the theater in Germany—in German—to 1850; "the emphasis on my work lies on the physical theater itself—the staging, building and problems of production." She studied "Tudor drama and Shakespeare . . . costuming, designing, directing, etc. etc." It was not only the theory and physical aspects of the stage that moved her; she also conceded candidly, "I want to write."[59]

And write she did. The following years were a highly productive period for her, though it was becoming evident that even as she gained a reputation as probably the leading playwright among African American women, this did not translate into a hefty income.

Still, her works of that period remain worthy of attention. Foreshadowing a theme raised decades later by Toni Morrison, her play *It's Morning* concerned an African American woman on a plantation who is about to murder her daughter rather than see her live as a slave. Taking place on the eve of emancipation from slavery, it dramatically evokes the upheavals produced as slavery ended and a form of freedom began.[60] The play *Elijah's Ravens*, a comedy in three acts with almost twenty characters, was based loosely on her experiences growing up in the home of a minister. *Coal Dust* (sometimes referred to as *Dust to Earth*), a three-act play about a mine disaster, incorporated Negro dialect and dealt with issues such as illegitimacy, a tricky brother-sister relationship, miscegenation, and class conflict. She wrote plays for radio on George Washington Carver and Phillis Wheatley. She cowrote a play on the Haitian revolution.[61] She was a prolific and wide-ranging playwright.

Not only were these years productive, they were also invigorating artistically. She had the opportunity to hone her craft and study the theory of drama. She danced and acted in various productions and did the music for others; in one play she "did the drumming backstage."[62] She composed the music and acted in Owen Dodson's play *Garden of Time.*[63] With Mary White Ovington and other Manhattan friends she became a habitué of Broadway and off-Broadway productions.[64]

She found Yale to be "all that I expected and more." She collaborated on a "special assignment" with the National Broadcasting Corporation (NBC) on "radio technique." She developed an innovative script involving "Negro voices singing." Then she began developing a "dramatization of a de Maupassant story." Again, this latter project was pursued for "sheer technique in order that I might not become one sided in working with Negro material." Yale was a "strong tonic. . . . There are so many things I don't know which there is no time to learn right now"; New Haven was like a "piece of bread to a starving man." She contemplated pursuing a "Ph.D. in Fine Arts."[65]

Her ideas about theater were typically idiosyncratic and, in a sense, "essentialist." At one point she said, "The Negro is a born actor because he had to express himself. During many ages he was oppressed and subdued and given no voice and he learned to make himself known by pantomime. As a result he acquired a special talent for projecting himself into any mood and any situation."[66] This statement—particularly the last sentence—may have been more accurate if used to describe Graham herself rather than "the Negro," whom she renders as male. Yet such words indicated that she was giving thought to the special role that theater could play among African Americans and how she could aid this process.

She also received stinging rejections. On one occasion such a rebuke was reported to have sparked her "fierce indignation." Apparently the Dramatic Guild did not want to accept her because of racial reasons; "can't you make them believe that you are an Arab?" a friend asked helpfully.[67] Some critics did not appreciate *Coal Dust,* a play that reflected her interest in class struggle even before she was reputed to have become a Communist. One called it an "old-fashioned type of play about workers"; "the appeal to pity for the workers' hard lot, be they white or colored, will no longer carry a labor play," she was told. True, "Miss Graham certainly has a flair for playwrighting, for dialogue and for characterization," but this was not enough to redeem the play. Mary White Ovington felt that this critic was right.[68]

Part of the problem—as her tiff with the guild demonstrated—was that Graham was having difficulty distinguishing legitimate criticism from outright bigotry. To reach the stage, plays required not only sprightly writing but investors or producers as well. The search for financial backers, which gave a significant role to those with capital, was infected inexorably with bias in a nation suffused with Jim Crow. Thus, when Ovington contacted Elmer Rice about examining Graham's work, she apologized in advance since she knew that "a Negro play isn't your line."[69]

These roadblocks and an inclination to reach her people deepened Graham's relationship with the Karamu Theatre of Cleveland and other African American producers. The director of the Karamu, Rowena Woodham Jelliffe, also attended Oberlin and had traveled to Africa in 1925, bringing back with her "relics and garments" for her theater, which opened two years later. She and Graham became quite close and shared many things in common besides Oberlin. Jelliffe too was a "premature Afrocentrist": the theater had an African motif, while Karamu itself was a Kiswahili term meaning "the place of entertainment or feasting, at the center of the community." The Karamu was small, seating only 120, and not very comfortable: "the stage was very small with a sixteen foot forscenium opening" and a "low ceiling."[70] In its use of theater to spur consciousness, particularly of Africa, it anticipated the "Black Arts" movement of the 1960s.

Like other theaters of this type, the Karamu was handicapped by the absence of African American playwrights. As late as 1940 they could still say, "We feel dependent 'almost entirely upon the output and promise of four [Negro] playwrights: Zora Neale Hurston, Shirley Graham, Owen Dodson and Langston Hughes.'" Otherwise, they were dependent on Euro-American playwrights, who often were not racially sensitive in their writing. This made it difficult to build audiences, though the theater in general at this point was far superior to its competitor, film, in avoiding racial stereotypes and providing opportunities for minority artists and technical workers.[71]

But the Karamu could not afford advertising. When Coal Dust was presented there, Jelliffe offered "our usual terms for royalty," "$75 for eight nights (consecutive) . . . that represents about our limit . . . that would mean about $26.00 clear for you after my debt is paid."[72] Although it was nice to be considered part of the pantheon with Hurston and Hughes, writing plays was not the surest route to prosperity.

Jelliffe did "like the play a lot. It has fine things in it. Also it has a [good] deal of artistry. It is not too obvious." However, to design a set for this play was "a stumper. We would try to hold attention by sound effects—shouts, winding winches, sirens, etc. through the blackouts," but how could one credibly present a coal mine on stage?[73] Jelliffe's fellow Clevelander, Ridgley Torrence, was concerned about the casting, feeling that the lead role was "by no means actor proof . . . the play could easily end feebly and falsely if the actor didn't handle it with great skill and power, particularly in the last scene."[74]

Coal Dust was produced there to mostly favorable reviews but the dilemma of the Negro playwright continued. Jelliffe was infuriated that "the great majority of Negro college drama groups and Negro drama groups in the larger universities continue to do Lady Windemere's Fan and other plays only a little more sensible. The reason being that there are not scripts of Negro life which are acceptable to them." The challenge she presented to Graham was to "give them some. Honest plays, good, well-constructed plays, and at the same time acceptable to actors and audience alike."[75]

Accepting this challenge was part of Graham's duties at Yale. In carrying out this herculean task she found Jelliffe a good partner and good friend. They had been friendly at least since her days at Oberlin, when Jelliffe steered Tom-Tom to the Cleveland Opera. During that time Graham was in frequent contact with her, including at one memorable breakfast—for "twenty people and of course that includes you"—for Jelliffe's "house guests" Countee Cullen (W. E. B. Du Bois's erstwhile son-in-law) and his close friend Harold Jackman.[76] Over the years Jelliffe not only exposed Graham to "house guests" with intriguing stories to tell but also offered wise counsel on writing plays. Both worked closely with the Gilpin Players—"America's oldest and foremost Negro Theater group"—in seeking to improve the quotient of dramatic excellence for the African American audience.[77]

This was no easy task. Even the bouquets tossed at her carried thorns. She won an award from Stanford University for Elijah's Ravens, which was termed a "gentle but sure satire" with a "warm human quality" and "easy understanding of not only the Negro but all human psychology." The noted actress Lynn Fontanne called it a "remarkably good play, the characterization is fine, amusing and original." But then another member of the award panel, while calling the play an "extremely important, thorough, humorous, and kindly study of humanity," added that it "happens to be for the moment expressed in darky form."[78]

One of her professors, Walter Lewisohn, dismissively suggested that she rewrite "'*Back Stairs*'" or "whatever it's called." He was dismissive of *Dust to Earth*, suggesting that the white characters were not "convincing." He denounced the draft of another play she had been laboring over:

> You don't know a damn thing about Father Divine except what you've read in the newspapers and that part isn't convincing to me . . . Yale is like Satan. It takes a playwright up to a high place, lets him survey the wonders of production and then pushes him off and he falls into the meshes and complexities of staging problems . . . I am trying to preach to you to keep your simplicity which is the hardest thing in the world for most people. I've seen a lot of people become complex, but I've never seen a complex person become simple.[79]

He suggested that she write a Broadway play with Ethel Waters as a cook with two spouses, one of whom would be Paul Robeson; Duke Ellington should be asked to do the music. Continuing in the Jim Crow mode, he suggested she find "Negro capital to back it. . . . You know Mrs. Robeson." Helpfully he included poor jokes in Negro dialect and racist dialogue for the characters. With a final twist of the knife, he told her that she might be a "Yalewright" and not a "Playwright, if you know what I mean?"[80]

Graham may not have understood what he meant—beyond the fact that it was intended as an insult—but by now she did understand that seeking to mount plays in a racially segregated nation was no simple task. One theater insider may not have intended insult when he informed her bluntly, "It's a rule in this business that no all-Negro play has ever been a good [seller]. *Emperor Jones* is a small exception and there's no telling when another will come along." He suggested that if she wanted to "get by with our public," she should write a "very light comedy." Actually, she had done that with *Elijah's Ravens*, but Graham was discovering that for an African American woman there was an infinite variety of ways to be denied opportunity in show business.[81]

The bad news and the not-so-good news kept rolling in. Another Yale professor expressed doubt about mounting *Elijah's Ravens*, which involved nontraditional casting, since when they performed *Cherry Orchard* it came across as "just Americans pretending to be Russians. The real play didn't come across . . . we'd be obviously pretending; the naturalistic flavor, the truth, the spontaneous quality, the comedy, would evaporate. Or so I hear."[82] She heard, just as she heard another remonstration from another Yale professor. He told her that *Dust to Earth* had a tad much "soap box oratory" and he totally disapproved of the killing of the leading female character, since "the murder of a woman on stage is always shocking to an audience and is not likely to be tolerated unless the dramatist has built up such strong motivation (as is done in *Othello*) that the motive seems stronger than the deed."[83]

Graham's career in drama could be killed off easily, though she was being counseled not to let such harm befall her fictional female creations. The discouraging news kept coming. An agent informed her, "frankly, I am somewhat skeptical about the commercial possibilities of a Negro comedy," though ironically the "reader's report" was "very favorable indeed."[84] It would have been easy for Graham to conclude that it was not meant for her to be a playwright, but she persevered. She tried to conform to what appeared to be "market forces" by emulating her past success with *Swing Mikado* by adapting *The Pirates of Penzance*. Maybe critics and producers preferred African Americans in such adaptations and did not appreciate original work. Predictably, Hallie Flanagan liked it and continued her effort to aid Graham by trying to find funding for her to write a history of the "Federal Negro Theatre" and have it "count toward" Graham's "doctoral degree."[85]

Fortunately for Graham, all of the news she received about her work was not so dispiriting. One of her mentors, the sociologist Charles Johnson, informed her that the famed scholar Bronislaw Malinowski saw one of her plays in New Haven and liked it.[86] A fellow student at Yale, Louis Laflin, saw *Dust to Earth* and loved it: "all the characters were treated as human beings. Even the villains had a certain dignity . . . and the mine-owners were not distorted into fiends." So impressed was he that he advocated that she tackle Jesus Christ as her next dramatic subject; she did not follow up on his counsel, perhaps recognizing that even divine inspiration seemed insufficient for her to get a financially successful play mounted.[87] Adam Clayton Powell, Jr., the son of her pastor, continued to scour Manhattan in search of opportunities for his "dear Shirley." That was the good news; the not so good news was that "nothing definite" had "turned up."[88]

Graham did not rely on the "invisible hand" of the marketplace to deliver audiences and acclaim. She invited the influential NAACP leader Arthur Spingarn to see a "serious drama" she had written; she added proudly, "Yale believes this is a good play."[89] Essie Robeson responded to her entreaties by expressing her delight that the "public has good taste and likes" Graham's work.[90] Still, it was becoming more difficult for Graham to ignore the clear message she was receiving about her career as a dramatist: things were not working out the way she would have liked.

Flanagan wanted her to stay in the field of scholarship and theater since she knew "so well your high resolution to work for your own people, and no less for all of us, on the actual writing and direction of plays."[91] This was heartening praise from a close friend, but Flanagan, though encouraging, was not a Yale professor who could shepherd her toward a doctorate. Moreover, it was the siege of Flanagan's own Federal Theater Project that helped convince Graham to retreat to Yale. Now New Haven itself did not seem as promising. It was time to move on and create another chapter in her life.

4

Crossroads

WHEN ONE OF her favorite professors at Yale returned to Great Britain, Graham abandoned graduate school and returned to Indiana.[1] Professor Allardyce Nicol "took more personal interest in what I was trying to do because I am a Negro"—which was the exact opposite of the responses she had encountered generally in New Haven.[2] By 1941 she was serving as director of "adult activities" for the Phillis Wheatley YWCA in Indianapolis.[3] By no means had she abandoned the theater, however. During the spring of 1941, for example, New Orleans's Dillard University featured a production of *Elijah's Ravens*; the renowned sculptor Elizabeth Catlett designed the sets, and the similarly reputable Randolph Edmonds directed. A program note mentioned that Graham was "perhaps the foremost playwright among Negro women," but by this point such predictably high praise rang hollow, for it did not seem to aid in securing a handsome livelihood.[4]

Yet theater was a love that was difficult to purge, so she persisted in seeking to bring entertainment and ideas to African Americans. She directed the Gilbert and Sullivan work *HMS Pinafore* and stressed the themes of equality and democracy.[5] Increasingly, however, as the clouds of war gathered in 1941, she turned more to ideas—particularly political ideas—in her attempt to influence masses.

Slowly but inexorably she was drifting away from the stage and toward direct political involvement. For example, she spoke at a conference in Evansville that year on how "Negro youth prepares for the social and economic challenges of a changing world."[6] That "changing world" was to include desegregation and decolonization, and Graham was arriving at the conclusion that she should play a central role in both processes.

This was a natural evolution for her. Her concern for Africa and her personal experience with harsh economic realities ineluctably drove her to make firmer political commitments. She continued to drive herself relentlessly to that end. One friend told her worriedly, "your list of labors sounds to me like the program poor old Hercules was forced to carry out."[7] Earlier another friend with evident distress reminded her, "you speak of doing double work, being too tired to see or to think straight, etc. Are your nerves holding up? Have you a good appetite? Do you sleep well?"[8]

Despite her Oberlin degrees, her matriculation at Yale, her riveting literary and musical creations, and her close connections with various celebrities, Shirley Graham, the mother of two teenagers, continued to have difficulty making a living—and sleeping well—in 1941. Before reaching Indiana, she was dickering for a "salary [of] 200 [dollars] for six weeks," which was barely enough for survival.[9] Such meager sums may help to explain why she was, sadly, gaining a reputation as a scofflaw. Sadie Alexander complained that Graham had "borrowed" four hundred dollars from "our sorority," Delta Sigma Theta, but "has not only failed to repay this money but has even given a check without having sufficient funds in [the] bank for the check to be honored." Worse, "she continues to refuse to meet her moral obligation to repay this money."[10] Another creditor sent Graham newspaper clippings that reflected the Yale matriculant's growing celebrity and added coyly, "it has occurred to me that with all the big things you are doing you may be able to redeem your note . . . maybe if you have not the money available, you will shift the loan; that is borrow from some friend or bank and repay me.[11] This creditor did not recognize that despite her frequent appearances in newspaper headlines, Graham remained virtually poverty-stricken and her new job in Indianapolis did not change things appreciably.

Hence, "when war with Hitler became imminent," Graham "'enlisted' as a YWCA-USO Director and was sent to Fort Huachuca in Arizona, which became the base of the largest contingent of Negro soldiers in the country."[12] Just as she had been forced to abandon music, economic conditions had now frog-marched her away from the theater.

The war did provide opportunity. As men were dispatched overseas, some jobs at home were opened for women. The defense industry boomed on the West Coast, and African Americans abandoned Texas and Louisiana for the region stretching from Seattle to San Diego and Arizona.[13] One scholar has observed that "the employment profile of black women during the 1940s shows large gains in service work outside homes (such as cleaning, serving, and cooking in hotels and restaurants) and in factory work . . . the war boom allowed black women to improve their status."[14] This "war boom" also allowed Graham to return to the West, a region of the United States then unfamiliar to many African Americans, but not to this vagabond who already had crisscrossed the nation.

Graham's new job meant not only increased income but also increased distance from her creditors. She was also further away from her sons and mother, but by now this woman in her mid-forties was accustomed to moving frequently, with all the dislocation and excitement it entailed. Her job as "director of Negro work" brought more money and responsibility, and consequently justified leaving Indiana.[15]

Race relations in the West were problematic. One of the larger nearby outposts, Las Vegas, which was in the process of acquiring the glitter that would make it a global symbol of hedonism, was marked cruelly by Jim Crow. In the 1930s as mobsters invaded, the authorities clamped down on the black variety, "but city officials did not maintain the same vigilance" over their white counterparts. The Ku Klux Klan was there; its aggressions against African Americans included flogging and running them out of town. Yet because the stereotype persisted that those of African descent could withstand the draining heat better, blacks continued to be attracted to the city during the war, though "many of the new arrivals found Las Vegas racism worse than [what] they had experienced in the South." There was a "major riot" in 1944 and "for a long period of time black entertainers at the resort hotels could not even stay at the hotels where they played."[16]

In 1942 the U.S. army decided to create the U.S. 93rd Infantry Division by combining the 25th, 368th, and 369th Regiments with various field companies and battalions. Fort Huachuca had been home to the 10th Calvary when it patrolled the U.S.-Mexican border in World War I. By December 1942 the 32nd and 33rd companies of the Women's Army Auxiliary Corps had joined the men of the 93rd in the desert.[17]

There were fifteen thousand black enlisted men and six hundred black officers at Fort Huachuca.

The 300 black women who made up the two companies at Fort Huachuca had their own mess, a large recreation area and barracks area. . . . In their off-duty hours, the women had access to the theater, service clubs, social activities, and recreational centers on the post, including the basketball court. At Fort Huachuca the women served as typists, stenographers, and clerks. They drove vehicles and served as chauffeurs, messengers, telephone operators, and librarians. They operated the theaters and the service clubs. They were medical, laboratory, and surgical technicians, physical therapists, and ward attendants. Some were even employed in light motor vehicle maintenance. There were no jobs or positions off-limits to them except those [proscribed] for all WACs.[18]

Fort Huachuca was no easy assignment for women. One female member of the U.S. military there recalled

strange weather in February. In the morning we put on full winter uniform with overcoat; by eleven the overcoat was off; and by two in the afternoon we shed the uniform jackets. Then the process was reversed, so that by ten in the evening, if one happened to be out of doors, the overcoat was needed. My lasting impression of the post was that it was large and desolate, so completely surrounded by mountains that I was puzzled as to how we got into that valley.

The discomfort caused by this "strange weather" was minor compared to the rampant sexual harassment the women were subjected to. When Charity Adams Earley first traveled there by train, "as we expected, on the first night some men, apparently intoxicated, attempted to break into our compartments."[19]

Race relations at Fort Huachuca were extremely tense. The future black businessman Dempsey Travis recalled that the "segregation" there was "demoralizing."[20] Here these soldiers were being instructed that they were fighting a war abroad against intolerance and bigotry, yet they were being subjected to the same thing at home. Such strains eventually were to force the nation to erode Jim Crow, but this prospect seemed far away in Arizona in the early 1940s.

Edward Soulds, a black lieutenant at Fort Huachuca, noticed that a white captain rarely spoke to minority soldiers. Soulds asked why and was told that this officer would be "compromising his dignity to work with niggers; that he hated them, didn't want to eat with them or talk to them or anything else. Furthermore, he would only do what he absolutely had to since he was in the Army."[21] Such rancid attitudes were resented deeply by African Americans. One unnamed black soldier complained that the colored officers are fed up. . . . They know that they are not being treated fairly but there is nothing they can do. Whenever they go over bounds, they are simply reclassified. Though we have some brilliant Negro officers they are never promoted. Some of these officers hold degrees from the nation's outstanding universities, while white officers from Fort Benning [are] ignorant as the days are long . . . morale is at as low an ebb as in a whorehouse. Nobody gives a [damn] about what happens. Unless something is done, there will be an internal revolution.

The black general Benjamin O. Davis was sent there to investigate but he was dismissed by some African Americans as a "military figurehead."[22]

Black soldiers not only complained about racism, they fought back—often violently—against it. U.S. army intelligence noted that

at the Negro camp, Fort Huachuca, a hand grenade was discovered attached to an automobile in which several white Army officers were about to take a trip. The grenade was so wired that if the starter switch had been pressed the grenade would have exploded, killing or seriously injuring the occupants of the car.[23]

In 1942 the New York Times reported that three were killed and twelve shot in a "Negro troop riot" at Fort Huachuca, a "3 hour gun battle" that involved "three hundred soldiers and 100 military and civil police." There were 152 black soldiers and some civilians held, "including two women." This conflict "was the result of antagonism between Negro soldiers" and "military police." It started when a military police officer (MP) was shot and wounded after resisting arrest as a result of hitting a black woman in the head with a bottle. The result was that five black soldiers were court-martialed; four were sentenced to fifty years each at hard labor, and the fifth, forty years. The NAACP intervened, focusing on the case of Ollie D. North, who was charged with mutiny. After seeing a black soldier beaten by an MP, he returned to camp, got a rifle and a vehicle, ignored a command to stop, and proceeded to try to halt the beating.[24]

Graham was deeply affected by this turmoil. It is little wonder that it had a catalytic impact on her political evolution. She intervened in this and other cases of racial injustice; in one instance she "reached the

General and influenced him to reopen the case and by military ruling had the soldier's sentence changed to ten years."[25] At this point her writing turned decisively from operas and plays to reporting and non-fiction generally. She now used her facility with words to defend African American soldiers. In an article published in *Common Sense* in early 1943, she criticized her own USO for capitulating to racism. Though it was alleged by Harold Cruse later that she was already a Communist in 1942, in this, one of her first political essays, she took positions inconsistent with those of the party. She praised A. Philip Randolph and his March on Washington Movement, which the Reds were then accusing of insufficient patriotism because of its threat to withdraw black enthusiasm for the war effort unless certain civil rights demands were met. With passion she concluded, "Is it the intention so to encircle and encompass the Negro by segregation and discrimination that finally we will have a separate and distinct 'nation within a nation?' Even if this were possible, is it desirable—in a Democracy?"[26] A "nation within a nation" was precisely the line espoused by the Communist Party, which had raised the issue of secession by plebiscite for African Americans.[27]

Graham was beginning to gain attention again, but this time it was not for writing plays or operas or directing but for her heartfelt defense of black soldiers. Her old friend Hallie Flanagan found it "magnificent" that "you are the USO Director of the largest aggregation of Negro troops in America. 'Mighty Winds a-blowing' is just the name for you and I am sure you are going to make history."[28] Another old friend, the sociologist Charles Johnson, was equally effusive, informing her that "several persons who have visited Camp Huachuca and have had an opportunity to observe your program have spoken of it in such high terms."[29]

These compliments from friends were a reflection of her labor on behalf of her brood of soldiers. Her penchant for caretaking was reflected in the fact that they called her "Mama." She sought to attend to their needs; they confided in her and sought her counsel. One black soldier, writing from Fort Benning, Georgia, told her,

> now hold your breath while I tell you "it can happen here." We rode all the way through the South on Pullman cars and ate in the dining cars smack into Georgia. But that's not the payoff. We are living in barracks with the white boys. . . . The colonel said that if [it] got out of line

to let him know. . . . On the way down we ran into separate waiting rooms and the other colored people rode Jim Crow cars. This is truly the Deep South.[30]

Yes, it was; the problem was that the Deep Southwest—Arizona—was little better. One correspondent was so concerned about his reporting of dire conditions in Needles, California—due west from Fort Huachuca—that he instructed her to destroy his letter after reading it. "It is just as bad here as it is in Huachuca. There are about one hundred colored people in the town all 'Hard Shell Baptist.'" He felt sufficiently comfortable with her to say, "the city officials ran all of the loose women out of town before we moved in, so there is not much means for diversion." Shooing away the prostitutes may have been motivated by a horror of miscegenation more than anything else, for Jim Crow there was rampant. The town had only one theater, "which discriminates . . . we have to sit on the left with the Indians and Mexicans."[31] Yet another soldier complained about racism in Victorville, California, at the USO; he warned ominously, "our lives are at stake as well as theirs," apparently referring to the fact that, since black soldiers were trained in warfare, they were capable of fighting back against racists. He did not necessarily object to the segregated dances—"we do not mind not going there when there is a dance for the white soldier"—since "we would want our dance to our self [sic]."[32]

Her relationships were not solely maternal. With war comes the smog-like imminence of death that, paradoxically, tends to drive individuals to romance and the process of creating life. While in Arizona, Graham struck up an intimate friendship with Captain Max Foresman of the Tenth Infantry, Field Artillery. This was a long-distance relationship since he was in Colorado, though this did not prevent him from averring that "I love you more than I can say." Interestingly, she had sent him a copy of a book by another close friend of hers, Du Bois's *Dusk of Dawn*. Perhaps sensing that he had become part of an incipient love triangle, he was a bit perplexed by the book—he "enjoyed it very much and would like to say something about it but haven't decided what it is."[33]

Captain Foresman may have sensed even then that her affections resided elsewhere. Soon not only her affections were elsewhere for Shirley Graham was ousted unceremoniously from Arizona, as her employer finally tired of her militance on behalf of black soldiers. As she told Du Bois, she did not leave as a result of

> free will . . . my ladies at YWCA-USO . . . ordered me to come into New York City for a conference. When I got here they coolly informed me that the USO was not interested in some of my activities which were outside the recreational program of the USO. . . . It seems that the FSA [Field Service Administration] man out there had written in that I was "using my position as a USO director to influence military and civic affairs" throughout the state. Which was perfectly true . . . not so much as to the "USO position" but as to the influence. . . . Also, following a riot in Tucson (little space in the papers) when a soldier had been given [a] life sentence I myself reached the General and influenced him to reopen the case. . . . No, I didn't want to leave Fort Huachuca.

But she was forced to do so.[34]

She departed with bitterness. In a rare display of a racialized temper, she conceded that she "did gradually become a threat to the complacency of USO," but "in the final analysis white supremacy has us by [the] throat because the white man has the money. Yet I'll be damned if I'm sorry."[35] Such an outburst was uncommon for her; it was indicative of the fact that the press of war and the open racial sores it exposed had a robust impact on her political sensitivities.

■

After being dispatched from Arizona, she moved again—this time to New York City—with "less than two hundred dollars" in her purse. New York was to remain her home until she departed for Accra in 1961 and was to be the site of some of her more important domestic triumphs. These victories were not on the horizon, however, as she arrived in Manhattan in the midst of an uncertain world war. As she explained later, she "took the cheapest room in the Theresa Hotel" in Harlem and "ate meals—when I did—at the Chock Full o' Nuts on the street floor of that building. I worked at whatever I could get—did not sell my body, but did manage to sell a few articles . . . God knows I had no wardrobe!"[36] Despite her penury, she managed to send Captain Foresman "the album of Sonata in A Minor, played by Jascha Heifetz and Arthur Rubinstein." This was a gracious gesture, though he flirtatiously complained about the folly of the expenditure: "I could [put] you over my knee and spank you until you couldn't sit down for being so utterly foolish."[37]

Graham no doubt could have used the appellation "foolish" to describe the situation whereby she found herself unemployed in the middle of a war. But she was not without resolve or resourcefulness. Tiring of the "crowded subways, the heat, people and a thousand distractions," she moved downtown to the Hotel Albert on University Place in Greenwich Village. "What I'd like," she said, "is a tiny apartment—the kind of thing one hears about but is never able to secure."[38] She was right. Instead, she found an apartment near Columbia University at 3111 Broadway, which she shared with Noma Jensen, a Euro-American woman.[39]

Her predilection for maintaining ties to the well-connected paid off, for she was able to secure a post with the NAACP as assistant field secretary. During her playwrighting days she had become friendly with Arthur Spingarn, who had long been influential within the highest ranks of the association. She had relationships of varying levels of intensity with power brokers like Adam Clayton Powell (father and son), Charles Johnson, Mary White Ovington, Essie Robeson, and Du Bois himself, an NAACP founder. Her role in Arizona had brought her notoriety (the NAACP itself was intimately involved with the cases of racial discrimination there) to add to her artistic luster. Thus, "complying" with the "request" of Walter White, in October 1942 she made a "formal application" to join the NAACP staff.

She explained that for the past eighteen months she had worked with the YWCA/USO but "could not keep quiet" about racial discrimination. "I have been disillusioned," was her mournful conclusion.[40]

On the other hand, her experience in Arizona had moved her to make firmer political commitments. Now she would not be seeking to influence masses with her deft characterizations on stage but instead with her organizing and nonfiction writing. As it turned out, the NAACP proved to be a halfway house between her life in the arts and her impending life in politics. After joining the NAACP she spent a good deal of time on the road, organizing chapters during the organization's most sustained boom in membership—before or since. Between 1940 and 1945 NAACP membership soared from approximately forty thousand to over four hundred thousand, a figure it has not reached since.[41] A central figure in this process—which meant so much for democratic advance during the war—was Shirley Graham.

Soon after arriving she told Walter White that "a goal of one million NAACP members by 1945" was feasible; "every modern technique of public relations must be utilized." Having lived in the Pacific Northwest, then Arizona, she was aware of the epochal change that had taken place in the dispersal of African Americans nationally; thus, she advised that "western sections of the United States in many places offer untouched territory" for the NAACP.[42]

In some ways, this job was designed with Graham in mind. A tireless worker who relied on her organizing skills to accomplish many tasks—not to mention being a person who enjoyed interacting with people—Graham found that organizing NAACP chapters was a sound match for her capabilities. A typical period in July 1943 involved a 4:20 P.M. dinner with local NAACP leadership in New Britain, Connecticut, an 8 P.M. meeting with the pastor of Shiloh Baptist Church in Hartford, then a departure for Bordentown, New Jersey, where she met the next day with the State Federation of Colored Women's Clubs. Then she substituted for Walter White as she gave the principal address at the state's convention of branches.[43]

Later in Memphis she "bearded Boss Crump in his den and received permission from him to present the work of the NAACP over the city's radio, an unheard of concession from the dictatorial old-line Democrat."[44] She traveled to St. Louis for five days, then to Little Rock, where she spoke on the radio and, possibly, helped to lay the basis for the black resistance exhibited during the 1957 school desegregation crisis. "I came down here in full armour against the 'white folks.' I meet a curious kind of wall of resistance from the Negroes themselves. These are people who 'use to have' and 'use to do.'" "Folks from New York can't tell us how to run our business" she was told. "Not that I have been met with personal resentment. I have been invited to speak three and four times every day and dined, wined, and feted. . . . Tomorrow I'm going to a group of laborers who are afraid to come to me."

She was appalled by the casual outrages of the Deep South, even in military camps she visited. "Our men are becoming more brutalized each day." But what angered her was what she saw as the narcotizing effect of the church, which she felt was not sufficiently militant in confronting wrongs. "Believe me, I can more clearly see why the Russians closed all the churches! Come the revolution—that would be the first thing I should advise—*throughout the south*. These fat, thieving, ignorant preachers! All of them should be put to work" (emphasis in original). When this daughter of a preacher expressed alienation from the church, it was a clear signal that she was in the midst of an ideological evolution.

In addition, Graham was being sexually harassed by the local NAACP head. "He's a slight problem! . . . I'm hard pressed to keep him working on a purely professional basis. I can handle it—but the whole thing becomes wearing at times. What price glory!"[45]

Though most of her duties took her away from headquarters in New York City to the wilds of Arkansas and elsewhere, she was on the scene when Harlem exploded in a riot in 1943 as allegations spread about a brutal racist murder of a black soldier. Such events as these helped to shape her developing political consciousness, pushing her to the left. Excitedly, she told her friend Mary White Ovington that during the conflagration,

> The Theresa Hotel was the very hub of everything. It was the most fantastic, unbelievable night anybody could imagine. Unless you read all the papers—especially *PM,* you could have not [a] conception of those eight hours! The five million dollars worth of damage done is no exaggeration. Streets looked as if they had been bombed! . . . Harlem blew up! Literally and thoroughly! Later in a police car, equipped with a loud speaker Walter [White] and Roy [Wilkins] drove through the streets saying "the soldier is not dead—justice will be done—go home—stop!" But they stopped only after they were exhausted. Terrible—Yes. As to the harm done—I'm not so sure . . . the Negroes in New York in five hours destroyed five million dollars worth of "white" property—and you should hear the phone calls we're getting and the committees being formed. Everybody's trying to do *something.* (Emphasis in original)[46]

Graham was coming to recognize that the powerful tended to "do *something*" only when pressured, either through the chaos of a riot or the organization of an NAACP.

However, all was not well with the association, as she breathlessly told Mary White Ovington.

> Things are happening at such a pace and scenes are shifting so completely and without warning, that anything short of a telephone communication seems like a waste of time. . . . The NAACP is in a state of

ferment! . . . William Hastie . . . is now employed (at the rate of five hundred dollars a month!) to "evaluate" all the work and workings of the organization; two weeks ago we held a week-end conference of all national staff . . . Walter, backed by the Board is using every known influence to get William Hastie to accept the position of "Associate Executive Secretary"; the *Crisis* has been simply torn to shreds with criticism—opening gun being fired at a Board meeting by John Hammond . . . I express[ed] the conviction that Negroes and whites in the United States are begging for intelligent leadership, that the NAACP can and does offer that leadership but *that up to this day the people do not know what the NAACP has to offer.* I want to do promotion, publicity, writing, speaking—rather than just money raising. . . . They acknowledge the need of a Public Relations Director—and that's as far as we get. That's the job I really want. It's the job where every ability, talent, skill I have can be utilized to its fullest extent and that's the job which needs to be done for the NAACP. (Emphasis in original)[47]

"Meanwhile," her jaunts across the nation organizing chapters also meant that money was "coming in as never before—the other day I spoke one evening in Connecticut—and the very next night at a state convention in New Jersey—hardly time between trains to wash my face!" Per usual, she was working herself to the limit and was "really frightfully tired." She wanted Mary White Ovington to contact Hastie about her desire to be "Public Relations Director . . . Daisy [Lampkin] praises me as a money raiser." But that praise was part of the problem. "The fact that I raised over eight thousand dollars in Cleveland may prove my undoing!"[48] Her skill at that task hampered her ability to move up to broader responsibility.

Her dream was not to be realized. By all accounts, Shirley Graham was extraordinarily talented as an organizer, but her tenure with the NAACP lasted less than a year. She resigned in the fall of 1943. The NAACP leader Arthur Spingarn sympathized with her ostensible reason for leaving, her "urge to do creative work," knowing that this was a temptation "too great for an artist to resist."[49] Spingarn might well have asked how the notoriously impecunious Graham planned to survive now that she was no longer gainfully employed. This must have occurred to her too; a few months after resigning, she was back in touch with Roy Wilkins and Walter White, trying to return to the staff. She had talked with her former NAACP coworker "Ella [Baker] about it and said that I was ready to acknowledge that I hadn't made a wise move. . . . Yes, I know you offered me the opportunity to take a leave of absence. I wish now that I had done so . . . I'm not going to whine now."[50] Instead of whining, she found a job at the Open Door Community Center in Brooklyn and then became executive secretary of the Brooklyn Inter-Racial Assembly; in the latter capacity she campaigned vigorously against police misconduct and for improved housing opportunities, health care, and jobs.[51] In her spare time and in rapid succession she wrote a series of popular biographies, first on George Washington Carver, then on Paul Robeson, next on Frederick Douglass. Sales from these works finally put her on the road to prosperity, but as her economic fortunes rose, her personal fortunes declined; she suffered a crushing blow when her firstborn, Robert, died tragically.

■

Though she wrote to them and spoke to them on the telephone, Shirley Graham had been away from her sons since they were young children and she had taken a ship to France. She was an absentee parent, though she tried to attend to their material needs and spend time with them during the summer.[52] She sought to use the connections she had developed with the influential not solely for herself; for example, she tried to get Hallie Flanagan to contact Eleanor Roosevelt in order to secure an appointment to West Point for her son David.[53] In 1941 when her son Robert traveled to Los Angeles with the dream of entering UCLA, he did not hesitate to contact his mother for funds; she scrambled to respond.[54] In turn, he reversed the relationship and, just before he died, advised her to settle down and marry: the potential spouse was a "'small town big shot' but he does have security which makes things just about even."[55]

She still felt guilty for being away from her sons, and no amount of money or gifts could salve her wounded conscience. It seemed that she had transferred her maternal gifts to others—soldiers in Arizona, for example. The newspaper *PM*, reporting on her job at the youth center in Brooklyn, where she worked from morning until midnight, observed that she was a "combination mother, probation officer and kindergarten teacher."[56] Somehow she was able to do for strangers what she had difficulty in providing directly for her own sons.

So when her son Robert died in 1944, this understandably painful blow hit Shirley Graham especially hard. He had married as a teenager and had children and, as a result, had debts that she could not always help him with. Though she wrote and called him regularly, her absences made it difficult to forge a relationship as close as she would have preferred. Her son David suggests that she walked with a slight limp because of complications during childbirth; this limp was a metaphor for her at times infirm relationship with her children. And so when Robert died prematurely, she found this tragedy even more difficult to endure. Perhaps this is why she fabricated the story that his death resulted from racism when he was denied proper medical treatment at a hospital. David states that this story was not accurate, that Robert perished after contracting tuberculosis. This fable at least had the virtue of providing a rationale for her to become more deeply involved in antiracist politics and politically tinged writing.[57]

When his brother died, David was crushed. "I felt alone in the world since I had never felt any closeness" to his mother.[58] Graham found some solace in condolences from friends. While working in Brooklyn, she had become friendly with the Communist councilman from that borough, Pete Cacchione. The words of comfort he provided were a credo of her remaining years: "We must remember that there are other Roberts, and therein lies your work, to make your contribution in creating that better world so that other mothers will not have to go through the sorrow you are today."[59] After the emotional devastation of this tragedy, she proceeded to work to insure that "other mothers" might enjoy a "better world." This tragic death, the unique wartime climate of diminished anticommunism, the "popular front" milieu in which she had become enmeshed, and her escalating involvement in politics all helped to push her closer to the Communist Party.

Her son's death had another unintended consequence. As she told her friend Roselyn Richardson, "since Robert's death I've become almost a recluse."[60] This self-imposed isolation allowed more time for writing the series of biographies that propelled her into the rarefied atmosphere of financial security.

Indeed, it seemed that with her son's death, Graham's already high level of productivity accelerated further. She remained determined to obtain a doctorate and enrolled at New York University. She impressed her professor when she was able to bring her Columbia neighbor Carl Van Doren to class—a "rare treat," according to her teacher.[61] By 1945 she had passed her "preliminary comprehensive examination" for a doctorate in education.[62]

She had completed all her "class work" and "the outline for [her] thesis" was "accepted and approved"; thus, she said, "my entire life is work." She continued,

> This isn't a pose or an affectation. It's simply a fact that the world is in pretty much of a mess. I seem to have the capacity for doing something about it, for helping people to understand each other a little better and for dispelling some of the lowering clouds. I accept this responsibility. It gives me a reason for living when all my normal goals and land marks have been swept away.[63]

Of course, she remained gregarious and enjoyed the pleasures of life. In late 1944 she was scheduled to fly to Haiti with an old friend with whom she had become closer, W. E. B. Du Bois.[64] After being ousted from Atlanta University, he too had returned to New York City, where for a while he had shared office space with her brother Bill Graham. She indicated that "everybody is quite pleased with this arrangement," which was suggestive of the blossoming friendship between her and her erstwhile mentor.[65]

Shirley Graham was approaching the age of fifty. The death of her son and the natural evolution of life were making her recognize that perhaps there were alternatives to the unmarried life. Besides, it was not easy being a single woman in Manhattan. One morning, she told her surviving son, "about five thirty I rolled out, reached for my slip and staggered out into the hall on the way to the bathroom. Imagine my amazement to find myself staring into the face of a man who [was] climbing into [the] kitchen window!"[66] He scurried away, but incidents like this were a stark reminder of the dangers a single woman faced in the big city.

This chilling incident was even more alarming for her since she was now spending more time at home writing. Her first biography, *Dr. George Washington Carver, Scientist,* was published in 1944 to critical acclaim.[67] She had been in the top ranks of playwrights, but this had not secured for her a suitable standard of living. Her biographies—though at times criticized sharply for their inclusion of imagined dialogue—may not have been at the apex of the biographical art but, unlike her work on the stage, they did bring in a decent income.

Actually the critics were a bit unfair, for Graham did conduct primary research for these works, scouring archives and libraries. When she wrote a biography of Benjamin Banneker she excavated primary material from the Library of Congress and the Maryland Historical Society. To immerse herself in the details of her subject's life she would "[walk] up and down the streets where [the] person was."[68] For her biography of George Washington Carver, she "went to Tuskeegee, wandered about the countryside, grew to know the people he had served."[69] For her award-winning biography of Frederick Douglass, she met with his descendants and others who knew him.[70]

Still, her invention of dialogue for her biographies was an extension of her life, for if she could create—and unmake—details of her own life, why couldn't she do it for someone else? To be fair, Graham in her memoir characterized this genre as the "biographical novel," though this was not the impression provided to contemporary readers and critics.[71] That these biographies were successful both critically and financially could only encourage her to continue reinventing her own autobiography.

As the day approached for publication of her Carver book, her excitement rose. "The publishers tell me that it is also going to take some literary prize—a movie producer is waiting for the corrected galley sheets." She had written with a purpose in mind; "my Carver book is designed to melt the heart of the most ignorant 'cracker'—while at the same time offering no compromise."[72]

In addition to courting movie moguls and influencing "crackers," she was also writing radio dramas about other important subjects. These works were almost exclusively dialogue-driven—not to mention more lucrative than the lines she had written for the stage—and this encouraged her further to imagine the lives of famous personalities. Her Carver radio play was broadcast on CBS to "universal acclaim." A CBS executive told her, "they liked it particularly in Canada." Canada Lee starred and the play was introduced by her friend Carl Van Doren.[73] Soon she was being mentioned in *Variety* and other trade journals as she began to duplicate her success as a playwright.[74] An analyst from the film company Twentieth Century Fox did inquire about her Carver biography, which he found "most colorful as well as interesting."[75] Her radio script on the life of Phillis Wheatley was broadcast nationally on CBS to even wider acclaim.[76]

Though her success as a writer was largely due to her own efforts, she had help. The leading Communist writer Howard Fast became the latest in a series of influential men who assisted her, encouraging her in her writing efforts. In turn, she became a black female equivalent of Fast—the engaged writer as political activist.[77]

In some ways her books are more revealing about herself than her plays and operas. In her Carver book she expressed admiration for his asceticism and his "alone-ness"; wistfully she spoke of his ability to construct a "sheltered place where every day, alone and undisturbed, unhurried, he could work—could dream, and plan to improve the good earth." This book, written during the war, reflected the multi-class soli darity of that era, hailing Carver's recycling and conservation activities, along with his expert use of weeds and other supposed useless plants. Though she was moving to the left, one could not guess it from this book, which had nothing bad to say about Henry Ford and Andrew Carnegie and other plutocrats whose names were scattered throughout the text.[78] It was telling, as well, that her first book concerned Carver: he reminded her of her father because of his reverence for nature and all things living.[79]

Though some critics railed at her re-creations of dialogue, others found this aspect trailblazing, adding a new dimension to the recounting of history, postmodern in import. Walter Prichard Eaton, an acquaintance from her days at Yale, was of this latter camp, complimenting the "dramatic effectiveness" and "imagination . . . with which" Graham sought to re-create Carver's boyhood.[80] Another acquaintance, writing from Black Mountain, North Carolina, could "only compare" this biography "to an Arabian night story in its interest and in its fabulous content. How did you learn to write so well! You make history read like a novel."[81] That latter point was part of the problem, according to her critics—but if Graham could make her own life read like a novel, why couldn't she do the same for Carver and others?

Her recounting of the life of Paul Robeson was also greeted positively. The novelist Ann Petry found it "wonderful!" and added, "I must confess to feeling very smug because I am able to say that I know you."[82] Carl Van Doren, who wrote the foreword to this 1946 biography, found it both "charming and moving."[83] The anticommunist upsurge that was to batter Robeson—and Graham—had not reached its zenith at the time of publication; thus, this book too sold respectably. Again, more so than her plays, this biography was revealing of Graham herself. She included high praise for her former supervisor, Walter White, hailing him as the "social and cultural arbiter of Harlem." She wrote with knowing detail about the artistic luminaries of the era, including James

Weldon Johnson, Carl Van Vechten, Miguel Covarrubias, Fredi Washington, and others. At one point she noted expansively that "everybody came to Paris that summer—Langston Hughes and Countee Cullen, Alain Locke, Lloyd and Edna Thomas, and young Adam Powell"—all friends of Shirley Graham, by the way. She wrote that her old friend Eric Walrond was "handsome as a Greek god, done in ebony." But besides the knowing references to the literati, there were commendations of Robeson's identification with Africa and intimations of Graham's own political trajectory: "What he said was that the Negro race should redeem its African heritage. He stated that he definitely believed the future of Africa was tied up with that of the peoples of the East." This was combined with exaltation of the Soviet Union; she approvingly quoted the dean of Canterbury:

> All that I hear of the Russian program grips and inspires me. If what we hear is true, it is majestic in range, practical in detail, scientific in form, Christian in spirit. Russia would seem to have embarked on a task never yet attempted by modern or ancient State. It is a plan well worth studying.[84]

Her biography of Robeson and praise of Moscow reflected Graham's own political evolution; unlike many in the United States, she moved more to the left as her economic fortunes improved and her age increased. Her presence in New York, the capital of the U.S. Left, facilitated her budding friendship with Paul Robeson and his spouse, Eslanda. She was ecstatic when he agreed to cooperate with her biography of him.

> In most important moments I can be strangely dumb. I had no words last night to express my feelings when you told me I might present you between the covers of a book to the men and women in whose hands lie the glorious task of building our "new world." I was so excited I couldn't sleep.

The details of his life were not altogether foreign to her, since she had "followed the intense drama" of his life "for years." As with her other biographies, she would conduct research. "I'll go to Philadelphia and acquaint myself with the scenes and friends of your childhood." However, she reminded him, "the most important material of my research must come from you . . . I'd like to follow you about and just listen to you talk." The agreement to write his biography, she concluded, was a "Red Letter day for me."[85]

Her biography of Robeson was followed quickly by a book on the life of Frederick Douglass. In many ways, this was her breakthrough work. A panel consisting of Carl Van Doren, Lewis Gannett, and Clifton Fadiman awarded her the Julian Messner Award for the Best Book Combating Intolerance in a competition involving over six hundred manuscripts; it came with a hefty stipend of $6,500. Finally, after an arduous struggle, Graham had attained a measure of financial security.[86] Like the death of her son, which had driven her to the typewriter, this was a turning point in her life.[87] That a powerful man she had cultivated—Carl Van Doren—sat on the panel making this award was not coincidental and would only encourage her to continue forging such relationships.

Yet the award came at a paradoxical moment. By 1947 the political climate was changing dramatically as a Red Scare gathered strength. She was not an opportunist—Graham had come to the Left just as it was about to enter a very bleak period. A portent of this was provided by a critic for the *Washington Star*, who assailed the "enmity" for the South that was supposedly reflected in her biography.[88]

The broader point, however, was that at this juncture Graham's books were not being ignored; they were reviewed in mainstream publications and consumed ravenously by hungry readers eager to acquire images of Negroes that contrasted with dominant representations that too often portrayed them harshly—if at all. Finally, Graham was beginning to reap the fruits of a celebrity that she had long since attained. When she arrived in Norfolk to promote her book, she was "besieged with requests for autographs."[89] Her stature was confirmed in 1947 when along with Gwendolyn Brooks she was awarded a prestigious fellowship from the Guggenheim Foundation.[90] It seemed as if she were marching from triumph to triumph; however, when her book signing in Boston was nearly "broken up at one point" by a protester consumed with disgust at her leftist politics, this should have served as a warning that setbacks loomed.[91]

But as 1946 was turning into 1947, such sobering visions were difficult to foresee. For the first time in her life, Graham had hired a lawyer to handle her taxes, indicative of her increased income.[92] She was about to buy a charming home in St. Albans, Queens, the neighborhood that

was to become the headquarters nationally for a flourishing black middle class.[93] Her old friend Arthur Spingarn of the NAACP was enlisted
to handle her "business affairs."

Despite her increased bank balance—or perhaps because of it—one
thing had not changed: Shirley Graham remained a tireless worker. In
1947 she told Spingarn, "my work has me going night and day. At this
point I can't say whether I'm making progress or not."[94] She was
equally ill-humored when she reached her old friend from Indianapolis, Roselyn Richardson:

> Perhaps I'm not thoroughly well, or perhaps a long gathering fatigue
> has caught up with me, or perhaps the overall condition of the world
> has produced mental depression within me—but the fact remains that
> I almost have to hold a gun at my head these days to get anything writ-
> ten! A thousand petty, unimportant details seem to fill my days, re-
> ducing me to a dull rag of indifference by nightfall. That I manage to
> arouse myself to go out and make speeches, push forward projects, au-
> tograph books and meet more and more people is only because there
> is inside of me a flame of wrath which [I] am anxious to apply to so
> many things in this world. . . . Not yet do I have a phone and so am
> greatly handicapped in picking up information.[95]

The enforced solitude of being without a telephone did facilitate her
writing—her maunderings about writer's block aside—and her reading. For example, she found Sinclair Lewis's *Kingsblood Royal* to be "the
last word on the 'Negro Question'" and "dynamite. . . . After this, I'm
glad I'm not writing about another Negro."[96] As was her wont, this latter comment was a slight exaggeration; Shirley Graham was to tackle a
number of subjects dealing with the "Negro Question." Though her
lack of a telephone may have made it easier for her to read novels, one
wonders how she could be so active politically in the absence of this
basic tool of communication.

■

Late in life, Shirley Graham recalled that she "had grown up in a family where politics were not discussed. My father usually preceded the
word with the adjective 'dirty.'"[97] Certainly she had an abiding interest
in Africa early on but, by all accounts, her turn to the left only began de-

cisively during World War II, under the twin pressures of her tumultuous wartime experience in Arizona and the death of her son Robert. Her son David recognized this transformation while he was in the military, serving in the Philippines. He noticed that all of a sudden his mother began sending him issues of the *Daily Worker* and another left-wing publication, the *Compass*.[98]

> And I found her to be very actively involved in the left progressive movement of the mid-forties. I think one of the important influences was in the person of the writer Howard Fast . . . [he] had been very instrumental in assisting my mother in getting published. . . . he encouraged her really in her writing . . . biographies for young people of color . . . he was very influential in a circle of intellectuals and writers into which my mother was introduced.[99]

Soon Graham was to be found in deed—and word—in a tight embrace with the much-reviled U.S. Left. In Adam Powell, Jr.'s newspaper *People's Voice* she enunciated her evolving philosophy: "Every writer owes a responsibility to his readers, to all the forces and events which have brought him to the place where he now stands, to the surging masses all around him, to history and the people who come after him." Again, she referred to her own role in masculine terms; however, her coda remained relevant to male and female writers alike: "The revelation of character," she concluded, "is the prime and most important function of the creative writer; characterization is the core of the good novel."[100] She who had done so much to obscure her own character revealed the core of the character of her writing in these few words. She had found a form of writing—popular biography—that allowed her to incorporate the best elements of the novel while creating a story grounded in fact. In revealing the character of figures like Douglass and Robeson, she was simultaneously communicating political ideas that soon were to be denoted as subversive.

As her notoriety as a writer increased, she became even more valuable to a political Left that was rapidly being smothered by a miasma of anticommunism. However, the African American constituency to which she owed her primary allegiance was less influenced by this rightward turn, not least because this turn was often championed by those who pioneered in ever more innovative Jim Crow practices.

The boxer Joe Louis, for example—who was not a Communist but reflected a viewpoint that was not unique to himself—later recalled that Graham's colleague Paul Robeson

> did more for the Negroes than anyone else. . . . Robeson went to Russia in '36 and he said this place is better for the Negro than in America, more opportunity, better treatment. What happened was the American politician got mad and said it was a lie. Ralph Bunche is a result of that. They gave him a chance after that.[101]

The heavyweight champion was not singular in feeling that desegregation was a "Cold War imperative" driven by the influence of the much-despised Left.

Of course, then as now critics charged that the U.S. Communist Party—which Graham and Robeson were presumed to have joined—was solely a creature of the wily Stalin, fueled by "Moscow Gold." But then as now dispute raged as to the full extent of civil liberties deprivations in the Soviet Union, just as dispute raged about the extent to which Communists were subsidized by Moscow.[102] This dispute about basic understandings made it easier for budding Reds to resolve doubt in favor of the party and then dismiss doubt as resulting from "imperialist propaganda." Moreover, Graham was being influenced by stalwarts like Robeson and Fast; it was difficult for a political novice like herself to imagine that her knowledge was more expert than theirs. A photograph from 1947 pictures her with two of the major influences on her—Communist leaders Pete Cacchione and Fast flank her at a rally to save the Communist-initiated publication *New Masses*.[103] This photograph neatly conveyed an idea of the political company she was now keeping.

That same year the House Committee on Un-American Activities listed her as a member of a number of so-called Communist fronts, including the George Washington Carver School in Harlem, where she served as a faculty member, and the Committee to Aid the Fighting South, of which she was the vice-chair. The purpose of the latter grouping was to furnish aid to the Southern Negro Youth Congress "in the battle against white supremacy," "to help finance the southern edition of the *Worker*," and to aid "the Communists and other militant forces in the South."[104] These were not the kind of causes guaranteed to win favor in Washington.

There was an obvious downside, in sum, involved in alignment with the unpopular Left. But coincidentally, this involvement brought Shirley Graham into closer contact with the aging scholar she had long admired: W. E. B. Du Bois. They were now in the same city after years of communication at a distance. Just as the distance between them narrowed, they came to find that their political ideas were converging as well, for Du Bois also was on a glide path that had brought him closer to the ranks of the Communist Party. He had returned to the city in 1944 to work with the NAACP and in 1947 he drafted a petition to the United Nations charging the U.S. government with human rights violations. When he moved to present the petition formally, he called on Graham to accompany him.[105] Likewise when he sought tickets to baseball's World Series—the "first" he "ever attended"—to view the newest symbol of desegregation, Jackie Robinson, he turned to her brother Bill for tickets.[106] She also collaborated with him on a series of lectures he presented at the New School for Social Research on "The Negro in American History."[107] But their already close relationship deepened when Du Bois was ousted in September 1948 from the leadership of the NAACP because of his failure to go along with the gathering Cold War consensus, his support for Henry Wallace in his third-party challenge to President Harry Truman, and his fervent desire to continue pressing the U.S. government in international fora on the issue of human rights violations. Shirley Graham, who had displayed her own organizing skills during her tenure with the NAACP, became a one-woman committee on his behalf. She scorned the "middle class" origins of the association and its "bureaucracy," and noted the fact that Ella Baker also felt compelled to resign. "How dare they insult Negroes all over the world," she asked, "by treating so contemptuously the one man who has been our foremost spokesman, our most eminent statesman for half a century."[108]

For African Americans, the sacking of Du Bois was a turning point in the Cold War; from then on, a popular front that united left and center began to fragment. Soon those who had been lionized—Du Bois, Robeson, and Shirley Graham—became virtual pariahs. The costs were immense. A critical and radical perspective was removed from the scene at the precise moment that U.S. elites determined that Jim Crow was an aching Achilles' heel hampering the execution of U.S. foreign policy. However, rendering mute the voice of figures like Graham meant that the civil rights movement that arose in the wake of the purge of the Left could only proceed so far—it could not reach the key questions of redistribution of wealth and reparations, measures now scorned as "Communist propaganda." Thus, the civil rights movement was faced with the dilemma that African Americans had the right to eat at a lunch counter but lacked the wherewithal to buy a hamburger, the right to check into a hotel but not the money necessary to check out. Moreover, when the Left—the natural predator of the Right—was weakened, it created something of an ecological imbalance that facilitated the rise of a form of black nationalism that stressed self-reliance and "do for self" that was much more compatible with the prevailing conservative consensus.

These developments would not come as a complete shock to Graham or her ever closer friend, Du Bois. Perhaps this is why she took to his defense with such ferocity. According to one scholar, after the sacking, Graham "threatened to destroy [Walter] White's reputation. She gave the *Chicago Defender* and *New York Post* the lengthy correspondence between White and Du Bois on the 'non-partisan' policy and encouraged the reporters to 'get that s.o.b. Walter White.'" She initiated the "Emergency Committee" to get him reinstated, which "flooded the NAACP branches" with her "unrelenting attack." In her "confrontational tactics" she derided White and his comrade Roy Wilkins as "lesser men" who "had seized 'the controls of a bureaucratically run organization'" and "had tried to 'drive [Du Bois] away' with 'vindictive' and 'petty heckling.'" The firing, she cried, was a "'brazen act' of sheer 'political persecution' that 'illuminate[d] the archaic and anti-democratic character of the NAACP's structure.'" Wilkins, in reply, charged that "Graham's committee relied upon 'numerous inaccuracies, distortions and partial truths.'" Graham, a blackbelt in the art of verbal facility, charged that the NAACP leadership had "fastened a cord around its own neck . . . that would [eventually] strangle it."[109]

As it turned out, the NAACP leadership felt vindicated when Truman was reelected and began to move against racial segregation, particularly in the armed forces. Graham and Du Bois in 1948 backed the losing campaign of Henry Wallace's Progressive Party, which mounted a left-wing challenge to Truman's reelection. Reputedly, Mao Zedong, when asked his evaluation of the French Revolution, replied that it was too soon to tell. Is it too soon to tell if Graham took the proper course when she resisted the tidal wave of anticommunism that drove the organized Left out of the NAACP and the civil rights movement gener-

Left: Shirley Graham's mother, Etta Graham, circa 1932-33. She played a major role in raising Shirley Graham's children as Graham pursued her career. *Right:* Shirley Graham's father, David Graham. He was a major influence on her life and spurred her interest in writing. He was also a firm taskmaster, whose strictness helped push her into an early marriage, which quickly ended in divorce.

Shirley Graham as a little girl. Because of her father's job as a pastor the family moved around quite a bit, and she spent her childhood in the Midwest, the South, and the West. She continued this pattern as an adult, residing intermittently in New York, Ghana, Egypt, and China.

Shirley Graham with her son and mother, 1931. Graham sought to compensate for her frequent absences from her children by writing to them frequently and buying them gifts.

The young Shirley Graham. In addition to her skill as a writer, early on she gained an excellent reputation as a musician. She pursued her interests in the arts in Paris in the 1920s.

Shirley Graham at the time of the opening of her opera *Tom-Tom,* circa 1932. This work, a frank homage to Africa, catapulted her to prominence.

Yale University production of *Dust to Earth,* Yale University Theatre in the late 1930s. Shirley Graham attended the School of Drama at Yale, where she honed her skill as a playwright.

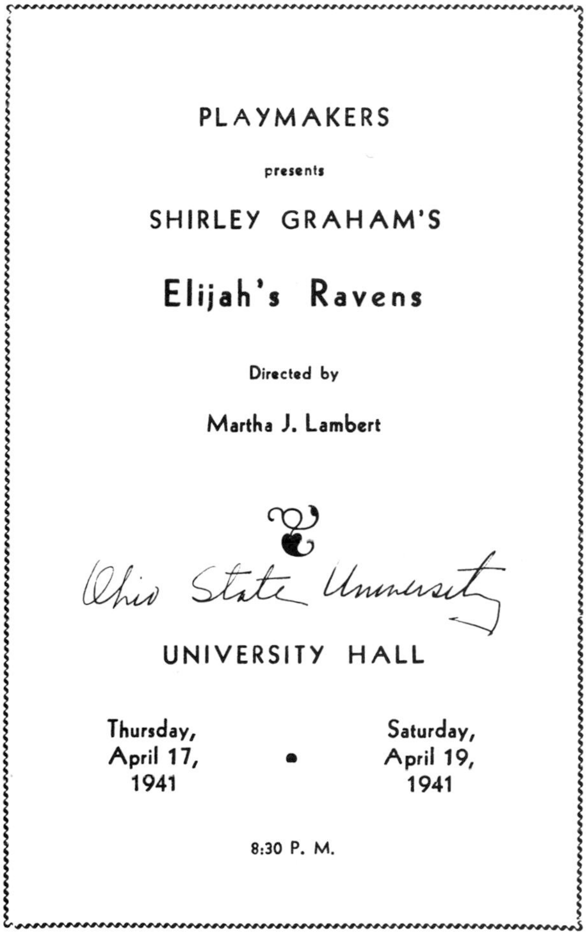

PLAYMAKERS

presents

SHIRLEY GRAHAM'S

Elijah's Ravens

Directed by

Martha J. Lambert

Ohio State University

UNIVERSITY HALL

Thursday,		Saturday,
April 17,	●	April 19,
1941		1941

8:30 P. M.

Playbill from *Elijah's Ravens.* By the late 1930s, Graham was ranked with Langston Hughes as a leading play-wright among African Americans.

A party at Fort Huachuca, Arizona, circa 1942, where Shirley Graham served during World War II. It was here that her political activism blossomed as she protested vigorously against the maltreatment of African American soldiers.

Shirley Graham and her son Robert, Capistrano, early 1940s. His premature death caused her to make firmer political commitments and forge a deeper engagement with the organized Left.

Shirley Graham, 1944. By this juncture, she was in the midst of leaving her position on the staff at the NAACP, where she had helped preside over the largest membership spurt in the organization's history.

Shirley Graham with her mother, son David (third from right), and brother Lorenz (far right) receiving an award for her writing in the 1940s. When she turned to writing popular biographies, she attained the commercial success that had eluded her previously.

Shirley Graham in the study of her St. Alban's, Queens, home, 1940s. During her career she wrote continuously, churning out plays, novels, biographies, and operas, along with newspaper and journal articles.

Shirley Graham's home in St. Albans, Queens, late 1940s.

Shirley Graham with her mother, brothers, and sisters-in-law. *Back row, left to right*: Orville, Bill, Lorenz, D.A. *Front row, left to right*: Elaine Graham, Ruth Graham, Etta Graham, Shirley Graham.

Shirley Graham in the library of W. E. B. Du Bois. When Du Bois returned to New York City during World War II, they began to spend more time together.

in spite of my very earnest intention to stick only to my writing I find myself . . . meeting in all sorts of executive groups, sitting down with all kinds of nationally known people, hobnobbing and lunching and dining with men whose names appear daily in the headlines. It's all rather incredible, but it's happening.

The authorities in Washington had taken note of her activity: "Naturally I am also running the risk of being called to Washington by the Thomas Committee since a large number of my personal friends and associates are already under indictment. Henry Wallace tells us not to give way to fear and intimidation," but this was becoming more difficult with each passing day.[116]

Despite Graham's passionate words and frenetic campaigning, the Progressive Party suffered a staggering defeat in 1948. As one of the party's most vocal and visible supporters, Graham was bound to be targeted by those who saw this electoral effort as no more than a trojan horse for the Communists. Though the political climate was becoming increasingly chilly, she refused adamantly to back down. She took a leading role in the campaign to elect Frances Smith, "rank and file leader of the workers of Local 6 of the Hotel and Club Employees" to the state assembly on the American Labor Party ticket. "The impact of a Negro woman fighting for her people," Graham concluded in a burst of race feminism, "would be tremendous."[117] Within five years of this 1950 race, this affiliate of the Progressive Party would be virtually defunct, "red-baited" out of existence, but that did not deter her. She took a leading role in the effort to oust May Quinn, a local teacher who attained notoriety for her penchant for expressions of racism and anti-Semitism. Signing on to her letter of protest were E. Y. Harburg, Alice Childress, and two up and coming entertainers, "Harry Bellefonte" [sic] and "Sidney Portier" [sic].[118]

At this juncture, along with Claudia Jones, Shirley Graham was the living symbol of left-wing political activism among African American women. This came clear when she played a leading role in the unsuccessful effort by the ALP to elect one of its own to the U.S. Senate in 1950. However, all was not grim and glum as a result of this campaign; after all, the electoral race had brought her into closer contact with the ALP senatorial candidate who was to become her second husband, W. E. B. Du Bois.

5

Shirley Graham Du Bois

AS THE RED SCARE was dawning in the late 1940s, Shirley Graham found herself uncomfortably close to the main target of this crusade: the Communist Party. The proximity inevitably left her singed and scorched. She was a closeted Communist, but that deliberate disguise hardly fooled those who were hunting for Reds. Inexorably, because of Du Bois's increasingly close relationship with her, he was drawn as well into these circles and, ultimately, joined the party himself in 1961. As their political relationship deepened, their personal relationship reached a new level when his spouse passed away.

■

Beginning in 1943, after she left Arizona, it seemed that Shirley Graham's name started popping up regularly in the *Daily Worker*. The youth center she worked for in Brooklyn was affiliated to the church of Reverend Thomas Harten, who was suspected of being all too close to the Reds.[1]

These developments had not escaped the attention of the vigilant FBI, particularly as the critical year of 1948 unfolded. When she spoke at Washington's "Cooperative Bookshop"—deemed "subversive" by the U.S. attorney general—the diligent agent present carefully observed that "she used as her notes the Negro Section of the Sunday *Worker* and lauded the Communist Party as the only American political institution which was truly a democratic party."[2]

Like latter-day equivalents of the hounds that hunted down escaped slaves, the FBI trailed Graham doggedly, noting her presence at an anti-HUAC rally at New York's Madison Square Garden. When she joined the lobbying of the U.S. Senate against the "Mundt Police-State Bill," an FBI operative was there to note that she was "one of the leading Negroes in the above mentioned delegation." *Counter-Attack,* the newsletter of record for those seeking to uncover Red affiliations, stated bluntly that "it isn't necessary to seek whether [she] is a member of the Communist Party. That question becomes largely irrelevant in view of her known record. She openly supported Communist Party nominees for public office in 1946." Perhaps the final insult came when she joined Du Bois in 1949 in sending greetings to Josef Stalin, hailing his "leadership in uprooting racial discrimination."[3] When in 1951 a "Security Index Card" was prepared for her, which would facilitate her detention in case of national emergency, this was simply confirmation of her journey beyond the political mainstream.[4]

Though the National Council of Arts, Sciences, and Professions included leading lights like Lillian Hellman, John Howard Lawson, Langston Hughes, Howard Fast, Robeson, and Du Bois, the authorities still found the time and energy to monitor what Graham was doing in this organization. Perhaps this was because of her leadership role, both formally and politically. NCASP was meeting in late July 1948 as the entire Communist leadership was about to be placed on trial and many others were fleeing. The minutes of that meeting reflect that it was "Miss Graham" who adamantly "indicated that we must think of ASP as a permanent organization over and above the Wallace campaign."[5] She refused to buckle. In the eyes of the FBI, Graham appeared to be an unrepentant "Stalinist" at a time when such a designation was viewed as akin to the mark of the devil.

At NCASP, she recalled, "I found myself attending meetings and having cocktails with Carl Van Doren; Ring Lardner, Jr.; the war correspondent and novelist, Ira Wolfert; the 'thriller' writer Dashiell Hammett; and the artist, Rockwell Kent." Through this process, she helped introduce her frequent companion, W. E. B. Du Bois, to the organized Left: "few had ever seen him, largely because he kept himself in a world apart from them." She was "drawing him into New York's young, eager and progressive circles. . . . Heretofore, Du Bois had pointedly and decidedly avoided having any but business or professional contacts with American whites."

Once when she had sent a Euro-American woman to be his secretary at the NAACP, he became upset. Du Bois, who had lived in Jim Crow Atlanta and attended school in racially segregated Nashville, was not eager to interact with a group that was not generally well-known for its enlightened attitudes on race. Such an attitude—a reaction to white chauvinism—helps explain the oft-repeated statements about his haughtiness. One result of his relationship with Shirley Graham was to convince him that there might be a few redeemable Euro-Americans, and this was a step on his path to the Communist Party.[6]

What was particularly galling to anticommunists was that Graham's popularity as a writer guaranteed her entree into diverse circles where her presumed Stalinist virus could be spread. During the 1946-48 period, she fulfilled a steady stream of speaking engagements, sponsored by an array of organizations ranging from the American Jewish Congress to the Howard University Alumni Association, the Sigma Gamma Rho sorority, the Cultural Committee of the Beth Israel Center in her home borough of Queens, the Teachers' Union of Philadelphia, and the National Association of Negro Business and Professional Women's Clubs.[7] All the while, her books continued to be reviewed in mainstream newspapers and she continued to garner relatively favorable publicity there.[8] When she spoke at Bennett College (a school that specialized in educating black women) in North Carolina in 1947 she was greeted by the president of the institution, and the event made headlines in the black press.[9] That same year there was no surprise when the Schomburg Library in Harlem named her to the "Race Relations Honor Roll," joining the relatively non-controversial Frank Yerby.[10]

This tranquility for Graham was crudely interrupted at Peekskill, New York, in 1949. She was one of the unfortunates who had come to this community for a rally sponsored by the Civil Rights Congress—a so-called Communist front—that Paul Robeson was to address. Instead a riot erupted, sparked by an inflamed right wing that amassed opposition and objected strenuously to the existence of presumed Communists and their allies.[11] Graham reported, "I felt a sharp sting on my face and put up my hands to wipe it away. There was blood on my fingers. I stared at it rather stupidly." The culprit

> hurled the rock—straight at me. He hurled it hard and swift and sure! I saw it coming but I could not move, I could not take my eyes from his face. The rock struck the thin pane of glass at my head and it bent and seared like paper in a flame but the rock fell, its force broken. I sat there, seeing his face, the face of Fascism—knowing I was marked for his next victim.[12]

It was her mother who "had never heard Paul Robeson and insisted on going though we were warned there might be trouble. So it happened we were in one of those buses which were almost completely wrecked and barely escaped being killed."[13]

Graham was coming to recognize that her recently minted political affiliations were not without cost. If this realization had not dawned at Peekskill, certainly it must have crossed her mind when she traveled to Paris for a major peace conference sponsored by left-wing forces. After her friend Paul Robeson was reported at this conference to have cast doubt on the willingness of African Americans to join in a war against the Soviet Union, a volcano of protest erupted in the United States.

This trip was no hardship for her in that she stayed in "one of the finest hotels on the continent . . . my bills . . . for the [conference] were paid by one of the committees of the Congress Mondial." This 1949 gathering was conceived as a blunt rejection of those who lusted for nuclear war. "Never in the history of the world has there been such a gathering of peoples from every part of the globe!" There were "large numbers of colored peoples of all shades and descriptions who took prominent parts [including] delegates from 60 different countries." The increasingly prominent Graham "sat with dignitaries from all over the world: The Dean of Canterbury, the Archbishop, members of the British and other Parliaments, [Madame Eve] Curie . . . scientists and writers from the Soviet Union." There was dinner in a "beautiful castle on the Champs-Elysees." This was quite a switch from her penny-pinching days in Paris over two decades ago. She was thoroughly impressed with Paris in part because "in France writers are aristocrats!"[14] No doubt she was reacting to the fact that left-wing writers in Paris were hardly on the margins; this was a far cry from the persecution her kind faced back home as evidenced by the volcanic reaction to Robeson's reported remarks. Such thoughts made Graham consider relocating there after she married Du Bois and persecution of both of them increased. Graham also included a trip to Denmark on this journey, where she helped the famed writer Martin Anderson Nexo mark his eightieth birthday.

Graham had embarked on a personal peace offensive, seeking to rally forces globally against nuclear war. Like Du Bois, she played a prominent role in the 1949 Scientific and Cultural Conference for World Peace held at the Waldorf Hotel in Manhattan. This rally for peace perversely stirred bellicose sentiments. The hotel was surrounded by "a mob" barely "held back by the police, walking through that narrow passage was an ordeal as insults, boos and curses were hurled at us."[15]

All the while, the authorities were taking careful note of her activism. The House Un-American Activities Committee cited her protest of the arrest of the fabled Chilean Communist poet Pablo Neruda; her support for the reelection of Harlem's Communist city councilman, Ben Davis; her participation in various May Day celebrations sponsored by the Communist Party.[16] Graham had become accustomed to her books attaining respectable sales and receiving favorable reviews in the mainstream press; this had allowed her to buy a nice home in Queens to which she brought her mother and, for a while, her son. Finally she had achieved the financial security she had been striving toward for so many years, a journey that had caused her to depart from her sons in the first place. But now she faced another, perhaps larger, problem: she began receiving reports about various libraries seeking to bar her books from their shelves because of her political affiliations.[17] She had begun writing biographies, as she recalled, "because I am anxious and concerned that young Negroes know their country and know their own place in it"; that is, her motives were largely patriotic. But now she was being charged with the exact opposite of what she intended; "this I protest[ed] with all the power of my being."[18] The process of discrediting Graham could ultimately erode the security she had strived so assiduously to attain. It seemed that her entire world might collapse around her.

After the Waldorf conference, "things simply fell apart. Our offices had been sacked, our files stolen. Everyone who had anything to do with the peace conference or was in any way connected with the Council knew that he might well lose his job."[19] The life of Shirley Graham, which had recently been charmed, was about to undergo yet another metamorphosis, only this time she was to have a partner in her journey: W. E. B. Du Bois.

■

By early 1950 the fifty-three-year-old Shirley Graham had developed a comfortable life in Queens. By that year her community, St. Albans, had attracted a stellar array of black artists and intellectuals, including Count Basie, Ella Fitzgerald, and Lena Horne; nearby in Corona was Louis Armstrong; in Flushing there was Billie Holliday. Like Graham, they too were attracted by the sturdy brick cottages and sparkling green lawns that characterized these neighborhoods.[20] In such an atmosphere, Graham's already immense productivity escalated further.

As the newspaper the *Afro-American* put it in an admiring profile, "her work room is the library of her attractive, English style home on a quiet street in St. Albans," where she lived with her mother and, intermittently, her son.

> The sun streams in the huge windows of the first-floor library where Miss Graham works at a large oak desk piled high with papers and books, including two fat volumes of research material. . . . Leisure time games are not for her. She shuns bridge . . . preferring to read, attend the theater or meet people.

When on deadline she

> is likely to work 12 or 15 hours at a clip. 'I do my best work like this,' she explains 'because in the wee hours I can be sure of no interruptions.' Miss Graham is also an accomplished cook. . . . Friends especially go for her cornbread, hot biscuits, creole jumbo, fried chicken and salads.

But above all, she was a working writer, "composing at a typewriter, making innumerable copies, each time adding corrections and improving her style. She never stops rewriting until her publisher demands that she make a certain deadline. She uses a small noiseless typewriter."[21]

This sylvan stability allowed Graham to turn her attention to the family she had neglected during her years of economic sacrifice. Her surviving son, David, had entered the military in 1943 and after one year graduated as a second lieutenant from officer candidates school. He spent a year in Alabama before being shipped to the Philippines. He entered Hunter College in Manhattan in 1946 and after a stint with the Wallace campaign in 1948 graduated in 1950.[22]

Perhaps because of guilt as a result of the years she was away from him, Graham became quite concerned with the evolution of her youngest son. She objected vehemently when he contemplated marriage in the mid-1940s, feeling that he was much too young.[23] He, on the other hand, was equally adamant, reminding his divorced mother, "in our family I have seen four marriages, two divorces, two remarriages, the same two remarriages without children, one marriage saved by the Navy, and one slowly going to the dogs with five beautiful children."[24]

He wondered openly how he could do worse. Shirley Graham, in turn, tried to use her developing celebrity on his behalf; in fact, she saw her increasing prominence as a bit of redemption for her perceived failures as a mother in that she could now use her good name on her son's behalf.[25]

Her son discounted her advice and married, thus leaving her with an empty room and a growing sense of her own mortality. She had been growing closer to Cuban diplomats at the United Nations, a development spurred by her visit to Havana in 1949 for a peace conference.[26] So not wanting to be "left . . . alone in a large house" with her elderly mother, she allowed a "son of friends of mine in Cuba," who happened to be in New York "with the Cuban delegation to the United Nations," to take her son's room.[27] Later, in the eyes of the FBI, this innocent gesture was to raise the specter of Graham's early friendship with Cuban revolutionaries, but this was not on her mind at the time; like many, she simply wanted company.

And when her mother passed away and the spouse of W. E. B. Du Bois died, there was a converging recognition that he too would provide pleasant company. Perhaps she thought that their intimate friendship could be better served in a marriage.

■

December 1950 was a bleak time for the dwindling ranks of the U.S. Left. The war in Korea had hastened an already escalating anticommunism; many in the United States were beginning to wonder why Communists should be tolerated at home when blood was being shed to subdue this same force abroad. Du Bois himself was about to be handcuffed, indicted, and tried for being the agent of an unnamed foreign power—presumably the Soviet Union—because of his activism against nuclear weapons. Graham herself was vulnerable in this regard because of her outspokenness about the war.

However, when Graham repaired to her typewriter on 12 December to compose a letter to her old friend from Indiana, Roselyn Richardson, this was not the primary subject she addressed. With barely concealed glee, she said,

> I have one more Christmas present which you are going to be the very
> first *friend to hear about*. And darling, please keep this secret for a while.
> It is going to cause a lot of talk—*on three continents*—and when the

announcement is made I want to be fully prepared. I'm going to marry W. E. B. Du Bois the last week in February. He's had a ring made for me at Cartier's which is different from any engagement ring you ever saw. Wait until you see it! [My son] Robert's birthday is February 27 so that is the day I have chosen. (Emphasis in original)

She was going to sell her home in Queens because "it's too far out from the center of our activities—takes too long to get back and forth. It's too large and too nice a house for me really to maintain the proper kind of establishment and it's impossible to get competent help these days—*especially so far from Harlem*" (emphasis in original). Even before becoming Shirley Graham Du Bois, she was already exhibiting the signs of imperiousness that were to disgust Maya Angelou in Ghana years later; moreover, there was a *class* pressure on Graham to conform to a hegemonic style of life that valorized domesticity, "consumerism," and all the rest. It was more difficult for her to resist aspects of antifeminism than white supremacy.

Continuing to muse about her future, she added,

We both love Europe. Dr. Du Bois has close and warm ties in at least three countries in Europe. It is our plan to spend a good part of our time in France . . . after February 27th I'm going to have a beautifully ordered life. I assure you it will not be dull. Du Bois is actually one of the most daring men I know. He has a youthful zest for life and living and I anticipate a lot of sheer fun. I will have a "position" to maintain but we both love the same kind of people and have not the slightest concern about what certain other kinds of people think about us. We both dislike publicity, yet we know that people have a right to know something about the lives of folks who write and speak publicly and a lot of folks will have decided opinions about our marriage. It is, however, our opinion about it that will make or break the marriage.

Her ecstasy about her marriage did not erode her activism for peace. That evening she was

speaking . . . for the Women for Peace Committee. We're bringing pressure on the United Nations to stop the shooting in Korea. Unless women everywhere come out very strong in the struggle *for peace* selfish men are going to drag us into war. And the heaviest responsibility

lies on the women of America. We are the only women in the world
who have not suffered horribly in wars. (Emphasis in original)[28]

This progressive incantation revealed part of the paradox of Graham: in
the same train of thought she could express class-drenched disdain
about the difficulty in finding a "competent" maid, then express sentiments about war and peace that few were sufficiently courageous to
utter. The burst of gender consciousness about women and war with
which she concluded her letter to Roselyn Richardson was even more
ironic in that her impending marriage did not turn out to be an exemplar of feminism. In fact, the years she was married to Du Bois, 1951 to
1963, were in many ways the least interesting and least productive of
her long life, in part because of the subordinate role she felt obligated to
adopt—but that is not to say they were the least enjoyable. She reveled
in and thoroughly enjoyed the "position" that she had "to maintain" as
Shirley Graham Du Bois; her critics would suggest that she enjoyed this
"position" much too much.

■

As Shirley Graham recalled it, she had known her second husband most
of her life. In her memoir she recounts when she first met him, when she
was a young girl and he, already a prominent personality, was visiting
her home.

"'Hello,'" he said, "'you must be the daughter of the family. How
do you do, Miss Graham. My name is Du Bois.' And he extended his
hand. Nobody had ever called me 'Miss Graham' before." Years later he
told her, "you were such a nosy little thing . . . wanted to know everything. The questions you put to me that day!" They discussed Paris and
two of her favorite writers, Victor Hugo and Charles Dickens. Already
she was enthralled with Dr. Du Bois.[29]

She told the writer Andrew Paschal that Du Bois held her "on his
lap" when she was a child, and that her father read every issue of the
Crisis, the journal Du Bois edited, to her when she was very small. Since
she was thirteen by the time the NAACP was founded in 1909—and
could read quite well at that time—perhaps Graham did not remember
the precise details of her childhood accurately, insofar as it concerned
the NAACP journal.

When she was a young woman in college, Du Bois used to take
her to "all the great educational meetings that he was to address," she

recalled.[30] Her sister-in-law, Ruth Morris Graham, reports that the eighteen-year-old Graham "fell in love" with Du Bois when he visited their home in Colorado Springs and she gave him her bedroom since they did not have a guest room.[31] Like the dialogue between herself and Du Bois that she recalled verbatim decades later, these accounts—which are evidently not in exact accord—must all be read cautiously. Yet there is little doubt that her attraction to Du Bois had begun decades before their marriage, and this attraction only increased with time.

Their contact increased in the 1930s when she was seeking to establish herself as a composer and Du Bois—who also happened to be married—was the patron saint of struggling artists. Graham, at this point, gushed with platitudes when writing to Du Bois. "We who are about to live, salute you, our chief" was one of her milder remarks. She told him that he had "been the inspiration and moving force" in the writing of her Oberlin M.A. thesis.[32] Once she told him, "I am quite consciously working for your approval."[33] She spoke of trying to "write the opera which will reveal the 'Souls of Black Folk'" in music.[34]

Du Bois, in turn, provided her advice on employment—keep Dillard and Prairie View in mind, stay away from Howard since it was "tied up with so many musicians of the older sort."[35] When she began teaching in Nashville, she reached desperately out to the man who was akin to a mentor and father confessor:

> I am stifling, I am strangling . . . I cannot go into a cafeteria and push and shove my way to a table, grab food from under other frantic hands, fight my way to a seat. . . . What is the matter with me? There are over a thousand students here. The things that we are doing to them are criminal. They are asking for food. We are giving them stones.

Besides, the teaching was not stimulating; "most of the things I'm doing could be done by any high school graduate."[36] He commiserated with her plight, recounting his difficulties at Wilberforce decades earlier.[37] This early exchange was indicative of a pattern that characterized their premarriage relationship: though she was an uncommonly competent and strong woman, it seemed that when communicating with Du Bois she was always on the verge of falling apart and needing rescue.

They began meeting periodically; he intended to meet her in Nashville in 1936 since he was going to be there for an Alpha Phi Alpha meeting anyway.[38] Enigmatically, he added that he wanted to "discuss some things which had better not be written."[39] A snowstorm prevented their meeting. He was "terribly disappointed."[40] So was she.[41] But he was not far from her thoughts, since she was now reading his novel *Dark Princess* and "passages from it sang in my heart." She assured him that Nashville "offers me no temptations" because of the "immorality of the spirit and soul which is so much more deadly than mere physical immorality." There was "some amusement when it was learned" that she was listening to Wagner's *Götterdämmerung*, "now that is something—to have the opportunity to lead hungry, young Negroes to Wagner!"

She was finding Nashville to be a difficult assignment. Though she denied being "presumptuous," she encouraged Du Bois to "free" her by taking her to Germany as his assistant. "Take me with you, I beg you . . . I'm dying here. . . . Fear of the future has me by the throat. Nine months ago I was so happy as I prepared for the 'work' I was going to do. . . . I have five hundred students under me."[42]

No, taking her to Germany was not possible, Du Bois chided her, but he could meet her in Louisville. He asked her to "find lodging . . . near where I am staying."[43] One could presume that by this point—around 1936—the forty-year-old Graham and the sixty-eight-year-old Du Bois were conducting an illicit affair, though his request for separate lodging is not necessarily consistent with that notion. The main point, however, was that Graham—who had an uncanny habit, in any case, of becoming friendly with the influential, such as Du Bois and Mary White Ovington—had developed an intensely personal relationship with a leading black intellectual.[44] Being able to see him made her "ecstatic with joy!" "I'm so excited," she gushed, "I'll probably be burned to a cinder before you get here."[45]

After this encounter, it seemed that their relationship became even closer. When her father died in 1936, she reached out to him, confiding that "my father's death plunges me into an inconsolable pit of darkness. We loved each other as each of us loved no one else."[46] When she needed a recommendation for a fellowship from the Rosenwald Fund, he complied readily, calling her a "woman not only of ability but of unusual energy in the face of great and almost overwhelming difficulties."[47] Now he was calling her "My dear Shirley" instead of "Miss Graham." He helped her with her work still; after he viewed a production of *Elijah's Ravens*, he told her, "it was a good play. It held the audience

. . . I heard them say on campus 'you must see *Elijah's Ravens.*' I think you have got a very good piece of dramatic work which will live a long time."[48] She, in turn, reported to him on her progress, noting her study of German, the production of two of her scripts on radio, her "debut" as a dancer. "*Swing Mikado,*" she said, "fulfilled the highest dreams of those promoting Federal projects. This has been one of the most satisfying events of my life. All in all, the gods are very kind. But I want more."[49] She got more, thanks in part to Du Bois. As she drolly put it, "Mr. Rosenwald takes very good care of his 'favorite' child"; the grant, for which he provided a recommendation, allowed her to repay a loan she had obtained from him. But it was not his money—such as it was— that she was after: "for twilight, and soft ruby wine and golden bubbles sparkling [on] my tongue—there is no repaying, only warm memories"; such was her pleasant recollection of their most recent encounter in the late summer of 1939.[50] There were logistical barriers to their encounters. She was in New Haven, he in Atlanta. But the miles that separated them did not bar the development of mutually intense emotions. She was becoming more fond of him, encouraging him to see *The Man Who Came to Dinner* since "the leading character bears a startling resemblance to you."[51] Despite the warm words, Du Bois—who, after all, did have a wife to attend to—and Graham lived in different cities and had difficulty meeting. Once he complained of not being able "to get anything articulate out of you these days"; later he regretted that he had "neglected" her "shamefully and will not try to account for the reasons except that [I] really have been busy. The one-legged clog dancer has nothing on me."[52] Graham had other romantic interests, he had a wife; constant and frequent communication could be problematic in this context. Yet despite the barriers, they shared too much of an intellectual bond to remain distant for too long. The publication of Richard Wright's *Native Son* turned Graham's "blood to vinegar and" made "her heart weep for having borne two sons. They say it is a great book. Why?"[53] Wright's success had reminded Graham of her advancing years and that she was "not old enough to have achieved anything worth having and . . . too old to laugh at everything worthwhile." She knew that she had "something to give—a great deal—I believe, but—The prospect is terrifying. I don't like the world outside. I'm afraid of it." She turned for comfort to Du Bois, adding tellingly, "I can't imagine saying [this] to anyone else."[54] Du Bois disagreed with her evaluation of *Native Son*, calling it "great."[55] It appeared as if she considered Wright's success both a benchmark for what was possible and a reproach for what she had not achieved. She told her "beloved and honored friend" Du Bois that the theatrical opening of *Native Son* "gives me hope—much hope." "No real money has been made on a Negro show since 'Green Pastures' until 'Cabin in the Sky,'" but Wright's work might prove to be the breakthrough for black dramatists generally.[56]

But Wright's success brought no immediate benefit to her. Du Bois tried to help her by providing contacts with Arthur Spingarn and other influential persons who might be able to help her. But this proved unavailing as Graham still felt compelled to abandon the stage. Yale and the Federal Theater had given her "an equipment for work in the theatre such as few of us have. I have made strong and influential contacts in the professional work. . . . Some one of us must be in [a] position of authority," she continued, referring to African Americans. "Until that happens we can get no plays produced and most of our acting is turned into a burlesque." She wanted to be that person "in a position of authority," and given her academic and professional background, she should have been that person, but that did not happen. She had to leave Yale, though if she "had no responsibility other than" herself, she could have tried to tough it out but she had two sons and needed economic "security." Writhing "in the blackest despair," she reached out to Du Bois again: "I am trained to work, I am anxious to work, I must have work. . . . You see, I really have no home to go to. I must work."[57] Should she stick with playwrighting? "Few white directors can do a Negro show" but, inevitably, this was what she was stuck with, particularly if she wanted to garner the income that only Broadway could provide; what to do?[58]

Du Bois could not help her find work, so she moved to Indianapolis to work for the YWCA, where she would seek—among other things—to build a theater. Her spirits were lifting a bit, in part because of the succor Du Bois provided: "Somebody read my palm the other day and predicted a 'stormy, turbulent and brilliant' career."[59] But "stormy" and "turbulent" proved to be the dominant themes. In the spring of 1941, as she was contemplating leaving Indiana for Arizona, she told Du Bois candidly, "I need more money." She now realized that "what I continue to build is a 'reputation' not financial security . . . I did a 'choric-drama' for the white YWCA last night. It went very successfully, a good house and lots of applause," but a very small economic return.[60] She revealed her vulnerabilities to him, confiding, "I have been so beaten down lately that I know I'm weak."[61] Was this intelligent and determined woman discussing genuine vulnerabilities with a person she admired? Or was she pushed to portray herself as vulnerable so as to conform to a presumed feminine norm that a man supposedly would find irresistible?

Whether consciously or not, her exposing of various sides of herself—her downs and her ups—was bringing Du Bois closer to her; interestingly, he was not as open about his feelings as she. Inevitably her letters to him were written in such a way as to call on him to provide her with uplift or the like; his had become the shoulder she rested on and the counsel she valued. This was a major theme of their premarriage relationship. It was probably flattering for Du Bois to acknowledge that a woman who could easily pass for his daughter was coming to see him in a role that surpassed the paternal.

Du Bois came to visit her in Indiana and she held a small dinner party in his honor. Being able to flaunt his presence was an emblem of her own success. A friend told her that she was honored to have been invited to meet this "truly . . . great man. I certainly do not wonder at your conceit when he considers you a friend . . . it was one of the most delightful experiences of my life."[62] Thus, when she left Indiana for Arizona he was one of the first to know of her bellowing pride in working with the "largest aggregation of Negro soldiers" in the nation—"I suppose in the world"; it was "the most amazing job!" "The skies [sic] the limit," she said. "I can do anything!" "I'm the boss."[63] Of course, Du Bois was not the only man with whom she shared intimacy. In the fall of 1940 a friend contemplated Shirley Graham's "marriage to one of three suitors," adding knowingly, "'tis a tale full of sound and [fury] signifying that you'll be of another frame of mind next month. A little better for the compliments to your charm and a little brighter for the polish applied to your vanity!"[64] Graham, like any other person, was desirous of both economic and emotional security. With his letters of recommendation and loans, Du Bois might be able to assist with the former, but his own marriage and his distance from her complicated his ability to provide the latter. For that, she often had to look elsewhere.

Still, despite being surrounded by thousands of Negro men in the middle of nowhere in Arizona, she stayed in touch with him and continued sharing her innermost thoughts with him. Yes, she liked her job; it was "amazing," but "last night, as I lay far into the night, unable to sleep I suddenly realized that my own salvation demands that I do write." But this dream might not be realized, since she felt exposed in Arizona: Tokyo had struck in Hawaii, where the United States was in "no way prepared," and Fort Huachuca was "the outpost guarding this lower border" near Mexico. "I too know the terror of waking in the night and hearing planes." Yet she was not sufficiently egotistical to worry only about herself; she felt that "every soldier here becomes my son in uniform."[65] Fort Huachuca was "the last stopping place before our soldiers go into active combat . . . our soldiers are now guarding most of the strategic positions along the west coast." The smell of impending death hung heavily.[66] Though military censors counseled stringently against writing precisely what she had just communicated, she did not hesitate to share her innermost apprehensions with Du Bois.

She continued to apprise him of her personal setbacks also. While in Arizona she had a serious accident when going to Tucson to meet the contralto Marian Anderson, and suffered a severe leg injury. It gave her "more trouble than anticipated. I can walk only with crutches . . . I'm rather wan and thin . . . I make a very bad invalid." Still bedridden, she reproved an officer who sought to improve troubled race relations in Arizona by having soldiers read *Native Son*. She objected to this "one-sided" book and instead recommended Du Bois's books—a gesture he certainly appreciated.[67] When she ran afoul of the authorities in Arizona, again she turned to Du Bois, telling him that her activism had caused her "to be interviewed by high Army officials. Some people were afraid of me."[68] These authorities were not too "afraid" of her to oust her, so when she wound up at the Hotel Theresa in Harlem she found herself "rushing" to Du Bois "for help and comfort"—a recurrent process over the years.[69]

Though she was an extraordinarily hardy woman, she showed another side to Du Bois. She told him about the "briny tears" that she shed "into her pillow" on the "many nights I've been in New York." Yes, it did seem she was having a "'roaring' good time" criss-crossing the nation and all, but now she was alone in the big city and was "forced to ask for another loan. My prospects are so dazzling," she said sardonically, "that I could quite easily eat cheese and crackers around here until the 'break' comes."[70] Apparently Du Bois chivalrously provided the loan, as he had done in the past, which only encouraged Graham to rely on him more. "I really would like so much to see you," she said. "In fact, I need to see you. I'm really tired." Just recently she had "fainted." "I probably did slightly crack that tiny and very delicate bone at the very end of the spine"; this put her "in bed [for] a couple of days."[71] It would have been difficult for Du Bois to have been unmoved.

When her son was drafted to fight in World War II she was concerned since she knew "too much about the U.S. Army! At this moment I can visualize myself going crazy."[72] She wanted Du Bois to write a letter for her son so he might qualify for the air corps. Her son's father was from South Carolina, she said accurately; his "mother [was] left a widow," she said falsely. It is unclear if she ever explained to Du Bois that her ex-husband remained alive, well after their marriage.

As she left Arizona for New York and the NAACP, she continued to rely on Du Bois for solace. Working with the NAACP involved "deadly monotony . . . circumstances are driving me almost beyond my limit. I'm caught and don't know how to untangle myself." It is difficult to imagine a time when the ever busy Graham's "brain" did not function up to par, but this is what she suggested to Du Bois in yet another attempt to garner his sympathy.[73]

Her pattern of informing him of her worthiness, praising him lavishly, while gently reminding him of her vulnerability continued. "I never quite get over the miracle of being able to say to people—oh so quietly and with . . . dignity—'Yes—I know Dr. Du Bois' . . . I've recently been taken into a rather important writers' club—me being the only and first of the darker brothers." She had "recently been called into the southern part of New Jersey to assist with relations in the schools. . . . I'm using up my passionate protest in speeches rather than in writing." This was unfortunate, because, she said, "I WANT TO WRITE!" The speaking and campaigning had taken a toll. "I've lost weight and have to fight discouragement and depression."[74]

These baleful words did not engender the response she wanted for days later she was remonstrating him for leaving her in a "deep and very dark valley." "At this moment," she continued dramatically, "I am sitting under a weeping willow, dolefully and wholeheartedly feeling sorry for myself." Why? "To think that you 'passed through' New York and never said a word to me!" Poor Shirley Graham had "lost contact with the few friends I had in this vicinity" and "'with the veil of work' drawn over [her] face," she had little time to pursue friends, old and new. Her mother had been with her for a few weeks, she said sadly; "I was doing all I could to keep my own problems from her. This was nothing new. I assumed that attitude along with papa when I was about ten years old. Practically all my life I've been older than mama. Well, I lost several pounds." The depressed Graham wanted to "go home tonight, crawl in bed and stay there for a long, long time. There must be something radically wrong with me."[75] Presumably Graham and Du Bois reconciled. By 1945 he was telling her, "we have been blessed beyond most folk to have so free and happy a love without scandal or criticism." Graham had groused about his aide, Irene Diggs, a talented anthropologist, arranging things for him that she—Graham—should have been doing; she wanted to be his caretaker and he was resisting. He continued,

> I'm definitely in your debt for all you have done for me. It was unforgivable to make you act at once as secretary, maid, cook, errand-boy, while you were doing two persons' work for yourself. . . . You shall not be a servant to me. I don't want that. I want a lover, rested and free . . . I long for your arms.[76]

But Graham felt that solidifying this relationship would require more than holding him in her arms—she would have to display other qualities as well. She had the opportunity to do so after their marriage.

By August 1946 he had requested that his "sweetheart" meet him in Manhattan. "I'm coming to New York late Friday night. Come to me Saturday at 4 p.m. and stay until Sunday night. I'll call you Saturday morning to talk cuisine. Until, my dear, love." At some point in the mid-1940s after Graham moved to New York City, their relationship had become closer as his notes were punctuated with phrases like, "I love and long to see you! . . . with love and kisses. . . . I ached for you this morning." Once he asked, "do you remember the time when I only needed to share you with the 'Party'? And later when the Son came in for a share?" Perhaps he meant the Communist "Party." This was 1947, when, supposedly, she had become a member; if so, it is presumptive evidence that she was a Communist. The point was that as early as the mid-1940s Du Bois and Graham had become quite close.[77]

Now it seemed that as her celebrity increased and her income from writing improved, he became as emotionally available as she. "If at any future time you find me planning to be away from you two months," he said in 1947, "will you kindly call in a psychiatrist and have me thoroughly examined for incipient homicidal tendencies[?]" He too could drench a lover with praise: "Your book is here and I am reading it. It is a splendid piece of work and I am proud of you."[78]

His emotional availability did not cause her to retreat. When she visited Paris for the peace conference of 1949 she exceeded him in feeling: "I am wrapped in sweet loneliness which keeps me warm and happy even while I ache for you . . . the world is really beautiful for me, my dear, because of you." She was apologetic: "I know I'm a demanding, selfish, small one when I'm around. I don't mean to be, my precious one, but I really want all of you—that's all." She continued her verbal caress: "*And you are such a really great man.* Every night before I go to sleep I thank whatever powers there be for my wonderful good fortune. Truly, I am most blessed among women!" (emphasis in original).[79] By 1947 Shirley Graham had attained that rare feat of having both economic and emotional security, albeit with a man who happened to be already married. It was difficult for her to keep her newfound joy hidden. Howard Fast recalls bumping into her at a political meeting in Chicago.

> She said to me, "Howard, I have an interesting announcement for you." "What is that, Shirley?" She said, "Dr. Du Bois proposed to me and I'm going to marry him." I said, "Shirley, my god, you're a woman in your forties." [Actually, she was about fifty-one at that time.] "You marry a man in his 80's, you're giving up all hope of sex for the rest of your life." She said, "Howard, how little you know about sex." And now as I approach the age of eighty, I am inclined to agree with her.[80]

Certainly she was happier in her second marriage than her first and, it appeared, the same could be said for him—at least that was her opinion. He "had married this pretty girl at Wilberforce" (his first wife), and was "absorbed in his work" though he never "neglected [her] intentionally. . . . I was older when I married him . . . I had worked . . . I was closer [to] what he was doing . . . we did many things together. . . . we travelled together . . . we shared in [every] work that he was doing." She never felt "alienated" from him.[81] By the time his first wife died, she had grown into the habit of "helping him," she told an interviewer in 1971. Their difference in age was "something nobody thought about . . . who thought about age?" He "needed help in a lot of different ways" and she wanted to help him.

After his wife passed away, she "found him in his apartment shaken and sunk in silent depression." He grieved his loss and expressed remorse about leaving his wife alone so often because she didn't want to travel with him. Graham suggested that he come to her place in Queens for a few days. She cooked for him, pampered him. He was impressed, stating, "It's unusual to find a woman who can write, speak, *and* cook."

"Undoubtedly," she recalled, "I had been in love with him for a long time . . . my love had made no demands. The fact that we shared work together was enough." Though her mother had harbored misgivings about the relationship, they decided to marry. Shirley Graham "thought happily that soon I would not be going to dark houses alone."[82]

Du Bois, who called himself her "father confessor in literary affairs and difficulties of life for many years," was overjoyed that "her beautiful martyr complex, finally persuaded herself that I needed her help and companionship, as I certainly did."[83] As she had indicated, he was apologetic about his treatment of his first wife, acknowledging that "I was not, on the whole, what one would describe as a good husband. The family and its interests were never the center of my life. . . . She must have been lonesome and wanted more regular and personal companionship than I gave."[84] He did need help, particularly in 1951, the year of their wedding. He had been indicted and he was lucky to have Shirley Graham Du Bois by his side, a talented organizer whose roots in the church gave her admittance into a vast circle of support. Though her years with Du Bois were not the most productive of her life, her talents in so many different areas helped to extend and enrich his life.

6

Home

SHIRLEY GRAHAM AND W. E. B. Du Bois married twice in 1951. They were planning to be married on 27 February at her Queens home, but he was indicted on 9 February because of his peace activism. She "insisted that we be married before his arraignment," but "he didn't want to." Well, she wisecracked, "you know women . . . I insisted just as strongly." They were married "secretly" on 14 February with only a minister and two witnesses present; the arraignment was on 16 February.[1] The second wedding took place later; her son David gave away the bride as friends from across the nation came to help them celebrate.[2]

This wedding was a major production. "News Reel called for permission to take pictures." After all, despite the forbidding political atmosphere, Du Bois remained a major public figure and she was no nonentity. For the event Du Bois was "faultlessly attired in gleaming black and white," and she was also fashionably dressed. "Flowers filled the house, candles flickered, soft music and the low murmur of voices" provided the sound track. Guests were served "sparkling punch," "platters of toasted sandwiches," "velvety ice cream," and "plates of dainty canapes." The pastor got lost but finally arrived in time to perform his duty. The newlyweds hurried to the airport to depart for their all too brief honeymoon in Nassau, the Bahamas.

Their friends were happy that the two had found each other's companionship. It was generally understood that Du Bois, an octogenarian, still had much to contribute. During a time when the forces of the Left were shrinking daily, it was well that he had such a staunch and talented partner as Shirley Graham. Others, however, who believed she was a Communist, looked askance at their union, even thinking that it was "Communist arranged."

She was less concerned about such speculation than about the political and legal difficulties facing her husband. Shirley Graham Du Bois realized that as a spouse she could not be forced to testify about politi-

cal activities of which she was an intimate part—for example, opposition to the war in Korea, the Paris peace conference, and so forth. Moreover, as a spouse, she could conceivably have better access to her octogenarian husband, in case he did wind up in a prison cell.

Even setting aside the question of the possibility of his imprisonment, February 1951 was not an easy time for the celebrated couple. The
weather during this tumultuous month was blustering with blizzards
of snow. Those opposed to the U.S. intervention in Korea were likewise
besieged with a blizzard of unfavorable stories in the press and, in some
instances, subpoenas. Du Bois's doctor ordered him to bed as a result of
the concomitant "mental strain, exposure to bad weather, extreme fa-
tigue." It was thought that he had pneumonia.[3]

His arraignment seemed to be more trying for her than him. According to the *Pittsburgh Courier*, when she saw her stolid husband
frisked and fingerprinted "she broke into uncontrollable, tearful sobs
that clearly echoed through the usually quiet corridors of the government courthouse."[4] In her memoir she spoke of being "hysterical when
they put handcuffs on him."[5] Du Bois's codefendant Abbott Simon recalled her as being "agitated," noting that she "was more upset because
she was a more emotional person. And, besides, it involved him and she
was very much in love with him and had been all her life and she was
very protective of him."[6]

Her son David was there and recalled her reaction when "she saw
them putting handcuffs on Dr. Du Bois. He's 81 years old"—actually
closer to eighty-three—"and my mother saw them putting handcuffs on
him and fingerprinting him. She almost had hysterics at the very [sight]
of this horror."[7] It was not just the fact that the person she loved might
face his dying days in jail, what moved her as well was the prospect of
facing the coming years alone after contemplating the happiness of
marriage.

This prospect helped concentrate her mind wonderfully and impelled her to become a whirlwind of activity in the campaign to set her
husband free. As in his sacking from the NAACP in 1948, during this
1951 crisis Du Bois was lucky to have a companion with inexhaustible
energy, expert organizing skills, and numerous contacts. As the filmmaker Carlton Moss remembered later, "she was the daughter of a minister, so she knew organization. Anybody that knows about black culture knows that these churches are very well organized." Her talents
were even more important because many who might have rallied to

Du Bois's banner had skulked away cravenly; this included the organization he founded, the NAACP, not to mention many in the so-called Talented Tenth whose existence he once hailed. Moss recalled that "Shirley told me, I have no way of documenting this, but . . . Walter White went right behind him telling everybody that the old man [Du Bois] didn't have a chance."[8] Whether he said this or not, the fact is that the NAACP was not eager to court the wrath of ascendant anticommunism by coming to the defense of a man whose effort to "ban the [nuclear] bomb" led federal authorities to charge him with being an agent of an unnamed foreign power that was presumed to be the Soviet Union. Aiding a leftist like Du Bois might compromise the ongoing effort to garner civil rights concessions.

Thanks in no small part to Shirley Graham Du Bois, a national committee arose to defend her spouse and his codefendants. As she noted in one of the many pieces of literature she wrote in their defense, "from Africa to Alabama to South America to the west coast, to Canada, England, France, the Balkans, north, south, east and west, the pendulum of indignation swings."[9] After making bail, the newlywed couple traversed the nation in search of support and funds. In Chicago, where the prominent black lawyer and businessman Earl Dickerson rallied to their side, funds were raised; "the ladies," she said, "swarmed about [her spouse] and regarded me with some speculation." In Milwaukee "our host there was a businessman who had become interested in my books." His wife, "one of the prettiest little Dresden-doll bits of femininity that could be imagined," was charmed when she was able to converse with Du Bois in German. In St. Paul, "home of my mother's family," there was overflowing support since "Lizzie Etta's little girl Shirley's husband" was involved; there was the "largest inter-racial meeting held in this community up to that time." In Seattle, mostly whites turned out. In Portland "there was not only a strong reactionary movement against us but a virulent drive to browbeat Negroes." The NAACP, the Urban League, and others from the mainstream bowed out. In San Francisco eight hundred came to a rally for Du Bois; in Oakland, twelve hundred. In Los Angeles they encountered "the biggest audience we had had."[10]

This coast-to-coast marathon of travel was both trying and heartwarming. In Detroit the harried couple "felt the shadow of the Terror"; they had "continuous bodyguard[s] day and night" because of the fear of physical attack and bodily harm. As they spoke to large crowds nationally the lurking fear persisted that someone drunk with the heady brew of anticommunism might decide to assault this frail black couple. On the other hand, in this crucible of anxiety irreparable bonds of love and solidarity were forged between the two: "years of normal marriage could have not knit us closer together than had" this unnerving experience.[11]

It was not preordained that Du Bois would be acquitted, so it was well that they campaigned so vigorously. During this era, many had languished in prison on flimsier charges than those that faced him. Thus, with gusto, Graham Du Bois took to the defense of her husband, saying in a typical stump speech, "They have told you much about an iron curtain," she began,

> I would speak tonight about a smudge curtain—a screen tight down which shuts our country in from the rest of the world—a screen which cuts even our country into bits and portions so that you out here on the Pacific coast do not know what we are doing in the east.[12]

Du Bois acknowledged that "Shirley spoke easily and interestingly, without notes and with an intense vigor which set the audiences on the edge of their seats."[13] Because of such campaigning by her and others— along with expert lawyering—Du Bois was freed.

Though she was no longer as poverty-stricken as she had been two decades earlier, the Red Scare took its toll on her and her new husband. Groups that as late as 1947 might have invited her to speak and assembled scores to purchase her books now hesitated. Du Bois's 1950 New York state income tax return stated that he was unemployed; he had an embarrassingly meager income. Various pensions did increase his income thereafter, but he was far from being affluent.[14] Her income was mostly from royalties, and now her husband "was leaving the handling of all financial matters to me—but he was beginning to worry about the lack of money."[15] Being a leftist writer in New York City during the Cold War was not the best guarantee of a prosperous standard of living. After the State Department seized their passports, they could not follow up on her earlier dream of moving to France and obtaining lucrative speaking fees and other emoluments there.[16]

As with many couples, this lack of wealth was of consequence for their relationship. Early in 1951 they were discussing a vacation. Du Bois told his wife that he had been worrying about the cost of the trip . . . which you say that I should bear wholly. In the ordinary marriage the husband bears all the costs of family life and the wife lives on what he gives her. This makes the wife the subordinate partner in the combination and the servant in the house. Such a marriage I lived through for 55 years. I could not enter another of this type for the plain fact that I have not enough income to support a wife. I would not do this if I could because I believe this whole set-up morally wrong and the cause of the failure of most marriages. The marriage I plan with you is based on economic equality: I pay my way and you pay yours; except of course in case of sickness or like calamity. My only hesitation is the calamity of old age, which may eventually incapacitate me and make me in part dependent on you.

At this juncture, she had twelve thousand dollars in savings and he had two thousand less. "I think that unconsciously and because in the past you have had no one to take care of you, you are looking for a husband who will pay your expenses as a duty." This was not his idea of the ideal marriage, he announced. He evinced interest in sharing: "that is the marriage for men and women, but not for parasites."[17] He sensed that her ideal leaned toward the traditional, though he did not vigorously object when she assumed the "subordinate" role of becoming his caretaker, which was similarly traditional.

They did pool their resources to buy the fashionable Brooklyn Heights home of the playwright Arthur Miller. They lived minutes away from the Brooklyn Bridge, linking them to the vibrancy of lower Manhattan; in the Bedford-Stuyvesant section of Brooklyn, due south from their lovely home, a huge African American community was forming. The location proved to be ideal.

For both political and racial reasons they hired an "anonymous purchaser . . . acting through an agent for fear that no one would sell to [them] directly."[18] She had sold her St. Albans home for $19,500 with a "fair profit" that padded their down payment.[19] Despite Du Bois's stated desire for equity in their relationship, her recollection is that he asked her to take care of this purchase since "homemaking is the wife's business, my dear. If you say it's all right I know it will suit me!"[20]

After the threat of his imprisonment passed, they quickly settled into a comfortable domestic routine, though she was plagued by concern about her husband's advanced age. In the spring of 1952 she and a worker "cut and dug and planted. . . . My husband suggested that we plant a tree in one corner. I didn't exactly say that he would not live long enough to enjoy it, but he understood my objection perfectly."[21] This hovering fear only forced her to savor every moment of happiness. "Our established routine was that he arose each morning shortly before eight o'clock, shaved, took a leisurely bath and was down to breakfast before nine."[22] Despite Du Bois's noble intentions about equality and sharing, she did almost all of the cooking. She was the one who would "fix him a bourbon and ginger ale, a quite tall one with Ritz crackers and blue cheese"; this was "almost a nightly affair."[23]

Despite his reputation for aloofness, he was not that way with his spouse or anyone he came to know well. Ethel Ray Nance, who had known him for decades, "never knew Dr. Du Bois to dislike anyone or if you had something in common he could be friendly with you, if you didn't he just didn't bother you at all"; the problem, as she saw it, was that the envious—like Walter White—"could never quite accept the greatness of Dr. Du Bois."[24]

His conviviality and her hospitality helped to make for a happy household. Herbert Aptheker found them to be a "splendid host and hostess."[25] Vicki Garvin, a black woman who once lived in both Ghana and China, also visited their Brooklyn abode. She recalled that when Du Bois "would . . . come back to the house right after he made his little stroll around the block, he would ring the doorbell and he would yell, 'Yoo-hoo, Shir—ley, I'm ho-o-ome.' He was really so delightful in announcing himself because they had a very warm relationship," and this warmth spilled over and encompassed their guests.[26] James and Esther Jackson, frequent visitors to their house in Brooklyn, have similarly fond memories. He was a Communist leader; she also had graduated from Oberlin and later was to found the quarterly *Freedomways* with Graham Du Bois. The party had brought him to New York City as the Red Scare dawned and, as a partial result, the Jacksons became ever closer to the Du Boises. Esther Jackson remembered

> children's parties that they often had for children who were of the McCarthy period, children whose parents had either been jailed or indicted. . . . often we went there for lunch or breakfast. They also had the opening celebration when the first issue of *Freedomways* magazine appeared in March of 1961. We had a big celebration at the Du Bois home. All of the writers were there, Ossie Davis was there, John Killens was there. And a whole number of—Alice Childress—a

whole number of the writers of my generation in the New York area [were there].[27]

Louise Patterson also had positive recollections of the Du Boises' hospitality: "it was always a pleasure to go to their home . . . you would find many different people there from everywhere."[28] In particular, diplomats from the United Nations and Africans fighting colonialism often made their way to their Brooklyn home.

Shirley Graham Du Bois had helped her husband understand that not all Euro-Americans were unenlightened when it came to the question of race. Howard Fast had been a decisive influence on her own life and he quickly became a part of the Du Boises' inner circle. Fast liked her above all, considering her a "rather gifted writer, interesting woman. Rather remarkable in her sensibility. I met her at a publishing house or a party of the publishing house doing a book of hers and a book of mine." This was in the mid-1940s. "We took her into our home and we were as kind to her as we possibly could and we became fast friends with her and this was a friendship that just grew over the years. My wife loved Shirley and they spent a great deal of time together." According to Fast, Graham Du Bois's sweet disposition made it easy for her to get along with most, even those with whom she was in basic disagreement. She was "an unflappable person; she had great inner strength, great solidity . . . she was a gentle, kind, forgiving person." Like most of her friends, he felt that "Dr. Du Bois was very fortunate to have her in those last years of his life."[29]

Even before she became Du Bois's spouse she had become his ideological shield. She interceded to prevent him from encountering those she felt were up to no good. When an inquiring scholar wanted to look at Du Bois's papers for his research, she turned him down,

> the purpose of this frantic interest in Negroes is to perfect the machinery of control and to continue the enslavement to which they have been subjected all these years. The enemy is aware that he has blundered badly in the past; he is now faced with the horrifying realization that Negroes hold the balance of power in the approaching struggle.

She added, "in the final analysis I trust only one white American" (she may have been referring to Herbert Aptheker, whom she was addressing). "White America has forced me to this position. White America will have to change before I change that position."[30] Her Communist friends may have flinched at this racial argument, but it was suggestive of something that would become apparent after she left the United States for exile: though Howard Fast and other Euro-Americans were among her closest friends and allies, the nagging persistence of Jim Crow had helped to convince her that "white America" did not merit the benefit of the doubt. This bloc was not to be trusted.

The flash of temper she displayed with this young scholar was indicative of her sometimes grave demeanor—yet another side of a woman who, after all, once acted and directed. Her son David recalls, "my mother had a tendency to be terribly, terribly serious at all times and under all circumstances regardless of the conditions." Du Bois "would very, very often have to or feel it necessary in fact to suggest to my mother that we can talk about those matters some other time but not at the dinner table . . . [since he] always felt that at the dinner table conversation should be light, conversation should be interaction."[31] Naturally, she complied with her husband's request for, as her friend Anna Grant put it, "she lived through him and loved it." This is not what one would expect from an accomplished artist, a "distinguished woman," but she was "dazzled by his scholarship and his presence" and felt "privileged" that "he wanted her to be his wife. She was a perfect lady and for that day and time when women were supposed to show deference to their husbands . . . I thought she pulled it off very well" and did not "seem disturbed that he was getting all of this attention."[32]

The contemporary cult of domesticity reinforced Graham Du Bois's tendency to be deferential to her husband. She told her friend Roselyn Richardson,

> you would have to see my marriage in operation to believe it. I am most fortunate among women and people who have known W. E. B. for years tell me that his bounding spirits and zest for life reflect his complete fulfillment. We have a home worthy of the man, reflecting our tastes and cultural needs; we have engrossing, important, constructive work, we have extraordinary health. I purposely avoided using the word "happiness" because happiness implies contentment. If we could shut ourselves away just with ourselves and be content I could say we were very "happy" but we are one in having no desire in this.

But one thing she was apparently "happy" in doing was cooking, since her spouse was "a most appreciative diner and I love to cook for him."[33]

Perhaps not surprisingly, Du Bois felt his marriage to be "rich and rewarding."[34] He also appreciated the fact that she was so helpful with his intellectual endeavors. He once told Arna Bontemps that she "regarded it as her chief object in the world to preserve and arrange my library, and to write a definitive biography on the basis of my books, papers and letters." This was why they had bought their sizable Brooklyn home, "which is considerably larger than our needs."[35]

But Du Bois also loved his wife because she was always a political companion. As noted, Howard Fast claims that she was a Communist and that he—Fast—played no small part in her recruitment: "Now it has been said that one of the reasons Shirley Graham joined the party was in terms of my own friendship. I never urged her to join but she probably felt that in terms of my work and my attitude toward black people, here was something that she could admire." But after the revelations about Stalin's rule in 1956, he left the party and, presumably because she did not, they saw each other less: "much to my sorrow, [we didn't see each other for] a period of four or five years. I again met Shirley quite by chance on 59th Street one day in [Manhattan]. We embraced; she was well, we were both so happy to see each other . . . that however, was the last time I met Shirley." The party brought them together and moved them apart. But, assuming she was a Communist, why did she stay on after 1956 when so many left? "Well, Shirley and Dr. Du Bois, I would guess, had a position which said we are part of a totally repressed group. This [party] is the only group willing to go out on a limb and fight for us with no holds barred." Fast compared the United States to South Africa, where Africans have been heavily represented in the ranks of the Communist Party; he added, "so the attitude toward the Communist Party on the part of Africans and even Black Americans, I would suspect, would be very different from what my attitude is. This is only natural." It seemed that Fast was suggesting that white privilege and black lack of same were factors in an individual's commitment to radicalism. He had a point.[36] Fewer African Americans proportionally and in absolute numbers left the party after the convulsions of 1956.[37] Presumably, one of those who did not leave in 1956 was Shirley Graham Du Bois.

Paul Robeson was another example of an African American who did not flee from the orbit of the Communists after 1956. He and his spouse, Eslanda, along with Shirley Graham and W. E. B. Du Bois were the premier couples of the Left during a very difficult era. All were accomplished—Eslanda Robeson was a distinguished writer—and all were mutually supportive, generally speaking. They visited each other's homes and shared confidences at a time when the shriveling Left was being shunned by many. Du Bois's granddaughter recalls a time in the 1950s when Robeson was "invited . . . to come over" to the Du Boises' Brooklyn home to test a "new piano" that Graham Du Bois had just bought. She had neglected to purchase "the [appropriate] bench" for this instrument. "Paul came bounding up the spiral staircase . . . and immediately saw the new piano, and off he went and sat down on the bench" by the piano, "which immediately splintered into 10,000 pieces of wood. And he just landed up on the floor in the most ungraceful position possible." Nonplussed, the basso profundo still immediately launched into a rousing rendition of "Ol' Man River."[38]

Shirley Graham had written a biography of Paul and was friendly for years with Eslanda Robeson. During one of her trips to Paris before entering Oberlin Graham had visited their home in London and left with words of praise for him: "he has genius, he has brains and he has a wife."[39] This curious and oblique reference to Eslanda Robeson may not have been unintentional. Graham Du Bois's son David recalls his mother having an "intense" friendship with Eslanda Robeson: it was "not a smooth relationship"; "they fed on each other." This was an "important relationship" for Graham Du Bois and had "rather intimate elements," though it was "bumpy" and "highly personal." However, like others, Graham Du Bois felt that Eslanda Robeson "didn't treat Paul right"; besides, there was "a certain kind of competition between the two of them" as talented spouses of internationally recognized men. Moreover, as a reflection of her tendency to be more capable in confronting white supremacy rather than male supremacy, Graham Du Bois had a "built in tendency to glorify male personalities, put them before everybody else, [her] attitude toward her father to a great extent [was extended to other men], you see it repeated over and over in her relationships with men."[40] This tendency did not extend to a woman like Essie Robeson.

Still, this image of Graham Du Bois as a woman easily led and misled by men does not rest easily with the then prevailing notion that she inveigled Du Bois into the ranks of the Communist Party. In 1955 a witness appearing before the House Un-American Activities Committee portrayed her as much more radical than her better-known spouse.[41] And despite her general lack of militance on feminist concerns, she was a lodestar in one of the early black feminist organizations, Sojourners for Truth and Justice. Along with Eslanda Robeson, the publisher Charlotta Bass, the activist Louise Thompson Patterson, the writer Alice Childress, and the actresses Beulah Richardson and Frances Williams, Graham played a leading role in this small but ideologically potent organization. The case of Rosa Lee Ingram, a black woman tenant farmer in rural Georgia who fought back when assaulted by her landlord, was one of their principal concerns.[42] Their call was a precursor of a kind of "race feminism," though more globally minded than contemporary iterations. "Our action will carry forward the tradition of Harriet Tubman and Sojourner Truth," they declared, "and will give inspiration and courage to women the world over, the colored women of Africa and Asia who expect us to make this challenge."[43]

Sojourners was not the only organization to which Graham devoted time after her marriage. Though she spent a considerable amount of time tending to the needs of her elderly spouse, she also found time for increased political commitments. FBI reports in 1956 listed her as a "concealed Communist" with over seventy political affiliations, including Sojourners, the American Committee for the Protection of the Foreign Born, the Council on African Affairs, the Civil Rights Congress, defense committees designed to spare from prison the Communist leaders V. J. Jerome and Alexander Trachtenberg, and a host of others.[44] Part of this information was gleaned as a result of an FBI interview with her conducted under "pretext." Graham, five feet two inches tall, was described as "slender-frail" with hair "streaked with gray; wavy, worn shoulder length." This information would be useful in case she had to be found—and detained—pursuant to a national emergency.[45]

This was not an easy time for a black woman to align herself with an increasingly unpopular Left. Cold War pressures were obligating the United States to move away from the more egregious aspects of Jim Crow: how could this nation purport to charge Moscow with human rights violations when darker peoples in this nation were treated so horribly? However, the price paid for this bargain was the bludgeoning of a Left besieged on all sides with political trials, persecution, and harassment: the weakened Left had to spend more time defending itself than fighting for its ideals. In such an atmosphere, the relative tranquility of a trial—even if it was a comrade in the dock—was almost a respite from what awaited beyond the realm of the judiciary. The stool pigeon Julia Brown, who infiltrated the Communist Party on behalf of the FBI, recalled that "there were so many meetings, rallies and other fund-raising pitches that I longed for the final courtroom sessions to get under way."[46]

In such an environment, many black women in particular decided that the better part of wisdom was to avoid the enforced marginalizing that the Left represented, in favor of what was becoming a mainstream civil rights movement. Modjeska Simkins had worked with Sojourners but had also been a leader of the South Carolina NAACP. She was ousted from NAACP leadership in 1957 apparently because of her ties to other alleged "Communist fronts," for example, the Southern Negro Youth Congress, the Southern Conference for Human Welfare, and others. As one analyst notes, "Simkins was a friend and supporter of many leaders of the American [sic] Communist Party."[47] Simkins's experiences transmitted the message that African Americans could win basic rights only if they did not press for more far-reaching reforms in alliance with radical organizations, particularly those that adopted controversial stances on foreign policy.

Graham Du Bois refused to heed this message and, instead, opted for the loneliness of the Left; eventually she decided that she could maintain her radical beliefs and avoid isolation only if she left the United States. She reinforced her shrinking circle of associates on the Left by deepening her ties with diplomats from socialist countries and anticolonial movements who were posted at the United Nations and/or living in New York City. Serving on the board of the National Council of American-Soviet Friendship facilitated this process for her; moreover, she continued her friendship with figures like Langston Hughes, who felt compelled to retreat from more overt ties with the Left.[48]

In the meantime, she preached avidly—though at times futilely— her socialist philosophy. After Du Bois was spared imprisonment, they continued to speak across the continent—and faced harassment every step of the way. In 1952 they were both deported from Toronto for "refusing to undergo an examination"; this was a "flat lie," said Du Bois, whose beliefs had just been examined with a microscope at a federal trial. They had come to address the "left-wing Canadian Peace Congress" and, as was customary during the 1950s, they found it difficult to escape from the United States.[49] That same year the couple were invited to attend the American Intercontinental Peace Conference in Brazil.

They immediately sought to renew their passports; she had held one for twenty-four years, he for fifty-nine. They were denied.[50]

When they were able to actually fulfill speaking engagements, she usually spoke on the same platform with her spouse, often on questions of peace and war. She also addressed other audiences on her own, for example, American Women for Peace, the Emma Lazarus Club, and various church groups.[51] One 1953 peroration by Graham Du Bois at Taylor Memorial Methodist Church in San Francisco, recorded by the FBI, was typical:

> Do not let anyone keep you from working for peace or using the word peace. Do not let anyone tell you that those who work for peace are subversive. Do not let anyone tell you that those who [work] for peace are subversive. Our own American boys, those sons and husbands of ours now fighting in Korea, are murdering and making human torches of the women and little helpless Korean children by dropping jelly fire bombs on them. We must and can stop this terrible war.[52]

These fiery words notwithstanding, she and Du Bois were still wary about campaigning for peace. She was asked to join the World Peace Council, but this might have meant filing documents indicating that she was the agent of a foreign power. Dismissing the congealed Russo-phobia of the era, Graham Du Bois boldly scribbled "nyet" in response to the suggestion that she file.[53]

She refused to say "nyet" to those who wanted her to become involved in helping those charged with espionage on behalf of Moscow. One of her most endearing and important political roles was as trustee of the fund established to benefit the orphaned children of Julius and Ethel Rosenberg, executed for alleged atomic espionage. They had been convicted and killed for a crime—aiding the Soviet Union—not dissimilar from what her husband was charged with; thus, the dilemma of the children left behind resonated with her, not least because it dovetailed with Graham Du Bois's own role as a "mother" in politics. Despite subsequent sympathy for the Rosenbergs and their children, in the early 1950s this sympathy was in short supply; hence, it took some courage to accept the assignment she did. The intimidating atmosphere meant that even liberals and social democrats who charged the Soviet Union with anti-Semitism—respected intellectuals like Michael Harrington, Irving Howe, and others[54]—were mute about similar allegations of anti-Jewish fervor bolstering the persecution of the Rosenbergs.[55]

This intimidation did not deter Graham Du Bois. She felt that the defenders of the Rosenbergs should "stress" their abject "innocence."[56] Above all, it seemed, she worried about the children of the defendants and their ruined "innocence" as they confronted a loneliness that her own two sons were compelled to endure. The Rosenberg sons, Robert and Michael, recalled a particular Christmas vacation when they were boys when they attended a festive party at the Du Bois home in Brooklyn.[57] Now known as Robert Meeropol, the son of the Rosenbergs recalls fondly that "Shirley Graham was in charge of finding people to adopt my brother and I . . . I remember coming into their house" and there was this "large Christmas tree" with "all sorts of light all over it and a huge mound of presents and a lot [of] children"; at this Christmas party he and his brother met Abe and Ann Meeropol, who adopted them. "This," Robert Meeropol recalls with gratitude, "was the best possible place to bring us together with them and hold this event." No one from his mother's or father's family would take them in for fear of further persecution.

Meeropol recollected that in the Du Boises' house "there'd be a vase from China . . . something else from the Soviet Union. Something else from Brazil. It was like a small museum from the world," at a time when many U.S. households were bathed in parochialism and certainly apprehensive about displaying items from nations led by Communists.[58]

In addition to seeking deliverance of their children, Graham Du Bois also campaigned for the freedom of the defendants themselves. A congressional committee took note of her letter of appeal demanding that those concerned write the president and attorney general and "tell them what you think."[59] One positive result of her campaign was its influence on the career of Ruby Dee, who replicated Graham Du Bois's combination of activism and interest in theater: "through friends she had made while protesting the treatment of Julius and Ethel Rosenberg, Dee received a role in *The World of Sholem Aleichem*. She credits that production with changing her consciousness about theater and about the universality of oppression."[60] This historical accident also suggests that though the influence of Graham Du Bois and others on the Left was thwarted in the 1950s, it was not squelched altogether.

To be sure, Graham Du Bois did suffer a certain political isolation during the 1950s. Her friend the actress Frances Williams recalls when the Du Boises visited Los Angeles, "people we had gone to see together many times" now shunned them; when Graham Du Bois and her husband

> drove up to the home of these two doctors and rang the doorbell . . . no one answered. We rang and we rang and we decided they were not home. And as we got in the car to drive away I looked up and the curtains upstairs moved and I could see that these people who were "good" friends of Dr. Du Bois were at home and they were avoiding him.[61]

This was a bitter reminder to Du Bois of the fatuousness of his notion of a "talented tenth"; racial heritage or even the oppression that accompanied it did not guarantee political clarity, particularly given a privileged class background. It was fortunate that Graham Du Bois introduced him to new friends on the Left; otherwise he would have wound up more isolated than he was.

Sadly, the negative attention that Graham Du Bois received—as one of the few prominent left intellectuals of the 1950s—impacted her son David as well. With regret she told her friend Roselyn Richardson that he "has been a victim of the oppression and senseless hysteria sweeping our country . . . [his] passport was taken away and he had had other difficulties." This was caused in part by his own activism but also because of his filial ties. His was a typical example of a growing and disturbing pattern—the spreading influence of McCarthyism. "The other night," Graham Du Bois wrote, "we had dinner with a great scholar who has been 'laid off' one of the big universities—a brilliant and productive career cut away!"[62]

The same could be said about her famed spouse: he was a "great scholar" who also had been sidelined, though he was well past retirement age. The careers of certain writers were boosted because they were more in accord with the prevailing conservative atmosphere, while others suffered correspondingly.[63] Graham Du Bois and her spouse were in the latter category. They were not alone. Strikingly, many in this category were Jewish or African American.[64] Since many of their friends were of this ethno-religious or racial background, their already small circle began to wither correspondingly; this increased isolation sparked their desire to live abroad.

This persecution also impacted the work of many creative artists. In response to the swing to the right nationally,

> many artists moved to more abstract concerns . . . out of fear of being labeled political, or worse, a Communist during the Cold War years. . . . this "evolution" was not simply a modernist improvement. . . . many artists successfully retreated from overt political content and . . . this retreat was often praised by critics who said, essentially, that politics was no business for true, visionary artists. . . . criticism in the Cold War era effectively silenced the political artist in American society.

Even worse, certain anticommunist critics felt that "mere social interaction with African-Americans could signify leftist sympathies."[65]

As an artist with sympathies for the plight of African Americans, Graham Du Bois was doubly affected by this trend. Still, she persevered, working on her own books and helping her husband with his. Du Bois recalled later that "my manuscripts and those of Shirley Graham were refused publication" by mainstream publishers during the height of the 1950s repression.[66] Her productivity was limited further because she was so involved with her husband's work. She "assisted in editing the Fiftieth Anniversary Edition of my husband's *Souls of Black Folk*," for example.[67] Still, she also found the time to lend her formidable skills to the left-wing journal *Masses & Mainstream*, where she served as a contributing editor, and a pressure group called the Committee for the Negro in the Arts, which was also a "laboratory" where up and coming actors like Harry Belafonte "worked out [his] repertoire."[68]

She also found the time to work on her own writing. Though the number of her readers in the United States may have shrunk, her readership in Europe was expanding. In 1954 she received a check for almost eight hundred dollars in royalties from a Berlin publisher for her biography of Benjamin Banneker. Her works were translated into many languages, including Czech, German, and Russian. In the United States, however, her Banneker book suffered the fate of many of her works; it had been published in 1949 and "less than 7000 copies have been sold." She continued, "Very shortly after its publication it was practically dropped from circulation and suppressed. It has been removed from most libraries and is not mentioned on book lists."[69]

Because of such dismal prospects, it was inevitable that she would turn more toward European publishers as outlets for her writing. In 1957 she proposed to a Prague publisher a book about the case of Emmett Till, the African American youth who had been lynched in Mississippi because of a reputed violation of social norms.[70] Such a book would also add to the international pressure that was obligating the United States to address its pressing racial problem.

This book was not completed; however, she did finish a biography of her husband's old nemesis, Booker T. Washington. The book was surprisingly tame for such a militant socialist writer. There were her usual trademarks—fictionalized dialogue and shimmering prose, for example—but other aspects seemed more in accord with the looming conservatism of the day. She began the book with a quote from Washington that she did not interrogate: "No race can prosper till it learns that there is as much dignity in tilling a field as in writing a poem." When she wrote of Washington's collaboration with the tycoon Andrew Carnegie, there was no reproach of either party. Nor did she scrutinize certain core ideas expressed by Washington: "Long ago he had turned his back on politics. 'While politicians talk, I'll work,' he said. He advised other Negroes to 'let white folks have their politics; you buy a farm!'" There was no discussion of the challenge posed by the Niagara Movement—in which her spouse had played a prominent part—to Washington's pusillanimous leadership. Overall, the book seemed more in tune with an ascendant conservatism than a socialist ideal.[71]

In the Washington biography she evinced certain weaknesses on the race question, which was not her habit; in her biography of Pocahontas she evinced weaknesses on gender, which was more in keeping with her pattern. In telling the story of the life of this Native American woman, Graham was surprisingly uncritical of the role of John Smith; when she discussed the effort of the European colonists to arrange a marriage with Pocahontas for reasons of political alliance, Graham Du Bois expressed no opinion of this tactic. Though this nation was founded on expropriation of Native Americans, she evinced no interest in a critique of this process. The biography was far from being an anti-imperialist or even an anticolonialist work, which was all the more surprising considering that it was written by a supposed Communist during the height of the Cold War.[72] It reflected the times in which it was written.

Perhaps Graham Du Bois should not bear the exclusive blame for such work, since there was enormous pressure on her and other writers to conform to certain conservative norms, particularly when discussing the founding myths of the nation. Thus, when she contemplated writing a "bit of satirical fiction which I have already called 'The Trials and Tribulations of Xantippe,'" she turned to her Prague publisher. Her intentions were serious and seemingly at odds with the cautious lineaments of some of her other work of this era. "(What does Socrates say on the Woman Question?) It is my personal contention that Xantippe has been a much maligned woman. I'd like to tell her side of the story." Her concluding words were also a coda for her own life, particularly her future life in Ghana: Graham Du Bois was also a "much maligned woman" whose "side of the story" was often ignored. Thus, when the international atmosphere eased and her passport was finally returned, she quickly left the country—her venerable husband in tow—in preparation for a more extended exile where compromises of her political vision were not mandatory.[73]

7

On the Road Again

BY THE TIME her passport was renewed in 1958, Shirley Graham Du Bois was more than ready to leave the United States for an extended period. She and her husband were revered abroad with the same fervor with which they were vilified at home. Moreover, though she had first stepped into the limelight as a result of an artistic creation that concerned Africa, she was far from being a frequent visitor to this continent. Thus, even before moving permanently to Ghana in 1961, she was determined to travel to Africa.

■

It was not easy to be a presumed Communist in the United States in the late 1950s. Though things had improved since the days of hysteria that accompanied the war in Korea, there were still proscriptions of various sorts: employers were reluctant to employ Reds, publishers were reluctant to publish them, people generally were reluctant to associate with them. On the other hand, the nascent civil rights movement was sprouting shoots in places like Montgomery and Little Rock. This threatened to push the nation in a more progressive direction. Yet a precondition for this movement's success—or so it was thought by many—was that it had to shun those who harbored the kind of seditious ideas expressed by Shirley Graham Du Bois. Given such an environment, she started thinking of leaving the country as soon as the government relented and restored her passport.

The changing atmosphere brought by the civil rights movement caused others to reconsider their evaluation of her and her once indicted spouse. When Du Bois was invited back to Fisk University in 1958, Arna Bontemps was impressed by how his employer greeted the seasoned intellectual. "Fisk went all out for Du Bois," he reported to Langston Hughes.

It was like the return of a king from exile. We had him and Shirley to dinner once and we attended a luncheon. . . . Shirley whispered to me that while he has made no public statement, he has felt in recent years that he was losing contact with his own folk—which he wished to reestablish. So I read a good bit into that statement.[1]

What Bontemps should have read into that statement was that as time passed, it was becoming more difficult to isolate the African American Left from the general African American community. Du Bois's triumphant return to Fisk symbolized that. This tardy détente notwithstanding, Shirley Graham remained eager to depart for a more sympathetic environment.

She was in the midst of her usual frantic pace: taking courses in Russian at Columbia University, working on various books, laying the foundation for a new magazine to be known as *Freedomways*, public speaking and attending to the needs of her aging spouse. By late 1959 she was complaining to her friend Roselyn Richardson, "When I stagger home . . . at the end of the day, I'm pooped—I haven't been too well lately, it takes me from then until rising time the next AM to rest up and start the same old grind. Interestingly enough, I don't mind."[2] She may not have minded at that moment, but it was difficult to engage in often unappreciated labor at home when adoring—and powerful—audiences awaited abroad. Moreover, Graham had been a peripatetic sort, ever since she had left her children behind and traveled to Paris in the 1920s. This frequent movement often was a spur to her political and artistic evolution. Thus, from the summer of 1958 through a good deal of 1959, she and her spouse traveled to Western and Eastern Europe (including the Soviet Union) and China. Doctors prevented Du Bois from going further, but his wife went on, as he put it, "to Belgrade, Athens, Cairo, the pyramids and sphinx; the Nile, Khartoum and Kano and Accra."[3] This extended travel was a complete turnabout from recent years and a signal that the political climate was changing, for when she had applied for a passport in 1955, she had been refused due to her Communist affiliations.[4]

This trip abroad was a transforming journey for her. Since she had moved to the left during World War II, she had not had the opportunity to visit any nation where a Communist party ruled. After doing so, she was more eager than ever to abandon the United States and move to a nation where she could assist in the construction of socialism. Two years after she returned from China in 1959, the opportunity arose in Ghana.

But Ghana was not her immediate concern when she embarked across the Atlantic in 1958. It was not easy traveling abroad with a man approaching his tenth decade. They had tried to make the trip easier by taking a ship to Great Britain. Still, she experienced "anxious hours" when her husband became ill, while he dismissed her concern: "aside from the fact that Shirley is hysterical," he reported, "all goes well."[5]

Despite these nervous moments, their trip was a respite from the stress of the Red Scare. In England she encountered firsthand the impact of the Afro-Caribbean immigration on Britain when she witnessed the "Nottingham Riots."[6] Graham Du Bois "simply fell in love with London." She stayed in the Robesons' home there and spent considerable time with the U.S. Communist leader Claudia Jones. Jones, who was of Trinidadian extraction, had been deported and wound up in Great Britain, where she quickly became a leader of the black community there.[7]

In Holland they were besieged by "reporters [and] photographers" who "called every day." They were greeted warmly by "the Suriname [sic] people in Amsterdam"; "people in the street recognized" her husband and greeted him warmly.[8] They arrived in Paris in time for the pivotal 1958 elections and viewed closely the impact of the war in Algeria on the French capital.[9]

In Moscow they received a rousing reception. This was the period after Sputnik, when there was optimism in the Soviet Union about the prospects for socialism and widespread unease in the United States for the same reason. While the civil rights movement they had left behind looked askance at the slightest hint of Communist influence, Shirley Graham Du Bois and her spouse met with the Soviet leader Nikita Khrushchev "for about two hours." They discussed the "peace movement in the United States and the Pan-African movement." The fruits of this meeting included a decision by the Soviet Union to establish an Institute on Africa.[10] Graham Du Bois was pleased by "the K. charm . . . it certainly took me in. That man is something!" She was also taken with the Soviet Union, adding, "I personally do not yet see why we should hurry back to the USA."[11]

Graham exaggerated about her "fluent Russian," yet it did seem it was easier for her to communicate ideas and be taken more seriously in Moscow than in the land of her birth. The royal treatment they received there made it easier for Graham Du Bois to take more seriously her own importance, as telltale signs of the attitudes Maya Angelou accused her of exhibiting in Ghana were becoming apparent.

They stayed in a charming dacha "about fifty miles outside of Moscow in a wonderful pine grove over a lake. The air is chilled like champagne. . . . Frankly, we both love the cold. It doesn't worry us the least bit. My 'There Was Once a Slave' was being translated here for publication when I arrived," she was proud to proclaim. "The Russian edition . . . will be infinitely better than the American edition. . . . Everything we'd [sic] doing is so incredible that it's hard to write about it."[12] Actually, it was not "hard to write" in the USSR, for she had "done more writing here in the last four weeks than I did in the U.S. in the last four years!"[13]

On New Year's Eve in 1958, revolutionaries in Cuba were poised to seize Havana. Meanwhile in Moscow their future patrons were feting Shirley Graham Du Bois, her spouse, and their friend Paul Robeson. As she told the *Pittsburgh Courier*,

> When the last stroke died away, the orchestra played, all the lights blazed and an array of butlers bearing large, silver trays began plying us with food. Ulanova danced, the Oistrakhs, father and son, played, and when the performing artists appeared together on stage for the finale, two of the opera stars unexpectedly went out into the audience to where Robeson was sitting and led him back to the stage.[14]

The black readers of this paper no doubt pondered the anomaly that their brethren in the Deep South were being battered by segregationists as they sought to exercise simple civil rights, while Shirley Graham Du Bois was receiving blue-chip treatment in a nation that was said to be tyrannical. Such pondering could ultimately compel some to conclude that, minimally, the Communists were not as hostile to blacks as capitalists were. Such tensions eventually forced Washington to move aggressively against the more egregious aspects of Jim Crow in the United States.

During the course of this trip, Graham Du Bois left her ailing spouse behind and traipsed off to "Egypt, the Sudan, Nigeria as well as Ghana." She had been "up to my eyebrows in other activities" in Moscow before being convinced to take this journey. She traveled with a group of merry Soviets who did not allow for dull moments:

I shall some day write a book entitled "Across the World with Five Mad Russians!" Five powerful, brilliant, fascinating, jolly, overpowering Soviet citizens, putting my luggage through on "diplomatic immunity," protecting me from all kinds of red tape, being met at various places by government representatives, filling me with hot tea! Our route: Moscow, Kiev, Budapest, Belgrade, Athens, Cairo! Stops everywhere but a real five day sight-seeing period in Cairo. The pyramids, Sphinx, Suez Canal, Red Sea, desert, desert, desert. Then down to Khartoum. . . . Visits to the historical scenes of the famous Sudanese Mahdi, across the Sahara desert to Nigeria, and finally, down to Ghana. . . . After one of the most exciting weeks of my life we stop back by way of Cairo with two days in the fascinating Adriatic country of Albania.

"Well, I wanted to travel," she concluded breathlessly, "and I must say I've had it! My only regret was that W. E. B. was not along . . . I was somewhat anxious about him."[15]

Though she was the most attentive of wives, she realized that she had something to offer the world before she married and that her light should not be extinguished because of the simple fact of a betrothal. Her trip to Ghana in late 1958 represented the duality of this life she was now leading. At an important international gathering hosted by the newly installed government of Kwame Nkrumah, she read Du Bois's remarks, "The Future of All Africa Lies in Socialism." Here, Du Bois presented ideas with which she heartily agreed: that Africa should not shun the socialist camp and should recognize that the ravages of the slave trade fueled the capitalism that continued to hamper African development. But here too in a crowded hall in Accra she took the initiative in personally removing the flag of Taiwan—a rebel province of China that Washington claimed was the legitimate government of the nation—and replaced it with the banner of the Communist regime in Beijing. For a U.S. government rather uneasy about Communist influence in the aftermath of Sputnik, this was more than a provocation. That she was assisted in this task by Tom Mboya, a Kenyan leader then being touted as a reliable friend of the United States, was even more disconcerting for some in Washington.[16]

Though she was away less than two weeks, she "returned to find an anxious and depressed W. E. B." Though he was healthy for someone his age, her absence did not aid his mental well-being: "The two letters

I had written him arrived after I reached Barvikha. He had missed me terribly, in spite of the unflagging attention he was receiving."[17] She was his caretaker, worrying about his health, taking him to various hospitals and doctors, taking his temperature, expressing concern about his appetite; and her special, personal touch meant that a substitute was insufficient. Though carried out with love, attending to Du Bois placed enormous strains on her time and hampered her ability to attend to herself and her work.

During their stay in the USSR, Graham Du Bois also traveled to Tashkent in Soviet Central Asia to speak for herself and her husband at an Asian-African Writers Conference. Just as her trip to Accra revealed a tendency that was to dominate her last years—her fascination with China—her trip here demonstrated another aspect of the twilight of her life: to the cacophony of "wild applause and cheers," she proclaimed, "I am an African . . . an American-African."[18] Her romance with her ancestral homeland was to bloom upon moving to Ghana, but this trip, where she encountered numerous African writers, had revealed both its existence and its ineradicable persistence.

From the Soviet Union Graham Du Bois and her husband took an arduous trip to China, a nation still deemed off-limits by the U.S. government and something of a mystery to her as well. While she had a "superficial knowledge of the Soviet Union," she "knew absolutely nothing about China." She had "known Russians in New York City, had studied the language and read some of their literary masterpieces." But her "only contact with Chinese in the United States" was shockingly stereotypical, consisting of encounters in "Chinese restaurants or laundries, and these Chinese I knew were either American-born or from Hong Kong or Taiwan." She "therefore came to Peking feeling like an interested tourist expecting to see strange sights."[19] She left a devoted advocate of China.

Again, she informed the readers of the *Pittsburgh Courier* of what she had seen and helped to lessen an anticommunism that was never as strong among African Americans as among others in the United States. Still, even after contact with China, her opinions often were influenced by stereotypes. While living in Ghana and after, she conceded that "the closest woman" to her "during [those] trying times" was the "wife of the Chinese Ambassador," Huang Hua. Yet she could still complain that there were times when her "oriental pattern of thought gets in the way."[20]

She found China to be a "lovely place," but she was worried since "the State Department has already voiced its displeasure . . . I guess they'll start getting our jail cells ready," she joked nervously. Apprehension about what fate awaited her upon her return could not suppress her joy, however; she found the people to be "wonderful! I didn't think any place could be better than the Soviet Union but I must say China takes my breath away."[21]

Writing from "the Yangtse, nearing Chunking," she mused about the "incredible saga" she was experiencing. They met with "Chairman Mao" in a "fairy-like lakeside villa. Now I feel that I have seen into the heart of China! Henceforth I'll be able to accept its miracles."[22] She did not mention famine or the dislocations caused by some of Mao's policies. In the world of realpolitik, it was enough for her that China was then hostile to those who were depriving her own people of their human rights. The idea that "enemy of my enemy is my friend" which drove Washington and Beijing together during the Nixon administration because of their mutual hostility to Moscow, was the philosophy that allowed her to look beyond pressing domestic problems in China. Many African Americans rationalized voting for a Democratic Party that had epitomized Jim Crow and that once had a de facto armed wing known as the Ku Klux Klan on the grounds that it was the "lesser of two evils"; Graham Du Bois rationalized her backing for less than perfect socialist nations on similar grounds, that is, Beijing was less dangerous to blacks than Washington. After all, China had not engaged in the trans-Atlantic slave trade nor pioneered in devising Jim Crow.

She visited Wuhan, "perhaps now the foremost industrial center in Asia. . . . We'll spend some time in Cheng-tu seeing something of Chinese minorities." She was a Red in a land ruled by Communists and a black in a nation of color. She was exhilarated: "THIS IS THE LIFE!" she wrote.

Of course, there were pressing concerns, including the health of her spouse.

> W. E. B. holds up well . . . they simply carry him around. Our entourage includes a trained nurse for him—the prettiest possible little girl who is constantly at his side. And if you think our dear doctor is bored by all this 'veneration,' forget it. He adores it! I don't know what I'll do when we get home.[23]

All of this "veneration" and cavorting with the likes of Chinese and Soviet Communists was not welcomed by her government, apparently.
While they were away their "home was broken into, desks pried open,
papers searched and scattered . . . a small radio [was] taken and the bedrooms searched." Her son David, who reported the incident, "could not
be certain about what of ours was taken since he had no way of knowing all the items." Because of the search of their papers, she assumed
that this was no ordinary burglary; nevertheless "this trip is worth any
harassment."[24]

Understandably. Moscow and Beijing, whose conflicted relationship was to be a dominant factor in global events over the next few
decades, seemed to be in rivalry over who could provide the warmest
welcome for these two visiting African American dignitaries. In Beijing
they were "guests of honor at a banquet" attended by "many leading
Chinese scholars, professors, historians, writers, public leaders."[25] Graham Du Bois was hailed for her temerity in hauling down the Tai-
wanese flag in Accra. Though her husband was the center of attention,
increasingly these host governments were beginning to recognize that
she was a major intellectual and political force in her own right. The
same held true for the perceptions of U.S. government agencies: the FBI
filed a report on this impressive banquet and her role in it.[26]

Sidney Rittenberg, a U.S. expatriate then living in China, has recalled the visit of Graham Du Bois and her spouse to China. She told
Rittenberg once that "to cheer [Du Bois] up when all else failed," she
would tell him that "if he listened to the doctor and got well, 'I would
take him back to Beijing. . . . That really perked him up and that's the
only thing that did.' From then on whenever he balked at the doctor's
orders, she would threaten not to take him to Beijing and he would behave." This anecdote is revealing not only for what it says about Du
Bois's affection for China but also for what it says about the nature of
his marriage: her approach to him reflected a bit of the maternal, which
is not overly surprising in a sense, given his age and fragility and her
history.

Another time they were having dinner and, according to Rittenberg, she "kept fussing over what her husband was eating—gently but
persistently urging him to take more vegetables and less red meat. 'My
wife always makes me [eat] a lot of grass,' he said . . . with his usual
broad twinkle. 'She says if I don't eat this grass it'll shorten my life.'"[27]
Again, her role as caretaker to her spouse is evident.

By her own admission, Graham Du Bois returned from China a changed person. The FBI reported that at a meeting of the National Council on American-Soviet Friendship, she spoke of returning from her trip "a new born woman."[28] If nothing else, this journey reconfirmed her socialist beliefs and provided her with an increased sympathy for Beijing, which she was to retain for her remaining days. Once more her ability to move around spurred an ideological journey—in this case her move toward Maoism. After residing abroad she found it even more difficult to accept the anticommunism and conservatism of the United States.

That was not all. While in China she met women who couldn't believe she was

> spending her days doing housework and waiting on her husband. "Look at yourself," they said, "you're a teacher, a writer, a musician, and you're giving up all these things for washing dishes." . . . "Well you know," Shirley said with a grin, "those Chinese women laid me right out! I went back home and hired a housekeeper and immediately I became editor of a magazine!"

This magazine was *Freedomways*.

She had returned with a more feminist outlook, apparently influenced by her encounter with Chinese women. As she told the readers of the *Afro-American*, even European women had "more guts" than their U.S. counterparts.[29]

Du Bois, she continued, was an altruistic spouse who backed her feminist-inspired ventures: "He supported everything I did, even if I wasn't there when he needed me. For example, I decided to learn Russian and I [had] to leave the house every morning at 7 a.m. so he had to get his own breakfast."[30] She had fled her father's home and that of her first husband because of a reluctance to be a mere caretaker. She had resisted a permanent union with a man in the 1930s because of a fear of becoming yet another "mad housewife." Yet by the 1950s she had settled into the role she had resisted. Why? Perhaps she felt that playing this role in a marriage to Du Bois—a great man in obvious need of help—made her sacrifice worthwhile.

She was surprised that their passports were not seized after their return and that "only two of our thirteen bags were even open[ed] . . . I can't explain it."[31] This fortuity did not lessen her paranoia about the U.S. authorities, however. After the activist "kind Abner Green" died and the daughter of Dick Morford, her colleague on the Council of American-Soviet Friendship, died "of a strange, 'unknown' malady," she remarked, "everybody knows the food in the New York area has been more or less poisoned but nobody talks about it."[32]

This paranoia was a reflection of how beleaguered she felt. It was not just that the Red Scare was still in force, causing the firing of workers, the pulling of books from library shelves, the "blacklisting" of artists. Worse, her Communist Party was splitting. Some argued that the party should distance itself from Moscow, while others maintained just as adamantly that this would be disastrous. She was decidedly in the latter camp but, ironically, was to drift away eventually from the party as a direct result of her transforming journey to China.

■

One of the tasks that occupied her during her remaining months in the United States was launching the magazine *Freedomways*. A lineal descendant of Paul Robeson's old newspaper, *Freedom,* this quarterly was designed to report on and shape the burgeoning "freedom movement" that was bursting forth in the Deep South. Shirley Graham served as an editor, along with her friend Esther Cooper Jackson, the spouse of the Communist Party leader James Jackson.

From its inception, this journal (which included on its masthead Jack O'Dell, an advisor to Martin Luther King, Jr., and yet another presumed Communist) was viewed with suspicion by the FBI as a "Communist front," a mole smuggled into the highest reaches of the civil rights movement. The bureau believed that at a high-level Communist Party meeting in 1961

> it was stated that the original plan called for the publication to be openly Marxist, but that it was later decided it would not be an avowedly Marxist publication. Editorial[s] are in the hands of a mixed group of Marxists and non-Marxists. It was stated that the central purpose of "Freedomways" is to develop a theory and positive criticism of currents in the Negro movement, as well as to raise the level of understanding and discussion taking place in Negro life today and to project a socialist and pro-Soviet orientation.[33]

Actually, this report was not wholly inaccurate. Graham Du Bois and many others of the small African American Left had hailed the onset of a mass movement against Jim Crow, but they also felt that even if it were successful in bringing basic rights like voting, these gains would be ultimately insufficient unless there were fundamental economic changes in society. In part, *Freedomways* was a vehicle designed to open debate on these and other issues. Ultimately, writers as diverse as Alice Walker and various members of the Congressional Black Caucus were to grace its pages. Despite opposition from the FBI, it played a role that the bureau's early report predicted.[34] Graham Du Bois's notion of calling the magazine *Forward: A Marxist Quarterly of the Negro Freedom Movement* was not realized, but the journal was successful nonetheless.[35]

"Editing this magazine," she wrote, "is really a maddening and exhausting job, but it is being so very well received that we are encouraged to stand by our guns."[36] But fighting the numerous battles required to generate a progressive magazine was taking its toll on her. It was inevitable that she would again seek to travel abroad, where she was not a hounded dissident but a valued intellectual. The FBI took note that on 25 June 1960 she and her husband flew on Sabena Airlines from New York City to Brussels; their destination was Prague, then on to Ghana for a mid-July conference on "African Women and Women of African Descent."[37]

The contrast between her effusive treatment abroad and her at times difficult reception at home was becoming all too glaring to her; likewise, it was becoming difficult for her not to believe in her own regal importance when she was being treated so royally abroad:

> This whole episode is incredible! Two weeks ago after travelling all night over the Atlantic Ocean and Western Europe we landed in Prague, were rushed to our hotel, bathed, rested for an hour, dressed and were taken to the Stadium where after being presented to the President of Czechoslovakia, we witnessed the most extraordinary sports festival I have ever seen. Imagine . . . sixteen thousand girls in colorful attire, with white hoops performing in the Stadium at the same time— music, rhythm, magical color! . . . Our five days and nights in Prague was a succession of banquets, state receptions, sport sessions at the stadium, surrounded by ardent, old and new friends.

Then it was on to Rome and Ghana. They had been invited to witness Ghana joining the Commonwealth as a republic. After they landed in Accra,

> an official came on board asking for "Dr. Du Bois". We were escorted from the plane and beheld a full military guard, a band began to play, officials stood waiting and behind barricades hundreds of waving people . . . . Everywhere W. E. B. is hailed as the "Father of Pan-African-ism." We are the private guests of the President.

Even more important was how this treatment invigorated her husband: "years have literally dropped from W. E. B.," she said with typically hyperbolic zest. "All of this happened so fast and so unexpectedly that we're having to make plans as we go along—just as we did before."[38]

A few months later she was in Cairo for yet another international conference on women, this time without her husband. Little did she know that this great, infuriating, ramshackle, remarkable city on the Nile would be her home a few years later. Once again she was besieged by journalists and politicians:

> Tomorrow I am having lunch at the home of the Tass man here. I was asked to arrange for a broadcast on Moscow radio at six o'clock this evening . . . I've been interviewed by two Cairo newspapers, the United Press and Pravda. I was the only [one] here from the western world until today when [someone] from Sweden arrived . . . I have been kissed, embraced and photographed by the Chinese delegation.

She told Du Bois, "all send love to you." The women there "paraded through the downtown district of Cairo, with police escort and people cheering us along the way. Afterwards, President Nasser received us in his home and gardens."[39]

The simple fact was that Graham Du Bois could play a larger role abroad than at home. This "first Afro-Asian Women's Conference" in Cairo was an example, as well as the "Extraordinary Session of the Afro-Asian Solidarity Council, called especially for discussion of the Congo crisis," which she also attended while there.[40] After leaving Cairo she signed an ad that appeared in the Trotskyite newspaper the *Militant* blasting U.S. policy toward Cuba in the wake of the disastrous

Bay of Pigs invasion.[41] U.S. citizens courageous enough to align with Nasser's Egypt (which had fought a war a few years earlier with the close U.S. ally Israel) and criticize U.S. foreign policy in the Congo and Cuba were not numerous. Hence, on the international scene the relative rarity of her being a U.S. citizen highly critical of her government's foreign policy made her even more valued, just as it brought her a purgatory at home. This made it relatively simple to decide that living abroad was preferable to living at home.

•

In 1961 W. E. B. Du Bois joined the Communist Party, then with his wife moved to Accra, Ghana. These events were not unconnected. Du Bois had been leaning to the left for some time, and the fact that the woman he loved was a party member no doubt facilitated his membership. His socialist sympathies and his wide-ranging critique of U.S. foreign policy were shared mostly by Reds and so-called fellow travelers. Certainly his former colleagues in the NAACP had long since abandoned *any* analysis of U.S. foreign policy and how it intersected with their domestic concerns. Impending decisions by the U.S. Supreme Court in 1961 made many on the left wonder if a new climate of repression was on the way, which could once again lead to the invalidation of the Du Boises' passports. This could jeopardize the kind of specialized medical treatment Du Bois increasingly required; he could more easily obtain it abroad, where he was a walking legend, than at home, where he was marginal. Above all, he had the opportunity to participate in the production of the *Encyclopedia Africana,* a projected definitive reference work on peoples of African descent.

They sold their Brooklyn Heights home for $69,000—about $20,500 in cash—and, as a "confidential source" of the FBI put it, they "would move from their residence into the St. George Hotel on October 4, 1961" for a departure the next evening for Ghana.[42]

Graham Du Bois was enthusiastic about this self-imposed exile. She was distraught when she was refused a passport to attend the independence celebration of Ghana in 1957.[43] After she received her passport in 1958 Ghana was one of her stops. At the First All African Peoples Congress in Ghana, where she hauled down the flag of Taiwan, she also "heard Patrice Lumumba speak." She was invited to speak at the university there and to her dismay, "a group of students (small but vocal) disturbed the gathering by shouting that they wanted 'Nothing to do with that All-African, 'red' Conference! I was shocked and could not understand this—until later I learned that a large portion of the teachers at the University were from South Africa!" This may have been true, but Graham Du Bois was to discover that official rhetoric aside, not everyone in Ghana was sold on Nkrumah's dream of building Africa's first socialist republic that would serve as the building block for a united, socialist continent.[44] In her mind that made it all the more crucial for her to reside in Accra.

Their arrival in Ghana was covered in the local press and monitored by the FBI.[45] The U.S. authorities had reason to believe that the growing fascination of African American youth with Africa could easily lead them to be influenced by socialist leaders like Sekou Toure of Guinea and Nkrumah of Ghana. Shirley Graham Du Bois and her spouse could facilitate this process, or so it was thought. Thus, when the Chinese ambassador, Huang Hua, and his wife called on them days after their arrival, this report was filed away as well.[46] Months later, the FBI took note of a report in the *Worker* noting that the radical couple had been honored at a reception in the Kremlin, where, said the FBI,

> President Breshnev [sic] spent nearly two hours with the guests. The subject [Graham Du Bois] spoke to a group of students from Cuba, Ghana, Guinea and other nations at Lumumba University in Moscow and spoke of Patrice Lumumba, the "martyred" Congo leader. They were also guests of the Union of Soviet Writers while in Moscow.[47]

Though they had crossed the Atlantic, scrutiny by the U.S. government survived the transoceanic journey.

By October 1961 Graham Du Bois and her spouse were residing "comfortably" in a hotel in Accra, "trying to be as inconspicuous and out of the way as possible."[48] However, this was difficult when their every step was seemingly being monitored. The FBI noticed when Graham Du Bois wrote articles for Soviet publications on Cuba and Africa. "The enclosed material," the bureau reported irritably, "clearly shows that Tass utilizes its wire service in the U.S. as a transmission belt for propaganda material of a type that American correspondents in the Soviet Union would never be allowed to send." The FBI also was not pleased when an article by Graham Du Bois appeared in the *China Daily News* praising the Communist regime in Beijing.[49] At a time when Washington was concerned about an anti-U.S. cabal spearheaded in Moscow and Beijing, Graham Du Bois seemed to represent this nightmare.

The house the Ghanaian government provided them was symbolic of their elevated status and their close relationship with the nation's leader, Kwame Nkrumah. According to Charles Howard, it was a "beautiful" seven-room residence with many windows, situated high on a hill in the center of an acre of land. The grounds were divided, "English style," by hedges and blooming trees. Two scarlet red flamingo trees guarded the entrance. The house had a library, a living room, a dining room, two bedrooms with private baths, a study room for Graham Du Bois, and a "screened porch of nylon netting." They had a steward, a cook, a driver and night watchman. They had two cars, one a Soviet model and the other an English make driven by Graham Du Bois. Their furnishings had been shipped from Brooklyn.[50] On the walls, according to the visiting journalist Ralph McGill, there were "richly and beautifully wrought red hangings of Chinese silk and a few paintings. There were busts of Marx, Lenin and Mao Tse-tung." With apparent relief, he informed his readers that "save for the sculptured head of Marx, there was no evidence of Russian art."[51]

The writer Leslie Lacy concluded that "by Ghanaian standards it was considered plush," but "by American standards it measured up to the homes lower-middle class whites would own in a very small Northern community."[52] Lacy was partially correct: there was nothing special about the structure itself, but only a select few in both Ghana and the United States had as many servants as did Graham Du Bois and her spouse. The home and accoutrements provided by the Nkrumah government were not only indicative of how Nkrumah felt about Du Bois, but were also suggestive of the flourishing friendship that developed between him and Shirley Graham Du Bois.

The Du Bois home quickly became a necessary stop for visiting African Americans in search of their "roots," Southern African exiles, Chinese diplomats, and the like. Her son David was struck by it all; he felt it was "like living in a glass house when you went to the home there in Ghana because it was a place of pilgrimage for people from all over the world and particularly all over Africa."[53]

It was clear that Graham Du Bois was enjoying this life she had made for herself. After facing virtual ostracism in the United States because of her ties to the Communists, she now discovered that this liability had been magically transformed into an asset: Nkrumah's gov-

ernment was busily constructing a network of ties with the then socialist camp, including China, and he considered himself something of a socialist too.

Besides attending to her increasingly frail husband, Graham carved
out a role for herself in Ghana that eventually let to her appointment as
director of television there. Her "first project" was "the remaking of
schoolbooks," which for some time had a distinctly procolonialist flavor.[54] Still, at this juncture she had plenty of time for conviviality. One
of her early house guests from the United States was Du Bois's codefendant in his 1951 trial, Abbott Simon. He recalled the routine there:
she "got up early to listen to the BBC news program and I bathed . . . we
breakfasted. . . . And, usually it was . . . almost like a symposium. We
would . . . start talking and we would talk about a topic and we would
exhaust it."[55] Graham Du Bois was a noted raconteur and conversa-
tionalist, and the unsophisticated telecommunications system in
Ghana, combined with difficulty in receiving mail, might have caused
her to prevail even more on visitors like Simon for news and analysis.
Cedric Belfrage, a close friend of both Graham Du Bois and her spouse,
"acted as a forwarding agent between Du Bois and the socialist countries since 'my mail' as he wrote to me 'is so tampered with that I am
afraid it may not reach.'"[56]

Even Graham Du Bois's most innocent activities became an opportunity for U.S. intelligence agencies to gather information about her.
Soon after arriving in Accra she informed Eslanda Robeson that "a
lovely Parisienne called on me . . . Madame will also be a good friend.
Her husband is connected with one of the big French firms. They came
out nine years ago, a bride and a groom. . . . [I] will be taking French lessons three times a week. Actually, I know basic French and concentrated
brush up" was her goal. This admirable quality of lifelong education—
she had begun studying Russian at the age of sixty—unbeknownst to
her was converted to a negative purpose. The station chief of the Central Intelligence Agency wrote, "My French teacher, Madame Bassguy
told me that she is now giving Dr. Du Bois and his wife French lessons.
The couple contacted the French Embassy for a teacher and they were
referred to her."[57] Wittingly or unwittingly, this French teacher had become a CIA "asset," sharing details that she may have deemed trivial
but that the agency considered pieces of a larger puzzle. This episode
also illustrated a disturbing aspect of Graham Du Bois's tenure in
Ghana: though she knew she was under intense scrutiny by the U.S.

authorities, she had a rather naive approach to this issue. She struck up a friendship with the U.S. ambassador in Ghana, William Mahoney, at a time when the U.S. government had become hostile to the government of which she was an official representative. At best this was curious.

More typical was Richard Wright's experience abroad. He had understandable suspicions about many of those from the United States he encountered while living in Paris in the 1950s, including the five hundred or so African Americans there.[58] Julian Mayfield, another African American in exile in Accra, assumed that "everyone" he encountered in Ghana "is . . . an agent."[59] By comparison, Graham Du Bois was an innocent abroad.[60] It was almost as if she had been transformed by the panegyrics she had been subject to and was grateful that she could now consort with ambassadors, even if they were from a government that was hostile to the nation she professed to love, Ghana.

Early in her residence in Ghana, Graham Du Bois should have recognized that she was no favorite of the U.S. government. Soon after her arrival in Accra she went to the embassy to renew her passport and was informed it was invalid. The historian Herbert Aptheker recalled that "Du Bois restrained her from physically assaulting this clerk. It was as a result of this experience and at Mrs. Du Bois' suggestion that they inquired of President Nkrumah if they might become citizens of Ghana."[61] Her son David recalls it differently, albeit with no less significance. When he had gone to the U.S. embassy in Cairo, where he was then residing, to renew his passport, he was refused; instead they stamped his document with the ominous words, "Good Only for Direct Return to the U.S.A." He went to Accra using a travel document provided by the Ghanaian embassy in Cairo to confer with his mother and Du Bois; there he and Du Bois decided to become citizens of Ghana and were granted this privilege by order of the Presidential Council.[62] Later Graham Du Bois did the same. This decision was significant for many reasons. Africans in North America for the longest time had been treated atrociously and with impunity in no small part because it was felt they had no recourse, nowhere to go. Shirley Graham Du Bois had shown that, no, they did have somewhere to go, there was recourse, at least for some. Given the competition between Washington and Moscow for friends and allies in Africa, the flocking of militant African Americans to their ancestral homeland could be seen as harmful to the long-term interests of the U.S. ruling elite.

This momentous development—renouncing U.S. citizenship—was interpreted by many to mean that they were giving up on the possibility of transforming the land of their birth. This was not necessarily the case. Global pressure, including pressure from Africa, was helping to bring about desegregation in the United States. However, the experience should have made Graham Du Bois realize that her friendship with the U.S. ambassador should have been leavened with realism and caution about the limits of their relationship. If he was so friendly toward her, why didn't he intervene so that she could renew her passport?

Although Graham Du Bois may not have been totally aware of the far-reaching significance of Ghana's independence, certainly Washington was. As early as 1953, *U.S. News and World Report*, a reliable barometer of conservative opinion, was blaring, "Africa: Next Goal of Communists."[63] When Ghana attained independence in 1957 under the leadership of Kwame Nkrumah, who was suspected of Communist ties during his sojourns in both the United States and Britain, the prospect of Red penetration into Africa seemingly had become reality.[64]

There was a high "level of communist influence" among anticolonial movements in Africa generally, and Ghana was no exception. As early as 1948 the U.S. consul in Accra had called Nkrumah a "dangerous man. He is recognized as a communist." While living in Britain he had become close to the British Communist leaders Emile Burns and R. Palme Dutt; Graham Du Bois's old friend Claudia Jones "knew him well."

In the post–World War II era, "communism and especially Marxist ideology were playing an increasingly important role in the politics of many of the [African] students in Britain, and to some extent this influence was spreading to West Africa."[65] Nkrumah was a veritable symbol of resistance to the kind of foreign policy that Washington advocated in Africa. C. L. R. James has averred that "to the Africans, and peoples of African descent everywhere, the name of Nkrumah became for many years a symbol of release from the subordination to which they had been subjected for so many years . . . Kwame Nkrumah was one of the greatest political leaders of our century."[66] Washington begged to differ; it considered him a dangerous demagogue, not least because of his presumed explosive impact on the anti–Jim Crow youth of the South.

Simultaneously, as one writer has observed, "scholars have tended to shortchange the fact that the shift to a more internationalist perspective injected an additional source of racial pride which aided the burgeoning civil rights movement."[67] This "internationalist perspective," which Graham Du Bois and her spouse symbolized, was strikingly apparent in the shock troops of the movement, the Student Non-Violent Coordinating Committee (SNCC).

Of course, this "internationalist perspective" was not shared universally in the civil rights movement. The Urban League's Lester Granger and some of his cohorts criticized the same Patrice Lumumba that Graham Du Bois hailed. "The NAACP Board of Directors never made more than passing reference to the Congo throughout 1960-63." To no avail, "numerous letters to the NAACP appealed for the organization to work on behalf of the Congolese."[68] Much of this leadership had concluded that civil rights reforms would be realized only if they steered clear of sticky foreign policy matters. Their acquiescence made Graham Du Bois' lack of reticence stand out even more.

It appeared that the traditional civil rights leadership was not alone in its skepticism about African radicalism. As early as 1953 the State Department filed a lengthy memorandum reputedly prepared by the writer Richard Wright; there it was written that Nkrumah's "ideal is Lenin . . . at the head of his bed in his sleeping room is a large portrait of" the Russian leader. In Leninist fashion, a "Secret Circle" dominated the ruling party in Ghana, the Convention Peoples' Party: "The other leaders and the general membership did not know of its existence." The CPP was "a Communist minded political party," it was said.[69] That Communists like Shirley Graham and W. E. B. Du Bois were being welcomed as citizens in Ghana was further confirmation of Washington's perception that Moscow had established a beachhead on the western coast of Africa.

Ghana's evolution was causing alarm bells to sound all over Washington; "By the time President John F. Kennedy's new ambassador arrived in Ghana in January 1961, relations were so sour that the Ghanaian cabinet debated whether to receive the new ambassador or not."[70] Yet "President Kennedy had quickly realized that Ghana was the key to his whole African strategy."[71] His successor, Lyndon Johnson, was less informed; reputedly he once said to Averill Harriman, "Tell me, Av, what's the goddam name of that place."[72] Even those who could not place Ghana on a map felt that it could subvert other "pro-Western" governments on the continent, threaten to nationalize U.S. interests, and exert a perilous influence on African Americans: Nkrumah's fabulous treatment of the radical couple from Brooklyn Heights did nothing to erase this perception.[73] Indeed, under Nkrumah Ghana became a haven for all manner of leftists, socialists, and anticolonial fighters from Africa and abroad.[74]

Washington may have been a bit more skittish than usual because it was suffering from an intelligence deficit—in every sense of the term—when it came to Africa: "regardless of their philosophical persuasion or research strategy, historians of American foreign relations have had little to say about Africa." They were no better—or worse—than their government, since "as recently as 1958 . . . the United States had more diplomats in West Germany than in all of Africa."[75] When African nations began asserting their independence, many in Washington viewed it as little more than a target of opportunity for the hated Communists.

At the same time, Nkrumah's domestic policies presented contradictions that Graham Du Bois either did not see or did not care to comment on. In 1962, for example, he apparently stated that trade unions' former role of "struggling against capitalists" was "obsolete" in Ghana. They were now to "inculcate in our working people the love for labour and increased productivity."[76] Though Wright's memorandum suggested that Nkrumah was a closet Red, as early as February 1954 the CPP "banned Communists from entering the civil service in the Gold Coast"; just before that, party members were suspended supposedly for attending meetings in Vienna of the Communist-led World Federation of Trade Unions.[77] Undoubtedly Nkrumah's government was under unjustifiable pressure from Washington, but those in his inner circle—for example, Graham Du Bois—should have been the first to tell him that circumscribing the role of unions and radicals was simply the first step toward disaster for a government that could not afford to isolate potential or actual allies.

On the other hand, Nkrumah may have been a paranoid with real enemies. Late in 1961 his Ministry of Information told of a "plot" of "the 'elite' and of some of the more unprincipled 'self-seekers.'" J. E. Appiah was accused of sending telegrams to "foreign trade unions" seeking aid for a "struggle against government control of unions and for survival." Also involved in this effort was "Ishmaila Annan" and a number of "traders." They were supposedly upset with a new system of taxation.

There were "explosions in Accra" and "illegal strikes" that were to provide "an excuse for a coup d'etat by the Army." They were backed by Togo, "certain expatriate interests," and "certain colonial and imperialist powers." Apparently, a number of anti-Nkrumah activists were in contact with the notorious Jay Lovestone, a leading U.S. trade unionist with known links to certain U.S. government agencies. The "Ghana Students' Association of the Americas" forwarded their newsletter to him, which demanded that Ghanaians "stand up . . . and be counted in the fight against communism in Ghana."[78]

Meanwhile, Graham Du Bois blithely went about her duties in Ghana. Ever busy, she outlined yet another book, this time "on British dissenters, Englishmen who at one time have been considered traitors, but who have only recently been vindicated." No doubt she had her own situation in mind as an inspiration for "this little study." "And believe me," she added, "I am never going to have more time on my hands than I have right now."[79] She may have been right: she had an increasingly ill husband to take care of but she had no job, which helps explain why she subjected visitors like Abbott Simon to a barrage of conversation. But that was to change soon. After her husband passed away, she began another life as an official of a Ghanaian government that the United States deemed to be on the wrong side of the Cold War divide.

8

Mother, Africa

WHEN DU BOIS DIED, his spouse was enervated, but only momentarily. Shorn of the role of caretaker for the first time in years, she quickly plunged into a swirl of activity, principally as a confidante and leading advisor to Nkrumah. In fact, the rapid resumption of work seemed to be therapeutic for her, helping to buffer her grief. However, the caviling notion persisted that the "position" she maintained as a result of adopting the surname Du Bois had led to a certain overbearing style.

■

By 1963 W. E. B. Du Bois was ninety-five years old; despite the tender care of the similarly aging sixty-six-year-old Shirley Graham Du Bois, his health continued to falter. She tried "to keep things on an even keel so that his strength is conserved . . . he never feels lonely or isolated. We have a beautiful Russian car—a Chaika—in which he has a ride every late afternoon"; nonetheless, he still suffered from an "extreme depression."[1] His strength, she concluded sadly, was "gradually failing. He is not sick, suffers no pain, but is extremely irked by his weakness."[2] Her well-being was so bound up with his that when he suffered, she did too: "Our dear William's health has become such an uncertain element that my days and nights go 'up and down.' . . . He is very weak, must be cared for patiently and tenderly." All "his faculties retain their efficiency," she reported, but his decline was taking a heavy toll on her.[3] When she went away briefly with Nkrumah to East Africa she made sure that he had a "day and night nurse"; plus, "one of the Supervisors of the Military Hospital, a charming and intelligent young woman came and lived here in the house with him. She devoted every hour to entertaining him, reading to him, enjoying music with him and accompanying him on his daily long drive." Du Bois had become melancholy and she tried to "surround him with every comfort and make him feel secure and loved."[4] Finally, in August 1963, as the March on Washington was marking a new stage in the struggle against Jim Crow in the United States, W. E. B. Du Bois died.

On 29 August 1963, Shirley Graham Du Bois received those who came to pay respects at her spouse's funeral. The visitors included a sizable section of the diplomatic corps, but none from the U.S. embassy. Her "friend" Ambassador William Mahoney was not able to make it; his gesture was interpreted widely as an intentional diplomatic rebuff.

Dressed in black with a veiled hat, she was accompanied by Kwame Nkrumah—a man she had grown quite fond of, even before her widowhood—who turned this sad affair into something amounting to a state funeral, with extensive press coverage, disciplined military contingents, and masses in attendance. Nkrumah and Graham Du Bois walked to the casket together. For a moment she placed her hand on her husband's body, perhaps contemplating their happy years together and the loneliness that was now surely to follow. Messages of regret and sorrow came from Mao Zedong and Zhou En-lai, Nikita Khrushchev and Jomo Kenyatta, Cheddi Jagan and Kim Il Sung. Boosted by their support and the good wishes of countless others from across the globe, Shirley Graham Du Bois buried her spouse, then proceeded to resurrect her career and construct one of the more intriguing of her many lives.[5]

Though she was given credit for strongly influencing Du Bois, with his passing it seemed that she floundered ideologically. She developed a sort of "left nationalism" that eventually led her to Maoism and disaffection from some of her allies in the U.S. Communist Party. On another level, her close relationship with Nkrumah, her acute cognizance of her own importance, and perhaps a kind of male supremacy that made it difficult for men and women alike to accept with equanimity a woman with power, led to strained relations with quite a few, not least Maya Angelou.

Even before her husband was laid to rest, it had become apparent that Nkrumah viewed her as someone whose counsel he could trust. When he went to Ethiopia for the founding of the Organization of African Unity in the spring of 1963, she traveled with him "in his private plane." This conference, she pronounced majestically, "was probably the most important gathering so far in this century."[6] She "managed to work on two levels" there, "as a delegate and as a journalist"; "and that means I didn't miss a thing." Nkrumah had come to recognize what was evident: she was a tireless worker, an excellent writer, and a competent administrator; unfortunately such a combination was not in great supply in a country that had been underdeveloped by British colonialism. When she began to study an indigenous language, "Twi-Fanti," it was further confirmation that she was not just another expatriate but a true citizen interested in nation building.[7]

Despite her love for Du Bois, his death did not paralyze her indefinitely. To the contrary, it seemed that work became her escape, her solace—certainly work was a familiar companion throughout her lives. Her regimen after his death was clear: "after six weeks in Europe for rest, pulling myself together and seeing friends, I shall begin preparation for a very important post . . . an educational and creative post." The job of director of television would be held by this former U.S. citizen who was now "proud to tell you that I am a Ghanaian citizen . . . this is my home."[8]

•

From 1963 until early 1966—from the death of Du Bois to the overthrow of Nkrumah—was a spectacularly busy period for Shirley Graham Du Bois, one of the most fruitful of her lives. Her calendar was jammed with dinners for visiting dignitaries like Zhou En-lai, conferences with ambassadors from Japan and the Soviet Union, cocktails with the Nigerian high commissioner; dinner with the Cuban ambassador.[9] One interesting event was her November 1965 "bon voyage" to the Indonesian ambassador. He was departing Ghana because of the bloody coup that had dislodged his government in Jakarta. The February 1966 coup in Ghana—one of a string of extraordinary political changes globally during a brief period—was to shatter her world and force her to depart the nation that she had only recently begun to call "home."[10]

To the casual observer it may have seemed that Graham Du Bois was reeling from one embassy reception or dinner to another in a kind of round-robin bacchanalian revel. This was far from the truth. As director of television—in fact, the "first woman TV director in the world"—she planned to "create, construct, train workers and program Ghana Television." To insure a diversity of programming that surpassed the drivel that too many viewers worldwide had to endure— which meant going beyond the programming from Hollywood that dominated most networks—she found it necessary to seek programs from across the globe and that meant frequent sessions with various diplomats.[11] Moreover, the name Du Bois may have lost its luster in the

United States, but in Africa and abroad it continued to shine brightly; as a result, many were eager for the opportunity to meet her.

Graham Du Bois took to the task of building Ghana Television with typical zeal and exuberance. In her humble opinion, she had "one of the heaviest jobs in all Africa." She "visited and studied the most advanced television systems throughout the world," examining "all phases—including a stiff course in television electronics in Japan." She informed the writer Cedric Belfrage that she "would need several hours" to explain her job, but suffice it to say that "the government of Ghana is spending near four million pounds to set up television throughout the country and to train Ghanaians to operate it. Even before" she took over, "a Television Training School had been set up . . . with the aid of Canadian experts and construction of the broadcast studio and three transmitters had been started." After her global tour of Britain, France, Italy, East Germany, Czechoslovakia, and Japan studying the "most advanced television systems," she "expanded the original plans and set about building a system which would be indigenous to Ghana in particular and Africa as a whole." Her plans, she thought, were "original, inventive and constructive—no commercials at all, television viewing centers set up in villages and rural areas—even some telecasting in colour." "Needless to say," she concluded, "I AM BUSY."[12]

That she was. Her sprawling 19,000-square-foot headquarters was a whirl of activity.[13] An agreement was made with a British company to build more studios. Classes for television writers were planned.[14] In a move that later generations may have found questionable, she planned special programs for women on, for example, "demonstrations on cooking, dress-making, exercises, fashion shows, beauty hints, interior decoration."[15] To bring television to villages that barely had electricity, let alone television, she intended to set up "television viewing centers" powered by generators until electricity came on line. In an updating of the African tradition of the "griot," there would be "traditional story tellers" present to explain in local languages what was taking place on the screen. Her ambitious plan was to insure that "85% of the material shown" would be "produced right here" in Ghana; "this rules out entirely the type of television which is being imposed by the West on the people of Nigeria," she boasted.[16] This plan would not go down well with those who could easily view it as a dangerous precedent for other nations to emulate, thus disrupting a traditional and steady profit stream for those in "the West" who controlled programming. Strikingly, after her ambitious plans were mentioned in the trade publication *Variety*, she received an immediate letter of inquiry from the U.K. office of the U.S. programming firm Desilu, which had been started by the television star Lucille Ball and her then husband, Desi Arnaz.[17]

Graham Du Bois's son David told her that the launching of Ghana Television "made news around the world."[18] Soon she was in a "battle" with the transnational corporation Philips of the Netherlands, because of its effort to nullify a contract she had made to make televisions and radios with the Japanese corporation Sanyo.[19] Earlier, the FBI had reported her appointment as director of Ghana Television and took special note of her trip to Japan "to learn television techniques."[20]

These were storm signals, but she sailed on cheerfully. By the spring of 1964 Graham Du Bois was writing happily about the construction of a

> two million dollar Television Broadcasting [center]. Giant transmitters are being erected in different regions so that when we begin televising about June 1st, 1965, Ghana's Television will reach three-quarters of the entire country. While the Volta River Dam is being completed, we shall be building additional transmitters so that by the end of 1966, television will not only expand throughout the country but will transmit across our borders. The government of Ghana is spending about four million pounds (that is approximately, twelve million dollars) in construction, the most modern equipment, training of personnel and organization.

The plan was to train specialists for neighboring nations and exert influence on their populations with Ghanaian broadcasts. She was involved with the effort to establish the Ghana State Publishing House, which would print books to be circulated continentally. This latter venture was "being built and equipped by advisors from the German Democratic Republic," that is, Communist-ruled East Germany.[21] These investments in communications media were strategic components of Nkrumah's Pan-African vision of a united continent.

Graham Du Bois felt that her past life had led her inexorably to this point where she could make a profound contribution to the Africa she had first portrayed in her opera *Tom-Tom*. "The television we are planning will be a tremendous channel for education, for increased understanding and for developing and unifying the peoples of Africa. It will

[lift] the African personality before the world in all its beauty and dignity."[22] Some of her plans were realized. When the OAU met in Accra in 1965, Ghana Television "covered all open sessions . . . live. . . . We had both Josephine Baker from Paris and Miriam Makeba from New York here as 'special entertainers.'" Baker was "happy to put" herself at Graham Du Bois's "disposal . . . to sing as many times as you wish."[23] Apparently, this offer was not as gracious as it appeared. Though Graham Du Bois was now being accused of being a "diva" of sorts, she felt that this label should have been applied to her old friend Baker and the South African exile Makeba. "God what I went through with those two temperamental dames!" she wrote to a friend. But it was all worth it, for "people all over Ghana [were] huddled in front of their televison sets watching." This was not just an occasion for political mobilization, it was also a massive educational event.[24]

Ghana Television under her leadership also initiated "school telecasting." They broadcast programs for schools in "Science, Geography, Literature." They also broadcast "an evening programme for illiterates." Her effort to diversify programming had gone in a direction that some in Washington—and Los Angeles—had feared; in 1965 on the forty-eighth anniversary of the Bolshevik Revolution, they featured the "long film 'Lenin in October'" in honor of our Happy Socialist Revolution."[25]

She may not have been pleasing Washington, but apparently Nkrumah was not dissatisfied. Soon she took on the added responsibility of serving as "chairman of the Board of [the] Electrical Manufacturing Corporation." This was a joint venture with the Japanese corporation Sanyo to make "television receiving sets and transistor radios" for Ghana and, presumably, the region.[26] Japan had taken a less hostile stance toward the Nkrumah government, and this operation was symbolic of this policy; on the other hand, Sanyo's competitors in the United States—which within decades were to be virtually driven out of the television manufacturing business—did not greet this coproduction agreement with euphoria.[27] Inevitably the deal helped cement U.S. opposition to the regime in Accra.

Graham Du Bois railed at the idea that her plans exceeded the capabilities of Ghana. "The next time somebody mentions illiteracy in 'just out of colonialism Ghana,'" she said huffily, "I shall send them to Italy—where folks have been 'free' for hundreds of years" and where illiteracy persisted. She was confident about her project and her own capabilities too; she recognized that she did "not know enough about the engineering, the mechanics of television," but she felt that heading Ghana Television should not be left to the "mercy of some technician," and she was sure that she—and Ghana—were up to the task.[28]

At this juncture Shirley Graham Du Bois was one of the most important women on the African continent, if not the world. One of her competitors for this hallowed position, the first woman in space, Valentina Tereshkova, made sure to visit her in Accra, and Graham Du Bois went "dashing about with her." When one of the most important men in the world came to Accra, the Chinese premier Zhou En-lai, he took time to have "a private tea" with her. In Ghana she had found a nation that was in the forefront of African independence and was looked to hopefully by Africans globally; she was a key advisor and intimate friend of Nkrumah, who was not only a political leader but a writer whose words influenced millions. She was giddy with it all: "for the first time in my life I am really part of a dynamic, progressive government which is doing something every day . . . AFRICA is leading the way! I am most fortunate and happy to be in the front ranks."[29]

Certainly the FBI was paying more attention to her, particularly her cozy relationship with Chinese leaders. It took note of the report from the *People's Daily* in China where she praised Mao Zedong and assailed the "hypocrisy and the real face [of] U.S. fascism" that "set dogs on defenceless American Negroes and dropped bombs on the Democratic Republic of Vietnam."[30]

Though her views may have been anathema in Washington, people elsewhere thought otherwise. In the spring of 1965 the United Nations invited her to "represent Ghana at an important continent of Africa conference meeting in Senegal. All expenses paid (handsomely!) by the United Nations." She was "brushing up" on her French, "which is now fairly good," so that if necessary she could fluently assault U.S. foreign and domestic policy. From Senegal she would be going to Liberia to inspect terrain once traveled by her father almost forty years before.[31] But unlike her father, she would be coming as an embodiment of another kind of gospel—the gospel of socialism.

Being interviewed by Chinese journalists, running a television network, entertaining visiting prime ministers and cosmonauts, globetrotting—all this made for a hectic schedule, and Graham Du Bois, who was no stranger to bustle, at times felt overwhelmed. She did have a refuge, her "lovely white and blue house in the midst of . . . beautiful gardens."[32] Her garden was "a thing of sheer beauty . . . [with] thick grass—a ripening bunch of bananas hanging from one tree, another tree is heavy with a luscious tropical fruit . . . the two orange trees stand slender and firm. In a few months they will burst into blossom."[33] It was here that she escaped the frenzy of Accra. This revitalization was necessary because, by her own admission, she had "become a real WORK DRUDGE." She knew she was "overworking," but she felt that the importance of her responsibility left her with few alternatives; ultimately she was to have "six hundred people working under" her, and the administrative burden alone was formidable.[34] This was why she complained in late 1965 that she had just had her "first non-working Sunday in five weeks."[35]

Her U.S. attorney, Bernard Jaffe, was "simply . . . dumbfounded" when he reflected on her immense

> responsibilities . . . Even with your fantastic energy, where on earth can you find the time to do all the things which are required, plus other things that have to be done as well? I dare say that it is no exaggeration to refer to you as the most influential woman in Africa. I have a very strong feeling that you are among the most influential women in the entire world.[36]

The problem with such prestige was that it tended to attract the envious, the jealous, and the simply xenophobic who wondered how someone born in the United States wound up as a leader of Ghana.

Graham Du Bois, who was well aware of her own prominence, did not help matters. Though she saw Josephine Baker and Miriam Makeba as "temperamental dames," others were using harsher language to describe her. In an unpublished memoir she wrote about her time in Ghana, the writer Ella Winter described Graham Du Bois derisively as "something of an old-style Stalinist communist" who "would inveigh against the U.S.'s imperialism at the drop of any pause in almost any conversation." The quick-with-a-quip Winter and her husband, the left-wing screenwriter Donald Ogden Stewart, came to Ghana at the invitation of Nkrumah and Graham Du Bois to assist in the training of writers for television. Rather quickly, Winter—who did not want to come to Africa in the first place—became disillusioned with Graham Du Bois. Why? One reason was the latter's "startlingly foolish" decisions, for example, seeking "to have a barbed wire fence built between Broadcasting House and the Film Corporation," presumably because of simple pique and Winter's key role in the latter. When Winter had the gall to go away for a week without informing her, Graham Du Bois exploded, "shouting and screaming"; this subjectivity combined with erratic behavior was not atypical for her, according to Winter. Graham Du Bois, she alleged, resented her programme director, who was South African, in part because she was "beauteous" and "young."

She also griped about Graham Du Bois's "magnificent, huge, white painted office, with deep leather chairs and sofa and mahogany desk, as befitted a reigning deity." Graham Du Bois, she said, had to be approached as if she were a potentate; "one rarely spoke with the Director. Every comment, question, request, suggestion had to be made in writing with four copies." Worse, Nkrumah himself was a micro-manager, presiding over an administration that was full of scheming. "I learned more about the ways of kings and courts through my nine months in Kwame Nkrumah's Ghana than in a lifetime of university studies."[37]

She described Ghana as wracked with "disaffection, disbelief, disillusion . . . apathy"; everywhere "I saw this inequality between the indigenous population and us white 'expatriates.'" Actually, Accra was a city of stark contrasts, featuring rather modern abodes, such as those of Winter and Graham Du Bois, and hovels that were the lot of all too many Africans.

Winter tended to blame the Accra regime for such abominations rather than the colonial power that had only recently been forced out. She was harshly critical of Nkrumah. She thought him dictatorial and found his determination to build socialism in Ghana absurd. He "did not like to hear bad news," she claimed, "so his subordinates not only kept it from him, they lied to him until finally he was surrounded by sycophants."

But Graham Du Bois was the target of her most bitter scorn. Once Winter accompanied her to Nkrumah's office and they were shunted aside to a reception room. In disbelief, Graham Du Bois wailed with "outraged pride," "'don't you know I'm Mrs. W. E. B. . . .', but we had to wait all the same."

Winter's acerbic comments must be balanced with the simple fact that some of her ideas about Africa and Africans were questionable. She barely acknowledged the ravages induced by colonialism. At one point she wrote, "most Ghanaians have been made lethargic and apathetic by their tropical climate," perhaps unaware of how British policies could have impacted spirit, motivation, and daily reality there.[38] Her comments about Ghana were so one-sided that it is easy to conclude that she may have been discomfited by the notion of having to work alongside a person whose skin was darker than hers. She may have been baffled and bewildered by the then startling idea of reporting to a woman who wielded real power. Still, it would be foolish to dismiss all of her barbs about Graham Du Bois, since so many of them were echoed by others.

Winter's spouse, Donald Ogden Stewart, was a bit more balanced. He liked Nkrumah, for example, and spoke engagingly of the "twenty-five students in [his] class, all around twenty or twenty-five years old. . . . What I had to do was take the lessons I learned in Hollywood and apply them in underdeveloped Ghana." He "did this by trying to get the students to write interestingly about their own lives."[39] Stewart worked hard to make this initiative a success; he also sacrificed, turning down an opportunity to adapt some P. G. Wodehouse stories for television in Britain in order to come to Ghana, though his agent "saw us both making a fortune if it clicked." With a left-wing insouciance, he added, "but what's a fortune, I often say."[40]

Graham Du Bois worked long and hard to bring the couple to Ghana, often referring to "marvellous Ella," enticing her by reminding her with her customary grandiosity that "THIS IS NOW THE FRONT LINE OF THE WORLD'S PROGRESS."[41] Nkrumah himself took time out from matters of state to court her: "Why can't we have in Ghana a Photograph State Enterprise Corporation? And why not set up a Cinema School to train producers, designers of sets, script writers, cameramen, projectionists, directors and artists?" He wanted her to find the "best in films," including documentaries, children's films, cartoons. He wanted her to "accept the Chairmanship of our Ghana Films Industry Corporation"— which unintentionally but perhaps inevitably created a conflict with the director of television.[42] Sooner than expected, Winter and her spouse departed Africa in a huff.

Graham Du Bois's experience with another expatriate she lured to Ghana was more positive. William Gardner Smith was one of the few hundred African Americans who came to Ghana during the time of Nkrumah to help rebuild the continent their ancestors had been torn from centuries ago. In late 1964 he was residing in Paris, serving as head of the Agence France Presse "Far East Section, living in a cozy apartment on the Avenue Gambetta with Solange and six-month old

Michelle."[43] But he left the comforts of France for the rigors of Ghana at Graham Du Bois' invitation. He came to "help organize the news department"; he was impressed with her operation, stating that the

> advance training program for television, for example, was the most comprehensive I had ever seen: every journalist, every producer and actor, learned not only the techniques of his specialty, but also all of the other aspects of television: directing, the use of film and video tape, the handling of cameras and lights, the preparation of sets, etc.

Though he was impressed with Graham Du Bois, his evaluation of some of those surrounding her was less benign. He was appalled with the "universal corruption in high places. Ministers and high officials were using their posts to promote private businesses; they were hiring relatives or fellow tribesmen at high salaries; many of them were salting away money in foreign banks . . . closets full of money were discovered in the homes of some ministers."[44]

Given Graham Du Bois's prominence and influence, her foreign birth, her naïveté in cultivating a friendship with the U.S. ambassador at a time when relations with Ghana were not ideal, and certain ministers' interest in deflecting attention from themselves by pointing to her real and imagined flaws, it was inevitable that not all Ghanaians would view her as positively as did Smith.

Some wondered why an indigenous Ghanaian did not hold the important post of heading the television network. According to her son David, the "established aristocracy" and the "political elite" there had a "general resentment" of Nkrumah's Pan-African policy of welcoming African Americans to toil on behalf of his nation. These Ghanaians were eventually able to outflank Nkrumah's cosmopolitanism with old-fashioned nationalism. There was "particular resentment" among the "personal and political circle" surrounding Nkrumah toward Graham Du Bois and her special relationship with him. "She had access" and others did not; this was "highly resented."

She did not reinforce ties with the United Kingdom, which had been the pattern of the preexisting Ghanaian elite; "powerful and wealthy" Ghanaians did not appreciate this. In fact, she was "determined" to disrupt these ties, which was one reason she cultivated relations with Japan and China. When she "resisted very forcibly" efforts to maintain ties with the United Kingdom—ties that bolstered profitable relationships of long standing—local elites were stunned, then choleric. When she "challenged" the hegemony of London by, for example, brokering deals with Sanyo and bringing in Canadian experts, she "undermined" the ability of some who had profited—"legally and illegally"— from the alliance with Britain. Above all, "upper crust" Ghanaians did not like the fact that foreigners, like Graham Du Bois held high-level posts, and they despised the fact that these expatriates were "progressives" and "socialists." Others did not quite understand her friendship with the U.S. ambassador; her own son "never understood" this "rather peculiar" relationship and why she was "susceptible" to his blandishments. When she intervened in the case of Richard Wright's daughter Julia, who was married to a foreign national suspected of espionage, Graham Du Bois's stock plummeted further.[45] The fact that Graham Du Bois—despite her obvious influence with Nkrumah—was not a member of the ruling party was not helpful in her attempt to maintain her prestige.[46]

Graham Du Bois's manner, which some interpreted as arrogance, did not help matters either. A few months before Nkrumah was overthrown she boasted,

> If I were not on the job watching every angle of television and now preparing for the opening of the Ghana-Sanyo factory—I repeat, if I were not right behind everything—NOTHING WOULD BE HAPPENING. I have been able to bring down the screws whenever certain heads were raised. I have done some spectacular things in the past two months— which I shall not put into writing.[47]

Her "bringing down the screws" was not always viewed fondly. Earlier she bragged of how she faced a "table of engineers and Ghanaian big shots" and told them that "THEY MUST UNDERTAKE A REVISION OF THE GHANAIAN POWER PLANT."[48]

She complained constantly about "enemies of socialism and Africa" who wanted to "infiltrate Ghana and are ready to and anxious to take jobs here." Because she was a member of the National Planning Commission, "which reaches into all national projects," she would make sure that these unnamed "enemies" would not accomplish their objectives.[49] She clashed with powerful Africans, for example, S. G. Ikoku of the Ideological Institute, who accused her of "sending television people

to Winneba to [break] into his house to get [a television] set." She refused to "listen to such accusations."[50]

She also became involved in a row with C. M. V. Forde, a high-level
bureaucrat in the Ghanaian government whose portfolio included
broadcasting. When Forde asked whether she was "responsible to the
Director of Sound Broadcasting" or to the "Engineer-in-Chief of Sound
Broadcasting," Graham Du Bois had a simple answer: she was "responsible" to neither. Forde sought to calm the irate Graham Du Bois;
he "would strongly plead that we avoid imputation of motives."[51] Her
idea that she was "at the hub of the world—making history!" was a
kind of hubris that not everyone understood.[52]

Still, by late 1965 her son was reporting with confidence that the
"opening and successful carrying through of Ghana TV" had made her
"situation considerably more secure and has placed those who want to
'do her in' on the defensive." Nevertheless, he felt compelled to raise
with Nkrumah "our concern about her safety and our wish to see her
withdraw from governmental and financial affairs." She did not withdraw from government, but soon Ghana's "chief architect and his chief
security man arrived at [her] house" to arrange to build a "wall around
the entire place." Her alienation of too many powerful individuals had
obligated her to acquiesce to exceptional security measures. Her son felt
that her "exaggerated militancy and her blind anti-Americanism,"
which clashed oddly with her friendship with the U.S. ambassador, was
creating an untenable situation. He was concerned about her "neglect
of the house and of herself," not to mention her "hesitancy" to spend
"all that money she [was] piling up" after her husband's death. Worse,
her lordly manner was now causing her to treat him, a man approaching forty, like "I am maybe twenty."[53]

Even if Nkrumah had not been overthrown, it is doubtful that
Shirley Graham Du Bois would have survived indefinitely as a prominent government official in Ghana.

■

W. Somerset Maugham once commented that the Euro-American expatriate Henry James wasted much of his life going to English garden parties in the late nineteenth century, thereby missing out on the greatest
story of the age, the emergence of the modern United States. Did
African American expatriates during the 1960s exercise a similar lack of

judgment?[54] More precisely, did African Americans in Ghana—notably Shirley Graham Du Bois—miss out on the greatest domestic story of their age, the mass assault on Jim Crow?

Not necessarily, for she was involved in another story for the ages: the decolonization of Africa. In any case, she was well aware of events back in the United States—her continuing relationship with *Freedomways* guaranteed this—and a constant stream of visitors from the United States to Ghana meant that she could stay abreast of developments. She did feel she was at the "hub" of the world and felt that the example of Ghana and her growing influence could be deployed effectively on behalf of African Americans. When massive civil disobedience hit Birmingham in the spring of 1963, she was quick to react, terming it

> too horrible[.] I turn cold at the thought of children being shut up in those jails! And I feel so helpless to do anything. I am trying to involve Negroes in the North. I have sent editorials and clippings and cartoons from our papers to both the *Afro-American* and the *Pittsburgh Courier* telling them how sincerely and with what deep feeling Ghanaians are following this struggle.[55]

Further evidence of the fact that the African and African American struggles were linked symbiotically was her recollection of the time "details of rioting in Harlem, Brooklyn and Rochester" reached delegates to the OAU meeting in Egypt in 1964. These reports "swept Cairo like wildfire. Every head of state in Cairo was concerned and all felt that a strong and united Africa will be able to alleviate the plight of her dispossessed children."[56] In sum, black expatriates in Ghana not only did not miss out on the epochal events in the United States, they contributed to it mightily by dint of their participation in the other landmark event of the era: Africa's decolonization.

The headline "Big Anti-US Protest in Accra" became a staple in Ghanaian newspapers. Not only were transgressions against what the Ghanaians had begun to term "Afro-Americans" a cause for dismay, but various U.S. policies in Africa riled Ghanaians as well. One front-page editorial exclaimed, "Damn the Yankees!" A spokesman at one demonstration said, "We are telling the Americans that whether they like it or not, Ghana has said YES to Socialism and NO to capitalism."[57] Ghanaians were irked further when K. A. Gbedemah, a former finance minister, was accused of being a CIA agent bent on fomenting a coup, and had embezzled ten million pounds besides.[58]

Washington was displeased when Ghanaian newspapers turned their pages over to U.S. Communists, like Graham Du Bois's friend William Patterson; this "famed U.S. jurist," who was "Afro-American," praised "socialism in Romania."[59] The State Department took note that Ghana trained guerrilla fighters (whom some in Washington felt were no more than "terrorists") for struggles in Southern Africa.[60] To a growing number of U.S. officials it seemed that Ghana was becoming a base for subversion, not only of white minority regimes in Southern Africa but of the United States itself. Not only were suspected Communists like Graham Du Bois—who were reviled in elite circles in the United States—now accorded the highest positions in Ghana, but actual U.S. Communists like James Jackson, Claude Lightfoot, and others were visiting Ghana for reasons that remained mysterious in Washington.

Then Malcolm X, who had only recently departed from the Nation of Islam and was embarking on an ideological journey that seemed unclear, turned up in Ghana in 1964. The conservative columnist Victor Riesel wrote that he witnessed the defrocked Muslim minister meeting with Graham Du Bois at the Hotel Omar Khayyam in Cairo; this was not good news, for "Mrs. Du Bois has long been active in world Communist circles. Her background is important here to show the strange inter-weaving of characters now attempting to infiltrate and agitate the Negro communities of the U.S. Mrs. Du Bois knew the Castro brothers, Fidel and Raoul, in Mexico as far back as the late '40s."[61] The possibility of a "black-red" coalition—black Communists merging with black nationalists—was cause for great anxiety in a United States that was seized with fear of Reds and worried about the rise of black nationalism.

Malcolm X's visit to Ghana may have played a role in his own evolution too. After a local columnist criticized what he saw as Malcolm X's racialist viewpoint, both Graham Du Bois and her friend Julian Mayfield sharply disagreed and tried to reassure Ghanaians that Malcolm was actually on the correct path to socialism.[62] Graham Du Bois denied vehemently that Malcolm was anticommunist—a cardinal sin in Ghana. His protest, she argued further, was against the "White government and the White ruling class" not against all "whites," contrary to the columnist's allegation.[63] The columnist fired back, noting that on returning to the United States, the former NOI leader had undergone a "conversion." The columnist saw as opportunism "the speed with which [Malcolm] shed the [narrow nationalist] views he had expressed at Lagos and Legon"; he assailed the "blind racialism" Malcolm reputedly expressed as "crippling and destructive." Graham Du Bois in her response had spoken of how the former NOI leader "took time out of his heavy schedule during the short visit here to come to our house and take pictures of the library, the summer house, the beautiful gardens." These words were rebuked as "irrelevancies" by her interlocutor; instead he noted—and not necessarily inaccurately—that Malcolm's "conversion" (his rejection of the idea that all whites were "devils") occurred when "he . . . saw white men from many different countries without any apparent interest in economic exploitation helping to develop emergent Africa."[64] Yet Malcolm, it was felt, was not sufficiently courageous to attribute his metamorphosis to socialist Ghana; instead he credited events in feudal Saudi Arabia.

This was part of the contradiction of U.S. politics: the influential Malcolm X had returned to the United States in 1964 claiming that his visit to Saudi Arabia, where he had seen fair-skinned Muslims, had convinced him to back away from his "racialist" ideas, but it was more likely that his trip to Ghana caused this effect; after all, he had first visited the Arab peninsula in 1959 and was not unfamiliar with the phenomenon of melanin-deficient Muslims. It was not only seeing Eastern Europeans, Canadians, and British exiles aiding "emergent Africa" that probably helped to change his mind, but also observing black radicals who had no problem with this. In any case, this "conversion" should have been welcomed in all quarters in the United States; however, if the "conversion" resulted from an experience in "socialist" Ghana—which was coming to be seen as a sworn enemy of the United States—this experience would not necessarily be greeted favorably.[65] Sadly, anticommunism hindered the progress of interracial harmony.

Months after his return from Ghana, Malcolm was still effervescent about his journey. Not only did this African pilgrimage influence his thinking on race, it also shaped his thinking on gender. In a December 1964 interview he talked at length about the role of women in postcolonial Africa, exhibiting a range and sensitivity he had rarely shown to that point. This view on gender may have been swayed by his rendezvous with Shirley Graham Du Bois, whom he characterized effusively as "one of the [most] intelligent women I've ever met." At length he described how she chaperoned him on his tour of her massive television studio and of various regions in the sprawling West African nation.[66]

To the chagrin of some of her fellow "Afro-Americans," Graham Du Bois was at the center of the controversy involving Malcolm X's visit. Maya Angelou, then residing in Ghana, complained that Graham Du Bois was "as elusive as smoke in high wind" and "deliberately inaccessible," yet when Minister Malcolm showed up, all of a sudden Graham Du Bois could be found readily—at his side.

Graham Du Bois, said Angelou, was "a medium-sized, light brown-skinned woman with large eyes, a long attractive face and the confidence of Mount Kilimanjaro." When Malcolm arrived at a party at the Chinese embassy, Graham Du Bois "walked immediately to Malcolm and, taking him by the arm, guided him to a corner where they sat. . . . After nearly an hour, Shirley and Malcolm emerged from their retreat and rejoined the party." Graham Du Bois then "said loudly, 'This man is brilliant. I am taking him for my son. He must meet Kwame. They have too much in common not to meet.'" Angelou may not have been aware of Graham Du Bois's penchant for "taking" men as "sons" and acting as a "mother" to them. In any event, Angelou "was in a rage." She fumed to her housemates that earlier, Graham Du Bois "could have arranged a meeting in seconds" for Malcolm with Nkrumah, but "before she wouldn't even see [Malcolm]. I can't stand that." When Malcolm himself asked Angelou what she thought of the target of her ire, she "let loose," condemning Graham Du Bois in virulent terms. Malcolm listened, then told Angelou that her attitude was "very childish, dangerously immature."[67] It was gallant of Malcolm X to come to the defense of Graham Du Bois, but Angelou's opinion was widely shared. The even-tempered, unflappable Jean Carey Bond, an African American living in Ghana at the time, was forced to say that Graham Du Bois viewed herself as "royalty."[68]

Part of this conflict over Malcolm X stemmed from the fact that some considered Graham Du Bois a "Juanita-come-lately" to a form of black nationalism that was bursting onto the scene. She was seen as a Communist who belatedly and opportunistically was trying to ride the wave of an ascending nationalism. Actually she was trying to meld both of these powerful ideologies, but this amalgamation was not widely recognized at this early date.

Whatever the case, she took to Malcolm as if he were a long lost son. She was his de facto hostess in Accra—which annoyed more than a few—and arranged a coveted meeting with Nkrumah. She told her *Freedomways* colleague John Henrik Clarke that she wanted him to "co-author" a book on Malcolm with her. She wanted to "dig deep into all this, showing the pain, frustrations and desperation of black boys with no money, no prestige of family and status . . . [and] expose all the reasons for delinquency, crime, fear and hate." "Keep this entirely confidential," she said, not missing an opportunity to signal her importance, for she would discuss this proposal with Ghana's "State Publishing House. (And I am one of the directors of this corporation.)"[69] Clarke, a self-proclaimed "left nationalist" who knew the former NOI leader, was a natural choice to work on this project. After Malcolm's return to Harlem, Clarke "talked with [him] about this visit with Nkrumah and his talk with him. He has the highest praise for you both," he told her reassuringly.[70]

Naturally, when Malcolm X later traveled to Cairo, Graham Du Bois's son David hosted him. He saw the former Nation of Islam minister "regularly" and assisted him with various tasks.

> He is growing in understanding and conviction every day. . . . I think he is an honest man who is beginning to realize how much he does *not* know about the world around him. . . . I am convinced that if he is only allowed to live he will emerge as the most important Negro leader since the days of Reconstruction—mass leader that he is. (Emphasis in original)[71]

Tragically, he was not "allowed to live"; he was murdered in February 1965. Graham Du Bois was more tormented than most when this happened, not least because she was evolving away from her bedrock socialist beliefs to a kind of "left nationalism" that Malcolm symbolized and John Henrik Clarke professed. This was evident in her written defense of Malcolm in the face of attacks from the Ghanaian press, as well as her idea that "Afro-American is a word most white people hate and *fear*" (emphasis in original).[72]

After Malcolm's death she shared her post mortem of him with Langston Hughes whom she had known since their playwrighting days in the 1930s. "Unlike the majority of Afro-Americans who make the 'tour of Africa,'" she confided, "Malcolm came and learned. He did not take his 'briefings' from foreign embassies. He sought out and listened to Africans—those in high places and on all levels. . . . As time passed we learned to honor and love him as we did no Afro-American who has crossed this continent."[73] These glowing words were accompanied by a material gesture of support: through their mutual friend Ruby Dee, she forwarded five hundred dollars to his widow, Betty Shabazz.[74]

Malcolm X's encounter with Africa was emblematic of a larger African American engagement with Ghana during this period. Many U.S. citizens of African descent began to identify with Africa in the 1960s. This not only meant using slogans like "Black is beautiful," it also meant ceasing to straighten their hair, adopting West African names and modes of dress, and using terms like "Afro-American." It also meant the glorification of figures like Nkrumah. It was ironic that the Red Scare, in undermining unions and class consciousness, helped spawn a kind of nationalism that led some African Americans, at least, back to a socialist icon like Nkrumah.[75]

Consequently, hundreds of "Afro-Americans" expatriated to Ghana to assist in nation building. Architects like Max Bond, librarians like Jean Blackwell Hutson, lawyers like Pauli Murray came, and there were many more who wanted to follow in their footsteps.[76] E. Franklin Frazier did not come to live in Ghana, but Graham Du Bois made sure that his vast collection of books was deposited in the library there.[77]

For most of these exiles, living in Ghana was a positive experience; not so for Murray, who complained of the "growing uneasiness and fear among civil servants and intellectuals. . . . I was told I might be deported if I wrote an article for publication in the United States that, in the opinion of the Ghana government, was critical of its policies." During the crisis in the Congo in the early 1960s, "the government controlled press contemptuously referred to Dr. Ralph Bunche as a 'stooge of imperialism' and soon began applying the same phrase to American Negroes generally." Agents of the government began attending her class, she recalled; then she fell ill with malaria. She did not mention that a former "American Negro" encouraging Ghana to stand fast against "U.S. imperialism" was Shirley Graham Du Bois.[78]

Murray finally departed Ghana, disillusioned and saddened by what she had experienced. Yet other "American Negroes" longed to take her place; this could be a burden for Graham Du Bois, a well-recognized personality known to have the ear of Nkrumah. She once remarked, "I am constantly receiving letters from Afro-Americans who want to come to Ghana."[79] Writing from Detroit, Fairfield Butler expressed the sentiments of many when he asked Graham Du Bois for information on expatriation "due to the racial climate in this country. I personally feel that conditions are going to become excruciatingly insufferable for the Negro here in the future. So leaving would be my attempt to offer my kids a wholesome and promising future."[80] These hopes found some sympathy in Accra. Regina Asamany, a member of Parliament, told Graham Du Bois that her "people of the Volta Region are willing to grant pieces of land to settle our black brothers and sisters from America."[81] This "'Back to Africa' deal," she continued, "is calculated to be symbolic of our consciousness and determination to emancipate all peoples of color." Like the U.S. Communists of the 1930s she stressed that this nationalist idea *"shall be ancillary to [the] fight for equality in the USA itself"* (emphasis in original). These fine intentions were never realized, however; a reason may have been that the plan was meant to apply only to "the most responsible Negroes who accept [Nkrumah's] progressive policies," people like Paul Robeson and the boxer Cassius Clay (soon to be known widely as Muhammad Ali), for example—not necessarily the less well-known, like Fairfield Butler of Detroit.[82]

African Americans had run into the bitter reality that an underdeveloped Africa could only use those with capital or well-defined skills. Thus, when she sought to attract the brethren from across the Atlantic to Ghana, Graham Du Bois reached out to figures like Duke Ellington, whom she wanted to "dig down into the marvelous stores of West African music and bring it to its highest development" and teach what he knew to Ghanaians.[83]

During this period, Ghana was becoming a regular stop for prominent African Americans. Thurgood Marshall, Horace Mann Bond, Congressman Charles Diggs, and the labor leader Maida Springer were among the many who made this journey. Usually they were debriefed by the State Department when they returned. After the spirited 28 August 1963 demonstration of many African Americans at the U.S. embassy in Accra, which was set to coincide with the massive March on Washington, concern about the impact of such activity on global public opinion escalated. Signifying the importance of the African–African American connection was the fact that U.S. government personnel not only transcribed the slogans on the demonstrators' placards but also tried to transcribe all the names on the petitions submitted in solidarity with the Washington march. This level of scrutiny was not accorded to those participating in other demonstrations of sympathy on that momentous day in cities as diverse as Paris, Munich, Tel Aviv, and Oslo.[84]

As Pauli Murray had suggested, the Ghanaian government increasingly viewed African Americans not as prodigal sons and daughters to be welcomed back home but as surrogates of imperialism. Increasingly, Graham Du Bois was leaning toward this viewpoint as well. "Some Afro-Americans here," she believed,

> proved to be as imperialistic and selfish as the oppressors whom Ghana were determined to throw off. . . . [they] were not above joining with those who plotted to wipe out the most cherished ideals of the state. . . . a goodly number of Afro-Americans in Ghana have come here for exactly the same reasons that Europeans have been coming to Africa for centuries: better and easier living and quick profits to take back home. . . . A large number of Afro-Americans, like Americans as a whole, feel quite capable of "enlightening" the "backward Africans" on anything and everything! Such people irritate the Ghanaians. . . . There are some Afro-Americans who quite clearly are in the pay of somebody or something outside of Ghana.[85]

She was living a paradox. She was developing a nationalism that tended to subsume class and ideological differences among African Americans under the guise of "race." Yet in her day-to-day existence she realized instinctively that it was impossible for anyone—even "Afro-Americans"—to reside in the United States for centuries without being influenced by its dominant culture and philosophy. She reminded the black journalist and activist George Murphy that this meant "it is far more important right now for Africans to speak clearly to each other than for us to speak to the people of the United States"—even those who happened to be black.[86]

This skepticism directed at Afro-Americans was extended to those whose political credentials were otherwise impeccable. When the journalist Bill Worthy, who courageously violated the ban on traveling to China during this same period, sought her aid in traveling with Nkrumah on his ill-fated journey to Hanoi, Graham Du Bois demurred. "I cannot presume to tell the President," she declared, "whom he should invite to accompany him on a confidential, diplomatic mission. I know he would not think of taking an American with him on such a mission!"[87]

She was similarly unhelpful to her old friend Cedric Belfrage, a man of the Left who was instrumental in initiating the progressive newspaper the *National Guardian*. He had inquired about the air force in Ghana and she reminded him that "all emphasis is on training and using Ghanaians in every project. This does not mean that experts are not here from all over the world." Anyway, she did "not have the slightest idea about how an outsider could contact" them.[88]

Rightly or wrongly, some of her closest friends resented the fact that she was not more helpful in securing posts for them in Ghana. What her friends did not always recognize is that her powers were not unlimited. Once she said wistfully, "nearly every Afro-American I meet who wants to work in Africa, wants to come to Ghana."[89] Her inability to help them bothered her: "my heart bleeds when talented young Afro-Americans are brought to my attention and I am asked to give them an opportunity to use their abilities!" But she could hire only "professional experts," particularly in television, and had to turn away droves of applicants.[90] Among those turned away was Robert F. Williams, the former NAACP leader who was forced to go into exile in Cuba, then China. Though finding him "brave" and "gallant," she concluded, "there is nothing he could do in Ghana. Africa doesn't need 'leaders.' It does need the help of skilled technicians, experienced and exceedingly well trained."[91]

She was not always unhelpful. When the musician Pete Seeger came there in January 1965, she arranged "good audiences" for him and facilitated his "research in music and culture."[92] However, when Nkrumah was toppled and Graham Du Bois found that she no longer was a powerful advisor to a powerful leader, some of her friends deserted her on the grounds that she had not helped them.[93]

As 1965 wound down, it was evident that the United States had become exasperated with Nkrumah, his government, and aides like Shirley Graham Du Bois. At first they tried to treat her gingerly. When in late 1963 she applied for a visa to come to the United States to attend a memorial for her late husband, the Accra embassy advised that "Kwame Nkrumah . . . and the Ghanaian press will be severely critical of the United States Government if subject is denied a visa."[94]

Graham Du Bois continued to write articles for Communist journals rebuking U.S. policy in the region. In some ways she was the United States' worst nightmare in that she not only condemned its policies in left publications, she also wrote for the journal of the Nation of Islam, *Muhammad Speaks*. On the day President Kennedy was murdered, this weekly carried an article by Graham Du Bois asking rhetorically, "should Negroes welcome moral support from Chinese foes of 'our white folks'?" Her evolving left nationalist philosophy saw no merit in the rejection of Mao Zedong by the NAACP leader Roy Wilkins and the civil rights leader James Farmer. Of the latter she said caustically, "what kind of brainwashing can bring a black man lying in a Louisiana jail, to bite the hand [of Mao that] is stretched out to help him?" She continued,

> decent people throughout the world hail Chairman Mao Tse-tung's call to unite against racial discrimination. . . . Never before has such an appeal been made to the world by the head of a large and powerful state. . . . the wealth, prosperity and advancement of the United States were built on the annihilation of one people (the American Indian) and the enslavement of another,

so, she thought, why should U.S. civil rights leaders repulse another "colored" group, Chinese leaders, who wanted to assist them?[95]

As time passed, Graham Du Bois began to lean more toward China in its ongoing ideological dispute with the Soviet Union because, in her estimation, China linked the battle for socialism with the struggle against white supremacy; this dovetailed neatly with her own evolving left nationalist philosophy. The problem was that the Chinese were left nationalists of a peculiar sort and at times, for example, in Angola in 1975, their perception of their national interests did not always coincide with the best interests of Africa.

Neither her time in Ghana nor her friendship with the U.S. ambassador lessened her hostility to white supremacy. As "Southern Rhodesia" in November 1965 approached its Unilateral Declaration of Independence, meant to thwart African majority rule, Graham Du Bois was indignant: "we are about to make war on Great Britain! I was in Parliament when my President made this speech"; if the U.K. did nothing to restrain its rebellious colony, "this will mean WORLD WAR!"[96] Not only "world war" was in the offing, but "race war" as well, and "the consequences will be terrible." "The situation is extremely critical," she noted with stark understatement; Ghana was "solid behind" Nkrumah, and "some African countries are ready to join Ghana in military action NOW!"[97] Not only Rhodesia was fomenting "race war" and "world war." "South Africa," she once told John

Henrik Clarke, "is rapidly bringing us to the brink of war—and this will mean THE THIRD WORLD WAR!"[98]

Finally, the United States and its allies had had enough of Nkrumah's government. In February 1966 while on his way to Hanoi, Nkrumah was overthrown by military officers, who quickly pledged their loyalty to the same U.S. government that Graham Du Bois had admonished repeatedly. She was ousted from Ghana, barely escaping the imprisonment, beatings—even murder—accorded other advisors of Nkrumah.

9

Detour

ON 24 FEBRUARY 1966, while Nkrumah was on his way to Hanoi in an effort to broker peace between the United States and Vietnam, he was overthrown by his military. The coup in Ghana was a decisive turning point in the life of Shirley Graham Du Bois, ranking with the death of her son Robert during World War II and her marriage to Du Bois in 1951. It forced her to conduct an excruciating reappraisal of her life to that point and compelled critical changes in her outlook.

■

Though the U.S. ambassador to Ghana, William Mahoney, may have been making nice with Graham Du Bois, he was not as generous toward her leader, Kwame Nkrumah whom he condescendingly described as "preeminently the 'mixed-up kid' . . . vain and easily bruised."[1] Nkrumah, according to another U.S. official who also portrayed the Ghanaian as infantile, "takes pleasure in receiving gifts of any kind, and he is entranced by mechanical toys and gadgets."[2]

The embassy was concerned about Communist influence in Ghana, demonstrations at its headquarters (particularly when its Afro-American employees were targeted with abuse), and negotiations between Accra and U.S. transnational corporations about building the Volta Dam. There was anxiety when China extended a $22.4 million credit to Ghana and worry about the growing number of left-wing exiles and Soviet citizens roaming around Accra.[3] There was uneasiness at the embassy—and at Texaco—when the Italian state oil corporation, ENI, contemplated marketing Soviet crude oil in Ghana.[4]

In early 1964 embassy officials concluded that Nkrumah—for reasons that eluded them—"has become thoroughly, probably irreversibly convinced that 'the Americans' are out to overthrow him by any means."[5] Despite their wonder at why Nkrumah would think such a thing, a CIA "intelligence information cable" in February 1964 did

reveal that "agents of the Ghana United Party will make another assassination attempt on the life" of Nkrumah, possibly within ten days.[6]
The agency, in short, had detailed information about the internal political dynamics of Ghana.

Still, they were taken aback when Malcolm X came to Accra; the
embassy sought urgent consultations with Nkrumah who "listened patiently if somewhat abstractedly while" the U.S. official "filled him in."
He instructed the Ghanaian leader that "it would be unfortunate if
[Malcolm X] was to use Ghana as [a] propaganda platform and [it]
would be particularly hard for responsible Negro leadership in [the]
United States to understand. Nkrumah nodded but made no response."[7] The embassy was heartened when a "responsible Negro"
leader, James Farmer, came to Accra; he was "helpful" and "able [to]
undo in part [the] damage caused by two Malcolm X visits." But officials were angered that Farmer's press coverage was minuscule compared to that accorded the charismatic former NOI leader. There was
growing apprehension that alignment with or opposition to Ghana
would precipitate rifts among Afro-Americans in the United States,
with serious consequences for U.S. foreign policy. Thus, when an Afro-
American employee of the embassy, Adger Player, exhibited "bravery
in protecting the American Flag" during a demonstration in Accra, he
heard directly from President Lyndon Baines Johnson.[8]

Junior officers at the Accra embassy were also dissatisfied with
Ghana's policies. This became evident when Ghana sought to improve
its energy resources by constructing a huge dam. Nkrumah sought aid
for this project from the socialist camp. James Engle, who served in
Ghana from 1961 to 1963, opposed the Volta Dam because of Accra's ties
to Moscow; these ties meant "we were spending a great deal of time
looking at Ghana, compared to other parts of Africa," which today, he
considers a "mistake." The U.S. transnational Kaiser, which was involved with the Volta Dam project, pressured the embassy to accommodate Nkrumah, he recalled. Chad Calhoun of Kaiser "was sort of our
second ambassador there . . . he had entree into the White House . . .
quite often his judgments were exactly the contrary" to the State Department's. Engle was hostile to Accra and, by comparison, felt there
was "Nkrumah worship" at Foggy Bottom.[9]

Robert Smith, served in Ghana from 1965 to 1966; Jack Matlock, a
"junior political officer" who later served in Moscow during the dissolution of the Soviet Union, was in Accra with him gaining useful expe-

rience. Smith felt that Nkrumah "seemed to be, at times, almost losing his mind." He confided that Ghana's ambassador to the United States, Michael Ribiero, "hated Nkrumah privately," which did not help Accra in arguing its case in Washington.[10]

Willard De Pree served in Ghana from 1964 to 1968 as "chief of the political section." He felt that cocoa farmers were "unhappy" since the government bought their produce "cheap" and tried to "sell it at a better price" in order to gain revenue for social programs. Nigeria was not happy with Nkrumah, he said, since Accra was "supporting opposition elements" there, so Lagos "readily shared their information" about Ghana "with us." He was unhappy not only with Soviet influence in Ghana but also with the "Fabian socialism" propagated by advisors from the London School of Economics. He too was a hard-liner toward Nkrumah, feeling that Ambassador Mahoney "had an exceptional relationship with Nkrumah" that "in retrospect maybe . . . was too close." He too felt that Kaiser had significant impact on U.S. policy. "Edgar Kaiser used to come to Ghana a couple of times a year. It was always seen as a big event in Ghana." His "smelter turned out to be one of Kaiser's most profitable investments."[11]

In sum, frustration with the Nkrumah government, which provided sinecures to Communists like Graham Du Bois, was growing apace in Washington, at all levels. Nkrumah's book published in late 1965, *Neo-Colonialism: The Last Stage of Imperialism*, particularly infuriated the U.S. assistant secretary of state for Africa, G. Mennen Williams. He viewed the volume as an insult to the United States and provided the embassy with a laundry list of actions to protest its publication; he added ominously, "other opportunities to show our displeasure will be utilized as they occur."[12] Robert Smith agreed that the book was "awful." When Ambassador Ribiero met with Assistant Secretary Williams, Smith was mesmerized. "I had never heard Soapy Williams raise his voice until that conversation" about Nkrumah's book; "neither have I ever heard an ambassador get a tongue lashing like Ribiero got." Williams "was raising his voice. He was shaking his finger in the ambassador's face. And it was . . . very painful." Reflecting on that event, Smith concluded that "the publication of that book might also have contributed in a . . . way to [Nkrumah's] overthrow shortly thereafter."[13]

Nkrumah consciously styled his book as a complement to V. I. Lenin's notion that "imperialism" was the "highest stage of capitalism." The book begins with a quotation from the Bolshevik leader on "finance capital" and how it is "concentrated in a few hands." In its well-documented pages, Nkrumah presents an unflattering portrait of the United States, indicting such hallowed institutions as the AFL-CIO, Hollywood, the Peace Corps, the CIA, and so on. On the other hand, he provides glowing compliments for the "impressive" aid coming from China and the Soviet Union, "since it is swift and flexible . . . interest rates on communist loans are only about two percent compared with five to six percent charged on loans from western countries." That this book was published in the United States by the Communist Party's publishing house could not have pleased Washington either.[14]

The United States countered Nkrumah's literature by flooding Ghana with its own. Henry Dunlap, who served in Ghana from 1957 to 1959, recalled later that "we helped newspapers that were established . . . we distributed pamphlets" in the tens of thousands. They had clear "psychological objectives." They also showed films—countering Graham Du Bois's efforts—at times "in an auditorium" and other times "at night under a banyan tree."[15]

Nkrumah's book by itself was not enough to incur significant anger in Washington, but in combination with his other activities—for example, welcoming Communists like Graham Du Bois to Accra—it was enough to cause the United States to turn violently against him.

On the day of the coup in February 1966, Robert Smith was at the State Department headquarters in Washington. He bumped into Secretary of State Dean Rusk and informed him of the epochal developments. The balding, rotund secretary "broke into an ear-splitting grin." Smith had "never seen [him] look so happy."[16]

It was understandable why Rusk, a scholar of international law, was so elated. The Ghana coup was another in a series of events welcomed by U.S. officials in recent months, including the virtual elimination of the Communist Party in Indonesia and the overthrow of the Ben Bella regime in Algeria. The *New York Times* concluded that "1966 seems to have become Africa's year of retribution, 'the year of the generals,'" as military coups erupted across the continent.[17] There may have been additional, more specific reasons for Rusk's joy, however: Washington played a material role in dislodging Nkrumah, supporting and advising the officers who led the coup.[18]

Washington's joy was Graham Du Bois's agony. The ousting of Nkrumah turned her into a woman without a country, sailing from port to port in search of refuge.

A pliant press corps demonized Nkrumah as a "Stalin-like enemy of the U.S."[19] John Stockwell, a former CIA operative in West Africa, has written that the

> Accra station . . . was given a generous budget and maintained inti-mate contact with the plotters as a coup was hatched. So close was the station's involvement that it was able to coordinate the recovery of some classified Soviet military equipment by the United States as the coup took place. . . . inside CIA headquarters the Accra station was given full, if unofficial, credit for the eventual coup in which eight So-viet advisors were killed. None of this was adequately reflected in the agency's written records.[20]

According to one writer, "not long before the coup the staff of the U.S. Embassy in Ghana mushroomed considerably, exceeding the personnel of the Russian and Chinese embassies together. . . . [there was also] rapid growth in the number of Peace Corps volunteers."[21] Washington viewed the coup as a staggering blow to its adversaries—and Graham Du Bois's friends—in Moscow and particularly Beijing.[22]

Weeks before Nkrumah was overthrown, Ambassador Mahoney was replaced by an Afro-American, Franklin Williams, a former NAACP official.[23] Williams's "possible involvement . . . in the 1966 coup" has been suggested.[24] His subsequent actions did nothing to erode this idea. Hours after the coup he told the White House aide Bill Moyers that "we have been extremely fortunate in what has occurred. All the personalities associated with the coup are strong friends of ours . . . this was a positive coup . . . Bill, this is the kind of change people like you and I hope for." He continued, "this government now deserves our fullest support—we wanted it, we have it, we can keep it—if repeat, if we do what is necessary."[25] Williams, a lawyer like Dean Rusk, did not ponder the legal implications of aiding the overthrow of a lawful regime.[26]

Apparently the United States had done what was "necessary," for it had cultivated the Ghanaian military. Willard De Pree, chief of the po-litical section in the Accra embassy in 1966, said the coup was "not that unexpected"; the army "was friendly to the West. Our Defense Attache had very good contacts. So too did many of us in the embassy . . . they had been trained by the British . . . [many] fought in World War II in Burma." The embassy and the CIA collected a considerable amount of information informally, he recalled, for example, by attending parties or engaging in casual conversations, such as those held between Ambassador Mahoney and Graham Du Bois. "Many" in the new "government were rather vindictive," he recalled sadly, but, as Franklin Williams had noted, the United States was "extremely fortunate" when the coup occurred.[27]

In retrospect, Graham Du Bois's and others' highly charged words about going to war over Rhodesia may have been the final straw for the army, which, after all, would have been the ones dodging bullets if the possibility had been realized. Or so said Colonel A. A. Afrifa, trained at Sandhurst, and already upset about being posted previously in the Congo. This white minority regime in Southern Africa had exasperated the Nkrumah government when it blocked the path to African majority rule. After Rhodesia's Unilateral Declaration of Independence in November 1965 and the subsequent rhetorical outbursts from Graham Du Bois and others, "it became common conversation among the officers and the men that military action against Nkrumah's regime was the only solution."[28] Likewise, one of Nkrumah's aides felt that the "presence of white commanders of our forces constituted a most serious embarrassment to Ghana" in light of its Pan-African verbiage; these mostly British officers were not necessarily politically reliable either, it was thought.[29]

Nkrumah's overthrow was part of an amazing wave of political instability in Africa, which was so widespread that it made the coup in Ghana seem almost "normal," thereby reducing the effectiveness of Graham Du Bois's impassioned defense of the Nkrumah regime. Nigeria during this period was rocked by political instability. In October 1965 there was an unsuccessful coup in Burundi that led to a bloody denouement months later. Southern Rhodesia illegally declared independence on 11 November 1965. On 25 November 1965 Joseph Mobutu came to power in the Congo. Shortly thereafter the government of the nation then known as Dahomey was toppled. A few weeks later the government of the Central African Republic was overthrown. After that a coup attempt in Congo-Brazzaville failed—barely. In February 1966 the coup in Ghana succeeded—decisively.[30]

■

By the time of the coup, Shirley Graham Du Bois was close to seventy years old, though she appeared—and professed to be—much younger.

The coup was a shattering experience for her; it sent her into a form of semiretirement, eroded her position as one of Africa's most influential women, forced her to move to Cairo (after a period of virtually homeless wandering), and pushed her in political directions that would alienate her from some of her oldest comrades.

Though she was surprised by the coup, there were signs of impending distress that could have alerted her to turbulence ahead. In early 1965 she complained of Ghana's "real economic squeeze . . . and unless we can pull some rabbits out of the hat—the enemies will succeed."[31] She had studied the "Latin American style military junta" that overthrew Nkrumah's African ally, Algeria's Ben Bella: "no one will ever convince me that the man who struck him down is anything but a power-mad traitor," she declared with her typical fervor.[32]

These signs were not heeded. Weeks before the coup, she applied for a thirty-day visa to visit the United States, noting that she had not been to the "land of my birth" since October 1961, but now she wanted to "visit my brothers in California, friends in the New York area," and others. To giver her application weight, she mentioned casually Ghana Television's relationship with Ampex International Operations in California. Despite her alleged friendship with the U.S. ambassador, her visa was denied.[33]

Perhaps a sense of approaching doom caused her to counsel Nkrumah not to make the fateful trip to Hanoi. He ignored her advice.[34] The recent clandestine visit of the Cuban revolutionary Che Guevara, who "came to see" them "just before [Nkrumah] got ready to go to Hanoi," may have persuaded Nkrumah that it was "neo-colonial" regimes that were on the verge of being dislodged, not his.[35]

Her schedule in February 1966 was typical. It included meetings with Sanyo executives and the ambassador from Lebanon, dinner with the Pakistan high commissioner and the U.S. ambassador, a reception hosted by Ceylon's high commissioner, and numerous meetings with officials of the Pan Africanist Congress, a South African resistance movement then leaning toward the Maoist outlook that she was to adopt.[36]

She lived near Flagstaff House, where Nkrumah resided, and there was a military base not far from her home. About 4 A.M. on 24 February 1966 a loud noise awakened her; she arose and noticed there were people in her yard. "In the garden were running feet." She called out, "What's the matter?" She then turned on her radio, and just before

6 A.M. "somebody came on . . . to say that the military had seized the government and all citizens were requested not to leave their homes." By this time she could hear a "real battle going on in front of Flagstaff House. It was by no means a bloodless coup."

She heard what sounded like "the clatter of machine guns." She called out her window, "Lock the gates!" The "noise came nearer." Her "house shook." She "heard glass breaking. . . . Around [her] home, always within hearing, raged a battle that continued intermittently throughout the day." By this point she "was thoroughly awake." Soldiers came to tell her that she "was under house arrest"; fortunately, they treated her "very much better than they treated other women."[37] However, the soldiers were certain she had privileged information about Nkrumah that might be useful.[38]

Shortly thereafter, her "brother from California and [her] lawyer from New York rushed" to Ghana to rescue her; she was not spared interrogation and detention, however. She

> learned afterwards that lots of people in various parts of the world cabled the "authorities" asking about me. And finally they let me leave with my brother and lawyer for "three months leave" in England. Then they seized my home, carted off W. E. B.'s library—including, of course, all my books and research papers—ordered my help and caretakers off the premises and put one of the "new judges" into it. . . . Before we left we packed a few cartons and sent them to storage. I could take nothing with me except my suitcases. Not even any of my own money which was in the bank.[39]

Her son later confessed that "she was unable to tell me anything about what had happened to her in Accra, but apparently it had been a horrifying experience for her. She could hardly talk."[40] This last fact was suggestive of the trauma that the normally loquacious Graham Du Bois had endured, a trauma that was heightened by what befell her friends. The wife of her friend Julian Mayfield was "taken away" and "deported."[41] Mayfield's spouse, Ana Livia Cordero, was a "very able Puerto Rican woman doctor who was head of an important clinic"; she "was taken from her home not long ago. . . . Two others, a Negro American and the English (a good man) head of the School of Administration, Ghana University, were deported at the same time. A very nasty editorial featuring me recently appeared in the Ghana press."[42]

Julian Mayfield, after reporting that Graham Du Bois was "in London in a state of shock," stated that "the death toll" in Accra was "conservatively . . . 1800." "I can't believe it," he continued, "Africans at Addis Ababa were saying that three to four thousand had been killed."[43] Though "the new regime is under great stress . . . Ghanaians were genuinely happy at the overthrow of Nkrumah, and they thought that freedom and prosperity had arrived on 24th February. Unfortunately things are much worse."[44]

Graham Du Bois and other Nkrumah supporters portrayed post-February Ghana as a sullen nation just waiting to rise up against the coupmakers; supposedly there were allies in Cairo willing to join in. In March 1966 her son David, writing from Cairo where he had gone a few years earlier to work as a journalist, said that "resistance continues daily and will grow. . . . The man-on-the-street here is ready to take gun in hand and join a liberation army for Ghana. He just awaits a way."[45]

Nkrumah himself was caustic in rebuking the coup plotters and those "politicians" who backed them, to whom he applied what he felt was the ultimate insult: they were, he said, "old women."[46] The actual "old woman" who was his aide, Graham Du Bois, got off comparatively easy. His British advisor Geoffrey Bing "had his clothes and shoes torn off him and was made to walk up and down barefoot and to stand up and sit down in repeated succession without being able to use his hands." He was tortured. "The soldiers, he said, tore all his clothes from his body except for his underpants. . . .[when] they tore the shoes from his feet" he suffered "injury and pain. . . . They stuck a bayonet into him and his back became smothered with blood." His "wife was attacked and molested." Other women were subjected to "brutality, sadism, molestation and rape." "Racketeers, smugglers, profiteers, spivs and swindlers" assumed hegemony in the new government. His opponents were responsible for the "shooting and killing of defenceless men and women . . . the arrest, detention and assassination of Ministers, the Party's civil servants, trade unionists." There were "2500 murdered; more than 3000 wounded, tortured, and maimed." He blamed the CIA for aiding the coup and noted pointedly that "not one of the officers trained in the Soviet Union took part in the February rising."[47] Liberation fighters from Southern Africa "have been sent back home."

Others on the scene did not share this outrage at the coup leaders. Sylvia Boone, a friend of Graham Du Bois and a future Yale professor then residing in Accra, recalled that "like the day of Kennedy's death,

one will always remember what one was doing the day of the coup."
She was "crying" as "thousands of people were rounded up and ar-
rested." But "after 2 days absolute hilarity broke out." People

> were (are) generally delighted. There was a parade everyday—stu-
> dents, market women, army wives, young pioneers (!), even the jock-
> eys on their horses—laughing, chanting, praising the new govern-
> ment, damning the old. . . . Since there were no more hated 'security
> men' everyone here felt free to express his opinions. . . . damnation of
> [Nkrumah] was total.

But even Boone had sad tales to report, for her friend, the writer
"Maryse Conde, had a very bitter experience. One of her very 'close
friends', in order to 'save' herself, informed that she was an agent for
[Guinea's] Sekou Toure. . . . She was jailed but by bribing a guard she
got him to call her boyfriend . . . who was able to get her out." Interestingly, "communists" were conflated with "Afro-Americans and the
rest" and condemned—this may have reflected the large role of the alleged Communist, the Afro-American Graham Du Bois.[48]

Later Graham Du Bois told the British Communist R. Palme Dutt
that she was "fully aware" that she was "wanted in Ghana and that" she
must be "careful not to be found in any country from which" she
"might be extradited." She added, "In my preliminary interrogation I
stated clearly that I had nothing to 'confess' or to 'condemn, retract or
regret.' In most cases uncooperative persons were eliminated."[49] But
her stature and her name saved her from this fate.

Despite the trauma she had suffered, some observers were quite
unsympathetic to her plight. Richard Gibson, a shady character who
flitted from continent to continent and knew quite a bit about guerrilla
movements in Africa, was caustic in his analysis of Graham Du Bois
and Ghana.[50] "She still doesn't seem to understand just what happened."[51] "In Ghana," he said, "there were many persons who understood what was wrong, but, once comfortably settled in sinecures, they
seem to have lost their vision and used their breath merely to add to the
praises of [Nkrumah]. It was very sad . . . [this] is the price you pay for
listening to sycophants and Russian 'advisers.'"[52] Gibson's sweeping
condemnation was made with Graham Du Bois in mind. Even her
son David was raising troublesome questions, remarking, "she's all
alone now. All who 'tolerated' her because of the Doctor are no longer

compelled to do so, and few, very few, among her acquaintances can be called upon to act as friend."[53] He was painfully accurate: those who had felt compelled to bow to her, not least because of her perceived insolence, now were eager to berate her.

■

Despite her high-level post in Ghana and her often inflamed revolutionary rhetoric, Graham Du Bois was not as politically sophisticated as she appeared to be. But one thing she did believe firmly: the Nkrumah regime was a boon and his downfall was a bane for Africa. Others, including some Communists and others on the Left, did not altogether agree; this upset her tremendously and was a factor pushing her away from her erstwhile U.S. Communist comrades and toward Maoist China.

The charge was made that the Nkrumah regime was corrupt from top to bottom. Days after Nkrumah was toppled, a local paper featured Genoveva Marias of "Ghana television fame," who "admitted to being one of [Nkrumah's] numerous girlfriends"; he had given her a hefty salary and an "expensive Ford Thunderbird car."[54] There were also salacious allegations concerning "regular air trips undertaken by the attractive widow of the Father of Pan-Africanism and the vivacious lissome head of Programmes."[55] The evident closeness of her ties to Nkrumah inevitably had given rise to rumors that Graham Du Bois's relationship with him was something more than comradely. This was one of the many reasons that criticism of her in Ghana seemed so personal in its reproach. Still, Nkrumah's admirable employment of women in key posts was now being turned against him—and Graham Du Bois.

Others, though not reaching the issue of corruption, felt that Nkrumah had to go for other reasons. Kofi Annan, the future secretary general of the United Nations, but then working with the U.N. high commissioner for refugees, "supported the coup," according to one who knew him, saying that "Nkrumah's leftist ideas and policies had hurt the economy of Ghana. In addition, he said, Nkrumah's fight with the West was adventurous."[56] He was not alone in this opinion.

But what really galled Graham Du Bois were negative evaluations of her government coming from those of the Left. The South African Communist Ruth First accused Nkrumah of "petty corruption . . . chicanery abounded." There was "sheer bungling of the economy and the state," she alleged.[57] Even her friend Julian Mayfield felt there was

"enough truth in most of the charges" against Nkrumah "to make any
. . . rebuttal, at least by me, impossible and dishonest."[58]

Yet Graham Du Bois's ferocious defense of Nkrumah was backed
by surprising sources. Years later, Willard De Pree of the U.S. embassy
confessed that he didn't find corruption "blatant or pervasive" in
Nkrumah's Ghana; yes, some funds may have reached Nkrumah's
hands, but "not so much for his own personal gain, as to promote his
political wishes throughout Africa."[59]

■

If Graham Du Bois and Nkrumah were close in Accra, they became
even closer after his overthrow. He was forced into exile in Guinea-
Conakry, where French, not English, was the primary language among
elites. Nkrumah struggled with the French language, and this made
him depend even more on Graham Du Bois.[60] She often visited him in
Guinea and wrote him regularly, though many of her letters arrived late
or not at all. Nkrumah had been deserted by many of his aides, who
made a separate peace with the new regime; Graham Du Bois stuck
with him, once telling him, "I know that in some tiny, secret place you
carry me with you."[61] Her defense of Nkrumah was as adamant and
sweeping as her defense of Du Bois after he had been ousted from the
NAACP in 1948. In turn, Nkrumah advised her, recommending that she
stay away from Tanzania in her search for a post-coup home, for "East
Africa at the moment is filled up with American agents—CIA and so
forth. I don't trust these 'guys.'"[62]

Graham Du Bois had learned a bitter lesson from her experience in
Ghana; though she did travel frequently to Dar es Salaam and at times
traveled on a Tanzanian passport, she did not move there permanently.
She was aware of tensions between the mainland and the offshore island of Zanzibar but refused to discuss it publicly, for she was now
"convinced that we idealistic 'African builders' have talked too much in
the past."[63]

Above all, she defended Nkrumah with an undying passion in
the face of skepticism often expressed by her friends and comrades
on the Left. She informed the doubting Julian Mayfield that she had
visited Nkrumah "in Guinea and I want to say that if I admired him
before I admire him even more now."[64] Others were not so sure about
the former Ghanaian leader, and their disbelief infuriated her. Vivian
Hallinan, a longtime friend from San Francisco, "could not under-

Shirley Graham Du Bois in China with W. E. B. Du Bois and Deng Xiaoping (second from right). It was Deng, China's "paramount leader" subsequently, who led the way in opening the Chinese market to massive foreign involvement in the 1970s.

W. E. B. Du Bois and Shirley Graham Du Bois with the
Chinese leader Zhou En-lai.

Shirley Graham Du Bois with Zhou En-lai. She became
quite close to the leadership of the Chinese Communist Party and resided in Beijing from time to time.

Shirley Graham Du Bois speaking in Ghana, late 1950s. From early in life she
had displayed a distinct interest in Africa.

Shirley Graham Du Bois and W. E. B. Du Bois with the Soviet leader Nikita Khrushchev, circa 1959. Her spouse joined the Communist Party-USA before departing for voluntary exile in Ghana in 1961. Her critics charged that she—a presumed Communist herself since the 1940s—was akin to an "ideological courtesan" who had inveigled Du Bois to join the party.

Shirley Graham Du Bois and Kwame Nkrumah, 1960s. They became quite close during her years in Ghana, 1961–66.

A street scene from Ghana during the years of Nkrumah's rule. Ghana's opposition to U.S. policies in Africa and elsewhere and Nkrumah's welcoming of exiled dissidents—including African Americans—were not viewed benignly in Washington.

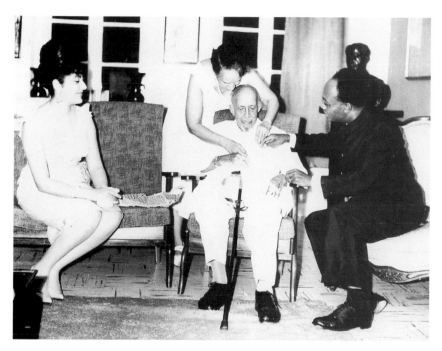

W. E. B. Du Bois and Shirley Graham Du Bois with Fathia and Kwame Nkrumah in the 1960s. Nkrumah provided Graham and her spouse with comfortable quarters in Accra, Ghana.

Shirley Graham Du Bois with Hannah Reitsch in Ghana. Reitsch, an accomplished pilot, established a flying school at Afienya in Ghana.

Shirley Graham Du Bois with Kwame Nkrumah in Ghana. Her close relationship with Nkrumah was resented by some, Ghanaians and African American exiles alike.

Opening of Ghana Television headquarters, 1964. As head of this enterprise, Graham Du Bois developed ambitious plans for the use of this medium. It was at this point that she was regarded as one of the most important women in the world.

Shirley Graham Du Bois visits the plant and headquarters of the manufacturer Sanyo in Japan during her tenure as director of television in Ghana, circa 1964–66. Though the United States became hostile to her and the Nkrumah regime, Japan

remained friendly. Sanyo and Ghana developed plans to manufacture electric appliances in West Africa. Even after Nkrumah's overthrow (with apparent U.S. complicity) in 1966, she continued a warm relationship with her Japanese hosts.

Shirley Graham Du Bois and Kwame Nkrumah (right). After his overthrow, Nkrumah moved to Guinea-Conakry, where she visited him periodically.

Stokeley Carmichael (Kwame Ture) and Kwame Nkrumah. Shirley Graham Du Bois was friendly with both men, who, like others, often referred to her in maternal terms.

Shirley Graham Du Bois during her "Maoist" phase poses in China during the Cultural Revolution, circa 1967.

Above: Shirley Graham Du Bois with Robert Williams, an African American in exile in Beijing, June 1967. *Left:* Shirley Graham Du Bois in the United States after a lengthy exile, February 14, 1975.

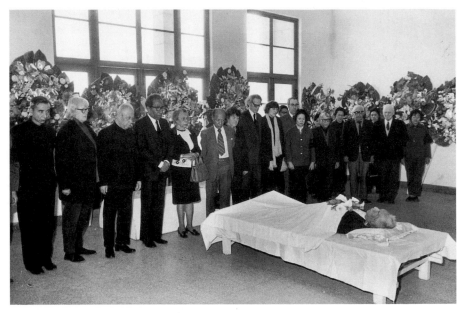

The funeral of Shirley Graham Du Bois, Beijing, April 1977.

stand why the people did not fight back, why they were not armed. The descriptions of the lack of protest and the corruption I do not get from the Western press, but from American progressives who stayed in Ghana, and those who visited after the coup."[65] Anna Louise Strong, a frequent visitor to Moscow and Beijing, asked, "and why should the man whom you call 'my president' expect people to rise up and call him back? He is supposed to have kept several million pounds to his personal credit in Britain; if so, is he using any of this to organize an armed uprising that would bring about his return?" She conceded tellingly that she did not "pretend to keep informed on Africa," but Graham Du Bois found her rebuke maddening nonetheless.[66] The doubts expressed about Nkrumah emanating from old comrades caused her to reassess her own allegiances. Though it did not cause her to reconsider her anger with U.S. policies, this reassessment pushed her closer to Beijing and away from those who remained close to Moscow.

■

After escaping from Ghana, Graham Du Bois faced the dilemma of where she should live. This was a trying episode in her life. "Every day" became "a real battle to 'keep going!'" "Hell," she concluded morbidly, "has no future fears for me." Her "immediate plan" was "something like that of an old-maid aunt who pays long 'visits' to relatives in order to save money." Though she had stashed funds abroad before the coup, there were funds in Ghana she could not retrieve, which was creating a burden. By the spring of 1967 she was conceding with regret, "Frankly, I have spent a fantastique sum of money this past year—and with nothing coming in."[67]

Besides, she had to be quite careful in moving around the globe. Not only was there the constant danger of extradition to Ghana, but right after the coup Ghanaian officials kidnapped a Guinean delegation to an international conference when the plane on which they were traveling made an intermediate stop in Accra. Since Guinea had given refuge to Nkrumah, relations between the two West African states had deteriorated.[68] So now she had to worry about being kidnapped on her frequent jaunts to Guinea. Right after the coup she made a bold statement for publication to John Henrik Clarke condemning the new Accra government, but she cautioned him to "sign with my name but *do not give location*" (emphasis in original).[69]

This kind of fearful uncertainty caused her to consider residing in sites as diverse as Tanzania, East Germany, France, Mexico, and Algeria. During the final eleven years of her life she visited all of these places and others, though she resided for the most part in Cairo, with long stints in Guinea, China, and the United States.

She knew that "Great Britain is closed to me."[70] She considered trying to resume her U.S. citizenship but, as her attorney informed her, her "renunciation of American citizenship" and her "acceptance of other citizenship" meant that she would have to undergo a "regular nationalization process," which would be complicated by her Communist ties.[71] She consulted with her supposed friend, the former ambassador William Mahoney, but he was decidedly unhelpful.[72]

After the coup one of her immediate and longest stints was in East Berlin, then under Communist rule, where she received the "most thorough physical check-up I ever had." After her harried existence, this visit proved refreshing. Her brother from California came to visit her and they spent many hours sightseeing. She visited with Ollie Harrington, the former NAACP staff member and cartoonist, who was then living in the German Democratic Republic.[73] She read James Bond novels in French "so as to recognize a popular vocabulary." This was "fun," as was the trip as a whole.[74] As she told "Dear Comrade Gerhart Eisler," the noted musician, "every day I have been in the GDR has strengthened my desire to make Berlin my home—if I cannot go back to Ghana."[75]

But later in 1967 she traveled to Tanzania and began "talking of setting up a home on the island of Zanzibar, giving up the idea of moving to East Germany completely."[76] Though not wealthy, she did have those who admired her—many of whom were heads of state, like Julius Nyerere of Tanzania—and they longed to welcome the widow of the "Father of Pan-Africanism." Thus, when she traveled to the Bahamas in early 1968 she "was invited to attend a session of their National Assembly" and had a "frank talk" with the prime minister, L. O. Pindling.[77] When she traveled to Algiers, she found she had "fallen in love with the city"; evidently, she had changed her mind about the soldiers who had overthrown Ben Bella a few years earlier.[78] Given her range of choices, it was understandable why she was having difficulty deciding where to reside.

But finally in 1968 she settled on Cairo as her primary residence, though her constant travels often made it seem that she had no primary

residence at all. That her son David had moved to Cairo a few years earlier was one advantage; also, as a gateway to Asia and Europe, Egypt
had an ideal location. Most of all, it was in Africa, the continent she had
come to love. In 1967 she informed a friend in Berlin that

> events of the past six months in Africa and in the USA make it impos-
> sible for me to consider establishing a home outside the area of the in-
> tense struggle in which my people are now engaged. . . . It is clear that
> the liberation struggle in Africa (and this includes Egypt) has entered
> a new phase: the era of *peoples' armed struggle*; and linked closely with
> this is the vanguard of revolution already launched in the United
> States by Afro-Americans. (Emphasis in original)[79]

She was referring to the rise of the Black Panther Party in California and
SNCC in the South. She had received an "arm full of" the latter's material after a representative had crossed the Atlantic "to consult" her.[80] It
was heartening for her that these young people would take the time to
visit her, for despite the warm welcome she was receiving in various nations, she still felt like "something of a 'displaced person.'" Though she
was being feted in East Berlin and Dar es Salaam, her radical politics
meant she had "difficulty getting either to Paris or London," not to
mention New York.[81]

Difficulty in reaching London was problematic for an interesting
reason: this is where she purchased "Inecto Colour Crème," which she
felt was necessary for her skin—"a concession to feminine vanity," she
explained.[82] But access to skin lotion was not the only reason she
needed to travel to London. Even while in Ghana, she maintained an account there that contained tens of thousands of dollars: book royalties,
a capital gain from selling their Brooklyn home, an inheritance from her
spouse—it added up.[83] She also maintained a Swiss account, which she
used to purchase "World Bank bonds."[84] Thus, she was far from being
totally dependent on the benevolence of strangers. Unlike other "state-
less" persons, she had choices, though her state of mind was not the
best.

She acknowledged that the coup had left her "utterly shattered"
and that "it took some time to pull myself together and come to grips
with . . . responsibilities."[85] She arrived in North Africa fully chastened.
"If there is one thing I have learned from the disaster which caught me,
it is a confirmation of the uncertainty of life in our time . . . NEVER TO PUT

OFF ANYTHING I REALLY WANT TO DO FOR SOME FUTURE DATE."[86] Though
she was pushing seventy, she acknowledged, "I have been rudely
forced to *grow up* the past six months" (emphasis in original).[87]

However, there were problems in Cairo too. She unsettled the life of
her son, for one. Initially, she was "alone and lonely" in Cairo and her
"coming made it necessary" for him to "give up" some work he was
doing "in order to spend time with her." She missed the "round of activity that characterized her life" in Ghana.[88] She was also doleful about
the drastic change in her life. "A year ago," she said dejectedly in the fall
of 1966, "I [felt] that I was making a decided contribution all along the
line. But with the reversal I am sort of dumped into a hole."[89]

Then there was the problem of adjusting to the heat. When she first
arrived to live there, she was "practically in a state of collapse. . . . You
see, we never have such heat in Ghana. . . . Even in Ghana's hottest
weather, as soon as the sun goes down, cool breezes from the ocean . . .
chill the air." But Cairo was different.[90]

She was in and out of Cairo for a few years before deciding to settle down there in 1968. She moved to a "large, 'old-fashioned', beautifully built building with spacious room and a view of the Nile from
every room." The building at 76 Nile Street in the Giza district was "on
a corner, with huge, spreading flowers and [a] shrub nursery on the
other side of the street."[91] She had bought the place for a mere seven
thousand dollars from a Saudi student who was moving to Beirut; it
came replete with tasteful Persian carpets and other attractive furnishings.[92] A lifelong student, she "began an intensive course at the University in Arabic—a four month course—five days a week."[93] Eventually
she learned "enough Arabic for necessary and practical use . . . [though]
whatever time I can find for languages" was spent on "improving" her
French; still, Arabic study imposed a "disciplined mental effort" on her
"at a time" when she "needed it."[94] Early on she decided that she "must
learn Arabic," for "the moment I open my mouth and begin speaking
American English, a cold, preoccupied look passes over people's face.
Nobody likes Americans! Oddly enough people do not react this way
even to my poor French."[95]

She made Cairo, a crowded metropolis of millions, where the
homeless often slept in cemeteries, seem pastoral and bucolic:

Palm trees, green grass and flowering shrubs border the Nile River.
People are always about—children playing, watched by buxom ma-

trons, enjoying the sunshine, seated on the grass or on convenient benches. In front of my house is usually a pushcart which sells hot tea and various kinds of "snacks" (this frequently includes roasted ears of corn or roasted yams). . . . Since Ghana I do not have a car. But taxis are cheap and plentiful in Cairo so I use them all the time.[96]

Her "apartment" was "just off the Nile River Drive where the three largest and most fashionable hotels are located. . . . So every time I walk out . . . I am usually accosted by some 'tourist agent' who wants to take me to see the pyramids!"[97]

Cairo was an endlessly fascinating city. For centuries it had been the citadel of Islamic learning and thought, yet it was also secular, enlightened, and chic. It was home to the Islamic world's most prominent university and preeminent press. Political dissidents since the days of the Ottoman empire sought refuge there; foreign students flocked to its universities. Publishing, cinema, and intellectual debate formed its core. Though it was an intellectual lodestar, it was also a city of decay, with crumbling buildings, torn-up sidewalks, leaking sewage pipes, unreliable electricity, overwhelmed schools and hospitals, noise levels rising to an ear-impairing ninety decibels, the highest lead blood levels in the world, and irregular garbage pickup. After fifty centuries of continuous habitation, Cairo stood as a nonstop din of dust and disorder, having survived countless invasions, booms and busts, famines, plagues, and calamities. By some accounts, it remains the most densely populated large urban area on earth. The uneven distribution of wealth was shocking, even for one, like Graham, who had lived in Manhattan.[98]

By way of contrast, a "European friend" of hers "lamented that [Graham Du Bois] had simply jumped 'out of the frying pan into the fire' by coming here as all kinds of 'disturbances' are liable to occur." As she was writing these words on an early visit to Cairo in the summer of 1966, "a fleet of powerful jets just passed overhead reminding . . . that we are having blackouts and air raid drills which are extremely realistic!"[99]

It did seem that Graham Du Bois had a predilection for arriving in zones of turmoil. During the 1967 Mid-East war, she had her "first experience of being in a bombed city. Particularly distasteful" was "being huddled into the improvised, hotel air-raid shelter, there in the quivering darkness to hear the muffled crash of bombs."[100]

Later, she rationalized that

people inside a war zone are not nearly so upset by a little bombing as their friends and relatives outside the said zone. . . . I was crossing the big square in front of the Hilton on my way to the American University the other morning when the air was shattered by a blast. Every[one] stopped, looked up and in a few moments we could see the smoke—came another—and I hurried to get inside the university gate. . . . "That seemed pretty close" commented the gateman (in Arabic). I nodded. Then we heard guns firing and I started across the campus. I wanted to get inside the Library, and go on with my work. But by then whistles were sounded all around me—and the university civilian guards with their bright arm bands were herding everybody into an air-raid shelter (the basement of the library). By the time I reached the Library, of course, the doors were closed and there was nothing for me to do but to obey sharply shouted orders and "Get into that shelter." There were others on the other side of campus. I thought—"Darn it! Nobody knows how long I'll be stuck in here!" . . . all women [and] girls were literally pushed into a huge lounge, furnished with sofas and great armchairs. . . . Later we all learned that this raid was on an outskirts of the city where several women and a child were killed. . . . It would be stupid to tell you there is no war going on out here. There is—but the danger to me is less than there would be in many parts of the U.S.[101]

The often harrowing experience of living in Cairo further sharpened her antagonism to the foreign policy of the United States, the nation seen as Israel's chief supporter. This did not help her in her subsequent attempts to obtain a visa to visit family members in the United States. Living in Egypt also spurred her to develop "Egypt-centric" ideas, which became popularized later as "Afrocentrism." After the 1967 war she concluded, "Egypt is Africa and the ambitions of Israel aim westward into Africa and not eastward towards Asia."[102] There could be "no peace with Zionism," she thundered, until the legitimate interests of the Palestinians were met.[103] In the 1960s these were not popular ideas in the United States, though they were quite commonly expressed in Africa; her identification with Africa was bonding her with the continent, just as it was creating a chasm between her and the United States—and many Afro-Americans.

However, Graham Du Bois had a ringside seat in this war zone and had access to sources of information about the conflict unavailable to

many in the United States. For example, she was devoted to the Egyptian leader Gamal Abdel Nasser and wrote a book about his life. The
book was in the same vein as her previous biographies, though this time
she noted pointedly, "conversations in the book are based on fact and
are an attempt to delineate character. They are not taken from any
records or tapes." Like her previous books, this one too reflected more
than cursory research; it revealed a significant understanding of Egyptian history. She wrote that Nasser "always respected women; he understood and appreciated their value. . . . He appointed the first woman
Cabinet member in Egypt. . . . Under Nasser all technical schools and all
departments of the universities were opened to girls." She also suggested that dark-skinned Nubians had it better under Nasser than previously and observed, "it is significant to note that in Egypt's long history, [Nasser] was the first indigenous Egyptian Head of State in more
than two thousand years." However, she rationalized Nasser's suppression of Communists while having Marxists as advisors. The book,
like so many of her previous biographies, said as much about her as it
did about Nasser.[104] Yet it struck a chord in Cairo also, receiving significant publicity there.[105]

Her book on Nasser was one of a number of writing projects she
completed in between dashing off to China, Conakry, and other
points on the globe. Her son was amazed at "how easily she writes.
She turns out chapters by the day, almost." Writing was therapeutic
for her now, he thought, since she missed "the glamour of Ghana and
the fight of the U.S. . . . I do my best to keep her at her typewriter and
out of the complicated and tradition laden Middle East politics. It is
not easy but I keep reminding her of the Ghana coup. This tends to
sober her somewhat."[106] Or so he thought, but she quickly plunged
into the whirlpool of Middle East politics. Indeed, her often fervent
defense of the Palestinians and Egypt inevitably exposed her to
charges in the United States that she and the Egyptian leadership
were anti-Semitic—which she just as fervently denied. Nasser, she argued in the increasingly "left nationalist" language she adopted after
the coup, "has raised a blockade against white imperialism and aggression rather than against Zionism or the Jewish people."[107] In response to these serious allegations of anti-Semitism, she initiated a
"private campaign to get Americans to visit Egypt—and see for themselves—especially Jewish people."[108] This was an understandable response, for her long experience with the Left had brought her into

close contact and friendship with many Jewish people, some of whom became her closest friends and comrades.

Yet her response to these charges of bigotry suggest why she would also downplay negative allegations about Maoist China. With no flippancy intended, she observed that "we became so used to lies about the socialist countries as they were told in the U.S. that I can take lies about Africa in my stride."[109] After a while, U.S.-born leftists like Graham Du Bois began to ignore critiques of socialist and many "Third World" regimes, assuming that all were savagely biased and distorted.

The longer she lived in Cairo, the more animated became her defense of her latest adopted home. To her it was "one of the most interesting and 'lively' places on the globe. The longer I stay here the better I like it—and this past year of really going into all parts of the country has strengthened my attachment to this valley and its diverse peoples."[110] The hazard of dodging falling bombs was dismissed as part of the city's charm; she didn't "intend to run away—Israeli bombs or no Israeli bombs."[111]

After the 1973 war, she did "a little war work in the hospitals. The wounded soldiers are simply marvelous," she said. "All they talk about is getting well so that they can return to the front." She warned a friend from the University of Massachusetts about the "oil weapon," adding, pointedly, "I do hope heating is not going to be a crucial problem in Amherst this winter . . . well, put on woolies and keep sweaters handy."[112]

■

After the dislocation of the Ghana coup, Graham Du Bois had found a new home in Egypt; she had left the paroxysms of Accra for the periodic convulsions of Cairo. Though she still had access to leaders across the globe, no longer could she rank as one of the most powerful women in the world. At this point, she began spending more time in China, a move that also served to distance her from many of her Communist friends who looked askance at Beijing's anti-Sovietism. She also grew closer to black nationalists from Southern Africa and the United States, which also brought her closer to China and pushed her further away from U.S. Communists.

10

Black, to the Left

SHIRLEY GRAHAM DU BOIS began her career as a musician, playwright, and author of biographies that had huge appeal for young adults. She moved to the left during World War II, when Moscow was Washington's ally, and became friendly with Communists like Howard Fast. She is given credit for lassoing Du Bois into the Left but, simultaneously, his more extensive knowledge of history and sociology also influenced—and anchored—her. With his passing, followed by the shock of the coup, she was by her own admission disoriented. This took place at a time of increasing tensions between China and the Soviet Union and rising nationalism in Southern Africa and among African Americans. Her frequent trips to China and Tanzania guaranteed that these ideological trends would not leave her unaffected. Fundamentally, she maintained her previous socialist outlook, though it was indelibly affected by the rise of nationalism. These two trends—one seeking to encompass all of humanity and the other speaking bluntly to Africans— were not always perfectly reconcilable, and led to some inconsistency in her thought and actions.

■

For some time she had been close to James Jackson, a Communist Party-USA leader, and his spouse, Esther Cooper Jackson, an editor of *Freedomways* and fellow graduate of Oberlin. They had all relocated to Brooklyn at roughly the same time and they became quite friendly. James Jackson has been given credit for recruiting Du Bois into the Communist Party before his departure for Ghana; Esther Jackson recalls that it was Shirley who sat "down and type[d] the letter" of application, which Du Bois "gave me to take and hold."[1]

It was not surprising that these two couples were together at this historic moment when Du Bois joined the Communist Party. They had collaborated in founding *Freedomways,* and even after she relocated across the Atlantic, Graham Du Bois continued to assist the struggling publication—writing articles, securing writers for other articles, peddling subscriptions.

In July 1961, while still in the United States and serving as an editor of the journal, she solicited an article from Dr. Lewis Wade Jones of Tuskeegee Institute. She described *Freedomways* generously as a "journal with no organizational ties, nonpolitical, nonpartisan, offered as a free forum open to all those who have something constructive to say." Would he be interested, she inquired, in writing a "thorough examination of the NAACP" or an article describing "what is happening in southern communities"?[2]

In the fall of 1962 Esther Jackson was "constantly amazed at all that" Graham Du Bois had "been able to do" for the quarterly "with all of the other responsibilities" that she had.[3] Because of Graham Du Bois and her many connections on the continent, it became easier for *Freedomways* to reach Tom Mboya of Kenya, Oliver Tambo of South Africa, Julius Nyerere of Tanzania, Leopold Senghor of Senegal, and "quite a few other literary people in Africa" concerning the submission of articles.[4]

Likewise, when Afro-American Communists like James Jackson and Claude Lightfoot traveled to Ghana, they were also sure to visit with Graham Du Bois; often they discussed the content of the magazine and how to make it a better vehicle to influence the civil rights movement.[5]

But the longer she lived in Accra, the more problems she had with *Freedomways*. Much of the controversy began when the magazine organized a memorial and a special issue to mark the passing of Du Bois. Part of the conflict stemmed from the fact that the magazine operated in a nation where the right wing was influential, while Graham Du Bois was living and working in a nation with a left-wing leader, Kwame Nkrumah. But the conflict also stemmed from the age-old problems involved when contending forces seek to appropriate a historic icon like Du Bois.

Thus, Graham Du Bois was outraged that *Freedomways* would deign to allow the NAACP's Roy Wilkins to play a role in the events: "I DO NOT BELIEVE THERE IS ONE PERSON IN THE WORLD WHO WANTS TO READ ROY WILKINS ON ANY PHASE OF W. E. B. DU BOIS." And how could they include Rufus Clement, the head of Atlanta University, who had sacked her spouse in 1944? "This man nearly broke W. E. B.'s heart and would have destroyed his work." As for Hugh Smythe, how could they include him since he "is known throughout Africa as a clever CIA agent." Langston Hughes, whom she had known since the 1930s? He "carefully excluded Du Bois from every book he has written for young people." Peter Abrahams? He is "considered a renegade by the Freedom Fighters of South Africa." There was more: "Ja-Ja Wachuku is now fighting every ideal to which Du Bois devoted his life. . . . And if Mrs. Amy Garvey was at the last Pan African Congress I certainly don't know anything about it." She was also dismissive of Sterling Brown and Rayford Logan. And she was annoyed because Lorraine Hansberry, who had been chosen to read Graham Du Bois's words at the memorial, did not provide a verbatim rendition.

In a sweeping condemnation, she had dismissed most of the leading intellectuals among the *Freedomways* constituency; it seemed to the editors that she was trying to paint the magazine into a sectarian corner.

She disagreed adamantly.

She was Du Bois's widow, after all, but she was much more than that, she argued:

> I was not only his wife, I was his close companion for the last twenty years of his life. Even before I married him he was the dominant force in my life. Every plan I make now—every detail of my work—every conference or discussion I hold with people from many parts of the world—every word I write—every action or dream or hope is carried out in close communion with him.

And so, she instructed *Freedomways*, "if this generation of Americans cannot accept him *as he is*—do not try to gild his image for them" by including Wilkins, Clement, and the like (emphasis in original).[6]

Esther Jackson did not accept this reprimand passively. Herbert Aptheker was the person who informed Graham Du Bois about Hansberry not reading her message faithfully. Jackson felt he was upset because he was not listed as a sponsor at the memorial; further, Jackson criticized him as being among the "whites [who] withdrew . . . when it became apparent they were not 'running the show.'" Anyway, the historian had "often been patronizing and arrogant, and has not patience to *listen* to Negroes" (emphasis in original).

Apparently, Graham Du Bois had also wondered why Malcolm X had not been included in *Freedomways'* efforts; Jackson was quite cool toward this proposal.[7] Graham Du Bois was left to wonder how the magazine could rationalize including an anticommunist like Wilkins while excluding a militant like Malcolm.

A quivering temblor had erupted as a result of the attempt to determine who had standing to claim the immense legacy of Du Bois. The *Freedomways* special issue and the memorial meeting would help settle the question, according to many. Aptheker, who would organize Du Bois's papers, felt that this task gave him standing.[8] James Aronson of the *National Guardian,* a newspaper that published Du Bois's writings in the 1950s when other publications flinched at the mention of his name, felt similarly. He was astonished that "there was not a single mention" of his weekly, which was viewed by some Communists as a not too friendly competitor to the *Worker.*[9]

Esther Jackson was aghast that Graham Du Bois would share with Aronson "your many differences over the years" with *Freedomways*; and how could Graham Du Bois claim that she "has a more world wide point of view" than the New York editors of *Freedomways*? This, Jackson responded, was a "disservice" to the magazine and "to the Negro movement"; how could Graham Du Bois write such a "slanderous letter," lacking in all "courtesy"?[10]

John Henrik Clarke, whose self-proclaimed "left nationalism" would ultimately drive him away from *Freedomways*, sided with Graham Du Bois: "speaking only for myself, I agree with you completely about our narrow approach to the African Revolution and its relationship to the Black Revolution in the United States."[11] Graham Du Bois told him she was "disappointed" with her "failure even to get [the magazine] to understand [that] what was happening here had a direct bearing upon what could be done in the United States."[12]

Clarke complained about the "Esther Jackson–Jack O'Dell partnership" at the magazine. "Esther's husband [James Jackson] determines the contents. . . . and Jack O'Dell and Esther are his puppets," he claimed. Graham Du Bois, he alleged, sent Esther Jackson material for the quarterly but got in reply a "number of nasty letters that were in poor taste. . . . she made it plain to Shirley that Freedomways would become, in effect, the house organ of the Southern Freedom Movement." This was much too tame a goal, he thought. Philosophically, he concluded, "there is nothing the American left movement hates more than an independent radical who is also a devout nationalist. That is what I am." The party, on the other hand, he asserted, was a "dwindling clan of middle class soreheads talking to themselves."[13] Increasingly, Graham Du Bois was sharing Clarke's viewpoint.

According to their mutual friend Calvin Sinette, Graham Du Bois also sensed the "long hand of James Jackson . . . again playing his obstructionist role" with the magazine.[14]

Though it seemed that Clarke and Graham Du Bois were aligning in a left nationalist bloc, Clarke had criticisms of Graham Du Bois too. He was irked that she had not found him a job in Ghana.[15] His friend Hodee Edwards was equally critical of Graham Du Bois. Without Du Bois, Edwards wrote to Clarke,

> let us put it this way: his widow "has no politics." I naturally tried to maintain the relationship after he died. But the last time I phoned her, she told me "Girl, don't you know I have one of the most important jobs in Ghana and don't have TIME for all this gabbing on the phone." Sorry! Oops! and so on.[16]

Like so many others, Edwards felt that Graham Du Bois had developed an inflated ego as a result of her status in Ghana.

And though it seemed that she was aligning with the *National Guardian* against *Freedomways* and the *Worker*, she had problems with Aronson's publication also. The *National Guardian* committed the capital offense of not printing her articles in defense of Nkrumah after the coup. It "simply wanted to *stay clear of black folks' business*," she snarled (emphasis in original).[17]

Graham Du Bois was in a bind. She was drifting away from the Communists, but the non-Communist Left and left nationalists were not altogether accepting of her either. According to Edwards, "angry Afro-Americans" charged that Nkrumah was a "'prisoner' of the Russians," which was why he was toppled, supposedly, and Graham Du Bois had to bear some responsibility for this.

Still, Clarke and Graham Du Bois simply reflected the difficulty in trying to build a progressive movement in a land saturated with white supremacy. As her conversation with Richard Wright two decades earlier suggested, a number of African American leftists felt that many of their Euro-American counterparts were more concerned with racial privilege than working-class solidarity; this forced African Americans into various brands of racial nationalism. According to Graham Du Bois, white supremacy was a transnational phenomenon. Even Ollie

Harrington, who once worked for the NAACP before going into exile in France, then East Germany, was leaning in this direction. Graham Du Bois told Clarke that "for the past fifteen years he's been knocking around Europe. . . . but as he said, 'No linguistic ability is going to make me a Frenchman, a Russian or a German. Here in Ghana I find not only my *roots* but a real *future*'" (emphasis in original).[18]

In a sense, she was responding to white supremacy while still trying to maintain a progressive outlook on humanity. This was not easy. Yet her molten responses to erstwhile comrades did not make things easier. After the coup, W. Alphaeus Hunton, her spouse's coworker with the Council on African Affairs who came to Ghana with him to work with the *Encyclopedia Africana,* did not adopt the same confrontational attitude to the military junta that she did. To her, this was a gross betrayal, though he eventually felt compelled to move to Zambia. Unpersuaded, Graham Du Bois continued to denounce this brilliant, intellectual leftist to any who would listen. He was a "lazy, selfish opportunist" and "a real rat."[19] He was "certainly without integrity or principle"; she found his actions so bizarre it made her "question [her] own sanity."[20] She accused him of "faithfully" trying to "cooperate with that bandit regime!" "I do feel pretty bitter about this," she wrote. Her outburst is more revealing about her than about Hunton, a true "unsung valiant" hero. It was suggestive of the fact that her analyses at times were driven by intense and highly idiosyncratic personal preoccupations. Her disillusionment with Hunton, however, was another step in her general alienation from friends and comrades on the left.

She never had a formal rupture with her comrades, she simply drifted away. She tried to get Conor Cruise O'Brien, Nkrumah, and other luminaries to work with *Freedomways* on a special issue, then became irritated when, in her opinion, there was inadequate follow-up.[21] Even after the coup, she maintained contact with the staff at *Freedomways,* though she did not have much good to say about their efforts. As they moved to mark the centenary of Du Bois's birth, she insisted that it not be a "love feast—not in these times and under these conditions," though she did not specify what would meet her tastes.[22] Writing from China, she observed, "I am not anxious for *Freedomways* to handle it. And when they learn that I am in China they probably won't want to handle it—if they believe I will actually be present."[23] She complained frequently to Nkrumah about the alleged treachery of the editors. The "extreme left" prevented the quarterly "from taking a positive position on Africa or even on the more positive movements of Afro-Americans in the states. They are so busy on 'peaceful coexistence' that they are wholly on the side of Martin Luther King." They had "reasoned that my article would unquestionably throw the weight of opinion towards BLACK POWER. . . . The idea makes me furious."[24] She was embracing the ideological trend of Black Power, while the editors were a bit more skeptical. According to her, this was because "they are under the influence of the great power which opposes the Black Power movement—and I don't mean the U.S." (she meant the Soviet Union).[25] She conflated the nonviolent resistance of King and Moscow's idea of "peaceful coexistence" with capitalism and contrasted that with the presumably more militant stances of Black Power advocates and Beijing: to her mind the Beijing–Black Power axis far surpassed the King-Moscow formulations.

Yet she continued to cooperate with the magazine because it was one of the few outlets in the United States that would publish her lengthy articles. But even here there were problems. Once Graham Du Bois was reduced to invective to describe what she perceived as unfair editing of one of her articles. It was explained patiently to her that this was done because the magazine was trying to avoid "libel suits" but she remained displeased.[26]

Though she occasionally complimented *Freedomways,* her general opinion was that it had become "so innocuous, so arty, so sentimental that while a real struggle is going on their pages give little reflection of the picture."[27] Still, she continued to make demands on this "innocuous" publication. She demanded that her critique of Ali Mazrui's analysis of Nkrumah be printed in its entirety and if not, "I must ask you to remove my name from the magazine's masthead. . . . The struggle in Africa today is too intense to be muffled by detractors."[28] In part, she was responding to pressure from pro-China forces who felt that "*Freedomways* does not represent the black liberation movement but is just another loudspeaker (for black dupes) of the American revisionists."[29]

Graham Du Bois was having trouble not only with *Freedomways* and its supposed black Communist influence, but also with Communists generally. Initially, while she was in Ghana, things appeared to be going smoothly. She arranged for U.S. Communist youth and their friends to travel to Accra.[30] She not only consented to the Communist youth organization to be called the "W. E. B. Du Bois Club," she also called the group "wonderful."[31] She was an intermediary between the party's publishing house and Nkrumah, who published some of his key texts with them.[32]

However, her relationships fluctuated here too. Though she had allied with Aptheker, the Communist historian, in his dispute with *Freedomways*, her opinion of him also was not consistent.[33] Soon she was falling out with other forces on the left. As in her contretemps with *Freedomways*, part of the reason was that many on the left were reluctant to accept her unalloyed, unwavering, uncompromising support for Nkrumah and his actions while in power. They would not accept her interpretations of African realities, though many were in the same category as Jessica Smith of the pro-Soviet publication *New World Review*, who once confessed revealingly, "It isn't at all that we are 'confused' by the latest events in Sierra Leone—we are simply ignorant about them!"[34]

Buoyed by the idea that this would mean recognition of her own expertise, Graham Du Bois then wrote a review of Nkrumah's book on the Congo for *New World Review*; but the editors changed "Hanoi" to "China," "which gave an entirely different connotation." Disgusted, she wrote to Nkrumah in the spring of 1967 that "experiences of the past year have brought me to the painful realization that many 'progressives' are Ghana's worst enemies. They are the ones we believed in and trusted. Now, in many respects they have utterly let us down." She declared ominously, "*We shall remember*" (emphasis in original).[35]

Like Jessica Smith, Graham Du Bois had difficulty getting accurate information about Africa—except she was not aware it was a problem. After the coup she spent a considerable amount of time in Tanzania, which happened to be one of China's closest allies in Africa, and her frequent presence in Dar es Salaam inevitably colored her opinions. As early as 1967 she was asking Smith about "widespread 'rumors' throughout Africa"—that mostly emanated from Dar—"that the socialist countries of Europe are 'betraying the African revolution.'" These countries' "untiring and nobly conceived efforts for peaceful co-existence have blurred their vision," she thought, and hampered their effort to aid Vietnam. This was a traditional line from China, and it had some credibility until Beijing itself—which was supposedly so concerned about Hanoi's fate—waged war against Vietnam after the United States was forced to pull out.[36] Because China was a "colored" nation, it was easier for some black leftists like Graham Du Bois to believe that it was

Beijing, not "white" Moscow, that was standing firm against U.S. imperialism. This perception persisted even after the entente between Beijing and Washington in the early 1970s in the wake of the momentous visits to China by Nixon and Kissinger.

Unlike others who drifted away from the U.S. Communist Party, Graham Du Bois was not influenced by the crimes of Stalin or Soviet interventions in Hungary in 1956 or Czechoslovakia in 1968. If anything, she was more gung ho than Communist leaders themselves about Stalin and about Moscow's foreign policy toward Warsaw Pact nations. She was quite critical of the 1956 report by the Soviet leadership that indicted Stalin: "Time and sober second thoughts would seem to be shaving down Khrushchev's revelations to proper proportions," she maintained. "It may be that history will label the speech as an inappropriate emotional outburst produced by the same kind of tensions, pressures and anxieties that tormented and drove the aging Stalin." Extraordinarily, *New World Review,* the pro-Soviet organ that published her remarks, added an editorial note of rebuke: "we now feel impelled to register editorial dissent."[37]

Like Mao Zedong, she was angry with Soviet Communists because they denounced Stalin. As in Southern Africa, the searing experience of white supremacy often made black comrades more willing than their nonblack comrades to rationalize stern administrative measures in the effort to construct a new society.[38]

Though some Communists globally joined with countless others in condemning the Soviet intervention in Prague in 1968, again Graham Du Bois disagreed with them. Instead she told Nkrumah, "I just wish a few Russian tanks had rolled into Ghana" when the coup began. Signaling her future distaste for Moscow, she added bitterly that "instead the Russians have been pleasantly cooperating with the 'criminal regime'. All right, I realize that the geography was different—but the *principle* is the same" (emphasis in original).[39] Jessica Smith of *New World Review* congratulated her this time.[40]

Graham Du Bois came to believe that Moscow was not sufficiently hostile to the Accra junta. Before this, her defense of the Soviet Union knew few bounds. And even after moving to Cairo, she was grateful to Moscow because of its assistance to Egypt during its intermittent wars.[41] In fact, though she became critical of Moscow when she turned so avidly toward Beijing, she never became vehemently anti-Soviet, though she had plenty of opportunity to do so.

Still, the Kremlin had taken notice of her coziness with the Chinese leadership and reacted accordingly. Her brother Lorenz Graham once sought her assistance in getting his books published in the Soviet Union; she was forced to tell him that her "contacts [there] are not what they once were."[42] With an audacious haughtiness she could still brag about "wrapping my sables about me" as she breezed off to the Soviet embassy for receptions, but after the coup, intimate and high-level encounters with Soviet officials became fewer and fewer.[43]

Graham Du Bois raised legitimate points about Soviet foreign policy that Moscow had difficulty answering. For example, she wondered why the USSR continued to have trade relations with South Africa (for example, Soviet diamonds were marketed via De Beers) despite its widely condemned policy of apartheid.[44] She was appalled by expressions of racism in Eastern Europe and seemed to view this phenomenon with more seriousness than similar expressions in China—perhaps because of the centuries-long tradition of white supremacy that fortified the colonization of Africa and the slave trade.[45] When she could not get satisfactory answers to her questions about race, it reinforced the idea that "whites"—irrespective of their socioeconomic system or ideology—were not reliable allies and that those who were "colored," for example, the Chinese, were. Unfortunately, reality was not that simple.[46]

When signs of the rift between Moscow and Beijing first became evident, she was reluctant to take sides and, instead, tried to bring the two sides together. In October 1962, as the Cuban Missile Crisis was riveting the world and raising the specter of thermonuclear war, she was advising Nkrumah that it would be "a healthy thing for the entire world if we can get Chinese and Russian scholars working together on an African undertaking." That would be Ghana's contribution to concord between the two powers.[47] The FBI took note of her mediation efforts; it retained on file her 1963 letter to a Communist publication explaining that

> we do not feel equipped to hand out advice to either of these socialist giants as to how they should handle their differences. . . . Meanwhile, world-wide problems are being created by loose talk. If people thousands of miles away from either country, who have never been in either and know nothing about either language, would attend to their own business . . . the clouds would roll away and we would have the peaceful coexistence all of us so much desire.[48]

This advice was directly contrary to a growing U.S. perception that the rift between these "socialist giants" was precisely what would allow Washington to prevail in the Cold War.[49]

Her perception that Moscow was somehow responsible for Nkrumah's fall and was too friendly with the Accra junta influenced her view of the dispute among Communist nations. Just after the coup, she advised Nkrumah that though "the rift between the Soviet Union and China is daily becoming worse[,] I feel it is essential that we remain absolutely neutral, though I confess this is becoming increasingly difficult."[50]

She did not remain "absolutely neutral" for long. By 1968 Jessica Smith was complaining that Graham Du Bois was "very wrong to include the USSR in your description of the Great Powers acting in concert for their own best interests—and by implication joining in the Chinese charges against the USSR as acting in collusion with the imperialists." "No one," Smith argued, "has done more for the freedom of colonial peoples" than Moscow.[51] In the period before Nixon's trip to China, Graham Du Bois felt that Moscow's "normalized" diplomatic relations with Washington were a betrayal; after Nixon's trip she had become so enamored with this way of thinking that she failed to adjust to the evident reality of a Beijing-Washington alliance targeting Moscow.[52]

However, pro-China forces also felt that Comrade Graham Du Bois was weak on certain questions. Anna Louise Strong, a longtime ally of China, explained why a journal with which she worked would not print Graham Du Bois's article: it was not because of the content but because Graham Du Bois was presumptuous in "attending and speaking at the conference of the revisionist organization of Afro-Asians"; "revisionist" was code for pro-Soviet.[53]

To her credit, Graham Du Bois did not impose her subsequent ideological sympathies on Du Bois posthumously. In 1974 when she was organizing an event in Cairo in honor of her husband, she observed that "of course, Chinese will be there—and I have told them to invite the Russians!" Of course, the fact that the Chinese were doing the "inviting" was telling, but in those days a fervent Maoist would not have considered any association with what Beijing referred to as "social imperialists."[54]

Nor were Maoists pleased when Graham Du Bois praised the CPUSA-affiliated "WEB Du Bois Clubs . . . who fearlessly carry his name like a red banner."[55] U.S. Maoists assailed her for praising "revisionists," but she would not back down.

Graham Du Bois was leaning toward China, but she was reluctant to break decisively with the USSR and the Communist Party-USA. When she finally was able to visit the United States in the 1970s, she sought to meet with Jessica Smith and her spouse, John Abt, who was the party's chief counsel. Why? "Recognized lines of demarcation have been swept away," Graham Du Bois asserted, "up is down—and east is west! I find myself dangling in the air! I need to both talk and *to listen*. . . . No matter how different your point of view I'd be glad if you would express it. I am trying to create better understanding" (emphasis in original). Her "preoccupation"—doctrinal disputes about "peaceful coexistence" aside—in "all" her work was "Justice and Peace or *Peace with Justice*" (emphasis in original).[56] As time passed, this ecumenism characterized her approach to disputes on the Left.

Graham Du Bois had fences to mend in part because of her "preoccupation" with her defense of Nkrumah and her growing belief that he was overthrown because "constantly at [his] elbow were Russian advisors. And he followed their advice."[57] Some felt this was a simplistic explanation that at once gave too much credit to Moscow and not enough to Ghanaians, the United States, and Nkrumah himself. Indeed, three of his key advisors were Graham Du Bois, an Afro-American, George Padmore, a Trinidadian who had broken with Moscow decades earlier, and Geoffrey Bing, who hailed from Great Britain.

But Graham Du Bois was in the midst of an ideological journey that led to China, and despite her admonitions about "neutrality," she had become alienated from the USSR and its U.S. Communist allies. Her son David has concluded that "certainly her early and insistent support for China over the USSR played an important role in her relation to the [Communist] Party and party individuals. And I doubt there would have been any formal leaving of the party."[58] As early as World War II, Shirley Graham had expressed deep admiration for China. "No American," she said, "can feel the suffering of China more keenly than does the American Negro."[59] She seemed to see a parallel between what African Americans had suffered domestically and what China had suffered globally at the hands of colonialists of various stripes.

While in Ghana, Shirley and W. E. B. Du Bois often spoke on Radio Peking for their "listeners" across the globe and in China itself.[60] As noted, she leaped to the defense of Mao Zedong after he had been criticized by U.S. civil rights leaders when he assailed Jim Crow; she raised the question sharply on Ghana Radio.[61] Her radio broadcasts, which conceivably reached millions, often blasted U.S. racial policies—not the sort of thing that endeared her to the authorities in Washington.

Just as her reaction to the persecution of black soldiers in Arizona helped push her to the left, her reaction to the overthrow of Nkrumah helped to push her toward China, for Beijing proved to be more helpful to him—and her—after the coup.[62] Her sympathies also might have been generated by the individual attention she received from the Chinese. During her stay in Accra, Huang Hua, the Chinese ambassador and a future foreign minister, and his wife cultivated her.[63] Bill Sutherland, an African American who lived in Ghana, then Tanzania, recalls that whenever she arrived in Dar es Salaam, Chinese embassy officials would pick her up at the airport, provide sumptuous dinners for her, and generally take good care of her.[64]

This was during the period following the Ghana coup, when she began to spend a considerable amount of time in China itself. Many in the United States had not recognized the significance of the Sino-Soviet dispute and, as a result, continued to associate visits to China with actions close to treason.[65] In addition, the so-called Cultural Revolution was under way at the time, and Graham Du Bois found that old friends like Huang Hua were under siege.[66] When she was there in 1967 on the fourth anniversary of her spouse's death, she had a striking meeting with Zhou En-lai. According to official Chinese sources, "he had taken time out to see Shirley only a day after the ordeal in which he was surrounded and harangued for 18 hours by a group of people sent against him by Lin Biao and the gang of four." She had a "cluster of questions which she was anxious to ask Zhou about the cultural revolution so that she could answer her associates in the black freedom movement in the United States."[67]

Sidney Rittenberg, a U.S. exile then living in China, recalls,

> that night about two-thirty, Chou En-Lai sent for Shirley and they talked till nearly dawn, with only Chou's interpreter present. Shirley called me at dawn and asked me to hurry down to the hotel. When I got there, she was obviously upset. She said that she had never seen [him] look like that. His face was drawn and anxious looking, he seemed to be under great stress—worst of all, he seemed to be in very poor spirits. . . . She reported that [he] told her, "It's possible that the

Chinese Revolution might go down to defeat in the Cultural Revolution. But it's O.K.—you'll have your own revolution in Africa, you'll develop your own Mao Zedong. . . . you'll do a better job of your revolution because you'll learn from our mistakes. . . ." She was thrilled that [he] confided in her as a trusted friend. I told her that I had never heard of a Chinese Communist leader expressing his personal misgivings in that fashion, to either Chinese or foreigners. In that sense, Shirley represented a very special tie between the African people, the American people, and one of China's finest sons.[68]

Evidently impressed with her experience there, in late 1967 she told Nkrumah that "when I go to the Far East this time I shall be there for a long time."[69] She had spent a good deal of that year in China and the same was to hold true for 1968. She "accepted an appointment on the Permanent Bureau of the Afro-Asian Writers, located in Peking."[70] It was a "revolutionary organization," she thought.[71] There in the midst of disorder created by the Cultural Revolution—a violent process of purging the Communist Party and society generally of so-called counterrevolutionaries and laggards—she found it all exhilarating.[72] It was a "real and necessary revolution," she said. After being "jailed by imperialist stooges" in Ghana and "bombed in Cairo," she found that "experience has stripped me of idealism—though not of vision." While in Asia she was "in that section of China, very close when the two American planes, having crossed the border, were shot down!" "The Third World War has already begun," she exclaimed.[73]

A recurrent critic of Graham Du Bois, Richard Gibson, told Julian Mayfield that the "Chinese comrades apparently aren't encouraging her too much. Perhaps they don't understand her continuing connections with *Freedomways*? I gather the Cultural Revolution has baffled her as much as many others and she still looks wistfully at the CPUSA and other revisionists."[74] Graham Du Bois had been misjudged. Her view of the agitation in China mirrored Gibson's. She arrived in China in June 1967 and "accompanied by young revolutionists . . . traveled to many parts of this vast land." She "mingled with crowds in the cities. . . . spent days with peasants on communes, with an Army division on its military post, with students . . . with Red Guard units." She was there for ten weeks and had high praise for an ostensible purpose of this "revolution": putting intellectuals and party "bureaucrats" in closer touch with the "masses" by, for example, sending them to the countryside to harvest crops and handle cow dung.[75] In June 1967, for example, she spent an "entire day . . . on the base of the 369th battalion of the Army"; she announced proudly, "I can now write a manual on army strategy, tactics and formation!"[76] Such varied experiences make it difficult to say that she was ignorant of the deaths and tumult resulting from the Cultural Revolution.

By February 1968 she was back in Beijing. After returning from the Bahamas and stopping in Cairo, she flew twenty-two hours to reach China. Now, outside her windows it was "several degrees below zero," but her "big room with balcony overlooking the boulevard" was "warm and bright with sunshine." She had become so "Africanized" that despite the chill she could not "stand to be inside an entirely closed room." She had to "have fresh air," so she threw open the balcony door. The Cultural Revolution was another breath of fresh air, she thought; it was proceeding apace, though "some 'intellectuals' and university groups" were "still dragging their feet." As she wrote, on her "tea table" was a "platter of oranges, pears and apples" that she would nibble on, providing food for thought. For some reason, Chinese officials didn't want her "to wander about alone. They fear something might happen." She could not "imagine what," since she didn't "speak a word of Chinese." Besides inspecting the Cultural Revolution, she planned to learn how to play chess and improve her swimming and French.[77]

Later she was moved into a "corner suite, with a magnificent view." It remained "frightfully cold—way below zero. . . . gales from Siberia lashed around this corner practically putting [her] three radiators out of business"; she longed, once more, for "African sunshine."[78]

Fortunately, while she was in China her "circle" was expanding; she was "learning more about people and the world in which we live. . . . paradoxically, this fact, in many cases only increases my uncertains [sic], my realisation of how much I do not know and the need to know more." She was studying the works of Patrice Lumumba and Sekou Toure in French, editing a publication for the Writers' Bureau magazine, and conversing regularly with a Japanese gentleman in French; just recently she "spent an hour and a half with the Guinean ambassador conversing only in French."[79] However, her increased language facility did not increase her insight into the pandemonium of the Cultural Revolution that was erupting all about her.

She was also spending considerable time with Gora Ebrahim, a representative in China of the Pan Africanist Congress (PAC) of South

Africa, which she and they called "Azania." The PAC was a staunch opponent of Nelson Mandela's African National Congress. He was her "best colleague"; he lived "just below" her and brought her "papers and magazines."[80] They often conversed and reinforced each other's perceptions about the validity of Maoism.

She also spent time speaking on international radio broadcasts, once commenting on Mao Zedong's latest "marvelous statement" on racial unrest in the United States She had "been dodging television and newsreel cameras ever since. For many reasons," she did "not want" her "face sent out to various parts of the world"; her "disembodied voice" was another matter.[81] Perhaps if her face were seen, her efforts to gain a visa and regain her citizenship would be compromised; or worse, she might be kidnapped by her enemies in Africa, if they could pinpoint her location.

But just as she was looking over one shoulder to gauge U.S. and other reaction, she had to look over the other shoulder at her pro-China comrades. In China she encountered Robert F. Williams, the African American exile who had bolted from the NAACP in North Carolina after offering to confront Jim Crow with armed struggle; he fled to Cuba, then Asia.[82] They had met years before in Brooklyn; indeed, when the FBI was searching for him they came to her door in Brooklyn.[83]

Before arriving in China in 1967 she had asked him if he could "put in a word for me to get there soon."[84] Williams was a friend of Richard Gibson, whom she knew as no friend; the elusive Gibson was suspected of having questionable ties with various intelligence agencies.[85] That is probably why the son of Elijah Muhammad of the Nation of Islam, Akbar Muhammad, who was a resident of Cairo, told Williams, "Shirley asked me to tell you NOT to mention anything about her plans to Gibson."[86]

However, as one of the few African Americans in China, she found it difficult to avoid other blacks, no matter how questionable. For example, Gibson was a good friend of her friend Gora Ebrahim; Gibson recommended him to Williams, calling him a "bright and honest fellow and a pleasure to work with."[87] All were friends of Carlos Moore, an anti-Castro Afro-Cuban; all spent time gossiping and condemning Cuba and the Soviet Union. This was not to Graham Du Bois's taste. However, in China these were the people she encountered.

During this period, 1967–68, China was trumpeting loudly its solidarity with Afro-Americans. The U.S. press worriedly reported that China was "exploiting racial unrest" in North America, while others

charged that it was directly responsible.[88] There were huge demonstrations in Canton and Shanghai with "red guards carrying red flags" on
behalf of Negroes. On 1 August 1967 an editorialist in China's *People's
Daily* blasted the "bankruptcy of non-violence," suggesting that sterner
stuff would be necessary to bring the imperialists to heel. The *Hong
Kong Star* of 20 April 1968 reported that China had established links
"with some of America's most militant Black Power Negroes and has
promised to smuggle them money, arms, and telecommunications
equipment." Graham Du Bois's old friend Huang Hua was said to be in
charge of China's "agents" in the United States. Nervously it was noted
that Mao Zedong had "put the Chinese on the side of the colored races
around the world in a barely disguised appeal to racist revolution." He
was quoted as saying, "we are in the majority [the colored races—black,
brown, and yellow] and they [the whites] are in a minority."[89] This bold
and gruff talk was in the aftermath of the murder of Dr. Martin Luther
King, Jr., when U.S. cities went up in flames and the country was in
chaos; hence, there was more reason than usual to take the Chinese
leader's words seriously.

Robert F. Williams was said to be organizing from his base in China
a plan for Afro-American soldiers in Vietnam to "eliminate" their
"white comrades." For the folks back home in the United States he helpfully provided tips on "clogging sewer lines and highways, burning fa-
cilities and smashing windows without getting caught."[90] *Newsweek's*
headlines roared about this new alliance between "China" and "The
Black Expatriate." It too viewed Williams's activities warily, particularly his "shortwave broadcasts" aimed at Afro-Americans; the "number of Chinese Communist publications entering the U.S. by indirect
means," it reported apprehensively, "has more than doubled."[91] Marvin
Liebman, a conservative friend of William F. Buckley, was informed that
China's offensive on race had made the United States "somewhat vulnerable at the moment."[92]

These were intoxicating times indeed for Graham Du Bois, who had
reason to believe that her foreign patron, China, would be lending militant aid to African Americans. This was a central reason that she sided
with Beijing, not Moscow.

As early as 20 August 1953 an editorial in the *California Eagle*, a
black-owned paper in Los Angeles, noted correctly that China had
"made the most of racial feelings" to "win the loyalty" of African American prisoners of war who had been embroiled in the war in Korea. Yet

this hope of an alliance between radical blacks and Beijing proved to be premature. Though left in form, China's policy proved right in essence, as this most populous of nations wound up collaborating with the United States in Southern Africa, Southeast Asia, and elsewhere. At this moment it turned out that China was the same "paper tiger" that it so often accused the United States of being.

Yet this was difficult for her to see in 1968 and later. For the time being she comforted herself with the bonhomie provided by her new-found comrades, one of whom was the Euro-American—and Jewish—exile from the Carolinas, Sidney Rittenberg.[93] He had come to China during World War II and had decided to stay on, working as an interpreter and writer. The first time he met the Du Boises was in 1959. He had gone to their suite at the Beijing Hotel one evening after being introduced by "remote control by mutual friends," though they "had never met." Graham Du Bois was reading an English-language newspaper as he entered, and as he started to remove his coat,

> Shirley waved the newspaper at me and said with feeling: "One of these days when we are in power, the first thing we're going to do is hang all these sell-outs—like . . . Roy Wilkins!" As I walked over to shake Du Bois' hand, he looked up at me with a twinkle and said, "Mr. Rittenberg, you have probably observed that my wife is something of a radical."

This was indicative of the effect that Maoist China had on her. The rampages of the Cultural Revolution, in particular, reinforced her own bent toward a kind of radicalism and settling scores with supposed ideologically retrograde elements.

Rittenberg acknowledges that the Chinese treated her and her spouse quite well. "They offered to make the State Guest House villa their own private home, and to give him a big limousine and a driver to take him driving whenever he wanted to go." "I think Shirley was a little tempted at the idea, but Du Bois was adamant" in opposition to relocating to China at that time.[94]

Rittenberg recalls that Graham Du Bois encountered the kind of antiblack racism in China that had made her reconsider her support for the Eastern European nations when she noticed it there. One of the African American soldiers who had defected during the war in Korea, a "former MP named Clarence Adams, from Memphis," had married a Chinese woman and they had several children. Clarence had fallen afoul of Great Han Chauvinism a number of times, running into various forms of attitudes based on the fears and misunderstandings that many Chinese have towards foreigners, especially when they are African but also when they're Afro-American. Clarence went to see the Du Boises and told them some stories about his own problems, and especially about the chronic strain and occasional conflict between Chinese and African students—especially in connection with Africans making friends with Chinese girls.

With urgency Graham Du Bois called Rittenberg to discuss this matter. He tried to explain the cultural clash, but the incident left her uneasy.

Rittenberg recalls another occasion when Zhou En-lai had sponsored a huge banquet for her and Du Bois before their return to Africa. At the gathering Du Bois had expressed "deep regret at the hostility" between the Soviet Union and China in the context of making other remarks. Then Graham Du Bois

> stood up and. . . . said, "When we go to meet Khrushchev, I'm going to dress him in his Chinese cadre suit with his Chinese People's Liberation Army cap on--with the Red Star on the visor!" There was a dead silence in the room. People stopped talking, the ice in the glasses stopped clinking, the servers stopped moving. Shirley looked around in wonderment as the whole room went dead. Then she turned and said to her husband, "I don't think they understood what I was saying." Du Bois answered in his deep bass, "From the silence, Shirley, I would judge that they understood exactly what you were saying." Shirley looked nonplussed, but dropped the subject. Tang Mingzhao, Director of the Department for Liaison with English Speaking Countries, came over and explained to her quietly that they hoped the Du Boises would avoid offending the Russians and would try to maintain a position from which they could do a little good. Shirley nodded, and seemed to understand

her diplomatic faux pas. This incident also seems to suggest that the seeds of her sympathy toward Beijing in its dispute with Moscow were already present even before the Ghana coup.

The last time Rittenberg saw her was in 1967.

On every trip to China Shirley had told me about her deep suspicion
of Eslanda Goode Robeson. China had been leaving no stone unturned
to get Paul Robeson to come to China. . . . [Graham Du Bois] believed
that Eslanda was preventing [the trip]. . . . Shirley thought that Eslanda
and the Soviet Ambassador [in London] had gotten the British to com-
mit Paul to a mental health institution just to keep him from going to
China—not because his health required it.[95]

When President Richard Nixon traveled to China to meet with Chinese leaders, Graham Du Bois, who still considered herself a staunch
anti-imperialist, was dumbfounded. A friend had told her earlier, "if a
million people can come out to see Nixon in Roumania, then why
should I hate him for his past anti-socialist activities. If he is good
enough for them, isn't he good enough for me?" With understatement,
she concluded, "confusion reigns in my mind."[96] The same could be
said for Graham Du Bois, who had been banking on Beijing to assist in
the overthrow of white supremacy in the United States, not Communist
Party rule in the USSR.

This same friend felt "rather bitter" about Nixon's warm welcome
in Beijing.[97] Graham Du Bois would have none of that. She decided to
go along with the new Beijing line, counseling her friend, "you must not
lose faith in China, my dear. Never mind any 'new friendships.' The
Chinese are very wise and farseeing. They plan for the future! . . . Even
if I do not understand some moves (I confess I do not) I'll still believe in
the ultimate victory of China."[98] Why did she not desert China when
the career anticommunist Richard M. Nixon, whom she despised, bro-
kered this open anti-Soviet alliance? She was still angry with Moscow
for various reasons, and if she had deserted China, where would she
have placed her socialist anchor? China was a major aid supplier to one
of her newer patrons, Tanzania (it was helping construct a major railway there, among other projects), and was a backer of the PAC of South
Africa, with which she was also close. And, as she told the writer John
Oliver Killens, after he had received acupuncture in China, "we 'colored folks' had better get together to help each other."[99] China was not
just socialist but "colored" as well and was more compatible with the
"left nationalist" approach she had developed.

She stuck with China to her last dying day in Beijing. When Brindley Benn of Guyana scored China for maintaining "good relations with
the reactionary Chilean junta" after the 1973 coup, she defended the

policy.[100] She resorted to elusive Chinese-type proverbs in her defense of such policies, speaking of how *"the willow tree bends in the storm and so it does not break"* (emphasis in original).[101] She spoke of her "two hours with the Chinese Ambassador" in Cairo and how he "pulled me out of that 'slough of despair.' . . . He showed me bright spots in the gloom. . . . he gave me a large tin of China's finest, fragrant tea and sent me home in the Embassy limousine!"[102] Apparently, such gestures also helped to retain her support.

When the facts did not fit her preconceptions, she bent them accordingly. In Angola, where China, South Africa, and the United States collaborated in backing a political faction that opposed the eventually triumphant MPLA (Popular Movement for the Liberation of Angola), she claimed that the latter faction was "generally thought to be pro-Mao" and resorted to lengthy biblical stories to explain her falsehood.[103] Her devotion to China at times made her lose sight of what was best for Africa.

To be fair, China was not the only nation with which she was fascinated. During her tenure as director of television, she had developed with the Japanese corporation Sanyo a factory in Ghana to produce television sets, electric fans, and other appliances. She visited Tokyo then and wrote Nkrumah that her visit had her "feeling like a charged rocket transistor!" Her hosts were "gentle, polite and very charming." She also met with Sony executives. She was enthusiastic about the possibilities of African-Japanese cooperation, noting that germanium, "the basic metal used in all transistors . . . is produced only in the Congo!"[104]

The contract she negotiated with Sanyo allowed for the training of Ghanaian technicians, the sole importation of Sanyo televisions, and the like, plus the construction of a factory to produce various appliances. A "furore" erupted because "European companies proclaimed that Japanese were robbing them of their rightful place. . . . And by various means," she charged, "including bribery—these Europeans succeeded in persuading many Ghanaian officials the Japanese were intruders. . . . I am certain now that what we were doing added fuel to determination to overthrow President Nkrumah!" She recalled speaking with Indonesians who praised Tokyo for training them when the Dutch would not. Ghana's relationship with Japan, she thought, showed that "the balance of power is shifting" against white supremacy.[105]

The coup obliterated these ambitious plans, but it did not destroy her relationship with Japan. The plant had assembled 1,100 electric fans and had sold 600 television sets before the coup, but the new government was not enthusiastic about continuing production. The Sanyo executive in charge told her with regret that the "future of Ghana Sanyo is not hopeless, however it will not be easy either." The new government in Accra, he said, increased the number of "television sets . . . imported from Philips and other European manufacturers, in quantity."[106] Graham Du Bois wondered, "with imported sets all over the place how can they expect our own factory to prosper?"[107] She was right; it didn't prosper.

But it did continue. Sanyo executives remained in contact with her after the coup and continued producing appliances, expanding to refrigerators, air conditioners, and other items that Ghana desperately needed. Though the executives had a justifiable "worry . . . [that] some elements of western powers influenced the government to discourage Ghana Sanyo's operation," this fear was not altogether realized. "Thanks to your efforts," Graham Du Bois was told in 1974, Ghana Sanyo was "now one of Ghana's solid medium enterprises which can resist any vicious challenge from others."[108]

Her experience with Japanese capitalists did compare favorably with her experience with European and Euro-American capitalists, and this reinforced, in her mind, the primacy of "race"—which pushed her toward China, a nation that shared the socialist philosophy she espoused. While in China she listened frequently to NHK radio from Tokyo and was at times surprised at its reporting on the war in Vietnam, which was often critical of the United States. "Often," she wrote with astonishment, "I am left wondering and would like to ask them the question: 'Hey, which side are you on?'"[109] According to her colleague John Bracey of the University of Massachusetts, after her ouster from Ghana and her hurried retreat to London, it was the Japanese ambassador there who packed her items from various places and flew them all to Cairo as a favor.[110] Again, such gestures—at a time when there was doubt she would even be allowed to enter Britain or the United States—strengthened both her opposition to white supremacy and her belief in the importance of the "colored" uniting against it.

Bolstering these ideas were her growing ties with a younger generation of Afro-Americans—particularly from SNCC—who were espousing Black Power. This new movement, she felt, was "uncertain and not steady to its goals," but "it is a very positive thing."[111] High on her list of advocates of Black Power was Stokeley Carmichael, who demonstrated his concord with Graham Du Bois by assuming the name Kwame (after Kwame Nkrumah) Ture (after Sekou Touré). After Carmichael's move to Guinea-Conakry, Nkrumah's home in exile, she met him and played a role in introducing him to his future spouse, the South African exile Miriam Makeba.[112] In fact, it was "through the intercession of Shirley Graham Du Bois" that he received an invitation from Nkrumah and Toure in 1967 to the "8th Congress of the Democratic Party of Guinea." This was during a time when the SNCC leader was coming under ever sharper attack because of his advocacy of Black Power. The two leaders invited him to "live, work, study and struggle there," an invitation he accepted promptly, making Guinea his home and, ultimately, the place where he was buried.[113]

Graham Du Bois and the young, sleek Carmichael frequently met in Conakry, described by Makeba as "an oversized village made up of fading French colonial buildings and tumbledown shacks where the poor try to live. The beaches have no sand, because the people took it all away to build with. But this type of sand makes poor concrete, and all over town walls and posts are crumbling down."[114] Carmichael was elated about being able to "work and study under Dr. Nkrumah, the most brilliant man this century has produced."[115] The situation was not as rosy as it sounded. Conakry was frequently under siege, for it continued to render assistance to its neighbor, Guinea-Bissau, in its armed struggle against Portuguese colonialism. In late 1970 Carmichael was lamenting the "state of emergency" because the nation was "expecting the fascists to attack at any moment."[116] Relations between Conakry and neighboring Senegal were "not very good" either, as the Senegalese leader, Leopold Senghor, was a favorite of France, the nation that Sekou Toure abjured when he opted for independence.[117] Carmichael also was facing difficulties back in the United States, worried about possible indictments and worse. Concern about his personal safety had helped to drive him to West Africa in the first place. Though in 1972 students at his alma mater, Howard University, had pushed the school to give him an honorary doctorate, "layers of conflict" prevented it.[118]

In this often tense environment, Nkrumah, Graham Du Bois, Carmichael, and Makeba all shared friendship and ideas. Graham Du Bois and Carmichael, both of whom had had some experience with Euro-Americans on the left, did not find it easy to explain their newfound fondness for Black Power to skeptics. Still, Carmichael wondered why black nationalists were accused of being "against everyone," while no one made similar allegations against their nationalist counterparts who were Irish or Italian.[119] Though his "ex-friends" were "condemning" him "out of hand," as early as 1966 he felt that the "discussion on Black Power in the white community is going well." In fact, he thought, "it is desperately needed."[120]

Unhappily, the export of Black Power abroad was not positive in all circumstances. Graham Du Bois received reports from Guyana that during Carmichael's visit there he "let loose a tirade of racial sentiments claiming to be a disciple of [Nkrumah] . . . in his first meeting he called upon the 'Africans' to develop by themselves, Indians by themselves, etc. This resulted in great controversy here. He was booed."[121] These nationalist sentiments were one thing in a society with a white majority, quite another in a place like Guyana, a South American nation almost equally balanced between Africans and migrants from India. Even Graham Du Bois became concerned about where the nationalism she had cultivated was going, writing that Carmichael "has been saying many things unworthy of our goals or even common sense."[122] Yet she continued to entertain him in her home in Cairo and he continued to refer to her as "ma" and "grandma."[123]

Grappling with the black nationalism that Black Power represented was vexing at times. As early as 1951 her friend Alice Childress confessed to having a "heated" debate with Theodore Ward about the need for a "Negro Theatre"; at first Childress said no, thinking "it might be a Jim Crow institution," but then she reconsidered.[124] Though the Communists particularly had boosted black nationalism by endorsing the idea of "self-determination" for African Americans, many under the influence of the party nonetheless had difficulty in assessing the implications of Black Power.

For her part, as early as 1960 Graham Du Bois had hailed the budding reassertion of African culture in Ghana, the "brilliantly colored kente," the judges ditching their powdered wigs. "Here is the key" she proclaimed, "a resurgence of Pride!"[125] The problem was that a revival of nationalism amidst the decline of a Left that preached class solidarity could portend an acceleration of chauvinism and xenophobia.

As a result of the legacy—and reality—of white supremacy, Graham Du Bois, like many younger Afro-Americans, found it difficult to trust or objectively assess many of European descent, even those who had displayed firm mettle. After the Mozambican patriot Eduoard Mondlane was murdered, she affirmed that "the fact that he was married to a white American caused certain understandable distrust of him in the African struggle."[126] Even Basil Davidson, the British historian who wrote voluminously and sympathetically about Africa, did not elude her censure; she railed at his latest "twenty-five dollar book. European (white) writers are now making fortunes out of Africa!"[127]

After her rupture with *Freedomways*, she began an association with the *Black Scholar*, initiated by younger Afro-Americans, many of whom shared her evolving philosophy of left nationalism. Esther Jackson and Jessica Smith urged her to criticize the new journal's occasional biting views of U.S. Communists and the Soviet Union and its praise of China, but she refused.[128]

She did draw the line at the Nation of Islam, however. She was friendly with the son of Elijah Muhammad, Akbar, who lived in Cairo and was disaffected from his father. Perhaps because of his influence, her appreciation of Malcolm X, and her own years living in a predominantly Muslim society, she was sharp in assailing the NOI's "dogmas, practices and aims," which were "as different from Islam as day and night—though like day and night they do [merge] at some points."[129] The NOI reciprocated by criticizing her for depositing Du Bois's papers at the University of Massachusetts, as opposed to, for example, Fisk; this only showed that Du Bois himself was—to use their most insulting epithet—an "integrationist."[130] But after they examined her ideas more carefully, they began to publish some of her articles and asked her to join the black conservative Tony Brown as one of their regular columnists.[131]

Her residence in Cairo cannot be discounted in explaining her political evolution. Many of the Egyptian leftists and intellectuals there were likewise marching toward nationalism during this period, a migration induced in part by the impact of racial chauvinism in the region, failures of working-class movements, and dissatisfaction with the Soviet Union. Consequently, her odyssey was not merely a personal matter but was influenced by larger, transnational trends.[132]

Despite the aid he received from Moscow, Gamal Abdel Nasser was no friend of Egyptian Communists. After he came to power, one of "Nasser's first measures was to crack down hard on the Egyptian Communist Party and imprison its leaders"; "left-wing" union leaders were hanged.[133] According to the Chinese writer Wang Suolao, however, Nasser was quite close to the Chinese leadership, becoming friendly with Zhou En-lai as early as the spring of 1955. Particularly after its own break with Moscow, Beijing encouraged Nasser to do the same. Supposedly, Zhou blamed Nasser's premature death in 1970 at the age of fifty-two on his "heartbreak at being betrayed by the Soviet leadership."[134] Thus, Graham Du Bois's journey to Cairo gave her more exposure to anti-Soviet—and pro-Beijing—opinion.

■

As her trips to the United States in the 1970s demonstrated, Graham Du Bois was becoming an icon for a new generation of black nationalists. A group of Afro-American immigrants to Tanzania who began a chicken farm were in touch with her during her frequent trips to that nation. They sent her a poem expressing their disdain for "pale white vipers" and their praise for "people of the sun"; this effort she termed "splendid."[135] She began to read the texts they recommended, for example, Chancellor Williams's *The Destruction of Black Civilization*, which she found to be revelatory: it "promises hours of intriguing study . . . on this subject I'm totally ignorant;" sheepishly, she added, "the only 'Chancellor' I know is Chancellor of the University of Massachusetts."[136]

Invigorating her born-again nationalism was her association with Gora Ebrahim, a leader of the Pan Africanist Congress, and other Southern African exiles in Egypt and China.[137] South Africa's PAC, with its slogan of "one settler, one bullet," mirrored similar trends occurring in the United States. She encountered many of these exiles in Dar es Salaam, a frequent port of call for her after 1966. She became quite friendly with the nation's leader, Julius Nyerere, whom she addressed as "my dear Mwalimu" or teacher.[138] He gave her the highest compliment, comparing her to "our Chinese friends" who "praise us for our ideals in spite of knowing our weaknesses."[139] When she traveled to the southeast African republic, she would meet with him "not only in his office, but with the family in his home."[140] Her affection for the Tanzanian leader was revealed in her hagiographic biography of him.[141]

Shirley Graham Du Bois had made a long journey from Ghana. From being regarded as some sort of Soviet mole in Flagstaff House in Accra, she was now viewed widely as the high priestess of black nationalism and Maoism. This perception became quite evident when she finally was able to obtain a visa and return to the United States.

11

The End of Her Journey

BY 1970 SHIRLEY Graham Du Bois was almost seventy-five years old; still spry, she had become an inveterate world traveler, journeying from her home in Cairo to Guinea, Tanzania, China, and points in between. However, she was still not welcome in the United States, the nation whose citizenship she had renounced when she became a Ghanaian.

In 1970 she and David had gone to the Ghanaian embassy in Cairo to renew her passport; unfortunately, they "were received with extreme discourtesy."[1] By this point Kwame Nkrumah, who initially had been seen as a virtual coleader of Guinea with Sekou Toure, was old news; she concluded with sadness that "it would appear" that Nkrumah "no longer has any influence where he is," so a Guinean passport seemed out of the question.[2] Eventually she was to obtain a Tanzanian passport, but this nation did not have ideal relations with Washington either. Ultimately she was to receive a visa to return to the United States, but not without considerable lobbying and protest. She returned to a land that in some ways seemed light years away from the nation she had departed only a few years earlier. Her evolving black nationalism was greeted warmly on campuses and in communities nationally, as she was treated as a latter-day heroine. Though her frequent speeches on the marvels of ancient Egypt were thoughtful, ineluctably they fed a form of Afrocentrism and inward-looking analysis that may have deflected her youthful audiences from the kind of political activism she herself had displayed in Ghana. On the other hand, few in her audience were ready for the socialist ideals of that era.

■

In March 1970 the FBI reported that Graham Du Bois had visited the U.S. interests section in the Spanish embassy in Cairo to obtain a visa in order to return "home." "She stated that she did not intend to engage in any public discourse of racial problems in the U.S. . . . she also said she wished to explore, at a later date, the possibility of regaining her U.S. citizenship." She had been invited to speak at her husband's alma mater, Fisk University, for a $2,000 fee on a subject not viewed as a threat to national security, "Ancient Egypt—Its Relation to Africa." This seemed sufficiently benign; besides, U.S. authorities were worried that "a refusal of a visa to Mrs. Du Bois might lead to adverse reaction in certain African nations as well as in the U.S."[3]

In addition to replenishing her coffers and speaking directly with a new generation of activists who knew her only from headlines, there were more personal reasons for her to want to come to the United States at that time. Though her brothers and relatives visited her in Africa, this was becoming more difficult as age crept up on them all. In addition, her brother Bill had encountered some nagging legal and health problems. Then there were other people she hoped to see, like William Allen, a fellow Oberlin musician, gourmet chef, frequent correspondent, and "bachelor."[4]

The problem, as she told Ho Li-Liang, was that she was on a "list of persons prohibited from entrance to the U.S. under any circumstances!"[5] She was initially pessimistic about getting a visa to the United States and cushioned her disappointment by rationalizing that she was "an idiot for even thinking about coming back there! I do not need any part of it."[6] The United States' "big talk about South Africa refusing a visa to [tennis star] Arthur Ashe to enter Africa sounds pretty hypocritical when they deny me a visa to come from Africa."[7] With her usual piquancy she added, "you can understand that I am in a war-like mood." Her mood was not improved when during the "last week in January government pressures caused Fisk to cancel the lecture series."[8]

In an inversion of an old Maoist dictum, the Nixon White House decided that the friend of a friend is an enemy: though Graham Du Bois was a friend of the administration's newest friend, Mao Zedong, she still was no friend of theirs, they thought. The White House aide John Erlichman was blunt: "I recommend that we not permit Mrs. Du Bois to enter the United States," because, inter alia, she "is still affiliated with thirty communist-controlled organizations with no change in view."[9] It was unclear if he had taken her—and their—new friendship with China into account in making this determination.

Egil Krogh of the White House staff was even blunter: why should they "grant her a visa to come back and talk to young people who currently are star-struck by representatives of the Third World and hard-core Communist revolutionaries"? The White House, feeling besieged on all sides by Vietnamese, Cuban, and assorted "revolutionaries"—not to mention Black Panthers at home—felt no need to add to this coalition. Further, Krogh didn't see "what benefit we will gain either in the academic community or the liberal domain at large by permitting Mrs. Du Bois to return."[10] Somehow he overlooked Afro-Americans, who demanded her entrance.

Soon the White House was being overrun by letters and petitions from members of Congress, including powerful senators like Jacob Javits of New York and Edward Brooke of Massachusetts, all protesting the visa denial. Black members of Congress like John Conyers and Shirley Chisholm weighed in.[11] Harlem's Congressman Adam Clayton Powell protested, as did Congressman Edward Koch of Greenwich Village. The pragmatic future mayor of New York City felt that "the outrage and sense of despair of our citizens arising as a result of the denial in this case . . . is more harmful to our government than the entry of Mrs. Shirley Graham Du Bois."[12]

Congresswoman Shirley Chisholm, a black woman with roots in Barbados, took to the floor of the House of Representatives to protest the visa denial "in the name of all black Americans." She had "received many letters of indignation and protest from many black intellectuals, organizations and individuals"; this, she concluded, was "but another manifestation of the oppression and suppression of blacks in this country."[13] Chisholm's remonstration was indicative of how the political climate had changed since the 1950s, when Du Bois was indicted; the civil rights and antiwar movements had created a climate that made it more difficult for the United States to marginalize Graham Du Bois because of her radicalism.

Even Whitney Young, the staid head of the centrist National Urban League—derisively termed by his militant detractors "Whitey" Young—called the visa denial "weird" and an "insult." "How can an elderly lady possibly be a menace to the security of the world's most powerful nation," he asked. "This latest fiasco," he argued tellingly, "is especially strange in the light of the State Department's policy of seeking better relations with Black Africa."[14]

The newly inaugurated Black Academy of Arts and Letters in the United States was a moving force in generating the flood of letters to which Chisholm referred. Its fifty founding members included Charles White, Jacob Lawrence, John Oliver Killens, Nina Simone,

Duke Ellington, Sidney Poitier, and Harry Belafonte. Many of them knew or admired Graham Du Bois and her husband, and they wanted her to speak. Graham Du Bois suggested that if she could not accept a citation they planned to award her because of the visa denial, then "Dr. John Hope Franklin . . . one of the younger scholars for whom my husband had high regard" should do so.[15] When Roy Wilkins—a man she had once threatened to hang—opposed the visa denial, it was clear that it would be difficult for the White House to withstand the pressure.[16]

She received support from a number of editorial writers, some of whom questioned why she could be refused while Stalin's daughter could be granted a visa. She was quick to tell the *New York Times* that despite the claim to the contrary, she had "absolutely no ties with organizations" in the United States, "'subversive' or otherwise."[17] With increasing irritation, she added forcefully—albeit disingenuously—"nor do I feel at this point in the mood to explain that I never joined the Communist Party."[18]

Later she conceded that her visa request was granted in the spring of 1970 because of the "tremendous pressures which were brought to bear in this case. All kinds of people were involved," but particularly significant was the "spontaneous reaction of *all the black people*" (emphasis in original).[19] She was right. Times had changed. The Justice Department, appropriately, overruled the Department of State.[20] She would be allowed to return.

It appeared that the tide of public opinion had shifted in her favor. Why? Perhaps it was because she denied the ultimate sin, Communist Party membership, or because her advanced age made her no longer seem threatening, or because the name Du Bois had regained its luster. Even some former opponents became conciliatory. Ralph Jones had been a U.S. Foreign Service officer in the late 1950s in Moscow; there he "developed a certain amount of hostility to Dr. and Mrs. Du Bois when they were visitors in the USSR." But now that he had been "swept up in civil rights activities back here in Washington," he "came to feel in [his] heart that [he] had grossly misunderstood and unconsciously maligned this dedicated couple."[21]

Her return was a triumph marked by tragedy: the death of her brother Bill. The shock of her brother's death seemed to inflame her nationalist ire. Writing to one of her newer nationalist friends, Nathan Hare of the *Black Scholar,* she insisted that the stress of the visa fight was a key factor leading to his death; she "lay the death at this time right at Whitey's door. . . . Whitey would like nothing better than to eliminate you" too, she thought.[22] Those "devils," she fumed, "prevented me from being with him in these last months. . . . His death has really diminished me. I am sure the disappointment, frustration and real anger about that refusal to me simply broke his heart."[23]

Thus, her happiness was tempered when she returned, as was her reaction to her former homeland. "Ten years ago," she told the *Washington Post*, "we were talking about gains made towards integration. I come back and nobody is talking about integration—nobody that I've talked to."[24] She found "wider cleavages between peoples in the United States than I was conscious of ten years ago." There were racial, ethnic, gender, age, and other conflicts, she said. "Struggles between these factions seems to have taken precedence over struggle between the 'haves' and the 'have-nots.'"[25] Perhaps her absence had dimmed her memory of the impact of the McCarthyism that had helped drive her from the United States: the assault on class-based organizations that defended the interests of the "have-nots" had left a vacuum filled by the acceleration of these other conflicts—just as this assault had brought terms to her vocabulary like "Whitey" that she would have used sparingly earlier. Previously she might have preferred a locution that signaled she was referring to the "haves," not to a particular "race" that included "have-nots."[26] Still, even during the apex of her Communist years, she retained a modicum of black nationalism. Perhaps even she did not realize that the decline of the Reds—and her drift away from them—facilitated her own resurgent nationalism.

The specter of these wider "cleavages" shadowed and haunted her tour from coast to coast. The range of topics she was asked to address had little to do with socialism in Ghana or China, but rather were oriented toward nationalist and Afrocentric themes. At Fordham University she spoke on "Africa and the Middle East"; at Syracuse, "Eduardo Chivambo Mondlane"; at Morehouse, "Africa and Pan-Africanism"; at Columbia, "Egypt Is Africa"; at Dartmouth, "Egyptian Civilization." At a meeting of the Congress of African Peoples in Kansas City, her theme was "We Are an African People, We Shall Win!" The publicity poster used to advertise this gathering featured her next to Minister Louis Farrakhan of the Nation of Islam.[27]

A symptomatic controversy erupted at Harvard during her three-day visit there. Students like the future historian Nell Irvin Painter, the future journalist Lee Daniels, and the future businessman Peter Bynoe came to greet her, according to her old friend from the Left, Professor Ewart Guinier, who had invited her.[28] It had been a wonderful tour, thus far, she told the father of the future law professor Lani Guinier. But what happened during her formal talk there cast a cloud over her visit and raised sharp questions about the "cleavages" that had so concerned her. Eight black students barred fifty to a hundred white students from attending her talk in Sanders Theater. One of those excluded, Richard Green, said he was handing out "pro-Israel political literature" when he was asked to stop; then he was prevented from entering the hall because, he said, of the color of his skin.[29] Apparently Graham Du Bois was unaware of this exclusion, and later she called it "wrong": the students were "off on a dangerous and defeating course, but I understood—and I love them."[30]

As one who had resided for a decade in Africa, she was acutely aware of the need and importance for African Americans to identify with their ancestral homeland. She often appeared for her jam-packed addresses clad in West African garb, and Africa was inevitably the theme she presented to her overwhelmingly black audiences. However, she did not seem to recognize that with the decline of the Left, she was courting the danger of reinforcing an identification with Africa that could be easily hijacked by misogynist, xenophobic, right-wing nationalists—as her appearance in Kansas City suggested. These larger questions were far from her mind—and the minds of most in her audiences.

Her old friend from Ghana Sylvia Boone, now of Yale, was overwhelmed with joy to see her since she "always learn[s] so much *new* stuff from your work and your musings" (emphasis in original). Professor Boone organized a conference on women for Graham Du Bois to address that garnered headline coverage in the *New York Times*.[31] This conference was an early expression of a "critical race feminism" that was to flourish in coming decades; that it was barely visible in 1970 also suggests why Graham Du Bois's own feminist consciousness seems so underdeveloped in retrospect.

Nathan Hare of the *Black Scholar*, based in the San Francisco Bay area, was "making plans" for Graham Du Bois "to take the [region] by storm."[32] Perhaps concerned about having her visa renewed, she denied she was a "revolutionary" during this visit; in contrast, the Black Panther Party proudly claimed this sobriquet.[33] Still, she vigorously defended the BPP in the face of sharp questioning.[34]

This defense was admirable, not only because the party was under siege, but also because it provided an alternative to the kind of nationalism that she was inadvertently promoting. In Los Angeles she expressed concern over the talk she had heard about "independence and a sort of separatism" and was "hesitant to link her husband's influence" ("'I've known him since I was 13 years old'") "to changes in this country, such as the growing emphasis on black separatism. . . . she doubts that he would have supported today's separatists."[35]

Her trip to Atlanta was typical. She met with the dowager of the movement, Coretta Scott King, and was feted by the Black Academy of Arts and Letters, which was also honoring Lena Horne, C. L. R. James, and Amiri Baraka. Richard Hatcher, one of the first of the new wave of black mayors, exulted that "they" could not

> ban her from this August assemblage; or prevent our breaking [bread] together. They could not interdict our embrace, that entwining of arms which fleetingly recaptures the agonies and joys of three and a half centuries of struggle. We have overpowered the troglodytes who dwell on high in the contemporary caves and caverns of the Department of State. . . . for everything you are, Shirley Graham, everything you stand for, is with us tonight, like a shining presence.[36]

Later, looking back on this visit to the United States, she claimed that "Every black writer in the country gave me books." This was an exaggeration, though she did have to construct new shelves in Cairo to house her bounty. She was like a Pied Piper leading her legions, some of whom "followed" her to Cairo. She was "overwhelmed with visitors" after returning to Egypt; "some I expected, but many were folks I did not know but who knew me: students who had heard me speak at some university, community workers from the west, who knew my brothers, etc. etc."[37]

■

During the 1970s Graham Du Bois was not simply circumnavigating the globe, accepting the hosannas of the worshipful. She spent a considerable amount of time at her typewriter, churning out articles, essays, fiction, and her loving memoir of Du Bois, *His Day Is Marching On*. Though Alice Walker was not impressed with this latter work, the black lawyer and activist Earl Dickerson found it "utterly fascinating and full of sharp recollections often reminiscent of Proust in the vividness of their reconstruction."[38]

Because she was an expert in creating "vividness," it was natural that she turned to writing fiction—what her critics charged she had been writing all along when she was prolifically writing biographies. Novels were a logical step for a writer who found this "planet the mad house of the universe"; her discerning eye and her gift for dialogue made the fiction format more suitable for her talents. Though "fiction bored" her comrade Nkrumah, she disagreed: "*good fiction* is bound to be humanistic—it opens up human beings and their circumstances to each other" (emphasis in original). She wrote a novel about Anne Royall, a feminist heroine of the early history of the United States—it was her "first real novel"—but it was rejected and never published.[39]

Her second effort in this genre, *Zulu Heart*, an imaginative novel about South Africa, was the work of a fully mature artist and, quite possibly, the most significant work of art she produced during her long and fertile career. According to a reviewer in the *New York Amsterdam News*, "in this novel . . . her narrative talents and especially her ability to convince have been brought to the fullest test."[40]

The crux of the novel, inspired by contemporary headlines, concerned a transplant operation in which a man of European descent in apartheid South Africa received the heart of an African. It allowed her to muse about race relations in a wholly political—indeed, Du Boisian—fashion: "The Republic of South Africa, caught up in the 'problem of the 20th century'—that of colour—was trying to cope with it on its own terms." It involved elaborate dream sequences; the characters included contract workers from Mozambique, Botswana, and "Southern Rhodesia" and Japanese servants. After the operation, the recipient of the organ had

> dreams! I'm having dreams in which I seem to be . . . a kaffir—no, rather—a Zulu . . . . you see, sir. It isn't only the dreams. . . . I'm beginning to feel different! And that is frightening. I ask myself what I let my wife in for. Am I a different one from the one she married.

Once he received his African heart, his ability to dance improved markedly; better still, he became more progressive.

There was a discourse in praise of Egypt that reflected her newfound interest in her new home; there was a fine etching of character—

particularly the character of white women, who come across as more humane than their male counterparts. Though the freedom fighters were trained in "Red China," an African character says sternly, "I am convinced that Africa must be liberated by Africans themselves from aggression, exploitation, pillage and rape."[41]

This tour de force had a simple point that may have been inspired by her experiences of racial "cleavages" during her tour of the United States: "the real point of the book is that black and white can live together if they will just face up to the fact."[42]

Her trip to the United States gave her more than just fodder for a novel. It increased her celebrity and her speaking fees, which provided more time for her writing. In a 1972 interview, while dodging coyly the issue of her age—"Don't think I'm about to take up knitting"—and speaking of her knowledge of Russian, German, French, Arabic, Italian, and Spanish, she mentioned casually that she was "debating whether her next book should be about the women of China or a novel giving Anthony and Cleopatra a better historical perspective than that offered by William Shakespeare."[43] Her productivity inspired her son David to write his own novel, which concerned black expatriates in Cairo.[44]

As Graham Du Bois's life illustrates, the journey of U.S. blacks back to Africa often distanced them from their counterparts in North America. For example, after she moved to Ghana, Graham Du Bois's advocacy of socialism did not rest well with many in the United States where anticommunism was strong. After moving to Egypt, she adopted the passion of that land, the struggle of the Palestinians; again, this was not popular in the United States where the Palestine Liberation Organization was routinely denounced as "terrorist."

A good deal of her writing and speaking in the United States concerned the volatile issue of the Middle East.[45] This was understandable. While living in Cairo she had to confront the reality of war, and these images were difficult to erase from her memory. In October 1973 the "airports were closed" as a "relatively short distance away armies are locked in a life and death struggle"; she was "fully seventy-five miles from the Mediterranean where naval battles are taking place." She found this not frightening but enlivening. She was "proud" and "glad to be here! I can rejoice now that my faith in these kindly, dark-skinned people has been vindicated. How much they have been humiliated!"[46] "Don't worry about me," she assured her son. "I'd rather be right here than in any other part [of] the world."[47] This war was an occasion for her to restate two major themes of her declining years. She savaged Israel, which she saw as a tool of white supremacy fighting a colored people. And she criticized the Soviet Union for allegedly selling Egypt only defensive weapons.[48] Both points were far from the mainstream in the United States.

She had the advantage of direct experience with headline-grabbing events that to many in the United States were no more than flickering images on a television screen. But she had the disadvantage of living in a nation where telephone calls were at times difficult to make because of "few circuits" and "great demands," where receiving letters and magazines through the mail was a constant struggle, and where paper shortages at times made it difficult to write the lengthy letters she specialized in.[49]

Thus, though Cairo was a great crossroads of the world, at times living there could be isolating. Combined with the yawning political gulf that separated her from the place where she spent the first six decades of her life, this isolation drove her closer to other intellectuals and activists who often operated on the margins, which reinforced her marginal viewpoints.

Such was the case with her association with the writer C. L. R. James and the ill-fated Sixth Pan-African Congress that took place in Tanzania in 1974. She had encountered James years earlier when she was living in Ghana and he was asked to write a foreword to *The Souls of Black Folk*. This was not an ideal match, and she quickly accused James, a veteran Trotskyite, of "unadulterated McCarthyism."[50] Herbert Aptheker, the Communist historian, speaking "frankly," was "worried about the James association" and was "relieved" when she "terminated" the relationship.[51]

But indicative of her transformation, by the time of the Tanzania conference she was lavishing James with praise. She spent time with him in Washington, D.C., and later confessed that "before that evening I had only admired you through your writings."[52] He was seeking to enlist her in the "6-PAC," as it was called, and she confided that she was dubious about the venture until she heard from him. The gathering was marked by a raging dispute featuring (mostly) African American delegates on one side arguing the primacy of race as an organizing principle and (mostly) Africans—principally Guineans and Southern Africans, who were receiving various forms of assistance from the Soviet Union—on the other side of the barricades stressing class struggle and dismissing their brethren as little more than racialists. It was a far cry from the Fifth Pan-African Congress in Manchester in 1945.[53] It would have been well if she had come to this 1974 meeting, not least because of the prestige she carried but also because she had operated on both sides of the barricades of this continuing ideological controversy of race versus class. Perhaps it would have forced her to clarify her positions or bring clarity to the minds of others.

One of her correspondents questioned the "wisdom" of James for "being involved in so questionable a project as this conference. Before meeting him I just assumed, like so many older men, he needed the visibility."[54] Though accustomed by now to being consigned to the margins, Graham Du Bois moved with alacrity to "firmly disassociate" herself from 6-PAC.[55] Later with her typical allure, she apologized—sort of—to a friend who remained involved with the project. "I guess you're mad at me," she said charmingly, "but I'm not at all at you, so now that all the 'Pan African' hullabalu [sic] is over let's kiss and make up." Increasingly contemplative as she reached the end of her journey, she acknowledged, "I am too far along in years to allow myself to use up energy and strength futilely and to be involved in arguments which nobody wants to hear."[56]

One of Graham Du Bois's endearing traits was that her eclectic philosophy could emit conflicting signals confusing to nationalists and socialists alike, but she did not necessarily berate one or the other for following what they perceived to be her lead. She once told Howard Fast, who had long since broken with the organized movement for socialism, that "there are many good, honest people about—even among leaders—and I'd like for you to believe that in spite of everything WE ARE ON THE WINNING SIDE! Nor do I attempt to define that WE. My illusions have all been swept away by wrestling with realities."[57] She was moving from the principle "all those who are not with us are against us" to "all those who are not against us are with us."

This did not involve the sacrifice of principle. "Our world is extremely complex today," she wrote in 1972, "yet, it's not too hard to understand. Some countries are on the side of imperialism—some countries are struggling against imperialism."[58] Her position was that she was with the latter.

She could be accused of applying such principles inconsistently, but as she grew older she tried "very hard to remain uninvolved in petty disputes among our people. They are all struggling against terrible odds, they have inferiority complexes, they are torn between conflicting powers and influences. I do not criticize because my heart is torn with sympathy."[59] Thus she tried "very hard not [to] get myself hemmed in by cliques."[60] In 1974 she recommended her current philosophy: "Take care of yourselves. As I get older I try to heed that advice—and realize that I can't change the world. I'll have to accept it and get as *much out of living as I can give!*" (emphasis in original).[61]

This outlook was put to the test when Martha Dodd, the daughter of the U.S. ambassador to Germany in the 1930s, and her husband, Alfred Stern—both now living in Czechoslovakia—reprimanded her after a houseguest of Graham Du Bois in Cairo in 1973 brought rich gossip back with him to Prague. According to Dodd, he said that Graham Du Bois "was never especially friendly with us" though she used to visit their "Connecticut house . . . quite often, spent a pre-marriage sojourn [there] and stayed week-ends later." "Could it be," Dodd wondered, that anger arose "because I questioned your Marxism."[62] Graham Du Bois responded that she had the "ordinary sense not to talk as you tell me he talked to *absolute strangers,*" and in any event, "how in the world could you possibly think that any exchange on Marxism could affect my feelings toward a friend? I am certainly not that narrowminded" (emphasis in original).[63] But in 1973 friendships all over the world were being broken because of the clash of Moscow versus Beijing, nationalism versus socialism, and all manner of ideological disputes. To her credit, Graham Du Bois tried to avoid these pitfalls.

■

Graham Du Bois did mellow as time passed, becoming more reluctant to plunge headlong into sectarian disputes. However, a constant throughout her life was her difficulty in embracing feminism overtly and the concomitant difficulties that arose from her relationships with certain men. Of course—before and after Du Bois—she was an exemplar of the independent, productive woman, and her generally positive relationship with her second husband demonstrated that she was able to make sound judgments about men; yet this was not necessarily the most accurate gauge of her own "gender trouble."

Graham Du Bois's opinion was that she was "well supplied with men counselors: brothers, presidents, Bernie, Abbott—and heaven knows I appreciate them." Abbott Simon, a codefendant of Du Bois during his trial, had grown closer to her over the years and had visited her in Ghana. Bernard Jaffe, her lawyer, helped to rescue her from Ghana when she found herself in the clutches of the military. He looked after her interests—particularly her financial interests—"in every way enabling me to live independently, comfortably and free to go about the writing which I consider important"; this she could "never repay."[64]

However, her friendship with Jaffe was not necessarily typical of her relationships with men. From the time she left her first husband, through the death of her first son, to her marriage to Du Bois, to her personal reaction to the overthrow of Nkrumah, relationships with men had been a driving force in her life—and these were not always in *her* best "interests." As she said more than once, she viewed herself as "the constant Mother anxious to straighten out tangles."[65] In this role she had adopted as "sons" figures as diverse as Malcolm X and Stokeley Carmichael. But this kindly and maternal attitude could backfire on her.

Joseph Opaku was a Nigerian living in the United States who was involved in a number of business deals. Though she realized that his businesses were not problem-free, after he visited her in Cairo she decided to invest a hefty ten thousand dollars in his firm and placed her novel with his publishing firm.[66] Then his wife sued him for divorce and "threatened to name" Graham Du Bois "as having alienated his affections if he puts up a fight to get the little boy! . . . He timidly told me that he might have to get an affidavit from me denying her allegations." At a time when most her age were settling into a comfortable dotage, Graham Du Bois was being accused of carrying on a torrid affair with a man who easily could have passed for her son.[67] Soon thereafter, she was "disgusted with Joe."[68] He was approaching her with another scheme—to invest in a picture book of a recent boxing match between Joe Frazier and Muhammad Ali.[69] Apparently she never recouped her ten thousand dollars. This was only one example of how her relationships with the "sons" she adopted could go awry.

The amateur therapist could conclude easily that her second husband was something of a substitute for the father she adored and that her adopted "sons"—even if one accepts the "oedipal" aspect—provided emotional compensation for the loss of her firstborn and her neglect of her children while she was clawing her way to success.[70] However, she still had a perpetual man in her life, her son David, and he was not always happy with how the person who he could legitimately call "mother" treated him. Once he went so far as to accuse her of "conspiring against me in her best interest." This was when she was cultivating

Opaku and was trying to influence her son to place his novel with Opaku's already shaky publishing house.[71] Though she could be quite solicitous toward her adopted sons, at times she seemed less than generous toward David. He helped her move to Cairo, where he had been staying previously, but then he moved to the United States for a while, and when he expressed an interest in returning to Egypt she was reluctant to facilitate his arrival.[72] After he became involved with the Black Panther Party—at one time editing its newspaper—she objected, calling it "utter folly!"[73] Parent-child relationships are inherently difficult, but unlike in her other relationships, she did not seem to be more forgiving with her own son as time passed. Perhaps he reminded her of a first husband she had long since tried to forget.

Her relationships with her son and Joseph Opaku, like her spectacularly ill-timed friendship with the U.S. ambassador to Ghana, were suggestive of a lack of judgment when it came to dealing with men. Her advice to friends reflected this at times also. Her friend Vivian Hallinan came to her with complaints about the wandering eye of her spouse, Vincent; "he is a difficult and unpredictable man," she said of her husband, a progressive and prosperous attorney. "I can go to jail for thirty days for equality for Negroes, but in my own home I'm a second class citizen. I have fought for years, gone without talking for days, weeks, months—but he always wins. He has to!"[74] Graham Du Bois reminded her mischievously that "there are plenty of women around who would be delighted to become 'Mrs. Vincent Hallinan'" and she should just try to accommodate him. "Men are trying under the best circumstances," she suggested properly, "and especially strong men who are determined to dominate. But then," she added strikingly,

> we *prefer strong men*—so what can we expect? It is much easier and simpler to let them dominate. It makes them happy and half of the time we have little to lose. . . . I am not sure I agree with the "screaming and yelling back." . . . In other words, you give in first—and save his masculine vanity. (Emphasis in original)[75]

She added that Du Bois did not have this urge to dominate, which made him "wonderful. He could laugh. It was not in my nature to laugh much—but *he gave me the gift of laughter*" (emphasis in original). Graham Du Bois's friend found all this "hard" to "stomach" and reminded her defensively that "there are a few men who would not be a marrying Vivian Hallinan."[76]

Hallinan realized that Graham Du Bois's views on gender relat. were not exactly avant-garde. Graham Du Bois had been raised in . era of runaway male supremacy. Her youthful experiences had in cluded united and militant assaults against Jim Crow, while she had reason to believe that her sisters across the color line might not include her in their definition of womanhood. In other circumstances, however, Graham Du Bois could display a feminist awareness. Though she willingly took the surname of her second husband, she did not appreciate the "promotion which has recently been used so widely on me 'the widow of so and so.' Except in the case of the 'Memoirs' being the widow of anybody is entirely irrelevant. I want to stand on my own feet and not lean on anybody's reputation or prestige."[77]

Throughout her life, she did stand on her own feet, most splendidly in Ghana from 1963 to 1966. In 1960 there were ten women in Ghana's parliament, and the *Ghanaian Times* proudly announced that the women of their nation had "surpassed the women of the United States in their political attainments."[78] Though her portfolio was television, Graham Du Bois took an abiding interest in women's affairs too.[79] This was no easy assignment, which sheds light on why some of her opinions on gender are seen today as retrograde. Put simply, on both sides of the Atlantic, she was operating in an environment infected with a male supremacy that some men defended on grounds of "tradition."[80] For example, when there was a push in Ghana for a positive quota to expand the representation of women in parliament, Victor Owusu of the opposition spoke insultingly of a "sprinkling of lip-sticked and pan-caked faces of doubtful utility to the deliberations of the House."[81] Just as it is difficult to improve one's tennis game while playing with total incompetents, it is difficult to generate a forward-looking view of gender when surrounded by male chauvinists.

Still, when it counted, Graham Du Bois could be counted on. The texture of her life resonated with the idea of women's self-assertion and independence. She was a bulwark of support when Angela Davis was indicted, rallying women in Cairo and beyond. She "managed to get together a number of journalists in the office of the largest Arabic language newspaper in the Middle East" to explain the case and rally support.[82] When Davis was freed, she had helped to make "elaborate preparations" for the "women of Tanzania" to greet her.[83]

addition to male supremacy, Graham Du Bois was influenced by she perceived as excesses of the early feminist movement of the Us and what she perceived as its difficulty in reaching women of olor. By way of contrast, she began a book on "Women in China"—for they were "really liberated"—as a way to counter "all the crazy 'women's liberation' doings in the West."[84] In short, though she was able to forcefully confront white supremacy, she was much less successful in confronting male supremacy; no doubt part of the reason was that she viewed the fundamentally antiracist projects of decolonization and desegregation as her leading priorities.

■

During the 1970s, the final decade of her life, Graham Du Bois belatedly began to receive the recognition and compensation she merited. Her lifelong quest for financial security reached a new plateau when the University of Massachusetts paid her approximately $150,000 for the papers of Du Bois.[85] This financial plateau had been reached via marriage, a striking indicator; but this only brought her more problems as the same institutions that had dodged her—like Fisk, which canceled her 1970 lecture under pressure—were now playing the nationalist card. Massachusetts "was truly mauled by the heads of certain black universities" for supposedly "seizing what properly belonged to one of them!"[86] Though many of these same institutions had hidden in the bushes and kept silent when Du Bois was indicted and then moved to Africa, now they were upset because he had been buried in Ghana instead of the United States.[87]

Times change. Another thing that changed after her tour of the United States was the numerous Afro-American tourists who showed up at her Cairo apartment. In 1972 she complained that "half of New York and Washington has been here."[88] This flood of visitors could be irritating; one noted historian whom she viewed as a "poor, little jerk" proved to be a "minor annoyance" who drove her to distraction.[89] On the other hand, the people who besieged her in Cairo often returned to the United States with a heightened appreciation for the Arabs' struggle against Israel and with the seeds of the philosophy that would eventually be termed Afrocentrism.

Perhaps in response, she fled her home for China; she also traveled to Japan, where she renewed acquaintances with Sanyo executives.[90] Her wanderlust was such that she did not stop there. Now nearing eighty, she was enticed to return to the United States, where she would teach at both Harvard and the University of Massachusetts. Such traveling was taxing for those in the best of health; it left her "frightfully tired," to the point where she was not sure she was "completely well or not."[91]

However, she found that entering the United States to work would not be so simple. In the summer of 1974 her lawyer informed her that

> getting your name removed from that [black]list has become almost as incredible as Watergate. Mr. Kailey [sic] the State Department man to whom we wrote . . . has informed us that your file has been lost. They simply can't locate it. When David Rein asked [if] the file was lost, no one would know that you're on the list, his response was that somehow the people in the State Department "remembered" it.[92]

When she went to the U.S. embassy in Cairo in the summer of 1975 to obtain a visa so she could teach in the fall, she found, "somewhat to my surprise . . . that I was still on the Prohibitive List as of the last publication, May 1975. This means that once more the Embassy here has to obtain from the State Department a *waiver* before they can issue the J-1 visa" (emphasis in original).[93] Again, the State Department underestimated the political support that she could muster: by the fall of 1975 she was in Amherst, teaching "What Is Literature? A Seminar in Creative Writing" two mornings per week. Her syllabus included works by James Baldwin, Gwendolyn Brooks, Han Suyin, Alexandre Dumas, Alexander Pushkin, Jacques Roumain, Sonia Sanchez, and other writers she admired.[94] Her department chair, John Bracey, informed the dean there that "as a result of feedback from our students and faculty and from other members of the university community," he was recommending that she be "reappointed as Distinguished Visiting Lecturer"; she was an "excellent teacher," he said.[95]

During this stay in the United States she became one of China's staunchest and most visible supporters. She was not alone. Though China was in league with U.S. imperialism in Southern Africa and elsewhere, a younger generation that was alienated by Soviet socialism yet yearned for an apparent challenge to Washington that was at once "socialist" and "colored" flocked to Beijing's banner. At a memorial in

Manhattan's Chinatown for her friend Zhou En-lai, 1,300 heard her speak.[96] On behalf of the U.S.-China People's Friendship Association she addressed 750 more.[97] In San Francisco she "received a standing ovation" from seven hundred as she blended two of her major interests by speaking on "Africa and China." According to the reporter present, "Du Bois pointed out the contrast between the comradely attitude of the Chinese and the elitist attitude of the Soviet Union's representatives in China."[98]

While in Oakland she was the guest of honor at a party sponsored by the Black Panthers. The FBI noted that she called the BPP leader Elaine Brown not "sister but daughter"—one of the rare instances when she embraced a younger woman in the same manner as she had embraced younger men. She praised the party leader Huey Newton, who "is recognized not only in [this] country, but in Africa and in China." She applauded her son David, then working for the party newspaper—"I am proud of him for that."[99] Later she worried that her son's political commitments meant he would be ambushed by "Eldridge Cleaver's ardent followers in Paris . . . [who] would not hesitate to kill him" or the "CIA in Cairo."[100] Cleaver, who ultimately became a right-winger, was threatening her surviving son as the BPP sank into a fratricidal dispute.

■

As early as 1973 the Ghana high commissioner in London—perhaps as wish fulfillment—had reported the death of Shirley Graham Du Bois.[101] This was premature, but it was understandable why they may have been moved to report her passing. For a woman of her advanced years, she pushed herself beyond the limits of reason. In 1973, for example, she flew east from Cairo to California, then on to Ohio and the East Coast of the United States, then a few days later to Tanzania—all within weeks.[102]

Living in underdeveloped areas was not easy for her either. While in Accra she had suffered through a "flooding of a cesspool," which was a "health menace to our neighborhood"; it was "truly a blight" with "foul odors."[103] Cairo had its own unique problems, not the least of which was air pollution.

Her mental health was not always the best either, particularly after the coup in Ghana. In 1966 she told one of her brothers she had the "worst case of what I suppose can be called 'flu' I've ever encountered"; worse, "the arrival of December, bringing the inevitable 'Christmas' had already depressed me. I had a feeling that I'd like to sleep the month out and just not know anything about it."[104] A few months later she took "sleeping pills" to force herself to "stop thinking and this morning I simply made myself stay in bed"; she felt like a "'displaced person.' . . . Where and how can I live?"[105] Later she developed a hearing problem and a stomach ailment and then "in addition to the swelling of my fingers, my left hand is beginning to pain."[106] She developed arthritis; then the "nightly blackouts" in Cairo "began to depress me."[107] By early 1974 she was moaning about being "harassed with all kind of 'old folks' aches and pains. . . . we had a frightfully cold January. . . . These have been exceedingly strenuous days for me. And I am very tired."[108] By mid-1975 she discovered a "hard lump in the soft tissues of my body which I do not understand and is cause for concern."[109]

While she was teaching in Amherst in 1975, John Bracey noticed her persistent "coughing" and her penchant for downing Scotch liquor. Shortly thereafter she was diagnosed with cancer, and Chinese doctors told her that if she came there for treatment they might be able to stave it off for four or five years. She could not leave until later—but by then it was too late.[110]

By early 1976 she was in Capital Hospital in Beijing; her "chief complaints" were "general weakness and loss of body weight for 3 months and discovery of a mass in her right breast of one and a half month's duration. In summary, the patient has been suffering from advanced carcinoma of the right breast with wide-spread metastasis." She was "in serious condition."[111]

This sobering diagnosis did not cause her to slow down. By the summer of 1976 she was telling her son that "after three weeks in tropical China I'll return to Cairo completely well and return to a year's intensive writing."[112] She wanted to travel alone from China to Cairo via Karachi—her usual route—then go on to London, but her doctors and son balked. A massive earthquake in China disrupted her plans and caused her to be evacuated to Shanghai. It was a shocking 8.3 on the Richter scale and according to her son, was "most exciting and not a little frightening."[113] Bedridden, she insisted on being active. She assembled a book of pictures on the life of Du Bois, worked on a book on

China and a novel, studied Mandarin Chinese, and admired the notification she had received about her biography of Julius Nyerere being judged "first runner up for the seventh annual Coretta Scott King Award."[114]

In the spring of 1976 she complained that her "treatment" was "rough. My bottom is sore from injections, my hands and arms are tender from repeated blood infusions, my stomach frequently rebels against the large amounts of pills I swallow."[115] To a visitor she continued to defend China, though he left with "serious doubts about [its] foreign policy—especially as it affects Angola and Chile."[116] In response she sent a message to her attorney that she wanted to give a political statement she had drafted the "widest possible circulation"; it was written to those "masses being exploited by 'social imperialism' and so-called detente."[117]

Despite her infirmities, a few months before her eightieth birthday she took off for London, where she spent "three delightful weeks."[118] This was not helpful to her recovery from cancer. She returned to China at an important moment: Mao and Zhou had died and the former's widow was under fire for leading a so-called gang of four that was being blamed for many of China's vast problems. Things were topsy-turvy, and Graham Du Bois, who was quite close to the leadership, could not help but feel the reverberations. One sympathetic friend writing from China in mid-1976 said that

> 2 weeks ago she was quite strong, but when I visited her yesterday she was weak and discouraged. She's lonely too, and eager for news from all her friends. . . . for such an old woman to be all alone so many miles from family and friends at the time when for the first time she is really ill is very hard.[119]

The news worsened. By March 1977 her son said despondently that "she is now in the final stages of terminal cancer. She can neither read, write or maintain a coherent conversation."[120] She did manage to scribble delusional ramblings in a diary that involved frequent references to the late Kwame Nkrumah (who had died in 1972) not wanting to greet Zhou at the airport and about the former Ghanaian leader telling Zhou that he wanted Graham Du Bois to stay in Ghana. There were also ramblings about her father beating one of her brothers.[121]

A few days after her son's sad words, she died; it was the first week of April 1977. A friend of her son summed up the meaning of Shirley Graham Du Bois's life:

> I felt about her that the face she turned to the world—even perhaps to those nearer was the harsher, more dominant side and that she may have feared the more loving, gentle aspect of herself. It is not easy to be a woman—even less easy to be a very gifted woman—and less still to be a black woman—she had all three hurdles to clear.[122]

Notes

Unless otherwise indicated, items of personal correspondence to and from Shirley Graham Du Bois are from the Shirley Graham Du Bois Papers, courtesy of David Du Bois, Cairo, Egypt

OTHER MANUSCRIPT COLLECTIONS CITED IN THE NOTES

American Labor Party Papers, Rutgers University–New Brunswick, Library
Cedric Belfrage Papers, New York University Library
Black Academy of Arts and Letters Papers, Schomburg Center, New York Public Library
Earl Browder Papers, Syracuse University Library
Stokeley Carmichael Papers, Stanford University Library
John Henrik Clarke Papers, Schomburg Center, New York Public Library
Peter Currie Papers, Hoover Institution, Palo Alto, California
David Du Bois Papers, Courtesy of David Du Bois, Cairo, Egypt
W. E. B. Du Bois Papers, University of Massachusetts–Amherst Library
Federal Theater Project Papers, Library of Congress, Washington, D.C.
Foreign Affairs Oral History Program–Georgetown University, Washington, D.C.
Oral History Collection Fisk University Library, Nashville, Tennessee
Hallie Flanagan Papers, New York Public Library
Lewis Gann-Peter Duignan Papers, Hoover Institution, Palo Alto, California
Shirley Graham File, Oberlin College, Oberlin, Ohio
Shirley Graham Du Bois Papers, Amistad Research Center, Tulane University, New Orleans
Paul Green Papers, University of North Carolina–Chapel Hill Library
Ewart Guinier Papers, Schomburg Center, New York Public Library
Dabu Gzinga Papers, Howard University Library, Washington, D.C.
Hatch-Billops Collection, Courtesy of James Hatch, New York, New York
Esther Jackson Papers, Courtesy of Esther Jackson, Brooklyn, New York
James Weldon Johnson–Langston Hughes Collection, Yale University, New Haven, Connecticut
Lyndon Baines Johnson Papers, University of Texas–Austin Library
Marvin Liebman Papers, Hoover Institution, Palo Alto, California

Jay Lovestone Papers, Hoover Institution, Palo Alto, California
Louis Massiah Papers, Courtesy of Louis Massiah, Philadelphia, Pennsylvania
Julian Mayfield Papers, Schomburg Center, New York Public Library
Miscellaneous American Letters, Schomburg Center, New York Public Library
George Murphy Papers, Howard University Library, Washington, D.C.
NAACP Papers, Library of Congress, Washington, D.C.
New Deal Agencies and Black America in the 1930s Papers, Schomburg Center, New York Public Library
Huey Newton Foundation Records, Stanford University Library
Nixon Presidential Materials Project, National Archives, College Park, Maryland
Kwame Nkrumah Papers, Howard University Library, Washington, D.C.
Mary White Ovington Papers, Wayne State University Library, Detroit, Michigan
P. L. Prattis Papers, Howard University Library, Washington, D.C.
Roselyn Richardson Papers, Indiana Historical Society, Indianapolis, Indiana
Eslanda Robeson Papers, Howard University Library, Washington, D.C.
Paul Robeson Papers, Howard University Library, Washington, D.C.
Arthur Spingarn Papers, Howard University Library, Washington, D.C.
Third Party Presidential Nominating Conventions, Proceedings, Records, Etc., Wayne State University, Detroit, Michigan
Van Deman Collection, Senate Internal Security Subcommittee Papers, Library of Congress, Washington, D.C.
Washington Conservatory of Music Papers, Howard University Library, Washington, D.C.
G. Mennen Williams Papers, University of Michigan Library, Ann Arbor, Michigan
Robert F. Williams Papers, University of Michigan Library, Ann Arbor, Michigan
Ella Winter Papers, Columbia University Library, New York, New York
Women in Journalism, Oral History Research Office, Columbia University Library, New York, New York

NOTES TO THE PREFACE

1. This trait was not unique to her. See, e.g., James Olney, ed., *Autobiography: Essays Theoretical and Critical* (Princeton: Princeton University Press, 1980), 28–48; Timothy Dow Adams, *Telling Lies in Modern American Autobiography* (Chapel Hill: University of North Carolina Press, 1990) pp. ix–xi, 1–16, passim. To be fair, recovering distant memories, particularly those inflected with racism and sexism, is not a simple process. See, e.g., Jennifer Fleischner, *Mastering Slavery: Memory, Family and Identity in Women's Slave Narratives* (New York: New York University Press, 1996).

2. See, e.g., Sara Alpern et al., eds., *The Challenge of Feminist Biography: Writ-*

ing the Lives of Modern American Women (Urbana: University of Illinois Press, 1992); Carol Ascher et al., eds., *Between Women: Biographers, Novelists, Critics, Teachers, and Artists Write about Their Work on Women* (New York: Routledge, 1993).

3. *People's Daily Graphic* (Ghana), 4 September 1986.

4. At times I will refer to her as Shirley Graham, particularly in the period before her marriage to W. E. B. Du Bois in 1951.

5. Darlene Clark Hine and Kathleen Thompson, *A Shining Thread of Hope: The History of Black Women in America* (New York: Broadway, 1998), 221. See also Kevin K. Gaines, *Uplifting the Race: Black Leadership, Politics and Culture in the Twentieth Century* (Chapel Hill: University of North Carolina Press, 1996).

6. Cheryl Lynn Greenberg, *Or Does It Explode? Black Harlem during the Great Depression* (New York: Oxford University Press, 1991), 122.

7. George S. Schuyler, *Black No More: Being an Account of the Strange and Wonderful Workings of Science in the Land of the Free, A.D., 1933–1940* (Boston: Northeastern University Press, 1989), 90. See also Oscar Renal Williams III, "The Making of a Black Conservative: George S. Schuyler" (Ph.D. diss., Ohio State University, 1997); Harry McKinley Williams, Jr., "When Black Is Right: The Life and Writings of George S. Schuyler" (Ph.D. diss., Brown University, 1988.)

8. See, e.g., Cheryl Wall, ed., *Changing Our Own Words: Essays on Criticism, Theory and Writing by Black Women* (New Brunswick: Rutgers University Press, 1989); Henry Louis Gates, Jr., *Reading Black, Reading Feminist: A Critical Anthology* (New York: Meridian, 1990); Patricia Hill Collins, *Black Feminist Thought: Knowledge, Consciousness and the Politics of Empowerment* (New York: Routledge, 1991).

9. Mary Helen Washington, ed., *Invented Lives: Narratives of Black Women, 1860–1960* (Garden City: Doubleday, 1987). See also Claudia Tate, ed., *Black Women Writers at Work* (New York: Continuum, 1983); Claudia Tate, *Psychoanalysis and Black Novels: Desire and the Protocols of Race* (New York: Oxford University Press, 1998).

10. See, e.g., Stanley Elkins, *Slavery: A Problem in American Institutional and Intellectual Life* (Chicago: University of Chicago Press, 1976; Naim Akbar, *Chains and Images of Psychological Slavery* (Jersey City: New Mind Productions, 1984); Paul Laurence Dunbar, *The Complete Poems of Paul Laurence Dunbar* (New York: Dodd Mead, 1980).

11. Ollie Harrington, *Why I Left America and Other Essays* (Jackson: University Press of Mississippi, 1993), 12.

12. Cf. Judith Rich Harris, *The Nurture Assumption: Why Children Turn Out the Way They Do* (New York: Free Press, 1998); Carol Gilligan, *In a Different Voice: Psychological Theory and Women's Development* (Cambridge: Harvard University Press, 1982); Nancy Friday, *My Mother/My Self: The Daughter's Search for Identity* (New York: Delta, 1997).

13. Shirley Graham Du Bois to Randolph Bromery, 12 August 1974.

14. Shirley Graham Du Bois, interview by Abigail Simon, 10 April 1974, Shirley Graham Du Bois Papers.

15. Shirley Graham Du Bois, "An Explanation," circa 1962, Shirley Graham Du Bois Papers.

16. Shirley Graham Du Bois, *His Day Is Marching On* (Philadelphia: Lippincott, 1971), 12, 28.

17. Gerald Horne, "Race for the Planet: African-Americans and U.S. Foreign Policy Reconsidered," *Diplomatic History* 19, no. 1 (winter 1995): 159–66; Gerald Horne, "Who Lost the Cold War? Africans and African-Americans," *Diplomatic History* 20, no. 4, (fall 1996): 613–26.

18. Gerald Horne, "Myth and the Making of 'Malcolm X,'" *American Historical Review* 98 (April 1993): 440–50. Gerald Horne, "Comment: Liberalism and the Left," *Radical History Review* 71 (1998): 34–40.

19. Robert Dee Thompson, Jr., "A Socio-Biography of Shirley Graham–Du Bois" (Ph.D. diss., University of California–Santa Cruz, 1997), 18, 19.

20. See, e.g., Stetson Kennedy, *Jim Crow Guide: The Way It Was* (Boca Raton: Florida Atlantic University Press, 1990).

21. Shirley Graham to Paul Green, 24 May 1940, box 8, Paul Green Papers.

22. Molly Ladd-Taylor and Lauri Umansky, eds., *"Bad" Mothers: The Politics of Blame in Twentieth Century America* (New York: New York University Press, 1998).

23. Shirley Graham Du Bois, *His Day Is Marching On*, 37–39.

24. Kevin K. Gaines, "The Cold War and the African-American Expatriate Community in Nkrumah's Ghana," in Christopher Simpson, ed., *Universities and Empire: Money and Politics in the Social Sciences during the Cold War* (New York: New Press, 1998), 135–58.

25. See, e.g., Gloria I. Joseph and Jill Lewis, *Common Differences: Conflicts in Black and White Feminist Perspectives* (New York: Anchor, 1981); Louise Newman, *White Women's Rights: The Racial Origins of American Feminism* (New York: Oxford University Press, 1998). The author sees a core contradiction in the heart of early feminist theory. At a time when U.S. elites were concerned with imperialist projects, "progressive" Euro-American women developed an explicitly racial ideology to promote their cause, defending patriarchy for "primitives" while calling for its elimination among the "civilized."

26. Roselyn Richardson, interview by author, 29 June 1998.

27. See, e.g., Molefi K. Asante, *Afrocentricity* (Trenton: Africa World Press, 1988); Wilson Jeremiah Moses, *Afrotopia: The Roots of African American Popular History* (New York: Cambridge University Press, 1998). Though this form of black nationalism is widely viewed as an exclusively U.S.-generated phenomenon, this is not altogether accurate. Kofi Ghanaba, a Ghanaian jazz musician also known as Guy Warren, exhibited "militant Afro-centric tendencies" in his

music and life, and he was not unique. Thus, residing in Nkrumah's Ghana was further impetus for Graham Du Bois's evolution toward black nationalism. See, e.g., Kwaku Sakyi-Addo, "Child of Ghana," *BBC: Focus on Africa* 9, no.4 (October–December 1998): 55–57. See also Ian Carr et al., *Jazz: The Essential Companion* (London: Grafton, 1987).

NOTES TO THE INTRODUCTION

1. *Baltimore Afro-American*, 5 April 1977; *Boston Herald-American*, 5 April 1977; *Xinhua*, 3 April 1977.

2. *Xinhua*, 3 April 1977.

3. Sidney Rittenberg, interview by author, 26 April 1997.

4. Shirley Graham Du Bois, interview undated (circa 1972), Shirley Graham Du Bois Papers; application for Guggenheim fellowship, 1934, Shirley Graham Du Bois Papers. But see Shirley Graham Du Bois to Maggie, 11 September 1973: "If I were twenty-five years younger and did not have the necessity immediately of earning a living, I would do nothing but *study foreign languages*. . . . I have studied several languages but never had the time and opportunity really to become fluent in any of them" (emphasis in original).

5. Elizabeth Brown-Guillory, ed., *Wines in the Wilderness: Plays by African-American Women from the Harlem Renaissance to the Present* (Westport: Greenwood, 1990), 80; see also Leo Hamalian and James V. Hatch, eds., *The Roots of African American Drama: An Anthology of Early Plays, 1858–1938* (Detroit: Wayne State University Press, 1991); Darwin T. Turner, ed., *An Anthology of Black Drama in America* (Washington, DC: Howard University Press, 1994).

6. Patricia R. Schroeder, "Transforming Images of Blackness: Dramatic Representations, Woman Playwrights and the Harlem Renaissance," in Janelle Reinelt, ed., *Crucibles of Crisis: Performing Social Change* (Ann Arbor: University of Michigan Press, 1996), 107–22, 117. The author continues, "During the course of the short play we hear both secular and religious songs, witness a variety of dances."

7. Carl Van Vechten to Shirley Graham, 22 March 1947. He added, "You see I had only read your books for young people before and this is such an advance in style, manner and thought that I am convinced you are going a long way and have only just begun your glorious journey." In his blurb for the book he called it "a pulsating reconstruction, which will leave the reader breathless of the triumphant melodrama that was the life of Frederick Douglass."

8. *Ghanaian Times*, 6 April 1964.

9. David Du Bois, interview by author, 16 May 1996; Shirley Graham to Frederick Artz, 11 August 1973: Graham had known her "for years" and after a recent Baker New York performance, she "went back stage to speak to her after the show. My publisher just happened to see how warmly I was welcomed and

he got an idea." The plan was for her to go to Monaco to write Baker's biography, but this project was not realized. See also Phyllis Rose, *Jazz Cleopatra: Josephine Baker in Her Time* (Garden City: Doubleday, 1989); and Sarah B. McCall, "The Musical Fallout of Political Activism: Government Investigations of Musicians in the United States, 1930–1960" (Ph.D. diss., University of North Texas, 1993).

10. Katherine Dunham to Shirley Graham, 10 January 1941. See also Ruth Beckford, *Katherine Dunham: A Biography* (New York: M. Dekker, 1979); Ethel Waters to Shirley Graham, 28 May 1940. See also Ethel Waters, *His Eye Is on the Sparrow: An Autobiography* (Garden City: Doubleday, 1951).

11. Maud Cuney-Hare to Shirley Graham, 9 December 1934. See also Maud Cuney-Hare, *Negro Musicians and Their Music* (Washington, DC: Associated Publishers, 1936).

12. Carol Mueller, "Ella Baker and the Origins of 'Participatory Democracy,'" in Vicki Crawford et al., eds., *Women in the Civil Rights Movement* (Bloomington: Indiana University Press, 1993), 51–70; Barbara J. Ransby, "Ella J. Baker and the Black Radical Tradition" (Ph.D. diss., University of Michigan, 1996). See also Joanne Grant, *Ella Baker: Freedom Bound* (New York: Wiley, 1998); Belinda Robnett, *How Long? How Long? African-American Women in the Struggle for Civil Rights* (New York: Oxford University Press, 1997).

13. Shirley Graham to Robert Nemiroff, 26 June 1973. Hansberry's first published work, a poem that adumbrated many of the themes in her future creations, was published in the left-wing journal *Masses & Mainstream*, where Graham Du Bois served as a contributing editor. See Lorraine Hansberry, "Flag from a Kitchenette Window," *Masses & Mainstream* 3, no. 9 (September 1950): 4. Hansberry is described here as a twenty-year-old "art student in Chicago." Julian Bond and Ishmael Reed also published some of their earliest work in this journal, which was widely viewed as being within the orbit of the Communist Party. See, e.g., Julian Bond, "Cambridge, Mass.," *Masses & Mainstream* 16, no. 7 (July 1963): 9; and Ishmael Reed, "The Arse Belching Muse," *Masses & Mainstream* 16, no. 7 (July 1963): 10–11. See also Carol Dawn Allen, "American Lives, Lived Positions: African-American Women Intellectuals" (Ph.D. diss., Rutgers University, 1997).

14. Ruth Morris Graham, *The Saga of the Morris Family* (Columbus, GA: Brentwood Christian Communications, 1984), 81.

15. Walter White to Shirley Graham, 30 June 1932. Graham was also friendly with the civil rights leader Leslie Pinckney Hill. Leslie Pinckney Hill to Shirley Graham, 3 August 1933.

16. Eric Walrond to Shirley Graham, 19 October 1931.

17. Rosalyn Richardson, interviewed by author, 29 June 1998.

18. Shirley Graham to Edwin Embree, 3 March 1944.

19. Alain Locke to Shirley Graham, undated. Locke felt that this book fell

"badly at the end—as did *Native Son* also—but the early and mid-sections are important social documentation." However, an "erroneous impression is given that this is the typical Negro Expression. It isn't, thank god."

20. Hastings Banda to Shirley Graham, 10 August 1932. See also Philip Short, *Banda* (London: Routledge and Kegan Paul, 1974).

21. Minutes of meeting between Shirley Graham Du Bois and Enver Hoxha, 27 November 1964, Shirley Graham Du Bois Papers; Shirley Graham Du Bois to "My Dear Comrade Vito," 13 December 1964. See also Miranda Vickers, *The Albanians: A Modern History* (New York: I. B. Tauris, 1995).

22. Ossie Davis and Ruby Dee to Shirley Graham Du Bois, circa 1964. See also Ossie Davis and Ruby Dee, *With Ossie and Ruby: In This Life Together* (New York: Morrow, 1998).

23. See, e.g., Cheryl Wall, *Women of the Harlem Renaissance* (Bloomington: Indiana University Press, 1995): Graham is not mentioned here; despite the book's title, W. E. B. Du Bois is. W. E. B. Du Bois is mentioned but Shirley Graham Du Bois is not in E. Quita Craig, *Black Drama of the Federal Theater: Beyond the Formal Horizons* (Amherst: University of Massachusetts Press, 1980). He is mentioned and she is not in Sally Burke, *American Feminist Playwrights: A Critical History* (Boston: Twayne, 1996). She is not mentioned in Elizabeth Ammons, *Conflicting Stories: American Women Writers at the Turn into the Twentieth Century* (New York: Oxford University Press, 1992). Graham Du Bois is not mentioned in Barbara Christian, *Black Feminist Criticism: Perspectives on Black Women Writers* (New York: Pergamon, 1985). James Young, in *Black Writers of the Thirties* (Baton Rouge: Louisiana State University Press, 1973), ignores women writers generally, not just Shirley Graham.

24. Maya Angelou, *All God's Children Need Traveling Shoes* (New York: Random House, 1986), 145; Maya Angelou, *The Heart of a Woman* (New York: Random House, 1981); see also *New York Times*, 9 July 1964, 16 July 1964.

25. Alice Walker, *Earthling Poems, 1965–1990* (New York: Harcourt Brace, 1991), 295: "Unfortunately, however, her version of Du Bois' career is perhaps more revealing of herself than of her late husband. The gaps in Mrs. Du Bois' memoir are more instructive than her recollections. . . . Instead she clutters her narrative with lengthy accounts of her father's work in the NAACP. . . . She assumes her romance with Du Bois to be as interesting as any other aspect of his career."

26. Dorothy Hunton, interview, 28 May 1992, Louis Massiah Papers: "I didn't know much about Shirley personally. She was rather distant to me for some reason, I don't know why. But we never had any real social contact, although we once in a while would visit. But she was on a different, what shall I say, not a different level but her ideas and things were not like mine. . . . [she] didn't get along with" Alphaeus Hunton either, "because I don't think he believed in a lot of things she was trying to do in Ghana."

27. James Jackson, interview by author, 10 December 1996.

28. Marvel Cooke, interview, 30 October 1989, Columbia University Oral History: Women in Journalism. See also David Levering Lewis, *W. E. B. Du Bois: Biography of a Race, 1868–1919* (New York: Henry Holt, 1993).

29. Shirley Graham Du Bois to Dorothy Markinko, 30 April 1974.

30. Shirley Graham Du Bois to Nathan Hare, 30 July 1972.

31. *Cleveland Plain-Dealer,* 27 February 1996.

32. *New York Times Book Review,* 7 November 1993. See also Sara Alpern et al., eds., *The Challenge of Feminist Biography: Writing the Lives of Modern American Women* (Urbana: University of Illinois Press, 1992); David Novarr, *The Lines of Life: Theories of Biography, 1880–1970* (West Lafayette: Purdue University Press, 1986); Joan Wallach Scott, *Gender and the Politics of History* (New York: Columbia University Press, 1988).

33. P. David Marshall, *Celebrity and Power: Fame in Contemporary Culture* (Minneapolis: University of Minnesota Press, 1997); Richard Schickel, *Intimate Strangers: The Culture of Celebrity* (Garden City: Doubleday, 1985); John C. Fout and Maura Shaw Tantillo, eds., *American Sexual Politics: Sex, Gender and Race Since the Civil War* (Chicago: University of Chicago Press, 1993); Roseann P. Bell, Bettye J. Parker, and Beverly Guy-Sheftall, eds., *Sturdy Black Bridges: Visions of Black Women in Literature* (Garden City: Doubleday, 1979); Esther Ngan-Ling Chow, Doris Wilkinson, and Maxine Baca Zinn, eds., *Race, Class and Gender: Common Bonds, Different Voices* (Thousand Oaks: Sage, 1996); Winnie Mandela, *Part of My Soul Went with Him* (New York: Norton, 1984); Arthur Zipser and Pearl Zipser, *Fire and Grace: The Life of Rose Pastor Stokes* (Athens: University of Georgia Press, 1989).

34. *Daily Worker,* 26 March 1947.

35. Shirley Graham Du Bois, "An Explanation" (summary of *The Woman in the Case,* her biography of Anne Royall), September 1962, Shirley Graham Du Bois Papers.

36. Patricia S. Misciagno, *Rethinking Feminist Identification: The Case for De Facto Feminism* (Westport: Praeger, 1997). Of course, Graham Du Bois's reluctance to identify with feminism may have been related to the historic difficulty that feminism has had in grappling with race and racism. See, e.g., Anne Marie Valk, "Separatism and Sisterhood: Race, Sex and Women's Activism in Washington, D.C., 1963–1980" (Ph.D. diss., Duke University, 1996); Kimberley Christensen, "'With Whom Do You Believe Your Lot Is Cast?' White Feminism and Racism," *Signs* 22 (spring 1997): 617–48; Micaela di Leonardo, ed., *Gender at the Crossroads of Knowledge: Feminist Anthropology in the Postmodern Era* (Berkeley: University of California Press, 1991). Graham Du Bois's lengthy sojourn in Egypt, a nation not known as being in the vanguard of the liberation of women, also may have influenced her often negative reaction to feminism. See Margot Badran, *Feminists, Islam and Nation: Gender and the Making of Modern Egypt*

(Princeton: Princeton University Press, 1995). See also Mary Murray, *The Law of the Father? Patriarchy in the Transition from Feudalism to Capitalism* (New York: Routledge, 1995).

37. Kenneth Greenberg, ed., *The Confessions of Nat Turner and Related Documents* (Boston: Bedford, 1996); John Henrik Clarke, *The Second Crucifixion of Nat Turner* (Baltimore: Black Classic Press, 1997).

38. Faith Davis Ruffins, "'Lifting as We Climb': Black Women and the Preservation of African-American History and Culture," *Gender and History* 6, no. 3 (November 1994): 376–96, 390. She notes how so many of these widows, including Graham Du Bois, were substantially younger than their husbands; she adds,

> The position of "famous widow" is a rather problematic one in the spectrum of cultural work. . . . The conundrum of the "famous widow" highlights a central problematic in the role of Black women in the preservation of African-American history and culture. How does one analyze as well as celebrate women's distinctive experiences within the context of a masculinist nationalist discourse?

See also Belinda Robnett, "African-American Women in the Civil Rights Movement, 1954–1965: Gender, Leadership and Micromobilization," *American Journal of Sociology* 101 (May 1996): 1661–93; Helena M. Pycior, Nancy G. Slack, and Pnina G. Abir-Am, eds., *Creative Couples in the Sciences* (New Brunswick: Rutgers University Press, 1996). Martha Millet, writing about Graham's Douglass biography in the *Daily Worker*, 2 May 1947, noted that "Miss Graham brings us an entirely different Anna—an intelligent free woman, a participant in the organized Abolition movement, a woman and mother who gladly seeks work and income to sustain the family while Frederick goes to England to further his grand undertaking."

39. Daniel Horowitz, "Rethinking Betty Friedan and the Feminist Mystique: Labor Union Radicalism and Feminism in Cold War America," *American Quarterly* 48, no. 1 (March 1996): 1–42. See also Patricia C. Walls, "Defending Their Liberties: Women's Organizations during the McCarthy Era" (Ph.D. diss., University of Maryland, 1994), 208, 211: "At the height of the McCarthy era, a number of women successfully combined anticommunism with their campaign to win equal rights for women. . . . Anna Kelton Wiley, a fellow member of the Connecticut Committee for ERA, combined anticommunism with racism, blaming communist agitators for instigating 'African-American violence and crime in Washington, D.C., in order to encourage racial strife.'" See also Elizabeth V. Spelman, *Inessential Woman: Problems of Exclusion in Feminist Thought* (Boston: Beacon Press, 1988).

40. Graham Hodges, ed., *The Black Loyalist Directory: African-Americans in Exile after the American Revolution* (New York: Garland, 1996); Ellen Gibson

Wilson, *The Loyal Blacks* (New York: Putnam, 1976); Bernard M. Magubane, *The Ties That Bind: African-American Consciousness of Africa* (Trenton: Africa World Press, 1987); Keletso E. Atkins, "'The Black Atlantic Communication Network': African-American Sailors in the Cape of Good Hope Connection," *Issue: A Journal of Opinion* 34, no. 2 (1996): 23–25; Tyler Stovall, *Paris Noir: African Americans in the City of Light* (Boston: Houghton Mifflin, 1996).

41. *Sepia,* January 1975, Hatch-Billops Collection. Graham's ambivalence about feminism should not discourage scholars, feminist or otherwise from re-examining her life. Nevertheless, it is also understandable why feminist scholars may have been ambivalent about Graham.

42. Doris Lessing, *Walking in the Shade: Volume Two of My Autobiography, 1949–1962* (New York: HarperCollins, 1997), 146.

43. John Henrik Clarke, interview, 29 September 1972, Oral History Collection Fisk University Library.

44. Angelou, *All God's Children Need Traveling Shoes,* 138. There was intense speculation about the precise nature of the Graham Du Bois-Nkrumah relationship, particularly after the 1966 coup. However, Nkrumah "seldom spoke of his personal life," once telling Graham Du Bois: "'It has always been my strong conviction that my domestic affairs . . . are purely private matters which should not be mixed up with my official and public life.'" See June Milne, *Kwame Nkrumah: A Biography* (London: Panaf, 1999), 81.

45. Kwame Nkrumah to Shirley Graham Du Bois, 12 November 1967, box 154, Kwame Nkrumah Papers.

46. Shirley Graham to Kwame Nkrumah, 26 November 1967, box 154, Kwame Nkrumah Papers.

47. Elaine May, *Homeward Bound: American Families in the Cold War Era* (New York: Basic, 1988). See, e.g. Amy Swerdlow, "The Congress of American Women: Left-Feminist Peace Politics in the Cold War," in Linda Kerber, Alice Kessler-Harris, and Kathryn Kish Sklar, eds., *U.S. History as Women's History* (Chapel Hill: University of North Carolina Press, 1995), 296–312. See also Lois West, ed., *Feminist Nationalism* (New York: Routledge, 1997); Ethel Klein, *Gender Politics: From Consciousness to Mass Politics* (Cambridge: Harvard University Press, 1984); Joanne Meyerowitz, ed., *Not June Cleaver: Women and Gender in the Postwar United States, 1945–1960* (Philadelphia: Temple University Press, 1994); Cynthia Harrison, *On Account of Sex: The Politics of Women's Issues, 1945–1968* (Berkeley: University of California Press, 1989).

48. Susan Lynn, *Progressive Women in Conservative Times: Racial Justice, Peace and Feminism, 1945 to the 1960s* (New Brunswick: Rutgers University Press, 1992), 4. See also Sara Ruddick, ed., *Between Women: Biographers, Novelists, Critics, Teachers and Artists Write about Their Work on Women* (New York: Routledge, 1993); Carolyn Heilbrun, *Writing a Woman's Life* (New York: Ballantine, 1988);

Nina Mjagkij, "A History of the Black YWCA in America, 1853–1946," (Ph.D. diss., University of Cincinnati, 1990).

49. See, e.g., Glen Jeansonne, *Women of the Far Right: The Mothers' Movement and World War II* (Chicago: University of Chicago Press, 1996); Kathleen Blee, ed., *No Middle Ground: Women and Radical Protest* (New York: New York University Press, 1998); Mary Beth Norton, *Founding Mothers and Fathers: Gendered Power and the Forming of American Society* (New York: Knopf, 1996).

50. John Bracey, interview by author, 4 December 1996.

51. Joanne Braxton, *Black Women Writing Autobiography* (Philadelphia: Temple University Press, 1989), 21. See also Patricia Hill Collins, "The Meaning of Motherhood in Black Culture and Black Mother/Daughter Relationships," *Sage,* fall 1987, 3–10; Elsa Barkley Brown, "Mothers of Mind," *Sage,* spring 1989, 4–11; Evelyn Brooks Higginbotham, "Afro-American Women's History and the Metalanguage of Race," *Signs,* 17 (winter 1992): 251–74; Deborah King, "Multiple Jeopardy, Multiple Consciousness: The Context of Black Feminist Ideology," *Signs,* 14 (autumn 1988): 42–72; Ruth Schwartz Cowan, *More Work for Mother: The Ironies of Household Technology from the Open Hearth to the Microwave* (New York: Basic, 1983). For a fascinating account of the intersection of black motherhood with black nationalism, see Lauri Umansky, *Motherhood Reconceived: Feminism and the Legacy of the Sixties* (New York: New York University Press, 1996); Karen Brodkin Sacks, *Caring by the Hour: Women, Work and Organizing at Duke Medical Center* (Urbana: University of Illinois Press, 1988), 120–21: here women union organizers, many of whom are black, are described as "centers and sustainers of workplace networks" and "key actors in network formation and consciousness shaping"; this was essential to the success of overall organizing.

52. Ben Burns, *Nitty Gritty: A White Editor in Black Journalism* (Jackson: University Press of Mississippi, 1996), 128.

53. *Parish News* (Church of Holy Trinity, Brooklyn) 57, no. 4 (February 1954): 1, Shirley Graham Du Bois Papers.

54. Shirley Graham Du Bois to "My dear, dear Friend," 13 April 1967.

55. See Miriam Johnson, *Strong Mothers/Weak Wives: The Search for Gender Equality* (Berkeley: University of California Press, 1988), 246: often the failure to conform to certain preconceptions about "femininity" has sidelined women; yet conforming to the prescribed role of "caretaker" often has disempowered women. Graham, like many women, was forced to adapt creatively to patriarchy.

56. Shirley Graham Du Bois to John Henrik Clarke, 13 October 1964, John Henrik Clarke Papers.

57. Casely Hayford, *Ethiopia Unbound: Studies in Race Emancipation* (London: C. M. Phillips, 1911), 172–73: "The African in America is in a worse plight than the Hebrew in Egypt. The one preserved his language, his manners and

customs, his religion and household goods; the other has committed suicide." See also David Kimble, *A Political History of Ghana: The Rise of Gold Coast Nationalism, 1850–1928* (London: Clarendon, 1963); Rina Lee Okonkwo, "The Emergence of Nationalism in British West Africa, 1912–1940" (Ph.D. diss., City University of New York, 1980); Akwasi B. Assensoh, "Kwame Nkrumah of Ghana: His Formative Years and the Shaping of His Nationalism and Pan-Africanism, 1935–1948" (Ph.D. diss., New York University, 1984).

58. See, e.g., Tunde Adeleke, *UnAfrican Americans: Nineteenth Century Black Nationalists and the Civilizing Mission* (Lexington: University Press of Kentucky, 1998); Valentin Y. Mudimbe, *The Invention of Africa* (Bloomington: Indiana University Press, 1988); K. Anthony Appiah, *In My Father's House: Africa in the Philosophy of Culture* (New York: Oxford University Press, 1992).

59. Shirley Graham Du Bois, interview by Charlayne Hunter, Joe Walker, and Esther Jackson, 19 February 1971, Shirley Graham Du Bois Papers; Shirley Graham Du Bois, "The Colonist," lecture at Stanford University, 12 November 1970, Shirley Graham Du Bois Papers; Shirley Graham Du Bois, "Egypt," in Robert Chrisman and Nathan Hare, eds., *Pan-Africanism* (Indianapolis: Bobbs-Merrill, 1974), 20–39. Her turn toward "Egypt-centric" and Afro-centric views may have been influenced by external factors; to wit, when she was applying for a visa to enter the United States in 1970, the State Department reported, "during conversation she stated that she did not . . . intend [to] engage in any public discussion [of] racial problems in U.S. . . . . She also indicated that she wished [to] explore, at [a] later date, [the] possibility of regaining U.S. citizenship and she did not wish to add to problems already existing [in] this area. Accordingly, her lecture topic at Fisk would be 'Ancient Egypt—Its Relation to Africa.'" She assumed, perhaps correctly, that discussing ancient Egyptian history would irk U.S. authorities less than discussion of contemporary "racial problems in U.S." See telegram, "FM USINT CAIRO" to "SECSTATE WASH DC 7140," 4 February 1970, file 100-370965-73, U.S. Department of State.

60. A major beneficiary of black nationalism, the Nation of Islam was not a profeminist organization; yet ironically, its origins in the 1930s in an alliance with Tokyo right-wingers (as evidenced by its continued references to the "Asiatic Black Man") also contributed to its "anti-African" biases—a phenomenon rarely examined. See Claude Andrew Clegg II, "An Original Man: The Life and Times of Elijah Muhammad, 1897–1960" (Ph.D. diss., University of Michigan, 1995), 97. For an examination of the impact of the Nation of Islam on one African American woman, see Sonsyrea Tate, *Little X: Growing Up in the Nation of Islam* (New York: HarperCollins, 1997). For references to the ties between the Nation of Islam and Tokyo and an account of the relationship between black nationalism and antifeminism, see Gerald Horne, *Fire This Time: The Watts Uprising and the 1960s* (Charlottesville: University Press of Virginia, 1995). One analyst has observed that in Europe nationalists "assigned everyone his place in

life, man and woman" and "any confusion between these categories threatened chaos and loss of control." These nationalists identified women as passive guardians of the traditional order, while men were to dominate and occupy the public realm. Thus, "the family was supposed to mirror state and society" with a hierarchical structure; and "through the role of father as patriarch, the family educated its members to respect authority." Despite the antipathy of many black nationalists to European conceptions, these ideas mirrored their own. See George L. Mosse, *Nationalism and Sexuality: Respectability and Abnormal Sexuality in Modern Europe* (New York: Howard Fertig, 1985), 19–20; Carol Boyce Davies, *Black Women Writing and Identity: Migration of the Subject* (New York: Routledge, 1994). Here the author observes that black nationalism often posits a monolithic identity that submerges, if not silences, women. See also Gail Bederman, *Manliness and Civilization: A Cultural History of Gender and Race in the United States, 1880–1917* (Chicago: University of Chicago Press, 1995); and Barry Chevannes, *Rastafari: Roots and Ideology* (Syracuse: Syracuse University Press, 1994).

61. See, e.g., Harold Cruse, "Revolutionary Nationalism and the Afro-American," in James Weinstein and David Eakins, eds., *For a New America: Essays in History and Politics from "Studies on the Left" 1959–1967* (New York: Random House, 1970), 345–69.

62. For an illustration of this trend, see, e.g., Roy Reed, *Faubus: The Life and Times of an American Prodigal* (Fayetteville: University of Arkansas Press, 1997). Like Faubus, Sam Yorty, the conservative mayor of Los Angeles when Watts exploded in 1965, moved decisively from the left to the far right. See, e.g., Ed Ainsworth, *Maverick Mayor: A Biography of Sam Yorty of Los Angeles* (Garden City: Doubleday, 1966). Ronald Reagan evolved similarly: see, e.g., Ronald Reagan, *Where's the Rest of Me?* (New York: Duell, Sloan, and Pearce, 1965); Lou Cannon, *President Reagan: The Role of a Lifetime* (New York: Simon and Schuster, 1991). This move from left to right also has been a transnational trend. See, e.g., Gerald Horne, "Race, Economics and Asian Socialism," *Peace Review* 9, no. 1 (1997): 79–84. The fact that U.S. foreign policy often has used right-wing nationalism to blunt left-wing class-based alliances also may have "blown back" and had domestic consequence. For example, U.S. policy toward Yugoslavia during the 1950s was designed to encourage the flowering of nationalism: see Lorraine M. Lees, *Keeping Tito Afloat: The United States, Yugoslavia and the Cold War* (University Park: Pennsylvania State University Press, 1997), 123, 146; Bennett Kovrig, *The Myth of Liberation: East Central Europe in U.S. Diplomacy and Politics Since 1941* (Baltimore: Johns Hopkins University Press, 1973).

63. *Muhammad Speaks*, 23 February 1968. As shall be seen, as the Sino-Soviet dispute deepened, Graham moved ever closer to Beijing.

64. Photographs, 1972, Black Panther Party Delegation to People's Republic of China, series 5, box 8, Huey Newton Foundation Records. The delegation visited Nanking, the Institute of National Minorities in Beijing, Shanghai, and

other places. See also photographs, 1971, Black Panther Party delegation to China, series 5, box 13, Huey Newton Foundation Records.

65. Amiri Baraka, *The Autobiography of Le Roi Jones* (Chicago: Lawrence Hill, 1997); Amiri Baraka, *Daggers and Javelins: Essays, 1974–1979* (New York: William Morrow, 1984); Amiri Baraka, *Wise, Why's, Y's* (Chicago: Third World Press, 1995).

66. See Timothy B. Tyson, "Radio Free Dixie: Robert F. Williams and the Roots of Black Power," (Ph.D. diss., Duke University, 1994).

67. John Stockwell, *In Search of Enemies: A CIA Story* (New York: Norton, 1978); Fred Bridgland, *Jonas Savimbi: A Key to Africa* (Edinburgh: Mainstream, 1986); Gerald Horne, *Race for the Planet: The U.S. and the New World Order* (Thousand Oaks: Kendall-Hunt, 1994). In 1975 as the African nation of Angola came to independence after centuries of Portuguese colonialism, three factions contended for power. While Havana and Moscow supported the faction that triumphed ultimately, Washington, Beijing, and Pretoria backed the losing group, led by Jonas Savimbi.

68. See, e.g., Rosemary Foot, *The Practice of Power: U.S. Relations with China Since 1949* (Oxford: Clarendon, 1995); John H. Holdridge, *Crossing the Divide: An Insider's Account of Normalization of U.S.-China Relations* (Lanham, MD: Rowman and Littlefield, 1997); Robert Ross, *Negotiating Cooperation: The United States and China, 1969–1989* (Stanford: Stanford University Press, 1995). Though it may have surprised his supporters in the United States, in a 1972 meeting with President Richard Nixon, Mao Zedong complimented this conservative leader, saying, "I like rightists. I am comparatively happy when people on the right come to power." See William Burr, ed., *The Kissinger Transcripts: The Top-Secret Talks with Beijing and Moscow* (New York: New Press, 1999), 61.

69. Reginald Kearney, *African American Views of the Japanese: Solidarity or Sedition?* (Albany: State University of New York Press, 1998). See also Gerald Horne, "Race from Power: U.S. Foreign Policy and the General Crisis of 'White Supremacy,'" *Diplomatic History* 23, no. 3 (Summer 1999): 437–61.

70. "Para Military Training and Sabotage Activities," "Special Branch Headquarters, 20th January 1965," "Secret," box 1, Peter Currie Papers.

71. Martin A. Bailey, "Tanzania and China," in K. Matthews and S. S. Mushi, eds., *Foreign Policy of Tanzania, 1961–1981: A Reader* (Dar es Salaam: Tanzania Publishing House, 1981), 175–85, 175.

72. *New York Times*, 13 August 1963. Strikingly, in 1964 the United States considered seriously a preemptive nuclear strike against China, an indication of heightened tensions between the two giants and a reminder that Graham Du Bois's dalliance with Maoism would not be greeted with indifference.

73. Richard Doyle Mahoney, "The Kennedy Policy in the Congo, 1961–1963," (Ph.D. diss., Johns Hopkins University, 1980), 76. See also Zachary

Karabell, "Architects of Intervention: The United States, the Third World and the Cold War, 1946–1961" (Ph.D. diss., Harvard University, 1996).

74. Ibid., Karabell, "Architects of Intervention," 17, passim.

75. Azza Salam Layton, "The International Context of the U.S. Civil Rights Movement: The Dynamics between Racial Policies and International Politics, 1941–1960" (Ph.D. diss., University of Texas, 1995), viii; Mary L. Dudziak, "Desegregation as a Cold War Imperative," *Stanford Law Review* 41 (November 1988): 61–120; see also David Guerin, *Negroes on the March: A Frenchman's Report on the American Negro Struggle* (New York: Weissman, 1956); Gerald Horne, *Black and Red: W. E. B. Du Bois and the Afro-American Response to the Cold War, 1944–1963* (Albany: State University of New York Press, 1986).

76. The dialectical relationship between Africans and African Americans has been examined at length. See, e.g., Yekutiel Gershoni, *Africans on African-Americans: The Creation and Uses of an African-American Myth* (New York: New York University Press, 1997); Adelaide Cromwell Hill and Martin Kilson, eds., *Apropos of Africa: Sentiments of Negro American Leaders on Africa from the 1800's to the 1950's* (London: Frank Cass, 1969); Bernard Magubane, "The American Negro's Conception of Africa: A Study in the Ideology of Pride and Prejudice" (Ph.D. diss., UCLA, 1967); Charles Alvis Bodie, "The Images of Africa in the Black American Press, 1890–1930" (Ph.D. diss., Indiana University, 1975); Codjo Achode, "The Negro Renaissance from America Back to Africa: A Study of the Harlem Renaissance as a Black and African Movement" (Ph.D. diss., University of Pennsylvania, 1986); Edwin Redkey, *Black Exodus: Black Nationalist and Back-to-Africa Movements, 1890–1910* (New Haven: Yale University Press, 1969); Elliott P. Skinner, *Afro-Americans and Africa: The Continuing Dialectic* (New York: Columbia University Press, 1973); Okon Edet Uya, ed., *Black Brotherhood: Afro-Americans and Africa* (Lexington, MA: D. C. Heath, 1971); J. Mutero Chirenje, *Ethiopianism and Afro-Americans in Southern Africa, 1883–1916* (Baton Rouge: Louisiana State University Press, 1987); Joseph Harris, ed., *Global Dimensions of the African Diaspora* (Washington, DC: Howard University Press, 1982).

77. With the dissolution of the Soviet Union and the escalation of tension between Beijing and Washington, a new situation has emerged that sheds new light on African American relations with China. Just as a central factor driving racial reform during the Cold War was the fear that Moscow could gain an advantage over the United States by pointing to Jim Crow, there are signs today that Beijing has begun to point to U.S. racial problems in order to combat Washington's charges about Chinese domestic policies; the question is: will this new process have any positive impact on U.S. minorities? See Horne, "Race, Economics and Asian Socialism."

78. Gerald Horne, *Black Liberation/Red Scare: Ben Davis and the Communist Party* (Newark: University of Delaware Press, 1994).

79. David Du Bois to Gerald Horne, 22 June 1996 (in possession of author): "I do not know for certain whether my mother was a member of the Party or not. It was my impression that she was. But she never told me she was. And Party membership for prominent folks at that time was a very loose affair—a membership card and paying dues. . . . If she was, it was Howard [Fast] who recruited her." See also David Du Bois, "W. E. B. Du Bois: The Last Years," *Race and Class*, 24, no. 2 (autumn 1982): 178–83, 180: during World War II, Graham joined a "writer's group which [carried]. . . . Marxist influence." See also John Abt with Michael Myerson, *Advocate and Activist: Memoirs of an American Communist Lawyer* (Urbana: University of Illinois Press, 1993).

80. Howard Fast, *Being Red* (Boston: Houghton Mifflin, 1990), 77. He adds that Graham, before her marriage in 1951 to Du Bois, was often at his—Fast's—home in New York City: she "was practically living with us; and her brother, Bill Graham, the largest beer and soda distributor in Harlem," was often with her. Her relationship to Fast, an influential Communist writer at the time, can be seen as yet another example of her attachment to powerful men who exerted influence on her. Interestingly, Fast wrote many novels with strong women characters, including *Shirley* (Garden City: Doubleday, 1963), written with the pseudonym E. V. Cunningham, a detective story featuring a "tough, wise-cracking diamond in the rough": see Andrew Macdonald, *Howard Fast: A Critical Companion* (Westport: Greenwood, 1996), 28.

81. Peter V. Cacchione to Earl Browder, 1 May 1945, Earl Browder Papers. My thanks to Alan Wald for bringing this correspondence to my attention.

82. Shirley Graham to Earl Browder, 27 April 1945, Earl Browder Papers. Even before joining the party, like so many others in the 1930s she found herself in circles where Communists were to be found. For example, as a student in Oberlin she was active in the defense of the Scottsboro Nine and acknowledged encountering Communists. She "turned in nearly five dollars given her in quarters and half dollars by students." See Shirley Graham, "Oberlin and the Negro," *Crisis* 42, no. 4 (April 1935): 118, 124.

83. *Los Angeles Tribune*, 2 February 1953. See also U.S. Congress, House of Representatives, Committee on Un-American Activities, *Subversive Influence in Riots, Looting and Burning*, Part 1, 90th Cong., 1st sess., 25–26, 31 October and 28 November 1967 (Washington, DC: GPO, 1968), 893.

84. Undated memorandum, box 143, Records of the Senate Internal Security Subcommittee, U.S. National Archives. See also Christopher John Gerard, "'A Program of Cooperation': The FBI, the Senate Internal Security Subcommittee, and the Communist Issue, 1950–1956" (Ph.D. diss., Marquette University, 1993).

85. Gerald Horne, *Communist Front? The Civil Rights Congress, 1946–1956* (London: Associated University Presses, 1988); *Worker*, 8 March 1964, 11 December 1960; file 100-370965, Federal Bureau of Investigation. *Daily Worker*, 18

May 1947: Graham is listed as vice-chair of the Committee to Aid the Fighting South. *Daily Worker,* 18 March 1949: Graham is listed as member of the board of the National Council of American-Soviet Friendship. *Daily Worker,* 21 April 1948: Graham is listed as a member of the Advisory Council of the American Labor Party. *Daily Worker,* 2 February 1948: Graham is listed as secretary of the Progressive Citizens of America of New York state. *Counterattack,* 4 February 1949: this right-wing publication listed her as a covert Communist. *Hoy* (Cuba), 7 August 1949: this publication of the Communist Party of Cuba reported that Graham addressed the National Congress for Peace and Democracy in Havana. *Counterattack,* 30 June 1950: Graham addresses a rally in Manhattan on behalf of the antinuclear Stockholm Peace Appeal. *Daily Worker,* 23 December 1949: Graham joins with W. E. B. Du Bois in cabling greetings to Josef Stalin. *Worker,* 12 January 1952: Graham sponsors a conference of trade unions and others at the Theresa Hotel in Harlem to establish a Frederick Douglass Educational Center. *Worker,* 8 April 1952: Graham listed as member of the editorial board of Paul Robeson's newspaper, *Freedom.* See also U.S. Congress, House of Representatives, Committee on Un-American Activities, *Communist Political Subversion,* part 2, 84th Cong., 2d sess., (Washington, DC: GPO, 1957), p. 7151: Graham in 1956 is listed as a member of the Citizens Emergency Defense Committee; p. 7208, she is listed as a member of the National Non-Partisan Committee to Defend the Rights of the 12 Communist Leaders; p. 7222, Graham joins Ossie Davis, Dashiell Hammett, and others in signing an advertisement calling for clemency for the Rosenbergs; p. 7290, Graham signs an appeal on behalf of the Joint Anti-Fascist Refugee Committee; p. 7379, Graham sponsors a program of the American Youth for Democracy concerning "A Tribute to Jewish Youth"; p. 7427, Graham signs a call marking May Day 1949; p. 8183, Graham signs an appeal for amnesty for jailed Communist leaders. See also U.S. Congress, House of Representatives, Committee on Un-American Activities. *Investigation of Communist Activities, New York Area,* part 8 (Entertainment), 84th Cong., 1st sess., 14 October 1955, Testimony of Zero Mostel, exhibit, *PM,* 30 April 1947: Mostel and Graham are listed as sponsors of May Day 1947; *House Un-American Committee Annual Report for the Year 1961* (Washington, DC: GPO, 1962): Graham was "identified before the Subversive Activities Control Board in 1954" as a Communist.

86. Manning Marable, *W. E. B. Du Bois: Black Radical Democrat* (Boston: Twayne, 1986), 196: in the late 1940s, according to David Du Bois, "my mother gradually drew Dr. Du Bois into contact with leading figures of this new progressive movement. . . . slowly Dr. Du Bois found these white Americans to be of a different breed from those who early in his career had discouraged him from seeking out or desiring white company."

87. Lloyd L. Brown, *The Young Paul Robeson: "On My Journey Now"* (Boulder: Westview, 1997), xiv. This charge of Communist women ideologically

seducing men has been made repeatedly. For example, Ronald Reagan's friend and comrade Roy Brewer alleged that the party "got" the actor John Garfield "married to a Communist woman so they could control him." See Griffin Fariello, *Red Scare: Memories of the American Inquisition: An Oral History* (New York: Norton, 1995), 116.

88. Harold Cruse, interview, 16 April 1994, Louis Massiah Papers; Harold Cruse, *The Crisis of the Negro Intellectual* (New York: William Morrow, 1967): Graham considered Cruse's "epic" to be "ridiculous." Shirley Graham Du Bois to Herbert Aptheker, 2 January 1973. Cruse joined the party in the mid-1940s in Harlem as a result of taking classes at the George Washington Carver School, with which Graham was affiliated. He was a member for ten years, sold the *Daily Worker* door to door, and compared the party to a "university." See Harold Cruse, interview, 25 April 1973, Oral History Collection Fisk University Library.

89. John Henrik Clarke, interview, 29 September 1972, Oral History Collection Fisk University Library.

90. Shirley Graham to Earl Browder, 27 April 1945, Earl Browder Papers.

91. Adam Fairclough, *Race and Democracy: The Civil Rights Struggle in Louisiana, 1915–1972* (Athens: University of Georgia Press, 1995), 146. For a contrasting view, see, e.g., Thomas Devine, "Dubious Alliance: Communists and Progressives at the 1948 Progressive Party Convention" (M.A. thesis, University of North Carolina, 1993); see also Angela Calomiris, *Red Masquerade: Undercover for the FBI* (Philadelphia: Lippincott, 1950).

92. Fast, *Being Red*, 77, 183.

93. Fon Louise Gordon, *Caste and Class: The Black Experience in Arkansas, 1880–1920* (Athens: University of Georgia Press, 1995). See also Kevin Gaines, *Uplifting the Race: Black Leadership, Politics and Culture in the Twentieth Century* (Chapel Hill: University of North Carolina Press, 1996).

94. William J. Maxwell, "Dialectical Engagements: The 'New Negro' and the 'Old Left,' 1918–1940" (Ph.D. diss., Duke University, 1993), 144.

95. Horne, *Black Liberation/Red Scare*. On the question of Stalin, see, e.g., Robert Thurston, *Life and Terror in Stalin's Russia, 1934–1941* (New Haven: Yale University Press, 1996); Hiroaki Kuromiya, *Stalin's Industrial Revolution: Politics and Workers, 1928–1932* (New York: Cambridge University Press, 1988); Lewis H. Siegelbaum, *Stakhanovism and the Politics of Productivity in the USSR, 1935–1941* (New York: Cambridge University Press, 1988). On the question of Mao Zedong, see, e.g., Yan Jiaq and Gao Gao, *Turbulent Decade: A History of the Cultural Revolution* (Honolulu: University of Hawaii Press, 1996); Dali L. Yang, *Calamity and Reform in China: State, Rural Society and Institutional Change Since the Great Leap Famine* (Stanford: Stanford University Press, 1996). The late South African Communist leader Joe Slovo, who served in the Mandela government before his death, commented on the dilemma of alignment with the USSR, which assisted their struggle when the United

States and its allies refused to lend a hand to the anti-apartheid movement: "In a world in which people, especially those involved in liberation politics, were compelled to choose sides, many found it very difficult to voice their misgivings about the flaws of existing socialism publicly. On both sides of that great divide, at the height of the Cold War, there was little room to accommodate critical supporters." Joe Slovo, *Slovo: The Unfinished Autobiography* (London: Hodder and Staughton, 1995), 232. For a similar view from Brazil, see Dulce Chaves Pandolfi, *Camaradas e Companheiros: Historia e Memoria do PCB* (Rio de Janeiro: Relume-Dumara, Fudacao Roberto Marinho, 1995).

96. Lessing, *Walking in the Shade,* 144, 167.

97. The reaction of the South African Communist leader Bram Fischer resembled that of many of his U.S. counterparts in responding to the Stalin revelations. In "addressing a querulous cell" he "listened carefully and respectfully to their concerns, but insisted on an overriding loyalty: For if one country in the socialist camp fell, he argued, it would be followed by all the others. Loyalty, acceptance, refusal, realpolitik: all these were superimposed upon one another." The collapse of the "socialist camp," it was thought, would have a devastating impact on the struggle for African liberation, given Moscow's arming of "freedom fighters" in Southern Africa particularly. See Stephen Clingman, *Bram Fischer: Afrikaner Revolutionary* (Amherst: University of Massachusetts Press, 1998).

98. Cf. Harvey Klehr et al., eds. *The Soviet World of American Communism* (New Haven: Yale University Press, 1998).

99. Ronald L. Filipelli and Mark McColloch, *Cold War in the Working Class: The Rise and Decline of the United Electrical Workers* (Albany: State University of New York Press, 1995), 186–87.

100. James Hunter Meriwether, "The African Connection and the Struggle for Freedom: Africa's Role in African American Life, 1935–1963" (Ph.D. diss., University of California–Los Angeles, 1995), 94, 115, 150. When A. Philip Randolph and Frank Crosswaith in 1952 protested the treatment of Soviet Jewry, a number of African Americans asked why they didn't say more about South Africa. "The NAACP Board of Directors never made more than passing reference to the Congo throughout 1960–1963," though "numerous letters appealed to the NAACP for the organization to work on behalf of the Congolese" (410–11).

101. Gerald Thomas, "The Black Revolt: The United States and Africa in the 1960s," in Diane B. Kunz, ed., *The Diplomacy of the Crucial Decade: American Foreign Relations during the 1960s* (New York: Columbia University Press, 1994), 320–60, 320: "The two major segments of the black revolt—in Africa and in the U.S.—strengthened each other with pride and political support during that decade." See also Brenda Gayle Plummer, *Rising Wind: Black Americans and U.S.*

Foreign Affairs, 1935–1960 (Chapel Hill: University of North Carolina Press, 1996); Penny M. Von Eschen, *Race against Empire: Black Americans and Anticolonialism, 1937–1957* (Ithaca: Cornell University Press, 1997).

102. Hakim Adi, *West Africans in Britain: Nationalism, Pan-Africanism and Communism* (London: Lawrence and Wishart, 1998), 142, 161. In the 1950s over "150 Nigerians joined the Party in London, where they were initially placed in their own 'Robeson branches.'"

103. Constance Coiner, *Better Red: The Writing and Resistance of Tillie Olsen and Meridel LeSueur* (New York: Oxford University Press, 1995); Jennifer Tyson, *Claudia Jones, 1915–1964: A Woman of Our Times* (London: Black Sister Publications, 1988); Zipser and Zipser, *Fire and Grace: The Life of Rose Pastor Stokes*; Marilyn Young, ed., *Promissory Notes: Women in the Transition to Socialism* (New York: Monthly Review Press, 1989); Elsa Jane Dixler, "The Woman Question: Women and the American Communist Party, 1929–1941" (Ph.D. diss., Yale University, 1974); Lisa Vogel, *Marxism and the Oppression of Women: Toward a Unitary Theory* (New Brunswick: Rutgers University Press, 1983); Carrie A. Foster, *The Women and the Warriors: The U.S. Section of the Women's International League for Peace and Freedom, 1915–1946* (Syracuse: Syracuse University Press, 1995).

104. Kathleen Anne Weigand, "Vanguard of Women's Liberation: The Old Left and the Continuity of the Women's Movement in the United States, 1945–1970s" (Ph.D. diss., Ohio State University, 1995), 16, 110, 215. See also Linn Shapiro, "American Communism and the Women's Rights Tradition, 1919–1956" (Ph.D. diss., American University, 1996), 34, 224, 62: "Between 1919 and 1956, no national organization promulgated a more feminist program than that of the CP. The CP orbit was one of the few sites that a left-wing female intellectual could create women's rights theory and practice." Thus, by 1944 women constituted 44 percent of party membership, up from 31.7 percent in 1938.

105. See generally Kim E. Nielsen, "The Security of the Nation: Anti-Radicalism and Gender in the Red Scare of 1918–1928" (Ph.D. diss., University of Iowa, 1996).

106. Kathleen A. Brown, "Ella Reeve Bloor: The Politics of the Personal in the American Communist Party" (Ph.D. diss., University of Washington, 1996), 112, 162; Paul C. Mishler, "The Littlest Proletariat: American Communists and Their Children, 1922–1950" (Ph.D. diss., Boston University, 1988). See also Melanie Tebbutt, *Women's Talk? A Social History of "Gossip" in Working Class Neighborhoods, 1880–1960* (Brookfield, VT: Ashgate, 1995).

107. Kate Fullbrook and Edward Fullbrook, *Simone de Beauvoir and Jean-Paul Sarte: The Remaking of a Twentieth Century Legend* (New York: Basic, 1994).

108. Gail Lumet Buckley, *The Hornes: An American Family* (New York: Knopf, 1986). Like the character in Nell Larsen's classic novel *Quicksand*, Gra-

ham may have been forced into this unwise marriage as the only way to express her sexuality. See also Cynthia Neverdon-Morton, *Afro-American Women of the South and the Advancement of the Race, 1895–1925* (Knoxville: University of Tennessee Press, 1989).

109. Louise Daniel Hutchinson, "Anna Julia Haywood Cooper," in Darlene Clark Hine, Elsa Barkley Brown, and Rosalyn Terborg-Penn, eds., *Black Women in America: An Historical Encyclopedia*, vol. 1 (Bloomington: Indiana University Press, 1993), 275–81; Mary Church Terrell, *A Colored Woman in a White World* (Washington, DC: Ransdell, 1940).

110. Tony Martin, "Amy Ashwood Garvey," in Hine et al., eds., *Black Women in America*, vol. 1, 481–82; Irma Watkins-Owens, *Blood Relations: Caribbean Immigrants and the Harlem Community, 1900–1930* (Bloomington: Indiana University Press, 1996), 155.

111. Dierdre Bibby, "Augusta Savage," in Hine et al., eds., *Black Women in America*, vol. 2, 1010–13; Thadious Davis, "Jesse Redmon Fauset," in Hine et al., eds., *Black Women in America*, vol. 1, 411–16. See also Stephanie J. Shaw, *What a Woman Ought to Be and Do: Black Professional Women Workers during the Jim Crow Era* (Chicago: University of Chicago Press, 1996); Miriam De Costa, ed., *The Memphis Diary of Ida B. Wells* (Boston: Beacon, 1995). See also Elzbieata Ettinger, *Hannah Arendt, Martin Heidegger* (New Haven: Yale University Press, 1998): Graham was not the only woman intellectual attracted to a man who was considerably older.

112. Buzz Johnson, *"I Think of My Mother": Notes on the Life and Times of Claudia Jones* (London: Karia, 1985).

113. Gloria T. Hull, "Alice Ruth Moore Dunbar-Nelson," in Hine et al., eds., *Black Women in America*, vol. 1, 359–63, 360. See also Jacqueline Anne Rouse, *Lugenia Burns Hope: Black Southern Reformer* (Athens: University of Georgia Press, 1989).

114. Elsie Arrington Williams, "Jackie 'Moms' Mabley," in Hine et al., eds., *Black Women in America*, vol. 2, 739–41, 740. See also Deborah Willis, *Malevolent Nature: Witch-Hunting and Maternal Power in Early Modern England* (Ithaca: Cornell University Press, 1995). In 1949 the writer Doris Lessing left two children and a spouse in south-central Africa and moved to London to pursue her career. "It is a decision which has pursued her ever since." Like Graham, she endured pangs of guilt about this decision. "'Now I know that it was about the most intelligent thing I ever did,'" she concluded years later, "'but at the time I was doing it, it was awful, dreadful.' She believes that if she had stayed, the misery would have turned her into an alcoholic." *Weekly Mail & Guardian*, 28 May–3 June 1999.

115. Shirley Graham Du Bois, "Letter from Tashkent," *Mainstream* 11, no. 12 (December 1958): 16–21, 18. See also Rosalyn Terborg-Penn and Andrea Benton Rushing, eds., *Women in Africa and the African Diaspora: A Reader* (Washington,

DC: Howard University Press, 1997); Gwendolyn Mikell, ed., *African Feminism: The Politics of Survival in Sub-Saharan Africa* (Philadelphia: University of Pennsylvania Press, 1997).

NOTES TO CHAPTER I

1. Certificate of birth for Lola Shirley Graham, Marion County Board of Health, Court House, Indianapolis, no. 30007. Date of Birth: 11 November 1896. Recorded November 1896 in book 7, p. 171: issued 24 October 1942, Shirley Graham Du Bois Papers; State of New York, Queens County, Deposition of Lizzie Etta Bell Graham, 21 March 1949 (signed by Etta Bell Graham), stating that on 11 November 1896 at 214 West Vermont Avenue in Indianapolis she gave birth to Lola Shirley Graham, Shirley Graham Du Bois Papers. See also sworn statement of William Jernagin, 11 April 1930: "on oath" he states that Shirley Graham does not use her given name, Lola, for reasons of her "profession." In *Current Biography*, October 1946, Graham's date of birth is given as 11 November 1907, Shirley Graham Du Bois Papers. In a 1971 interview her year of birth is given as 1906: Shirley Graham Du Bois, interview by Ann Shockley, 7 January 1971, Oral History Collection Fisk University Library. But see 11203, Board of Health and Charities, City Hall, Indianapolis, certified copy of birth certificate, "Zerelda Graham," born 11 November 1896, mother—23, father—36, Shirley Graham Du Bois Papers.

2. Kenneth T. Jackson, *The Ku Klux Klan in the City, 1915–1930* (New York: Oxford University Press, 1967), 144. See also Lionel Artis, "The Negro in Indiana, or the Struggle against Dixie Comes North," in Tom Lutz and Susanna Ashton, eds., *These "Colored" United States: African-American Essays from the 1920s* (New Brunswick: Rutgers University Press, 1996), 116–28; Emma Lou Thornbrough, *The Negro in Indiana: A Study of a Minority* (Indianapolis: Indiana Historical Bureau, 1957); William Vincent Moore, "A Sheet and a Cross: A Symbolic Analysis of the Ku Klux Klan" (Ph.D. diss., Tulane University, 1975); John Augustus Davis, "The Ku Klux Klan in Indiana, 1920–1930: An Historical Study" (Ph.D. diss., Northwestern University, 1966); Earline Rae Ferguson, "The Woman's Improvement Club of Indianapolis: Black Women Pioneers in Tuberculosis Work, 1903–1938," *Indiana Magazine of History* 84 (September 1988): 237–61.

3. Shirley Graham to Lin Yutang, 12 September 1943.

4. Shirley Graham to *New York Post*, 25 June, circa 1948.

5. Shirley Graham Du Bois, *I Got Wings!* (unpublished memoir), Shirley Graham Du Bois Papers.

6. Shirley Graham Du Bois, *I Got Wings!*

7. Biography of Etta Bell Graham, undated, Shirley Graham Du Bois Papers.

8. However, on his 1925 passport David Graham's birthdate is given as 11 January 1864, Shirley Graham Du Bois Papers.

9. Shirley Graham Du Bois, interview, 28 May 1975, Hatch-Billops Collection.

10. *Fourteenth U.S. Census*, 1920, Washington State, G650, Soundex, w. 17, E.D. 197, King, sheet 1, line 8.

11. Lorenz Graham, interview, 9 September 1993, Louis Massiah Papers. See also his novel: Lorenz Graham, *South Town* (Chicago: Follett, 1958).

12. Shirley Graham Du Bois, interview, 28 May 1975, Hatch-Billops Collection.

13. Ibid., Shirley Graham Du Bois, *I Got Wings!*

14. David Graham to Reverend James A. Handy, 11 April 1906, Shirley Graham Du Bois Papers.

15. Shirley Graham Du Bois, *I Got Wings!*

16. Shirley Graham Du Bois, *I Got Wings!* See also Robert Dee Thompson Jr., "A Socio-Biography of Shirley Graham–Du Bois: A Life in the Struggle" (Ph.D. diss., University of California–Santa Cruz, 1997), 14–17.

17. Shirley Graham Du Bois, interview, 28 May 1975, Hatch-Billops Collection.

18. Ibid.

19. Shirley Graham Du Bois to Randolph Bromery, 12 August 1974.

20. Shirley Graham Du Bois, interview by Abigail Simon, 10 April 1974, Shirley Graham Du Bois Papers.

21. Shirley Graham Du Bois, 7 January 1971, Oral History Collection Fisk University Library.

22. Ibid.

23. Shirley Graham Du Bois, interview by Abigail Simon, 10 April 1974, Shirley Graham Du Bois Papers.

24. Ibid., Shirley Graham Du Bois, interview, 28 May 1975, Hatch-Billops Collection.

25. Shirley Graham Du Bois, interview by Ann Schockley, 7 January 1971, Oral History Collection Fisk University Library.

26. Ibid., Thompson, "A Socio-Biography of Shirley Graham–Du Bois."

27. Ibid., Shirley Graham Du Bois *I Got Wings!*

28. Shirley Graham Du Bois, *His Day Is Marching On* (Philadelphia: Lippincott, 1971), 12, 28.

29. David Graham,"Ethics of the Pulpit and Pastorate," draft manuscript, chapter 8, undated, Shirley Graham Du Bois Papers.

30. David Graham, *Courtship, Marriage and Divorce* (Nashville: AMESS Union, 1916), 15, 17, 35, 46, 48.

31. Shirley Graham Du Bois, "An Explanation" (summary of her biography of Anne Royall), September 1962, Shirley Graham Du Bois Papers.

32. Shirley Graham Du Bois, interview by Abigail Simon, 10 April 1974, Shirley Graham Du Bois Papers.

33. Ibid.; Shirley Graham Du Bois, *His Day Is Marching On*, 30, 31; Thompson, "A Socio-Biography of Shirley Graham–Du Bois," 22–30.

34. Letter to the editor, 17 March 1914, Shirley Graham Du Bois Papers.

35. Shirley Graham Du Bois, interview by Ann Schockley, 7 January 1971, Shirley Graham Du Bois Papers.

36. Program, "Class of 1912" commencement, undated, unsourced clipping, Shirley Graham Du Bois Papers.

37. Undated, unsourced clipping in scrapbook, letter from D. A. Graham to Mrs. E. B. Butler, 1 June 1915, Shirley Graham Du Bois Papers.

38. Kathy Perkins, "The Unknown Career of Shirley Graham," *Freedomways* 25, no. 1 (1985): 6–17.

39. See, e.g., Quintard Taylor, *The Forging of a Black Community: Seattle's Central District from 1870 through the Civil Rights Era* (Seattle: University of Washington Press, 1994); Quintard Taylor, *In Search of the Racial Frontier: African Americans in the American West, 1528–1990* (New York: Norton, 1998).

40. Elizabeth Brown-Guillory, ed., *Wines in the Wilderness: Plays by African-American Women from the Harlem Renaissance to the Present* (Westport: Greenwood, 1990), 79. However, on her first passport application she listed her date of marriage as 16 July 1918: see file 100-99729-84A, 28 October 1958, Federal Bureau of Investigation.

41. Shirley Graham Du Bois, *His Day Is Marching On*, 37–39; "1935 Quinquennial Report Blank," 11 March 1935, Shirley Graham File, Oberlin College: Robert was born on 27 February 1923 in Oakland; Graham (David) was born on 10 March 1925 in Seattle. Her year of birth in this form is given as 1902.

42. Divorce decree, Circuit Court of Oregon, Multnomah, Portland, 4 August 1927, no. M-3046, no. 23993 (copy rendered 30 September 1940), motion of George Arthur Brown, attorney for Shirley Graham, Shirley Graham Du Bois Papers.

43. David Du Bois, interview by author, 16 May 1996; Kathy Perkins, National Endowment for the Humanities paper, August 1984, Hatch-Billops Collection.

44. David Du Bois, interview by author, 16 May 1996.

45. David Du Bois, interview by author, 26 December 1993.

46. David Du Bois, interview by author, 16 May 1996.

47. David Du Bois to D.A. Graham, 28 May 1970, Shirley Graham Du Bois Papers.

48. See Gillian Slovo, *Every Secret Thing: My Family, My Country* (Boston: Little, Brown, 1997).

49. Dorothy Ashpole to Shirley Graham Du Bois, 20 July 1969: commenting on Graham Du Bois's reaction to Ashpole's divorce, the writer said, "I want

to thank you again for your kindness, your love and human understanding. But for you I might have lost my faith in mankind. I often remember the words you and David said to me those last days we were together in Cairo. It was the things you both said which helped and saved me from becoming totally embittered; but it was your warmth and acceptance, your belief in me that gave me the courage and support I needed in what (I surely hope) was my life's darkest hours."

50. Ruth Morris Graham, interview, 9 September 1993, Louis Massiah Papers. See also Advertus A. Hoff, *A Short History of Liberia College and the University of Liberia* (Monrovia: Consolidated Publishers, 1962); Sylvia Jacobs, ed., *Black Americans and the Missionary Movement in Africa* (Westport: Greenwood, 1982); Walter L. Williams, *Black Americans and the Evangelization of Africa, 1877–1900* (Madison: University of Wisconsin Press, 1982); Wilson Jeremiah Moses, ed., *Liberian Dreams: Back-to-Africa Narratives from the 1850s* (University Park: Pennsylvania State University Press, 1998).

51. Undated and unsourced clippings in scrapbook, circa 1927, Shirley Graham Du Bois Papers. The AME church was not exactly the most democratic of institutions either: "The all-male leadership of the conference began making a definitive decision by first reprimanding Bishop Henry McNeal Turner for ordaining a woman. They then proceeded to issue a strongly worded resolution absolutely prohibiting women's ordination." Jualynne E. Dodson, "African Methodist Episcopal Preaching Women of the 19th Century," in Darlene Clark Hine, Elsa Barkley Brown, and Rosalyn Terborg-Penn, eds., *Black Women in America: An Historical Encyclopedia*, vol. 1 (Bloomington: Indiana University Press, 1993), 12–14, 13. See also Evelyn Brooks Higginbotham, *Righteous Discontent: The Women's Movement in the Black Baptist Church, 1880–1920* (Cambridge: Harvard University Press, 1993); Cheryl J. Sanders, *Saints in Exile: The Holiness-Pentecostal Experience in African American Religion and Culture* (New York: Oxford University Press, 1996); Susan Juster and Lisa MacFarlane, eds., *A Mighty Baptism: Race, Gender, and the Creation of American Protestantism* (Ithaca: Cornell University Press, 1996).

52. Hollis R. Lynch, *Edward Wilmot Blyden: Pan-Negro Patriot, 1832–1912* (New York: Oxford University Press, 1967).

53. Wilson Jeremiah Moses, *Alexander Crummel: A Study of Civilization and Discontent* (New York: Oxford University Press, 1989), 151–52. See also I. K. Sundiata, *Black Scandal: America and the Liberia Labor Crisis, 1929–1936* (Philadelphia: Institute for the Study of Human Issues, 1980).

54. Robert McCanns to Shirley Graham, 4 May 1936.

55. Robert McCanns to Shirley Graham, 5 April 1936.

56. Robert McCanns to Shirley Graham, 19 September 1938, 5 December 1938, 9 January 1939, 20 December 1938.

57. Graham (David) McCanns to Shirley Graham, 10 November 1938, 29

November 1938. Note that Graham McCann is referred to subsequently as David Du Bois.

NOTES TO CHAPTER 2

1. David Du Bois, interview by author, 16 May 1996.

2. File 100-99729-84A, 28 October 1958, Federal Bureau of Investigation.

3. Lorenz Graham, to Shirley Graham, undated (circa 1927).

4. *Portland Advocate,* 22 June 1930; Randolph Edmonds to Shirley Graham, 12 June 1930.

5. Tyler Stovall, *Paris Noir: African Americans in the City of Light* (Boston: Houghton Mifflin, 1996), 31, 99, 100, 111; Eslanda Robeson, "Black Paris," *Challenge* 1, no. 4 (January 1936): 12–13; Shari Benstock, *Women of the Left Bank: Paris, 1900–1940* (Austin: University of Texas Press, 1986).

6. Louis Parascandola, ed., *"Winds Can Wake Up the Dead": An Eric Walrond Reader* (Detroit: Wayne State University Press, 1999).

7. Irma Watkins-Owens, *Blood Relations: Caribbean Immigrants and the Harlem Community, 1900–1930* (Bloomington: Indiana University Press, 1996), 156–57; Eric Walrond, *Tropic Death* (New York: Collier, 1972).

8. Ethel Ray Nance, interview, 18 November 1970, 23 December 1970, Oral History Collection Fisk University Library.

9. Eric Walrond to Shirley Graham, 1 November 1930, 18 February 1931. Walrond also had a knack for borrowing money. See Eric Walrond to Montgomery Evans, 21 June 1929, box 9, Miscellaneous American Letters, Schomburg Center.

10. Eric Walrond to Shirley Graham, 18 February 1931, 22 March 1931, 22 April 1931.

11. *New Rochelle Standard Star,* 16 February 1929. See also Samuel A. Floyd, Jr., *The Power of Black Music: Interpreting Its History from Africa to the United States* (New York: Oxford University Press, 1995).

12. Program, 5 May 1931, Shirley Graham Du Bois Papers.

13. Rayford W. Logan, *Howard University: The First Hundred Years, 1867–1967* (New York: New York University Press, 1969), 220, 231.

14. Carlton Moss, interview, 19 June 1992, Louis Massiah Papers.

15. Charles Johnson to Shirley Graham, 10 April 1941. Abbott Simon, interview, 23 July 1992, Louis Massiah Papers.

16. Stephanie Shaw, *What a Woman Ought to Be and to Do: Black Professional Women Workers during the Jim Crow Era* (Chicago: University of Chicago Press, 1996), 197.

17. Jeane Weston, *Making Do: How Women Survived the '30s* (Chicago: Follett, 1976); Elizabeth Higginbotham, "Employment for Professional Black Women in the Twentieth Century," in Christine Bose and Glenna Spitzeg, eds.,

Ingredients for Women's Employment Policy (Albany: State University of New York Press, 1987), 73–91; Elizabeth Clark-Lewis, *Living In, Living Out: African-American Domestics in Washington, D.C., 1910–1940* (Washington, DC: Smithsonian Institution Press, 1994); Gwendolyn Etter-Lewis, *My Soul Is My Own: Oral Narratives of African American Women in the Professions* (New York: Routledge, 1993); Jonathan Scott Holloway, "Confronting the Veil: New Deal African American Intellectuals and the Evolution of a Radical Voice" (Ph.D. diss., Yale University, 1995).

18. Maureen Ngozi Eke, "Some of Us Are Brave: A Configuration of Revolutionary Black Woman Dramatists (Nigeria, South Africa and the United States)" (Ph.D. diss., Indiana University, 1994), viii. See also Sydne Mahone, ed., *Moon Marked and Touched by Sun: Plays by African-American Women* (New York: Theatre Communications Group, 1994).

19. Paul Nadler, "American Theater and the Civil Rights Movement, 1945–1965" (Ph.D. diss., City University of New York Graduate Center, 1995), 9. See also Nellie McKay, "'What Were They Saying?': Black Women Playwrights of the Harlem Renaissance," in Victor Kramer, ed., *The Harlem Renaissance Re-Examined* (New York: AMS Press, 1987), 129–48.

20. *New Yorker,* 3 February 1997, 49: the "influence" of "drug dealers" on black theater has been "unmistakable"; such has been the "sleazy world of popular theater."

21. Anthony Hill, *Pages from the Harlem Renaissance: A Chronicle of Performance* (New York: Peter Lang, 1996), xi.

22. Paul Cravath to Herbert Miller, 30 January 1933, Shirley Graham Du Bois Papers.

23. Ibid., Hill, *Pages from the Harlem Renaissance,* 8. See also Samuel A. Hay, *African American Theatre: An Historical and Critical Analysis* (New York: Cambridge University Press, 1994), 3.

24. W. E. B. Du Bois, "Krigwa Players' Little Negro Theatre," *Crisis* 32, no. 3 (July 1926): 134–36. See also Errol Hill, ed., *The Theatre of Black Americans: A Collection of Critical Essays* (New York: Applause, 1987).

25. Lionel Trilling, "A Novel of the Thirties," in *The Last Decade* (New York: Harcourt Brace Jovanovich, 1979), 15.

26. Michael Denning, *The Cultural Front: The Laboring of American Culture* (New York: Verso, 1997), 137. See also Paula Rabinowitz, *Labor and Desire: Women's Revolutionary Fiction in Depression America* (Chapel Hill: University of North Carolina Press, 1991); Barbara Foley, *Radical Representations: Politics and Form in U.S. Proletarian Fiction, 1929–1941* (Durham: Duke University Press, 1993).

27. Elizabeth Faue, *Community of Suffering and Struggle: Women, Men and the Labor Movement in Minneapolis, 1915–1945* (Chapel Hill: University of North Carolina Press, 1991), 71, 83.

28. Wendy Kozol, "Madonnas of the Fields: Photography, Gender and 1930s Farm Relief," *Genders* 2 (summer 1988): 1–23, 15. See also Terese L. Ebert, *Ludic Feminism and After: Postmodernism, Desire and Labor in Late Capitalism* (Ann Arbor: University of Michigan Press, 1996).

29. Susan Torrey Barstow, "Acting Like a Feminist: The Theatrical Origins of the Suffragette Movement" (Ph.D. diss., University of Virginia, 1994), 3, 15.

30. Mildred Denby Green, *Black Women Composers: A Genesis* (Boston: Twayne, 1983). See also Mildred Denby Green, "Composers," in Darlene Clark Hine, Elsa Barkley Brown, and Rosalyn Terborg-Penn, eds., *Black Women in America: An Historical Encyclopedia*, vol. 1 (Bloomington: Indiana University Press, 1993), 270–72.

31. Program, 31 May 1929, Shirley Graham Du Bois Papers.

32. *Afro-American,* 2 July 1932.

33. Lorenz Graham to Shirley Graham, 30 July 1931.

34. *Afro-American,* 2 July 1932.

35. Elizabeth Brown-Guillory, ed., *Wines in the Wilderness: Plays by African-American Women from the Harlem Renaissance to the Present* (Westport: Greenwood, 1990), 80.

36. Lorenz Graham to Shirley Graham, 30 July 1931.

37. Program for *Tom-Tom,* circa 1932, Shirley Graham file, Oberlin College.

38. Savannah Unit of the Georgia Writers Project of the Works Projects Administration, *Drums and Shadows: Survival Studies among the Georgia Coastal Negroes* (Athens: University of Georgia Press, 1986); William S. McFeely, *Sapelo's People: A Long Walk into Freedom* (New York: Norton, 1994); Allan D. Austin, *African Muslims in Antebellum America: Transatlantic Stories and Spiritual Struggles* (New York: Routledge, 1997).

39. Application for Guggenheim Fellowship, 1934, Shirley Graham Du Bois Papers.

40. Ibid.

41. Shirley Graham Du Bois, interview, 28 May 1975, Hatch-Billops Collection.

42. Program, 31 May 1929, Shirley Graham Du Bois Papers.

43. Alain Locke, *The Critical Temper of Alain Locke: A Selection of His Essays on Art and Culture* (New York: Garland, 1983). See also Norman G. Weinstein, *A Night in Tunisia: Imaginings of Africa in Jazz* (New York: Limelight, 1992).

44. *New York Times,* 19 September 1926.

45. Gary A. Reynolds and Beryl J. Wright, eds., *Against the Odds: African-American Artists and the Harmon Foundation* (Newark: Newark Museum, 1989), 188.

46. See, e.g., Susan Curtis, *The First Black Actors on the Great White Way* (Columbia: University of Missouri Press, 1998).

47. Kathy Perkins, "The Unknown Career of Shirley Graham," *Free-domways* 25, no. 1 (1985): 6–17.

48. Program, 31 May 1929, Shirley Graham Du Bois Papers.

49. Ibid., Program, 31 May 1929; *Cleveland News*, 30 June 1932; *Cleveland Press*, 21 June 1932.

50. Review, *Crisis* 39, no. 8 (August 1932): 258.

51. Kathy Perkins, National Endowment for the Humanities paper, August 1984, Hatch-Billops Collection; *Pittsburgh Courier*, 16 July 1932; *Afro-American*, 2 July 1932.

52. John Gruesser, "The Resonant Double-Consciousness of Shirley Graham's *Tom-Tom*," undated, Hatch-Billops Collection.

53. Ibid.

54. Shirley Graham Du Bois to Ora Williams, 3 March 1973.

55. *Cleveland News*, 30 June 1932.

56. *Cleveland Press*, 21 July 1932.

57. Perkins, "The Unknown Career of Shirley Graham," 10.

58. *Afro-American*, 9 July 1932. See also *Washington Tribune*, 8 July 1932; *Boston Chronicle*, 16 July 1932.

59. Kevin Dunn, "Lights . . . Camera . . . Africa: Images of Africa and Africans in Western Popular Films of the 1930s," *African Studies Review* 39, no. 1 (April 1996): 149–75. See also Jan Pieterse, *White on Black: Images of Blacks in Western Popular Culture* (New Haven: Yale University Press, 1992); Edgar Wallace, *Sanders of the River* (Garden City: Doubleday, 1930); Alfred Aloyius and Ethelreda Lewis, *Trader Horn* (New York: Literary Guild of America, 1927); James Hatch, "Some African Influences on the Afro-American Theatre," in Hill, ed., *The Theatre of Black Americans*, 13–29, 16, 17: Eugene O'Neill and Carl Van Vechten popularized the "cult of primitivism" in Africa; Eubie Blake's work *Blackbirds of 1930* featured Mozambique. Africa had been a recurrent theme in Afro-American theater since the nineteenth century. Doris Abramson, *Negro Playwrights in the American Theatre, 1925–1959* (New York: Columbia University Press, 1969); Frederick Bond, *The Negro and the Drama: The Direct and Indirect Contribution Which the American Negro Has Made to Drama and the Legitimate Stage, with the Underlying Conditions Responsible* (College Park, MD: McGrath, 1969); Leslie Catherine Sanders, *The Development of Black Theater in America: From Shadows to Selves* (Baton Rouge: Louisiana State University Press, 1988); Bernth Lindfors, ed., *Africans on Stage: Studies in Ethnological Show Business* (Bloomington: Indiana University Press, 1999).

60. Mary White Ovington to Shirley Graham, 2 August 1932. Later Ovington added, "I have been hearing about the great interest that is felt regarding primitive Negro music. . . . If I were you, I would get *Tom-Tom* out as soon as I could, even if it did not quite suit me. Evidently it was popular." Mary White Ovington to Shirley Graham, 14 May 1934.

61. Herbert Miller to Shirley Graham, 6 November 1933. Ovington was also not very sensitive about what had befallen the Jewish population in the 1930s. She once referred to "'climbers'" who try "to copy the new environment and frequently [copy] its worst phases . . . this is what makes the Jew so disliked." Mary White Ovington to Shirley Graham, 10 November 1935.

62. Shirley Graham to Hattie Gibbs Marshall, 6 August 1933, box 112-5, Washington Conservatory of Music Papers.

63. James Spady, biography of Shirley Graham, undated, Shirley Graham Du Bois Papers.

64. Shirley Graham to Hattie Gibbs Marshall, 6 August 1933, box 112-5, Washington Conservatory of Music Papers.

65. Letter of recommendation for Shirley Graham by Edward Dickinson, circa 1936, Shirley Graham File, Oberlin College.

66. Shirley Graham, "Black Man's Music," Crisis 40, no. 8 (August 1933): 178–79.

67. Shirley Graham to Hattie Gibbs Marshall, 4 February 1934, box 112-5, Washington Conservatory of Music Papers.

68. Application to Oberlin College of Shirley Graham, 1931, Shirley Graham File, Oberlin College.

69. Shirley Gibbs to Hattie Gibbs Marshall, 9 July 1935, box 112-5, Washington Conservatory of Music Papers.

70. Application to Oberlin College of Shirley Graham, 1931, Shirley Graham File, Oberlin College.

71. See, e.g., Elizabeth Clark-Lewis, Living In, Living Out: African-American Domestics in Washington, D.C., 1910–1940; Tera W. Hunter, To 'Joy My Freedom: Southern Black Women's Lives and Labors after the Civil War (Cambridge: Harvard University Press, 1997).

72. Dean C. N. Cole, Oberlin College, to Shirley Graham, 5 August 1932: "You have not been able to pay off $77.15 of your deferment of term bill last semester." See also Oberlin College to Shirley Graham, 22 October 1936: her $200 emergency loan note of 4 October 1934 became due with $10 interest. They had written her in June and had yet to hear from her. See also James H. Fairchild, Oberlin: The Colony and the College, 1833–1883 (New York: Garland, 1984).

73. Shirley Graham, "Oberlin and the Negro," Crisis 42, no. 4 (April 1935): 118, 124. "There are about sixty colored students in the conservatory, the college and the graduate school of theology."

74. Shirley Graham to Mary White Ovington, 2 February 1935, reel 6, part 2, NAACP Papers.

75. Edward Dickinson to Shirley Graham, 18 February 1936.

76. Edward Dickinson to Shirley Graham, 21 November 1937.

77. Edward Dickinson to Shirley Graham, 6 December 1937. Perhaps she

did open the letter but with the passage of time the glue on the envelope had caused it to be resealed.

78. Edward Dickinson to Shirley Graham, 12 October 1938.

79. Edward Dickinson to Shirley Graham, 7 December 1937.

80. Edward Dickinson to Shirley Graham, circa 26 August 1941.

81. Edward Dickinson to Shirley Graham, 14 January 1939. Shortly thereafter another Oberlin professor with whom Graham corresponded told her that "it is a gamble whether Mr. Dickinson comes out of this nervous collapse or not. My guess is that he will. He's miserable now, just like a sick and fretful child." Frederick Artz to Shirley Graham, 16 July 1940.

82. Joe Himes to Shirley Graham, 22 December 1932. See also Shirley Graham to W. E. B. Du Bois, circa 1932, reel 38, no. 370, W. E. B. Du Bois Papers.

83. Joe Himes to Shirley Graham, 4 September 1932.

84. Joe Himes to Shirley Graham, 12 April 1932.

85. Joe Himes to Shirley Graham, circa 3 June 1932, 6 November 1933.

86. Thomas L. Poston to Shirley Graham, 31 March 1940.

87. Application for Guggenheim Fellowship, 1934, Shirley Graham Du Bois Papers.

88. Raymond Paty to Shirley Graham, 27 October 1938.

89. Adam Clayton Powell to Shirley Graham, 20 December 1932.

90. Rosalie Young to Shirley Graham, 1 August 1940.

91. Edward Dickinson to Shirley Graham, 17 February 1939.

92. Edward Dickinson to Shirley Graham, 20 December 1938.

93. Adam Clayton Powell to Shirley Graham, 13 May 1933.

94. Mary White Ovington to Shirley Graham, 14 May 1934.

95. Edward Dickinson to Shirley Graham, 17 February 1939.

96. Edward Dickinson to Shirley Graham, 20 December 1938.

97. Edward Dickinson to Shirley Graham, 22 January 1939.

98. Mary White Ovington to Shirley Graham, 2 August 1932. It is unclear how Graham and Ovington met; however, over the years she was quite helpful to Graham in advancing her career goals—one of the few women in this category.

99. Edward Ellsworth Hipsher to Shirley Graham, 10 August 1935.

100. Shirley Graham to Hattie Gibbs Marshall, 16 March 1934, Washington Conservatory of Music Papers; program, 15 March 1934, "Caravanzia," Shirley Graham Du Bois Papers.

101. Shirley Graham McCanns to Dr. W. F. Bohn, 4 August 1935, Shirley Graham File, Oberlin College.

102. Shirley Graham to Frederick Artz, 11 August 1973.

103. Shirley Graham to Frederick Artz, 8 November 1972. See also Edward Tobias, director, Oberlin Annual Fund, to Shirley Graham, 3 July 1974 (thanking her for contribution).

104. See Shirley Graham McCanns, "The Survival of Africanism in Modern Music" (M.A. thesis, Oberlin College, 1935), 3, 78. In the preface she remarks that she is "deeply indebted" to Du Bois and James Weldon Johnson for their assistance in her research; she also notes that she consulted with W. C. Handy about some of her ideas concerning music.

NOTES TO CHAPTER 3

1. Shirley Graham Du Bois, *His Day Is Marching On* (Philadelphia: Lippincott, 1971), 42–43.

2. Raymond Wolters, *The New Negro on Campus: Black College Rebellions of the 1920s* (Princeton: Princeton University Press, 1975).

3. "1934 Class Letter" of Oberlin College, Shirley Graham Du Bois Papers.

4. W. J. Hale to Shirley Graham, 3 July 1935.

5. Frederick Artz to Shirley Graham, 25 October 1935.

6. Ibid.

7. Mary White Ovington to Shirley Graham, 10 November 1935.

8. Mary White Ovington to Shirley Graham, 4 February 1935, reel 6, part 2, no. 000483, NAACP Papers.

9. Shirley Graham Du Bois, interview, 28 May 1975, Hatch-Billops Collection.

10. See, e.g., Maxine D. Jones and Joe M. Richardson, *Talladega College: The First Century* (Tuscaloosa: University of Alabama Press, 1990), 21, 46, 115.

11. "1934 Class Letter," Shirley Graham Du Bois Papers.

12. See *Midwest Daily Record*, 17 February 1938, 1 November 1938, 10 January 1939. See also Robert Bone, "Richard Wright and the Chicago Renaissance," *Callaloo* 9, no. 3 (summer 1986): 446–68; Frank Marshall Davis, *Livin' the Blues: Memoirs of a Black Journalist and Poet* (Madison: University of Wisconsin Press, 1992).

13. Richard Wright, "I Tried to Be a Communist," *Atlantic Monthly*, September 1944, file 289882, Federal Bureau of Investigation.

14. See generally Colette A. Hyman, *Staging Strikes: Workers' Theatre and the American Labor Movement* (Philadelphia: Temple University Press, 1997); Raymond Williams, *Drama in a Dramatised Society: An Inaugural Lecture* (New York: Cambridge University Press, 1975); Malcolm Goldstein, *The Political Stage: American Drama and Theatre of the Great Depression* (New York: Oxford University Press, 1974); Ira A. Levine, *Left-Wing Dramatic Theory in the American Theatre* (Ann Arbor: UMI Research Press, 1985); Susan Duffy, ed., *The Political Left in the American Theatre of the 1930s* (Metuchen: Scarecrow Press, 1992); Richard Pells, *Radical Visions and American Dreams: Culture and Social Thought in the Depression Years* (New York: Harper and Row, 1973).

15. "701," newsletter of the Communist Party "unit," box 564, Federal Theater Project Papers. See also Kenneth J. Bindas, *All of This Music Belongs to the Nation: The WPA's Federal Music Project and American Society* (Knoxville: University of Tennessee Press, 1995).

16. Press release, 1 June 1936, reel 24, no. 771, New Deal Agencies and Black America Papers; Irwin Rubenstein to F. S. Belcher, 4 March 1938, reel 24, no. 861, New Deal Agencies and Black America Papers.

17. Glenda Gill, *White Grease Paint on Black Performers: A Study of the Federal Theater, 1935–1939* (New York: Peter Lang, 1988) 1. See also Fannin Belcher, "The Place of the Negro in the Evolution of the American Theater, 1767 to 1940" (Ph.D. diss., Yale University, 1945); Fannie Ella Frazier Hicklin, "The American Negro Playwright, 1920–1964" (Ph.D. diss., University of Wisconsin, 1965); Tina Redd, "The Struggle for Administrative and Artistic Control of the Federal Theatre Negro Units" (Ph.D. diss., University of Washington, 1996).

18. Warren Cochrane to Shirley Graham, 5 July 1940.

19. Jane De Hart, *The Federal Theatre, 1935–1939: Plays, Relief and Politics* (Princeton: Princeton University Press, 1967), 242.

20. Undated clipping in scrapbook, Shirley Graham Du Bois Papers.

21. Shirley Graham Du Bois to Hattie Gibbs Marshall, 27 November 1937, box 112-5, Washington Conservatory of Music Papers.

22. Andrew Paschal, "The Spirit of W. E. B. Du Bois," *Black Scholar* 2, no. 2 (October 1970): 17–28.

23. Shirley Graham to Hattie Gibbs Marshall, 19 November 1937, box 112-5, Washington Conservatory of Music Papers.

24. Hallie Flanagan to Anne M. Cook, 23 August 1943, box 6, folder 2, Hallie Flanagan Papers.

25. Melvin to Shirley Graham, 28 June 1937.

26. Shirley Graham, "Towards an American Theater," circa December 1937, Shirley Graham Du Bois Papers.

27. Rena Fraden, *Blueprints for a Black Federal Theatre, 1935–1939* (New York: Cambridge University Press, 1994), 59. See also Tony Buttita and Barry Witham, *Uncle Sam Presents: A Memoir of the Federal Theatre, 1935–1939* (Philadelphia: University of Pennsylvania Press, 1982).

28. Shirley Graham, *Little Black Sambo* (production script), circa 1938, Shirley Graham Du Bois Papers.

29. Hallie Flanagan, *Arena: The Story of the Federal Theater* (New York: Duell, Sloan and Pearce, 1940), 140, 144, 215.

30. Hallie Flanagan to Shirley Graham, 21 July 1938.

31. *Chicago Herald Examiner*, 31 August 1938.

32. Anna Maria Shawbaker to Shirley Graham, 22 October 1940.

33. Franklin Raymond to Shirley Graham, 18 January 1939; E. Kendell Davis to Shirley Graham, 19 January 1939.

34. Office of the president, University of Chicago, to Shirley Graham, 3 February 1938.

35. Fraden, *Blueprints for a Black Federal Theatre,* 121–22, 134.

36. Shirley Graham to W. E. B. Du Bois, 27 August 1937, reel 47, no. 508, W. E. B. Du Bois Papers.

37. Arthur Gelb and Barbara Gelb *O'Neill* (New York: Harper and Row, 1973); Joel Pfister, *Staging Depth: Eugene O'Neill and the Politics of Psychological Discourse* (Chapel Hill: University of North Carolina Press, 1995); Louis Sheaffer, *O'Neill: Son and Playwright* (Boston: Little, Brown, 1968).

38. Kathryn Baldwin, "The Color Line and Its Discontents: Passing through Russia and the United States" (Ph.D. diss., Yale University, 1995), 31. See also Michael E. Staub, *Voices of Persuasion: Politics of Representation in 1930s America* (New York: Cambridge University Press, 1994); James D. Bloom, *Left Letters: The Cultural Wars of Mike Gold and Joseph Freeman* (New York: Columbia University Press, 1992); Walter Kalaidjian, *American Culture between the Wars: Revisionary Modernism and Postmodern Critique* (New York: Columbia University Press, 1993).

39. This argument continues to resonate. Recently the prize-winning playwright August Wilson has raised similar points in an ongoing debate with the producer Robert Brustein; see *New York Times Magazine,* 8 June 1997. See also Redd, "The Struggle for Administrative and Artistic Control of the Federal Theatre Negro Units."

40. Shirley Graham to W. E. B. Du Bois, 1 October 1937, reel 47, no. 511, W. E. B. Du Bois Papers.

41. Arthur Sullivan and W. S. Gilbert, *The Mikado* (Boston: Oliver Ditson Company, n.d.).

42. Paul Sporn, *Against Itself: The Federal Theater and Writers' Projects in the Midwest* (Detroit: Wayne State University Press, 1995), 288.

43. *Midwest Daily Record,* 27 September 1938.

44. *St. Louis Post-Dispatch,* 4 December 1938. See also *New York Times,* 2 March 1939; *New York Herald Tribune,* 2 March 1939.

45. De Hart, *The Federal Theatre, 1935–1939,* 238.

46. Dorothy Eldridge to Shirley Graham, 9 November 1938.

47. Flanagan, *Arena: The History of the Federal Theater,* 338.

48. *Cleveland Plain-Dealer,* 11 February 1939; *Chicago Daily News,* 30 August 1938; *Chicago Defender,* 1 October 1938.

49. Art Cohn, *The Nine Lives of Michael Todd* (New York: Random House, 1958), 66.

50. Mary White Ovington to Shirley Graham, 27 February 1939.

51. Otis to Shirley Graham, 5 August 1940. See also Shirley Graham to Ora Williams, 3 March 1973:

> I did not write the *Swing Mikado*. It was produced in Chicago by what was then called the Negro Unit of the Chicago Federal Theatre, of which I was the director in 1937–38. It actually was a syncopated version of Gilbert and Sullivan's *Mikado*. We changed neither music or words only "swung" them. . . . The entire production was one of the most stimulating and exciting adventures of my life. It made a tremendous hit on Broadway. . . . I have done the music for a number of children's productions. . . . In those days I did plan to be a thorough musician. Life, circumstances, responsibilities necessitated my taking a job that paid "money." I have never, however, regretted my training or experience in music. I am sure my writing is better for it.

52. See also George Kazacoff, *Dangerous Theatre: The Federal Theatre Project as a Forum for New Plays* (New York: Peter Lang, 1989); Marsha Houston Stanback, "The Federal Theatre's Black Units: A Study of Their Social Relevance" (M.A. thesis, University of North Carolina–Chapel Hill, 1973); John O'Connor and Lorraine Brown, *Free, Adult, Uncensored: The History of the Federal Theatre Project* (Washington, DC: New Republic Books, 1978); Judith Ellen Brussell, "Government Investigations of Federal Theatre Project Personnel in the Works Progress Administration, 1935–1939 (The Show Must Not Go On!)" (Ph.D. diss., City University of New York Graduate Center, 1993); Dick Netzer, *The Subsidized Muse: Public Support for the Arts in the United States* (New York: Cambridge University Press, 1978), 56. The legacy of the FTP continues; National Public Radio, for example, had "its origins in the nearly 6000 FTP radio productions." One scholar has complained about "the 'infection' of anticommunism that plagues American cultural history" and how "women have remained invisible in standard accounts of the 1930s, particularly those written by literary radicals both then and now." Both tendencies have hindered an appreciation of Graham's contributions. See Paula Rabinowitz, *Labor and Desire: Women's Revolutionary Fiction in Depression America* (Chapel Hill: University of North Carolina Press, 1991), 3, 17. See also Granville Hicks et al., eds., *Proletarian Literature in the United States* (New York: International, 1935).

53. Shirley Graham to W. E. B. Du Bois, 25 February 1937, 4 April 1937, 9 April 1937, reel 47, nos. 493. 500, 501, W. E. B. Du Bois Papers.

54. Shirley Graham to W. E. B. Du Bois, 25 October 1937, reel 47, no. 514, W. E. B. Du Bois Papers.

55. Shirley Graham to W. E. B. Du Bois, 16 December 1937, reel 47, no. 516, W. E. B. Du Bois Papers.

56. George Reynolds, Rosenwald Fund, to Shirley Graham, 12 April 1939.

57. Flanagan, *Arena: The Story of the Federal Theater,* 215.

58. Shirley Graham, "A Critical Study of *The Good Earth,* Metro-Goldwyn-Mayer Picture Screened from the Novel of the Same Name by Pearl Buck, Directed by Sidney Franklin, Script Okayed by Irving G. Thalberg, March 14, 1936," for "Drama 136": this paper is a close, twenty-six-page analysis revealing an intimate knowledge of the nature of cinema and how it differs from theater. Shirley Graham to William Bohn, circa 1939; Reverend J. Raymond Henderson, Bethesda Baptist Church–New Rochelle, to Shirley Graham, 13 October 1938.

59. Shirley Graham to W. E. B. Du Bois, 6 March 1940, reel 51, no. 580, W. E. B. Du Bois Papers.

60. Shirley Graham Du Bois, interview, 28 May 1975, Hatch-Billops Collection. Graham said here that Alfred Hitchcock directed an early version of *It's Morning. Elijah's Ravens,* she said, was "very easy to produce." It was performed "all over the South." Another analyst has stated that *It's Morning* was directed by Otto Preminger. See Reuben Silver, "A History of the Karamu Theatre of Karamu House, 1915–1960" (Ph.D. diss., Ohio State University, 1961), 300; scripts of Graham's plays *Deep Rivers, The Revolutionists* (cowritten with Selden Rodman), and *Coal Dust* are in Shirley Graham Du Bois Papers.

61. Kathy Perkins, "The Unknown Career of Shirley Graham," *Freedomways* 25, no. 1 (1985): 6–17; Lorraine E. Ross and Ruth E. Randolph, *Harlem Renaissance and Beyond* (Boston: G. K. Hall, 1990); Constance Welch and Walter Prichard Eaton, eds., *Yale Radio Plays: The Listener's Theatre* (Boston: Expression, 1939).

62. Shirley Graham Du Bois, interview, 28 May 1975, Hatch-Billops Collection.

63. Program, Yale School of Fine Arts, Department of Drama, 17–19 May 1939, Shirley Graham Du Bois Papers.

64. Mary White Ovington to Shirley Graham, 7 December 1938.

65. Shirley Graham to W. E. B. Du Bois, 23 October 1938, Shirley Graham Du Bois Papers, Amistad Research Center.

66. *Canton Repository,* 5 June 1941, Shirley Graham Du Bois Papers.

67. Edward Dickinson to Shirley Graham, 30 January 1939.

68. Mary White Ovington to Shirley Graham, 21 March 1939.

69. Mary White Ovington to Elmer Rice, 21 May 1940, Shirley Graham Du Bois Papers. See also Elmer Rice, *Minority Report: An Autobiography* (New York: Simon and Schuster, 1963); Frank Durham, *Elmer Rice* (New York: Twayne, 1970).

70. Reuben Silver, "A History of the Karamu Theatre of Karamu House, 1915–1960," 8, 170, 171.

71. Ibid., 198.

72. Rowena W. Jelliffe to Shirley Graham, 29 March 1939.

73. Rowena W. Jelliffe to Shirley Graham, 22 March 1939.

74. Ridgley Torrence to Shirley Graham, 12 February 1939.

75. Rowena W. Jelliffe to Shirley Graham, 30 December 1940.

76. Rowena W. Jelliffe to Shirley Graham, 24 November 1933.

77. Program, undated, Shirley Graham File, Oberlin College.

78. Margaret Bailey to Shirley Graham, 7 March 1941, 20 July 1940.

79. Walter Lewisohn to Shirley Graham, 9 December 1940.

80. Walter Lewisohn to Shirley Graham, circa 28 February 1941.

81. Barrett Clark, Dramatist Play Service, to Audrey Wood, 27 January 1941, Shirley Graham Du Bois Papers (Wood, Graham's agent, forwarded her a copy).

82. Walter Prichard Eaton to Shirley Graham, 6 August 1941.

83. Allardyce Nicoll to Shirley Graham, 22 November 1940.

84. B. Case to Shirley Graham, 25 June 1940.

85. George Reynolds to Shirley Graham, 26 July 1940; Hallie Flanagan to Shirley Graham, 9 July 1940, 15 January 1940.

86. Charles Johnson to Shirley Graham, 3 February 1941.

87. Louis Laflin to Shirley Graham, 11 February 1941.

88. Adam Clayton Powell, Jr., to Shirley Graham, 1 July 1940.

89. Shirley Graham to Arthur Spingarn, 11 January 1941, Arthur Spingarn Papers.

90. Essie Robeson to Shirley Graham, 26 April 1940.

91. Hallie Flanagan to Shirley Graham, 15 January 1940.

NOTES TO CHAPTER 4

1. Shirley Graham Du Bois, interview, 28 May 1975, Hatch-Billops Collection.

2. Shirley Graham to W. E. B. Du Bois, 20 September 1939, reel 50, no. 192, W. E. B. Du Bois Papers.

3. Program, circa 1941, Shirley Graham Du Bois Papers.

4. Program, 1 May 1941, Dillard University, Shirley Graham Du Bois Papers.

5. Program, circa 1941, Shirley Graham Du Bois Papers. See also Alfred Farrell to Shirley Graham, circa 25 April 1941.

6. Conference, Evansville, Indiana, 3–4 April 1941, Shirley Graham Du Bois Papers.

7. Letter (indecipherable name) to Shirley Graham, 20 February 1941.

8. Edward Dickinson to Shirley Graham, 30 January 1939.

9. May Belcher to Shirley Graham, 4 June 1940.

10. Sadie Alexander to Walter White, 21 June 1943, group 2, box a585, NAACP Papers.

11. Letter to Shirley Graham, 8 November 1941.

12. Shirley Graham Du Bois, *His Day Is Marching On* (Philadelphia: Lippincott, 1971), 52. See also Judith Weisenfeld, *African American Women and Christian Activism: New York's Black YWCA, 1905–1945* (Cambridge: Harvard University Press, 1997).

13. Gerald Nash, *The American West Transformed: The Impact of the Second World War* (Bloomington: Indiana University Press, 1985); Kevin Allen Leonard, "The Impact of World War II on Race Relations in Los Angeles" (Ph.D. diss., University of California–Davis, 1992); Mark S. Foster, "Giant of the West: Henry J. Kaiser and Regional Industrialization, 1930–1950," *Business History Review* 59 (spring 1985): 1–23; Ruth Milkman, *Gender at Work: The Dynamics of Job Segregation during World War II* (Urbana: University of Illinois Press, 1987); Gretchen Lemke Santangelo, *Abiding Courage: African American Migrant Women and the East Bay Community* (Chapel Hill: University of North Carolina Press, 1996).

14. D'Ann Campbell, *Women at War with America: Private Lives in a Patriotic Era* (Cambridge: Harvard University Press, 1984), 74–75.

15. Program, USO Staff Institute, Hotel Whitcomb, San Francisco, 13–15 October 1941, Shirley Graham Du Bois Papers.

16. Perry Bruce Kaufman, "The Best City of Them All: A History of Las Vegas, 1930–1960" (Ph.D. diss., University of California–Santa Barbara, 1974), 232, 335, 343, 349, 350, 367.

17. Quintard Taylor *In Search of the Racial Frontier: African Americans in the American West, 1528–1990* (New York: Norton, 1998), 264; Robert Franklin Jefferson, "Making the Men of the 93rd: African American Servicemen in the Years of the Great Depression and the Second World War, 1935–1947" (Ph.D. diss., University of Michigan, 1995), 231–32, 234, 243.

18. Martha Putney, *When the Nation Was in Need: Blacks in the Women's Army Corps during World War II* (Metuchen: Scarecrow Press, 1992), 23; Danehower Wilson, *Jim Crow Joins Up: A Study of Negroes in the Armed Forces of the United States* (New York: William Clark, 1944).

19. Charity Adams Earley, *One Woman's Army: A Black Officer Remembers the WAC* (College Station: Texas A&M Press, 1989), 64. See also Leisa D. Meyer, *Creating G.I. Jane: Sexuality and Power in the Women's Army Corps during World War II* (New York: Columbia University Press, 1996); Paula Nassen Poulos, ed., *A Woman's War Too: U.S. Women in the Military in World War II* (Washington, DC: National Archives and Records Administration, 1997).

20. Dempsey Travis, *Views from the Back of the Bus during World War II and Beyond* (Chicago: Urban Research Press, 1995), 8.

21. Joyce Thomas, "The 'Double V' Was for Victory: Black Soldiers, Black Protest and World War II" (Ph.D. diss., Ohio State University, 1993), 297.

22. Phillip McGuire, ed., *Taps for a Jim Crow Army: Letters from Black Soldiers in World War II* (Santa Barbara: ABC-Clio, 1983), 45–47.

23. "Confidential," "Counter-intelligence Summary," November 1943, Eleventh Naval District, ND11/A9(1) (A8-By-ra), serial DIO-9949, box 32, record group 46, R-6661b, Van Deman Collection, Senate Internal Security Subcommittee Papers. The mass influx of African Americans to the Far West, where their numbers theretofore had been relatively small, apparently helped to spark severe clashes. This report also noted, "stabbings of whites by Negroes continue to fill police records in Los Angeles and San Diego."

24. *New York Times,* 28 November 1942, 17 February 1943; Leopold Johnson to NAACP, 8 April 1943; Otis Burns to James Davis, 5 May 1943; Leslie Perry to Charles Browning, 29 September 1944, box b159, group 2, NAACP Papers.

25. Shirley Graham to W. E. B. Du Bois, 9 November 1942, in Herbert Aptheker, ed., *The Correspondence of W. E. B. Du Bois,* vol. 2, *Selections, 1934–1944* (Amherst: University of Massachusetts Press, 1976), 346.

26. Shirley Graham, "Negroes are Fighting for Freedom," *Common Sense* 12, no. 2 (February 1943): 45–50, 46, 50.

27. Gerald Horne, *Black Liberation/Red Scare: Ben Davis and the Communist Party* (Newark: University of Delaware Press, 1994). See also Robert Hill, ed., *RACON: Racial Conditions in the United States during World War II* (Boston: Northeastern University Press, 1995).

28. Hallie Flanagan to Shirley Graham, 23 January 1942.

29. Charles Johnson to Shirley Graham, 6 April 1942.

30. Albert McKee to Shirley Graham, 3 March 1942.

31. Albert M. Hawkins to Shirley Graham, 25 January 1942.

32. "A Soldier" to Shirley Graham, 18 January 1942.

33. Max W. Foresman to Shirley Graham, 28 October 1943, circa 5 October 1943, circa 1 August 1942. Foresman was probably a Euro-American, as suggested by his frequent musings about interracial love. See Max W. Foresman to Shirley Graham, 16 July 1942. Later, he noted, "you probably wonder how I can say [I love you] without actually meeting you." Max W. Foresman to Shirley Graham, 28 October 1943.

34. Shirley Graham to W. E. B. Du Bois, 9 November 1942, in Aptheker, *The Correspondence,* vol. 2, 346.

35. Shirley Graham to W. E. B. Du Bois, 30 October 1942, reel 53, no. 1047, W. E. B. Du Bois Papers.

36. Shirley Graham to Bernard Jaffe, 30 August 1972.

37. Max W. Foresman to Shirley Graham, circa 26 March 1943.

38. Shirley Graham to Mary White Ovington, August 1943, Mary White Ovington Papers.

39. Shirley Graham Du Bois, *His Day Is Marching On,* 56.

40. Shirley Graham to Walter White, circa 1942, box a585, group 2, NAACP Papers.

41. See generally Gerald Horne, *Black and Red: W. E. B. Du Bois and the*

Afro-American Response to the Cold War, 1944–1963 (Albany: State University of New York Press, 1986).

42. Shirley Graham to Walter White, 14 July 1943, box a585, group 2, NAACP Papers.

43. Fred Clark to Shirley Graham, 24 July 1943; Shirley Graham to William Hastie, 20 July 1943; Roy Wilkins to Shirley Graham, 15 April 1943; Walter White to Shirley Graham, 16 June 1943. *Cleveland Plain-Dealer,* 18 April 1943: Graham speaks in Ohio in an effort to enlist ten thousand new members for the NAACP.

44. Shirley Graham Du Bois, *His Day Is Marching On,* 54

45. Shirley Graham to W. E. B. Du Bois, 1 April 1943, reel 55, no. 320, W. E. B. Du Bois Papers.

46. Shirley Graham to Mary White Ovington, August 1943, Mary White Ovington Papers; Nat Brandt, *Harlem at War: The Black Experience in World War II* (Syracuse: Syracuse University Press, 1996); Neil Wynn, *Afro-Americans and the Second World War* (New York: Holmes and Meier, 1976).

47. Shirley Graham to Mary White Ovington, 1 August 1943, Mary White Ovington Papers.

48. Ibid.

49. Arthur Spingarn to Shirley Graham, 5 October 1943. Shirley Graham to Walter White, 8 September 1943, box a585, group II, NAACP Papers.

50. Shirley Graham to Roy Wilkins, 6 January 1944; Shirley Graham to Walter White, 13 February 1944, box a585, group 2, NAACP Papers.

51. Shirley Graham to Charles Johnson, 22 May 1944, Shirley Graham Du Bois Papers, Amistad Research Center.

52. Julia Crockett to Shirley Graham, 1 August 1940. Here Graham was seeking to rent a cottage in Idlewild, Michigan, that would "accommodate you and the two boys"; "two large bedrooms" were available for the summer at a price of "$6 each."

53. Hallie Flanagan to Shirley Graham, 17 April 1941.

54. Robert McCanns to Shirley Graham, 11 September 1941.

55. Robert McCanns to Shirley Graham, 3 November 1943.

56. *PM,* 19 January 1944.

57. Shirley Graham Du Bois, *His Day Is Marching On,* 56; David Du Bois, interview by author, 26 December 1993.

58. David Du Bois, interview by author, 16 May 1996.

59. Pete Cacchione to Shirley Graham, 27 July 1944.

60. Shirley Graham to Roselyn Richardson, 3 July 1946, Roselyn Richardson Papers.

61. Adolph Meyer to Shirley Graham, 9 May 1946.

62. Edward Kastner to Shirley Graham, 10 December 1945.

63. Shirley Graham to Roselyn Richardson, 3 July 1946, Roselyn Richardson Papers.

64. Graham McCanns to Shirley Graham, 3 September 1944.

65. Shirley Graham to Graham McCanns, 6 July 1945.

66. Ibid.

67. Shirley Graham, *Dr. George Washington Carver, Scientist* (New York: Julian Messner, 1944).

68. Shirley Graham Du Bois, interview by Ann Schockley, 7 January 1971, Oral History Collection Fisk University Library.

69. Shirley Graham to Paul Robeson, 9 March 1944, Paul Robeson Papers.

70. Haley G. Douglass to Shirley Graham, 19 May 1946; Eva Ingersoll Wakefield to Shirley Graham, 11 December 1945.

71. Shirley Graham Du Bois, *His Day Is Marching On*, 86.

72. Shirley Graham to Mary White Ovington, 1 August 1943, Mary White Ovington Papers.

73. Leon Levine to Shirley Graham, circa February 1945.

74. *Variety*, 7 March 1945: "A second all-Negro serial entitled 'The Bannekers' by Shirley Graham has been going the rounds in New York City."

75. Marc Connelly to Walter White, 28 May 1943, Shirley Graham Du Bois Papers.

76. *New York Star*, 25 January 1949.

77. David Du Bois, interview, 3 June 1992, Louis Massiah Papers.

78. Shirley Graham, *Carver*, 187, 208.

79. *Christian Science Monitor*, 27 April 1950.

80. Walter Prichard Eaton to Shirley Graham, 16 April 1944.

81. Herbert Miller to Shirley Graham, 12 January 1945.

82. Ann Petry to Shirley Graham, 15 July 1946.

83. Shirley Graham, *Paul Robeson: Citizen of the World* (New York: Julian Messner, 1946).

84. Ibid., 146, 147, 185, 209, 210, 222.

85. Shirley Graham to Paul Robeson, 9 March 1944, Paul Robeson Papers.

86. Shirley Graham, *There Was Once a Slave: The Heroic Story of Frederick Douglass* (New York: Julian Messner, 1947).

87. *New York Times*, 6 April 1947: her book is sharply criticized here. The critic for the then liberal *Post* was also critical: see *New York Post*, 20 March 1947. However, the *Times* critic admired her biography of Benjamin Banneker: *New York Times*, 30 October 1949. Saunders Redding also wrote favorably of her Banneker biography: *Philadelphia Afro-American*, 12 November 1949. It was also reviewed favorably in the *San Francisco Examiner*, 29 October 1949. Redding expressed admiration for her Robeson biography though he questioned the fictionalized aspects: *Philadelphia Afro-American*, 31 August

1946; Her Douglass book was reviewed positively—twice—in the *Tribune*: *New York Herald Tribune*, 20 March 1947, 23 March 1947. Horace Cayton liked this book also, calling it a "competent story" but in addition to assailing her fictionalization, he observed that "there is not the breath [*sic*] of vision." *Chicago Sun*, 13 April 1947.

88. *Washington Star*, 6 April 1947.

89. *Norfolk Journal and Guide*, 22 November 1947.

90. *New York Herald Tribune*, 14 April 1947; *Chicago Defender*, 19 April 1947.

91. *Boston Chronicle*, 25 October 1947.

92. Shirley Graham to Arthur Spingarn, 28 November 1946, Arthur Spingarn Papers.

93. Shirley Graham to Arthur Spingarn, 3 January 1947, Arthur Spingarn Papers.

94. Shirley Graham to Arthur Spingarn, 15 October 1947, Arthur Spingarn Papers.

95. Shirley Graham to Roselyn Richardson, 23 May 1947, Roselyn Richardson Papers.

96. Ibid.

97. Shirley Graham Du Bois, *His Day Is Marching On*, 64.

98. David Du Bois, interview, 3 June 1992, Louis Massiah Papers.

99. Ibid.

100. *People's Voice*, 27 July 1946.

101. Quoted in *New York Times*, 22 April 1997. See also Keith Griffler, "The Black Radical Intellectual and the Black Worker: The Emergence of a Program for Black Labor, 1918–1938" (Ph.D. diss., Ohio State University, 1993); Raymond Wolters, *Negroes and the Great Depression: The Problem of Economic Recovery* (Westport: Greenwood, 1970); Christopher E. Linsin, "Not by Words, But by Deeds: Communists and African Americans during the Depression Era" (M.A. thesis, Florida Atlantic University, 1993). Linsin shows how Communist activity helped to drive African Americans to the left and toward militance, thereby helping to erode Jim Crow.

102. Arch Getty, Gabor Rittesporn, and Victor Zemskov, "Victims of the Soviet Penal System in the Pre-War Years: First Approach on the Basis of Archival Evidence," *American Historical Review* 98, no. 4 (October 1993): 1017–49; Michael Parenti, *Blackshirts and Reds: Rational Fascism and the Overthrow of Communism* (San Francisco: City Lights, 1997); Marion Miller, *I Was a Spy* (Indianapolis: Bobbs-Merrill, 1960), 117: this spy for the FBI implicitly called into question the impact of subsidies for local Reds from Moscow by observing how Communists lived "in a condition of furious, scrabbling famine as far as money goes. . . . There are major items of overhead—lawyers' fees, the support of Communist-led strikers, reasonably generous contributions to any and every cause that may be linked in some way to the master Communist plan."

103. *New Masses,* 13 May 1947.

104. U.S. Congress, House of Representatives, Committee on Un-American Activities, Testimony of Walter Steele, 80th Cong., 1st sess., 21 July 1947 (Washington, DC: Government Printing Office, 1947), 141.

105. W. E. B. Du Bois to Shirley Graham, 20 October 1947, reel 60, no. 66, W. E. B. Du Bois Papers.

106. W. E. B. Du Bois to Bill Graham, 15 October 1947, reel 69, no. 66, W. E. B. Du Bois Papers.

107. Hugh Smythe to Shirley Graham, 17 August 1948, reel 61, no. 1062, W. E. B. Du Bois Papers.

108. Shirley Graham, "Why Was Du Bois Fired?" *Masses & Mainstream* 1, no. 9 (November 1948): 15–26.

109. Carol Elaine Anderson, "Eyes off the Prize: African-Americans, the United Nations and the Struggle for Human Rights, 1944–1952" (Ph.D. diss., Ohio State University, 1995), 128, 130, 131.

110. Horne, *Black and Red,* 87, 88; Henry Wallace to Shirley Graham, 9 October 1945.

111. Shirley Graham address, 23 July 1948, Shirley Graham Du Bois Papers.

112. Curtis D. MacDougall, *Gideon's Army,* vol. 2 (New York: Marzani and Munsell, 1965), 510.

113. Ibid. See also Patricia Sullivan, *Days of Hope: Race and Democracy in the New Deal Era* (Chapel Hill: University of North Carolina Press, 1996).

114. David Du Bois, interview, 3 June 1992, Louis Massiah Papers.

115. Shirley Graham Speech, "National Founding Convention of the New Political Party at Convention Hall, Philadelphia, July 23–25, 1948," reel 2, Third Party Presidential Nominating Conventions, Proceedings, Records, etc. This evocation of the maternal had become a frequent theme for her. In an open letter to President Roosevelt published in *PM* on 24 June 1943, she announced, "The time has come for Negro mothers to speak."

116. Shirley Graham to Roselyn Richardson, 4 April 1948, Roselyn Richardson Papers.

117. Open letter from Shirley Graham, 20 October 1950, box 10, American Labor Party Papers.

118. Open letter from Shirley Graham, 1950, box 16, American Labor Party Papers.

NOTES TO CHAPTER 5

1. *Daily Worker,* 1 November 1943, 25 November 1943.

2. Memorandum, 27 February 1948, no. 100-370965-1, FBI.

3. Memorandum, 11 September 1950, no. 100-370965-8, FBI; *Daily Worker,*

26 March 1948, 31 May 1948, 23 December 1949; *New York Amsterdam News,* 31 December 1949; *Counter-Attack,* 1 July 1949.

4. Special Agent–New York to J. Edgar Hoover, 5 June 1951, 100-370965-2, FBI.

5. Minutes of meeting on membership, NCASP, 28 July 1948, Shirley Graham Du Bois Papers.

6. Shirley Graham Du Bois, *His Day Is Marching On* (Philadelphia: Lippincott, 1971), 90, 98.

7. List of speaking engagements, circa 1946–47, Shirley Graham Du Bois Papers.

8. *Washington Post,* 5 January 1947: here, like a female Jack Benny, Graham gave her age as thirty-nine; *Boston Globe,* 16 February 1950.

9. *Chicago Defender,* 29 November 1947.

10. *Publishers Weekly,* 22 February 1947.

11. See generally Gerald Horne, *Communist Front? The Civil Rights Congress, 1946–1956* (London: Associated University Presses, 1988), 235–38.

12. *Compass,* 7 September 1949.

13. Shirley Graham to Roselyn Richardson, 13 November 1949, Roselyn Richardson Papers.

14. Shirley Graham to "Dear Good Friends," 8 May 1949, Roselyn Richardson Papers.

15. Shirley Graham Du Bois, *His Day Is Marching On,* 115.

16. U.S. Congress, House of Representatives, Committee on Un-American Activities, Testimony of Walter Steele, 80th Cong., 1st sess., 21 July 1947 (Washington, DC: GPO, 1947); U.S. Congress, House of Representatives, Committee on Un-American Activities, *Review of the Scientific and Cultural Conference for World Peace. Arranged by the National Council of the Arts, Sciences and Professions,* 81st Cong., 1st sess., March 25–27, 1949 (Washington, DC: GPO, 1949).

17. *New York Herald-Tribune,* 8 October 1949.

18. Shirley Graham to Kathryn Messner, circa 1948, reel 61, no. 1062, W. E. B. Du Bois Papers.

19. Shirley Graham Du Bois, *His Day Is Marching On,* 115.

20. *New York Times,* 20 September 1998. See also Steven Gregory, *Black Corona: Race and the Politics of Place in an Urban Community* (Princeton: Princeton University Press, 1998).

21. *Afro-American,* 11 February 1950.

22. David Du Bois, interview, 3 September 1972, Hatch-Billops Collection.

23. Shirley Graham to Graham McCanns, 6 July 1945.

24. Graham McCanns to Shirley Graham, 1 July 1945.

25. Shirley Graham to Roselyn Richardson, 3 July 1946, Roselyn Richardson Papers.

26. *Afro-American*, 20 August 1949.

27. Shirley Graham to Mr. Zanich, 6 February 1950, Arthur Spingarn Papers.

28. Shirley Graham to Roselyn Richardson, 12 December 1950, Roselyn Richardson Papers.

29. Shirley Graham Du Bois, *His Day Is Marching On*, 16–17.

30. Andrew Paschal, "The Spirit of W. E. B. Du Bois," *Black Scholar* 2, no. 2 (October 1970): 17–28.

31. Ruth Morris Graham, interview, 9 September 1993, Louis Massiah Papers.

32. Shirley Graham to W. E. B. Du Bois, 16 May 1935, reel 44, no. 177, W. E. B. Du Bois Papers.

33. Shirley Graham to W. E. B. Du Bois, 9 September 1935, reel 44, no. 175, W. E. B. Du Bois Papers.

34. Shirley Graham to W. E. B. Du Bois, 23 June 1934, 8 December 1934, reel 42, nos. 318, 321, W. E. B. Du Bois Papers.

35. W. E. B. Du Bois to Shirley Graham, 17 November 1934.

36. Shirley Graham to W. E. B. Du Bois, 30 October 1935, reel 44, no. 177. W. E. B. Du Bois Papers.

37. W. E. B. Du Bois to Shirley Graham, 17 January 1936.

38. W. E. B. Du Bois to Shirley Graham, 3 January 1936.

39. W. E. B. Du Bois to Shirley Graham, 1 November 1935.

40. W. E. B. Du Bois to Shirley Graham, 3 January 1936, reel 45, no. 964, W. E. B. Du Bois Papers.

41. Shirley Graham to W. E. B. Du Bois, 11 January 1936, reel 45, no. 965, W. E. B. Du Bois Papers.

42. Shirley Graham to W. E. B. Du Bois, 6 April 1936, reel 45, no. 966, W. E. B. Du Bois Papers.

43. W. E. B. Du Bois to Shirley Graham, circa 1936, reel 45, no. 968, W. E. B. Du Bois Papers.

44. From the vantage point of the late twentieth century, it appears that Graham and Du Bois at some point during the 1930s consummated an adulterous relationship. On the other hand, such covert relationships are inherently difficult to ferret out: to my knowledge, no one else was present when this supposed intimate relationship was consummated. As her correspondence with her Oberlin professor indicated, Graham had been party to an intensely personal correspondence with an older man previously, and it is likewise unclear if this relationship extended to the sexual realm. Cf. Lillian Faderman, *Surpassing the Love of Men: Romantic Friendship and Love between Women, from the Renaissance to the Present* (New York: Morrow, 1981).

45. Shirley Graham to W. E. B. Du Bois, 10 April 1936, reel 45, no. 969, W. E. B. Du Bois Papers.

46. Shirley Graham to W. E. B. Du Bois, 23 April 1936, reel 45, no. 973, W. E. B. Du Bois Papers.

47. Du Bois recommendation, 10 December 1937, reel 48, no. 83, W. E. B. Du Bois Papers.

48. W. E. B. Du Bois to Shirley Graham, 7 July 1942.

49. Shirley Graham to W. E. B. Du Bois, 21 May 1939, reel 50, no. 190, W. E. B. Du Bois Papers.

50. Shirley Graham to W. E. B. Du Bois, 20 September 1939, reel 50, no. 192, W. E. B. Du Bois Papers.

51. Shirley Graham to W. E. B. Du Bois, 30 December 1939, reel 50, no. 193, W. E. B. Du Bois Papers.

52. W. E. B. Du Bois to Shirley Graham, 16 January 1942, 5 February 1940.

53. Shirley Graham to W. E. B. Du Bois, 6 March 1940, reel 51, no. 580, W. E. B. Du Bois Papers.

54. Ibid.

55. W. E. B. Du Bois to Shirley Graham, 12 April 1940, 28 May 1940, reel 51, nos. 581, 583, W. E. B. Du Bois Papers.

56. Shirley Graham to W. E. B. Du Bois, circa March 1941, reel 52, no. 1011, W. E. B. Du Bois Papers.

57. Shirley Graham to W. E. B. Du Bois, 25 April 1940, reel 51, no. 582, W. E. B. Du Bois Papers.

58. Shirley Graham to W. E. B. Du Bois, 21 April 1941, reel 52, no. 1012, W. E. B. Du Bois Papers.

59. Shirley Graham to W. E. B. Du Bois, 7 June 1940, reel 51, no. 585, W. E. B. Du Bois Papers.

60. Shirley Graham to W. E. B. Du Bois, 15 May 1941, reel 51, no. 1014, W. E. B. Du Bois Papers.

61. Shirley Graham to W. E. B. Du Bois, 1 July 1941, reel 52, no. 1019, W. E. B. Du Bois Papers.

62. Florence Keepers Lewis to Shirley Graham, 12 March 1941.

63. Shirley Graham to W. E. B. Du Bois, 1 October 1941, reel 52, no. 1020, W. E. B. Du Bois Papers.

64. Fannin to Shirley Graham, 20 September 1940.

65. Shirley Graham to W. E. B. Du Bois, 25 June 1942, reel 53, no. 1036, W. E. B. Du Bois Papers.

66. Shirley Graham to W. E. B. Du Bois, 19 March 1941, reel 53, no. 1044, W. E. B. Du Bois Papers.

67. Ibid.

68. Shirley Graham to W. E. B. Du Bois, 2 May 1942, reel 53, no. 1045, W. E. B. Du Bois Papers.

69. Shirley Graham to W. E. B. Du Bois, 30 October 1942, reel 53, no. 1047, W. E. B. Du Bois Papers.

70. Shirley Graham to W. E. B. Du Bois, 30 November 1942, reel 53, no. 1051, W. E. B. Du Bois Papers.

71. Shirley Graham to W. E. B. Du Bois, 8 March 1943, reel 55, no. 318, W. E. B. Du Bois Papers.

72. Shirley Graham to W. E. B. Du Bois, 19 June 1943, reel 55, no. 322, W. E. B. Du Bois Papers.

73. Shirley Graham to W. E. B. Du Bois, 23 August 1943, reel 55, no. 325, W. E. B. Du Bois Papers.

74. Shirley Graham to W. E. B. Du Bois, 24 February 1944, reel 56, no. 126, W. E. B. Du Bois Papers.

75. Shirley Graham to W. E. B. Du Bois, 6 March 1944, reel 56, no. 128, W. E. B. Du Bois Papers.

76. W. E. B. Du Bois to Shirley Graham, 9 November 1945.

77. W. E. B. Du Bois to Shirley Graham, 13 August 1946, 9 November 1945, 3 November 1946, 27 April 1947.

78. W. E. B. Du Bois to Shirley Graham, 14 March 1947.

79. Shirley Graham to W. E. B. Du Bois, 21 May 1949, reel 63, no. 1104, W. E. B. Du Bois Papers.

80. Howard Fast, interview, 3 August 1993, Louis Massiah Papers.

81. Shirley Graham Du Bois, interview by Ann Schockley, 7 January 1971, Oral History Collection Fisk University Library.

82. Shirley Graham Du Bois, *His Day Is Marching On,* 125, 131, 138.

83. W. E. B. Du Bois, *In Battle for Peace* (Millwood: Kraus-Thomson, 1976), 62.

84. W. E. B. Du Bois statement, *Chicago Globe,* reel 84, no. 45, W. E. B. Du Bois Papers.

NOTES TO CHAPTER 6

1. Shirley Graham Du Bois, interview by Ann Schockley, 7 January 1971, Oral History Fisk University Library.

2. David Du Bois, interview, 3 June 1992, Louis Massiah Papers.

3. W. E. B. Du Bois, *In Battle for Peace* (Millwood: Kraus-Thomson, 1976).

4. *Pittsburgh Courier,* 3 March 1951.

5. Shirley Graham Du Bois, *His Day Is Marching On* (Philadelphia: Lippincott, 1971), 143.

6. Abbott Simon, interview, 23 July 1992, Louis Massiah Papers.

7. David Du Bois, interview, 3 June 1992, Louis Massiah Papers.

8. Carlton Moss, interview, 19 June 1992, Louis Massiah Papers.

9. Literature by Shirley Graham Du Bois, circa 1951, reel 66, no. 535, W. E. B. Du Bois Papers.

10. Shirley Graham Du Bois, *His Day Is Marching On,* 157, 158, 160, 163, 164; *Daily Worker,* 8 June 1951.

11. W. E. B. Du Bois, *In Battle for Peace*, 104, 158.

12. Shirley Graham Du Bois speech, circa 1951, reel 89, no. 908, W. E. B. Du Bois Papers.

13. W. E. B. Du Bois, *In Battle for Peace*, 95.

14. Income tax return, 1950, reel 65, no. 373, W. E. B. Du Bois Papers.

15. Shirley Graham Du Bois, *His Day is Marching On*, 184.

16. Ibid., 188.

17. W. E. B. Du Bois to Shirley Graham, 23 January 1951.

18. Arthur Miller, *Timebends: A Life* (New York: Harper and Row, 1987), 328.

19. Shirley Graham to W. E. B. Du Bois, circa 1951, reel 65, no. 68, W. E. B. Du Bois Papers.

20. Shirley Graham Du Bois, *His Day Is Marching On*, 152.

21. Ibid., 195.

22. Ibid., 218.

23. David Du Bois, interview, 3 June 1992, Louis Massiah Papers.

24. Ethel Ray Nance, interview, 18 November 1970, 23 December 1970, Oral History Collection Fisk University Library.

25. Herbert Aptheker, interview, 12 June 1992, Louis Massiah Papers.

26. Vicki Garvin, interview, 27 May 1992, Louis Massiah Papers.

27. James Jackson and Esther Jackson, interview, 2 June 1992, Louis Massiah Papers.

28. Louise Patterson, interview, 13 June 1992, Louis Massiah Papers.

29. Howard Fast, interview, 3 August 1993, Louis Massiah Papers. See also Howard Fast, *Literature and Reality* (New York: International, 1950), 29: here Fast refers to "the heroic portraits of Shirley Graham" in the midst of castigating Orwell, Kafka, and others. Paul Robeson, Jr., agrees with Fast's analysis of her and her impact on Du Bois. "She was a person in her own right when she married him" and "managed at the same time that she continued her own career. . . . She was really able to support Dr. Du Bois and facilitate his continued career in his older years and that's a very difficult thing to do." Unlike Maya Angelou, he argues that she "didn't take advantage of her position as Mrs. Du Bois," though he adds quickly, "I didn't know her that well." Paul Robeson, Jr., interview, 15 April 1994, Louis Massiah Papers. Fast's wife and the poet Eve Merriam were part of a friendly triumvirate with Graham. Annette Rubinstein stated that "Eve was a very good friend of Shirley's." She added enigmatically that the poet "had known Du Bois well that way." Annette Rubinstein, interview, 29 May 1992, Louis Massiah Papers.

30. Shirley Graham to Herbert Aptheker, 10 June 1950, reel 65, no. 680, W. E. B. Du Bois Papers.

31. David Du Bois, interview, 3 June 1992, Louis Massiah Papers.

32. Anna Grant, interview, October 1992, Louis Massiah Papers.

33. Shirley Graham to Roselyn Richardson, 3 January 1954, Roselyn Richardson Papers.

34. W. E. B. Du Bois, *The Autobiography of W. E. B. Du Bois: A Soliloquy on Viewing My Life from the Last Decade of its First Century* (New York: International, 1971), 282.

35. W. E. B. Du Bois to Arna Bontemps, 3 November 1952, in Herbert Aptheker, ed., *The Correspondence of W. E. B. Du Bois*, vol. 3, 39.

36. Ibid., Howard Fast, interview, 3 August 1993, Louis Massiah Papers.

37. See generally Gerald Horne, *Black Liberation/Red Scare: Ben Davis and the Communist Party* (Newark: University of Delaware Press, 1994).

38. Du Bois Williams, interview, 18 September 1992, Louis Massiah Papers.

39. Shirley Graham, "Paul Robeson," *Opportunity* 9, no. 1 (January 1931): 14–15.

40. David Du Bois, interview by author, 16 May 1996.

41. Gerald Horne, *Black and Red: W. E. B. Du Bois and the Afro-American Response to the Cold War, 1944–1963* (Albany: State University of New York Press, 1986), 207.

42. Gerald Horne, *Communist Front? The Civil Rights Congress, 1946–1956* (London: Associated University Presses, 1988), 208.

43. Julia Brown, *I Testify: My Years as an Undercover Agent for the FBI* (Boston: Western Islands, 1966), x, 136. See generally Adrien Katherine Wing, ed., *Critical Race Feminism: A Reader* (New York: New York University Press, 1997).

44. Report, 12 January 1956, no. 100-370965; report, 16 May 1956, no. 100-370965, FBI.

45. Ibid., report, 12 January 1956; report, 16 May 1956, FBI.

46. Brown, *I Testify: My Years as an Undercover Agent for the FBI*, 83.

47. Barbara A. Woods, "Modjeska Simkins and the South Carolina Conference of the NAACP, 1939–1957," in Vicki Crawford et al., eds., *Women in the Civil Rights Movement: Trailblazers and Torchbearers, 1941–1965* (Bloomington: Indiana University Press, 1993), 99–120, 113.

48. Calendars of Shirley Graham Du Bois, 1951–59, Shirley Graham Du Bois Papers.

49. *New York Times*, 10 May 1952.

50. Ibid.; W. E. B. Du Bois, *In Battle for Peace*, 192.

51. Report, reel 69, no. 762, W. E. B. Du Bois Papers.

52. Report, 3 March 1953, no. 100-34259, FBI.

53. Shirley Graham to W. E. B. Du Bois, 13 May 1955, reel 71, no. 342, W. E. B. Du Bois Papers.

54. See, e.g., Michael Harrington, *The Long Distance Runner: An Autobiography* (New York: Holt, 1988); Edward Alexander, *Irving Howe: Socialist, Critic, Jew* (Bloomington: Indiana University Press, 1998).

55. Marjorie Garber and Rebecca L. Walkowitz, eds., *Secret Agents: The Rosenberg Case, McCarthyism and Fifties America* (New York: Routledge, 1995); Alvin H. Goldstein, *The Unquiet Death of Julius and Ethel Rosenberg* (New York: Lawrence Hill, 1975); Morton Sobell, *On Doing Time* (New York: Scribner's, 1974); Ronald Radosh and Joyce Milton, *The Rosenberg File: A Search for the Truth* (New York: Holt, Rinehart, Winston, 1983).

56. Letter from Shirley Graham, 8 March 1953.

57. Robert Meeropol and Michael Meeropol, *We Are Your Sons: The Legacy of Julius and Ethel Rosenberg* (Boston: Houghton Mifflin, 1975).

58. Robert Meeropol, interview, 3 June 1992, Louis Massiah Papers.

59. U.S. Congress, House of Representatives, *Investigation of Communist Activities (The Committee to Secure Justice in the Rosenberg Case and Affiliates)*, part 1, 84th Cong., 1st sess., 2–3 August 1955 (Washington, DC: GPO, 1955), 2138.

60. Margaret Pagan, "Ruby Dee," in Darlene Clark Hine, Elsa Barkley Brown, and Rosalyn Terborg-Penn, eds., *Black Women in America: An Historical Encyclopedia*, vol. 1 (Bloomington: Indiana University Press, 1993), 313–15, 314.

61. Frances Williams, interview, 9 September 1993, Louis Massiah Papers.

62. Shirley Graham Du Bois to Roselyn Richardson, 3 January 1954, Roselyn Richardson Papers.

63. Lawrence H. Schwartz, *Creating Faulkner's Reputation: The Politics of Modern Literary Criticism* (Knoxville: University of Tennessee Press, 1990).

64. See, e.g., Fiona M. Dejardin, "The Photo League: Aesthetics, Politics and the Cold War" (Ph.D. diss., University of Delaware, 1993), 63, 107; Christopher John Gerard, "'A Program of Cooperation': The FBI, the Senate Internal Security Subcommittee, and the Communist Issue, 1950–1956" (Ph.D. diss., Marquette University, 1993); Philip Goldstein, ed., *Styles of Cultural Activism: From Theory and Pedagogy to Women, Indians and Communism* (Newark: University of Delaware Press, 1994); Ronald Oakley West, "Left Out: The Seattle Repertory Playhouse, Audience Inscription and the Problem of Leftist Theater during the Depression Era" (Ph.D. diss., University of Washington, 1993); Hosoon Chang, "National Security v. First Amendment Freedoms: U.S. Supreme Court Decisions on Anti-Communist Regulations, 1919–1974" (Ph.D. diss., University of North Carolina–Chapel Hill, 1993); Judith Ellen Brussell, "Government Investigations of Federal Theatre Project Personnel in the Works Progress Administration, 1935–1939" (Ph.D. diss., City University of New York Graduate Center, 1993).

65. Belinda Corbus Bezner, "American Documentary Photography during the Cold War: The Decline of a Tradition" (Ph.D. diss., University of Texas–Austin, 1993), ix.

66. W. E. B. Du Bois, *The Autobiography*, 282.

67. Shirley Graham Du Bois to Roselyn Richardson, 3 January 1954, Roselyn Richardson Papers.

68. Report, 31 May 1957, no. 100-87531, FBI; Ellen Holly, *One Life: The Autobiography of an African-American Actress* (New York: Kodansha, 1996), 51.

69. Shirley Graham Du Bois to Director Schalike, Dietz Verlag Gmbh, Berlin, 4 August 1954.

70. Shirley Graham Du Bois to Dr. Vojtech Strnad, 23 June 1957.

71. Shirley Graham Du Bois, *Booker T. Washington: Educator of Hand, Head and Heart* (New York: Julian Messner, 1955).

72. Shirley Graham, *The Story of Pocahontas* (New York: Grosset and Dunlap, 1953), 71, 79, 129, 138. See also Robert S. Tilton, *Pocahontas: The Evolution of an American Narrative* (New York: Cambridge University Press, 1994).

73. Shirley Graham Du Bois to Dr. Vojtech Strnad, 23 June 1957.

NOTES TO CHAPTER 7

1. Arna Bontemps to Langston Hughes, 28 May 1958, in Arna Bontemps and Langston Hughes, *Letters, 1925–1967* (New York: Dodd, Mead, 1980).

2. Shirley Graham Du Bois to Roselyn Richardson, 19 December 1959, Roselyn Richardson Papers.

3. W. E. B. Du Bois to George Murphy, 26 December 1958, in Herbert Aptheker, ed., *The Correspondence of W. E. B. Du Bois*, vol. 3, 432.

4. Report, 28 October 1958, no. 100-370965, FBI.

5. Shirley Graham Du Bois to Essie Robeson, 23 September 1958, Eslanda Robeson Papers; W. E. B. Du Bois to Cedric Belfrage, 6 July 1958, box 2, Cedric Belfrage Papers. See also Jennifer S. Palmer, "Cedric Belfrage: Anglo-American Nonconformist" (Ph.D. diss., University of Delaware, 1993), ix. Belfrage joined the Communist Party in 1937 and apparently departed in the early 1940s. Sally Belfrage, *Un-American Activities: A Memoir of the Fifties* (New York: Harper-Collins, 1994); Cedric Belfrage and James Aronson, *Something to Guard: The Stormy Life of the National Guardian, 1948–1967* (New York: Columbia University Press, 1978); Jeff Broadwater, *Eisenhower and the Anti-Communist Crusade* (Chapel Hill: University of North Carolina Press, 1992).

6. Shirley Graham Du Bois to P. L. Prattis, 31 August 1958, box 144-22, P. L. Prattis Papers.

7. Shirley Graham Du Bois to Essie Robeson, 23 September 1958, Eslanda Robeson Papers.

8. Shirley Graham Du Bois to Cedric Belfrage, 15 September 1958, box 2, Cedric Belfrage Papers.

9. Shirley Graham Du Bois, "French Africa Dividing on De Gaulle Constitution," 26 September 1958, box 144-22, P. L. Prattis Papers; Margaret Walker, *Richard Wright, Daemonic Genius: A Portrait of the Man, A Critical Look at His Work* (New York: Warner, 1988); Tyler Stovall, *Paris Noir: African Americans in the City of Light* (Boston: Houghton Mifflin, 1996).

10. W. E. B. Du Bois, *The Autobiography of W. E. B. Du Bois: A Soliloquy on Viewing My Life from the Last Decade of Its First Century* (New York: International, 1971), 33.

11. Shirley Graham Du Bois to Cedric Belfrage, 7 February 1959, box 2, Cedric Belfrage Papers.

12. Shirley Graham Du Bois to Cedric Belfrage, 22 December 1958, box 2, Cedric Belfrage Papers.

13. Shirley Graham Du Bois to Cedric Belfrage, 14 January 1959, box 2, Cedric Belfrage Papers.

14. *Pittsburgh Courier,* 20 June 1959; Martin Duberman, *Paul Robeson* (New York: Knopf, 1989), 473. See also Shirley Graham Du Bois, "Heartwarming Memories," in Brigitte Boegelsack, ed., *Paul Robeson* (Berlin: Academy of Arts of the German Democratic Republic, 1978), 56.

15. Shirley Graham Du Bois to Cedric Belfrage, 22 December 1958, box 2, Cedric Belfrage Papers; *Baltimore Afro-American,* 3 February 1959: "Boy, I had some trip. I climbed the great pyramid and walked around the Sphinx, visited monuments of the greatest African rebellion in the Sudan and flew over the Sahara desert to Nigeria. I've slept beside the Nile and dipped my hands in the Red Sea."

16. W. E. B. Du Bois, *The Autobiography,* 404; Shirley Graham Du Bois, *His Day Is Marching On* (Philadelphia: Lippincott, 1971), 301.

17. Shirley Graham Du Bois, *His Day Is Marching On,* 266.

18. Du Bois speech, circa 1958, reel 89, no. 913, W. E. B. Du Bois Papers.

19. Shirley Graham Du Bois, *His Day Is Marching On,* 276.

20. Shirley Graham Du Bois to Edna, 30 May 1966.

21. Shirley Graham Du Bois to Cedric Belfrage, 22 February 1959, box 2, Cedric Belfrage Papers.

22. Shirley Graham Du Bois to Cedric Belfrage, 15 March 1959, box 2, Cedric Belfrage Papers.

23. Ibid.; Shirley Graham Du Bois to Cedric Belfrage, 31 March 1959, box 2, Cedric Belfrage Papers.

24. Shirley Graham Du Bois to Cedric Belfrage, 4 April 1959, box 2, Cedric Belfrage Papers.

25. New China News Agency, 17 February 1959, Louis Massiah Papers.

26. Report, 9 March 1959, no. 100-99729-91, FBI.

27. Sidney Rittenberg to Gerald Horne, 30 April 1997 (in possession of author).

28. Report, 11 November 1959, no. 100-99729-150, FBI.

29. *Baltimore Afro-American,* 29 September 1959. See also Annelise Orieck, *Common Sense and a Little Fire: Women and Working Class Politics in the U.S., 1900–1965* (Chapel Hill: University of North Carolina Press, 1995).

30. "Shirley Graham Du Bois," *Sepia*, January 1975, Hatch-Billops Collection.

31. Shirley Graham Du Bois to Cedric Belfrage, 6 July 1959, box 2, Cedric Belfrage Papers.

32. Shirley Graham Du Bois to Cedric Belfrage, 8 September 1959, box 2, Cedric Belfrage Papers.

33. Report, 19 June 1961, no. 100-87531, FBI. See also Shirley Graham Du Bois, "Negroes in the American Revolution," *Freedomways* 1, no. 2 (summer 1961): 125–35.

34. I wrote numerous book reviews and articles for *Freedomways* during the 1970s and 1980s.

35. Shirley Graham Du Bois to George Murphy, 13 February 1961.

36. Shirley Graham Du Bois to RP, 28 June 1961.

37. Report, 1 July 1960, no. 100-370965, FBI.

38. Shirley Graham Du Bois to Cedric Belfrage, 10 July 1960, box 2, Cedric Belfrage Papers. See also Shirley Graham Du Bois, "'Take Heart, My Brother!'" *New World Review* 29, no. 4 (April 1961): 24–28.

39. Shirley Graham Du Bois to W. E. B. Du Bois, 15 January 1961, reel 75, no. 127, W. E. B. Du Bois Papers.

40. Shirley Graham Du Bois to George Murphy, 13 February 1961.

41. *Militant*, 24 April 1961.

42. "Closing Statement," 2 October 1961, Shirley Graham Du Bois Papers; report, 6 October 1961, no. 100-87531, FBI.

43. Report, 31 May 1957, no. 100-370965, FBI.

44. Shirley Graham Du Bois to Joyce, 23 October 1969.

45. *Accra Evening News*, 11 October 1961.

46. *Accra Evening News*, 16 October 1961.

47. *Worker*, 16 November 1962; report, 27 November 1962, no. 100-87531, FBI.

48. Shirley Graham Du Bois to Essie Robeson, 29 October 1961, Eslanda Robeson Papers.

49. Report, 2 May 1961, no. 100-183386, FBI; *China Daily News*, 19 October 1959.

50. *National Guardian*, 6 August 1962.

51. Ralph McGill, "W. E. B. Du Bois," *Atlantic Monthly*, November 1965, John Henrik Clarke Papers.

52. Leslie Lacy, *The Rise and Fall of a Proper Negro: An Autobiography* (New York: Macmillan, 1970), 174.

53. David Du Bois, interview, 3 June 1992, Louis Massiah Papers.

54. Shirley Graham Du Bois, "Kwame Nkrumah: African Liberator," *Freedomways* 12, no. 3 (third quarter 1972): 197–206, 202; Shirley Graham Du Bois,

"Kwame Nkrumah and Pan-Africa," *Pan-Africanist: A Quarterly Journal of the International Black Movement* 1, no. 1 (fall 1972): 3–7.

55. Abbott Simon, interview, 23 July 1992, Louis Massiah Papers.

56. Belfrage and Aronson, *Something to Guard,* 250.

57. Gerald Horne, *Black and Red: W. E. B. Du Bois and the Afro-American Response to the Cold War, 1944–1963* (Albany: State University of New York Press, 1986), 352.

58. Stovall, *Paris Noir,* 219.

59. Julian Mayfield to John Henrik Clarke, 13 June 1965, John Henrik Clarke Papers.

60. Shirley Graham Du Bois to Laura McIlvain, 4 May 1964, reel 76, no. 525, W. E. B. Du Bois Papers: "Our friend Ambassador Mahoney will be paying a visit home next month. I had lunch with them Saturday (they have eight beautiful children!) and gave him your address."

61. Herbert Aptheker, "On Du Bois's Move to Africa," *Monthly Review* 45, no. 7 (December 1993): 36–40, 37.

62. David Du Bois to Gerald Horne, 28 July 1998 (in possession of author).

63. *U.S. News & World Report,* 1 May 1953.

64. Hakim Adi, "The Communist Movement in West Africa," *Science & Society* 61, no. 1 (spring 1997): 94–99, 98: "Nkrumah had himself been connected with the British CP while in London." Kofi Batsa, *The Spark: From Kwame Nkrumah to Limann* (London: Rex Collings, 1985); George Padmore, *The Gold Coast Revolution: The Struggle of African People from Slavery to Freedom* (London: Dennis Dobson, n.d.).

65. Hakim Adi, *West Africans in Britain: Nationalism, Pan-Africanism and Communism* (London: Lawrence and Wishart, 1998), 139.

66. Quoted in Marika Sherwood, *Kwame Nkrumah: The Years Abroad, 1935–1947* (Legon, Ghana: Freedom, 1996), 3, 176, 82, 1.

67. James Hunter Meriwether, "The African Connection and the Struggle for Freedom: Africa's Role in African American Life, 1935–1963" (Ph.D. diss., UCLA, 1995), 303.

68. Ibid., 410.

69. I would like to thank Hazel Rowley, author of a forthcoming definitive biography of Richard Wright, for bringing this document to my attention. Despite the clear statement on this memorandum that this report was prepared wittingly by Wright, it is possible that the information was obtained without his willing cooperation. See memorandum from Richard Wright, 29 August 1953, 745k.00/9-1553, American Consulate General–Accra, U.S. Department of State. See also Richard Wright, *Black Power: A Record of Reactions in a Land of Pathos* (New York: Harper & Row, 1954).

70. Gerald Thomas, "The Black Revolt: The United States and Africa in the 1960s," in Diane B. Kunz, ed., *The Diplomacy of the Crucial Decade: American For-*

eign Relations during the 1960s (New York: Columbia University Press, 1994), 320–60, 335.

71. David Rooney, *Kwame Nkrumah: The Political Kingdom in the Third World* (London: I. B. Tauris, 1988), 224.

72. Ibid., 230.

73. U.S. Congress, Senate, Committee on the Judiciary, Subcommittee to Investigate the Administration of the Internal Security Act and Other Internal Security Laws, *Ghana Students in U.S. Oppose Aid to Nkrumah,* 88th Cong., 2d sess., 29 August 1963 and 11 January 1964 (Washington, DC: GPO, 1964); *Nkrumah's Subversion in Africa: Documentary Evidence of Nkrumah's Interference in the Affairs of Other African States* (Accra: Ministry of Information, 1966): in this book there are numerous pictures purporting to show Chinese, Soviet, and other specialists training nationals from various African nations in techniques of demolition, constructing explosives, and so on. See also statements by Kwame Nkrumah, circa 1965, box 128-10, Dabu Gzinga Papers: herein are numerous statements by Nkrumah railing against the white minority government of Southern Rhodesia and their global supporters, many of whom resided in the United States.

74. Henry L. Bretton, *The Rise and Fall of Kwame Nkrumah: A Study of Personal Rule in Africa* (New York: Praeger, 1966), 24. See also Dennis Austin, *Ghana Observed: Essays on the Politics of a West African Republic* (New York: Africana, 1976); T. Peter Omari, *Kwame Nkrumah: The Anatomy of an African Dictatorship* (London: C. Hurst, 1970); Trevor Jones, *Africa's First Republic, 1960–1966* (London: Methuen, 1976); Ebenezer Babatope, *The Ghana Revolution: From Nkrumah to Jerry Rawlings* (Enugu, Nigeria: Fourth Dimension, 1982); Rooney, *Kwame Nkrumah: The Political Kingdom in the Third World.*

75. Thomas Noer, "'Non-Benign Neglect': The United States and Black Africa in the Twentieth Century," in Gerald K. Haines and J. Samuel Walker, eds., *American Foreign Relations: A Historiographic Review* (Westport: Greenwood, 1981), 271–292, 271; See also Thiedu Igwebuike Osakwe, "Conflict and Cooperation in Nigeria–United States Bilateral Relations, 1960–1964" (Ph.D. diss., New York University, 1996).

76. Jeff Crisp, *The Story of an African Working Class: Ghanaian Miners' Struggles, 1870–1980* (London: Zed, 1984), 134. See also Ebenezer Obiri Addo, "Kwame Nkrumah: A Case Study of Religion and Politics in Ghana" (Ph.D. diss., Drew University, 1994); W. Scott Thompson, *Ghana's Foreign Policy: 1957–1966* (Princeton: Princeton University Press, 1969).

77. Hakim Adi, *West Africans in Britain,* 163.

78. Ministry of Information and Broadcasting of Ghana, "Statement by the Government on the Recent Conspiracy," 11 December 1961; *Ghana Student* 2, no. 1 (November 1963): 1, box 73, Jay Lovestone Papers. See also Ronald Radosh, *American Labor and United States Foreign Policy* (New York: Random

House, 1969); George Morris, *American Labor, Which Way?* (New York: New Century, 1961); Robert Jackson Alexander, *The Right Opposition: The Lovestoneites and the International Communist Opposition of the 1930s* (Westport: Greenwood, 1981).

79. Shirley Graham Du Bois to Ella Winter, circa fall 1961, Ella Winter Papers.

NOTES TO CHAPTER 8

1. Shirley Graham Du Bois to Cedric Belfrage, 27 February 1963, box 2, Cedric Belfrage Papers.

2. Shirley Graham Du Bois to Cedric Belfrage, 7 June 1963, box 2, Cedric Belfrage Papers.

3. Shirley Graham Du Bois to Laura McIlvain, circa 1963, reel 76, no. 304, W. E. B. Du Bois Papers.

4. Shirley Graham Du Bois to Eslanda Robeson, 7 June 1963, Eslanda Robeson Papers.

5. David Levering Lewis, *W. E. B. Du Bois: Biography of a Race, 1868–1919* (New York: Henry Holt, 1993), 4–10.

6. Shirley Graham Du Bois to Cedric Belfrage, 7 June 1963, box 2, Cedric Belfrage Papers. See also Shirley Graham Du Bois, "5 Days That Made History," *Drum,* September 1963, box 128-19, Dabu Gzinga Papers.

7. Shirley Graham Du Bois to Eslanda Robeson, 7 June 1963, Eslanda Robeson Papers.

8. Shirley Graham Du Bois to P. L. Prattis, 16 October 1963.

9. 1964 calendar, Shirley Graham Du Bois Papers: 2 January reception at the Cuban embassy; 7 January dinner with singer Pete Seeger; 16 January dinner with Soviet ambassador, bids farewell to Zhou En-lai at airport; 4 March dinner with Senegalese ambassador; 5 April meeting with visiting delegation of women from China; 6 April reception at Chinese embassy; 8 April viewing films at USIS office; 28 April viewing Japanese films; 29 April reception at home of Japanese ambassador; 13 May dinner with Polish ambassador; 15 May meeting and cocktails with Achebe and Nigerian high commissioner. See also 1965 calendar, Shirley Graham Du Bois Papers: 18 March meeting at Chinese embassy; 24 March lunch with U.S. Communist leader James Jackson; 1 April cocktails with Japanese ambassador; 2 April meeting at Hungarian embassy; 19 April meeting with Cuban ambassador; 5 May meeting at Chinese embassy; 6 May meeting at Israeli embassy; 9 May reception at Soviet embassy; 10 May reception at Czechoslovak embassy; 12 May meeting at Egyptian embassy; 5 July reception at Zambian embassy; 16 July dinner with Polish ambassador; 19 July dinner with Cuban ambassador; 29 July dinner with Japanese ambassador; 10 August cocktails at East German embassy; 17 August reception at Indonesian

embassy; 23 August reception at Romanian embassy; 29 August dinner with Chinese ambassador; 2 September meeting with Bulgarian ambassador; 4 September meeting with Yugoslav ambassador and reception at North Korean embassy; 24 September meeting with first secretary of Indonesian embassy and meeting at residence of Australian high commissioner; 29 September meeting at embassy of Dahomey; 1 October meeting at home of Chinese ambassador; 8 October cocktails with Japanese ambassador; 13 October dinner with Bulgarian ambassador; 6 November reception at Soviet embassy; 12 November farewell meeting with Indonesian ambassador; 3 December cocktails with Cuban ambassador, meeting with Indian high commissioner; 4 December dinner at Chinese embassy.

10. Ibid, 1964 calendar, Shirley Graham Du Bois Papers.

11. *Ghanaian Times,* 17 August 1965; Sydney W. Head, "British Colonial Broadcasting Policies: The Case of the Gold Coast," *African Studies Review* 22, no. 2 (September 1979): 39–47; Shirley Graham Du Bois to Cedric Belfrage, 29 October 1964, box 2, Cedric Belfrage Papers.

12. Shirley Graham Du Bois to Cedric Belfrage, 29 October 1964, box 2, Cedric Belfrage Papers.

13. *Ghanaian Times,* 5 October 1963.

14. "This Is Ghana Television," circa 1963, Shirley Graham Du Bois Papers; *Mirror* (Ghana), 16 August 1964.

15. "This Is Ghana Television"; "British Colonial Broadcasting Policies," Head, 43. See also *Rhodesian Herald,* 19 July 1965.

16. Shirley Graham Du Bois to John Henrik Clarke, 20 December 1964, Julian Mayfield Papers.

17. Shirley Graham Du Bois to David Du Bois, 15 August 1965.

18. David Du Bois to Shirley Graham Du Bois, 20 August 1965.

19. David Du Bois to Bill, 15 August 1965, Shirley Graham Du Bois Papers.

20. Report, 13 April 1964, no. 100-370965, FBI.

21. Shirley Graham Du Bois to Soviet Peace Committee, 19 April 1964.

22. Shirley Graham Du Bois to Gladys, 16 December 1964.

23. Josephine Baker to Shirley Graham Du Bois, 26 July 1965.

24. Shirley Graham Du Bois to Bernard Jaffe, 21 November 1965.

25. Shirley Graham Du Bois to Mikhail Kotov, 7 November 1965.

26. Shirley Graham Du Bois to Sidney, 30 May 1965.

27. Jun Morikawa, *Japan and Africa: Big Business and Diplomacy* (Trenton: Africa World Press, 1997).

28. Shirley Graham Du Bois to George Murphy, 24 January 1964, George Murphy Papers.

29. Ibid.

30. *People's Daily,* 9 August 1964, no. 100-370965, FBI.

31. Shirley Graham Du Bois to Bernard Jaffe, 16 April 1965.

32. Shirley Graham Du Bois to George Murphy, 24 January 1964, George Murphy Papers.

33. Shirley Graham Du Bois to Bernard Jaffe, 16 April 1965.

34. Shirley Graham Du Bois to RP, 6 May 1964.

35. Shirley Graham Du Bois to Bill, 7 November 1965.

36. Bernard Jaffe to Shirley Graham Du Bois, 21 August 1964. Indira Gandhi of India, Margaret Chase Smith of the United States, and Golda Meir of Israel, to cite a few examples, would be among those who could challenge the assertion of Graham Du Bois's attorney; examples in Africa would be more difficult to find. See also Rhodri Jeffrey-Jones, *Changing Differences: Women and the Shaping of American Foreign Policy, 1917–1994* (New Brunswick: Rutgers University Press, 1995).

37. Ella Winter, "Africa Is Hot," box 16, Ella Winter Papers.

38. Ibid.

39. Donald Ogden Stewart, *By a Stroke of Luck: An Autobiography* (New York: Paddington Press, 1975), 300–301.

40. Donald Ogden Stewart to Shirley Graham Du Bois, 30 September 1964, box 1, Ella Winter Papers.

41. Shirley Graham Du Bois to Ella Winter, 14 October 1964, 23 October 1964, box 1, Ella Winter Papers.

42. Kwame Nkrumah to Ella Winter, 23 December 1964, 19 November 1964, box 2, Ella Winter Papers.

43. Michel Fabre, *From Harlem to Paris: Black American Writers in France, 1840–1980* (Champaign-Urbana: University of Illinois Press, 1991).

44. William Gardner Smith, *Return to Black America* (Englewood Cliffs: Prentice Hall, 1970), 96–97, 99.

45. David Du Bois, interview by author, 16 May 1996.

46. David Du Bois, interview by author, 26 August 1996.

47. Shirley Graham Du Bois to Bill, 7 November 1965.

48. Shirley Graham Du Bois to RP, 6 May 1964.

49. Shirley Graham Du Bois to the Soviet Peace Committee, 19 April 1964.

50. Shirley Graham Du Bois to E. K. Okoh, 10 October 1965.

51. Shirley Graham Du Bois to C. M. V. Forde, 3 September 1964; C. M. V. Forde to Shirley Graham Du Bois, 4 September 1964.

52. Shirley Graham Du Bois to David Du Bois, 17 September 1965, David Du Bois Papers.

53. David Du Bois to Bill, 15 November 1965, David Du Bois Papers.

54. Tyler Stovall, *Paris Noir: African Americans in the City of Light* (Boston: Houghton Mifflin, 1996), 271.

55. Shirley Graham Du Bois to Esther Jackson, 14 May 1963, Esther Jackson Papers.

56. Shirley Graham Du Bois to George Murphy, 26 July 1964, George Murphy Papers.

57. *Ghanaian Times,* 5 February 1964.

58. *Ghanaian Times,* 18 November 1964.

59. *Ghanaian Times,* 30 December 1964.

60. Memorandum, U.S. State Department, no. 5, 18 December 1962, National Security Archive: Alexandria, VA: Chadwyck-Healey, 1991.

61. *New York Journal American,* 5 August 1964; David Gallen, ed., *Malcolm X: The FBI File* (New York: Carroll and Graf, 1992), 331.

62. *Ghanaian Times,* 19 May 1964.

63. *Ghanaian Times,* 18 May 1964.

64. *Ghanaian Times,* 29 May 1964.

65. Karl Evanzz, *The Judas Factor: The Plot to Kill Malcolm X* (New York: Thunder's Mouth, 1992); David Gallen, ed., *Malcolm X as They Knew Him* (New York: Carroll and Graf, 1992); James Cone, *Martin and Malcolm and America: A Dream or a Nightmare* (Maryknoll, NY: Orbis, 1991); Bruce Perry, *Malcolm: The Life of a Man Who Changed Black America* (Barrytown, NY: Station Hill, 1991).

66. Bruce Perry, ed., *Malcolm X: The Last Speeches* (New York: Pathfinder, 1989), 96.

67. Maya Angelou, *All God's Children Need Traveling Shoes* (New York: Random House, 1986), 138, 141, 145.

68. Jean Carey Bond, interview by author, 28 September 1996.

69. Shirley Graham Du Bois to John Henrik Clarke, 13 March 1965.

70. John Henrik Clarke to Shirley Graham Du Bois, 5 June 1964.

71. David Du Bois to Shirley Graham Du Bois, 25 August 1964.

72. Shirley Graham Du Bois to editor, *Spark* (Ghana), 17 March 1965.

73. Shirley Graham Du Bois to Langston Hughes, 7 March 1965, box 52, James Weldon Johnson–Langston Hughes Collection.

74. Benard Jaffe to Shirley Graham Du Bois, 9 April 1965.

75. See generally Gerald Horne, *Fire This Time: The Watts Uprising and the 1960s* (Charlottesville: University Press of Virginia, 1995).

76. Arthur C. Gunn, "Jean Blackwell Hutson," in Darlene Clark Hine, Elsa Barkley Brown, and Rosalyn Terborg-Penn, eds., *Black Women in America: An Historical Encyclopedia,* vol. 1 (Bloomington: Indiana University Press, 1993), 603.

77. Anthony M. Platt, *E. Franklin Frazier Reconsidered* (New Brunswick: Rutgers University Press, 1991).

78. Pauli Murray, *Song in a Weary Throat* (New York: Harper and Row, 1987), 333, 334, 339. See also Donald Harman Akenson, *Conor: A Biography of Conor Cruise O'Brien* (Ithaca: Cornell University Press, 1994). The Irish writer and diplomat was at the university in Ghana during the Nkrumah years.

79. Shirley Graham Du Bois to Regina Asamany, 4 July 1964.

80. Fairfield Butler to Shirley Graham Du Bois, 1 August 1964.

81. Regina Asamany to Shirley Graham Du Bois, 8 June 1964.

82. Regina Asamany to Shirley Graham Du Bois, 17 July 1964.

83. Shirley Graham Du Bois to Gladys, 16 December 1964; Shirley Graham Du Bois to Bill Graham, 9 December 1964.

84. Kevin Gaines to Gerald Horne, 10 February 1997 (in possession of author). I thank Professor Gaines for this and other insights gleaned from his own research for his forthcoming book on African American expatriates in Ghana, 1957 to 1966.

85. Shirley Graham Du Bois to George Murphy, 5 May 1963.

86. Shirley Graham Du Bois to George Murphy, 26 July 1964.

87. George Murphy to Shirley Graham Du Bois, 19 November 1965; Shirley Graham Du Bois to George Murphy, undated, George Murphy Papers.

88. Shirley Graham Du Bois to Cedric Belfrage, 29 October 1964, box 2, Cedric Belfrage Papers.

89. Shirley Graham Du Bois to John Henrik Clarke, 28 December 1964, John Henrik Clarke Papers.

90. Shirley Graham Du Bois to John Henrik Clarke, 20 December 1964, John Henrik Clarke Papers.

91. Shirley Graham Du Bois to Cedric Belfrage, 7 June 1963, box 2, Cedric Belfrage Papers.

92. Shirley Graham Du Bois to Bernard Jaffe, 22 August 1966.

93. John Henrik Clarke to Julian Mayfield, 21 February 1966, John Henrik Clarke Papers.

94. Report, 10 October 1963, no. 100-370965, FBI.

95. *Muhammad Speaks,* 22 November 1963.

96. Shirley Graham Du Bois to George Murphy, circa November 1965, George Murphy Papers. See also Anthony Lake, *The "Tar Baby" Option: American Policy toward Southern Rhodesia* (New York: Columbia University Press, 1973); George W. Shepherd, ed., *Racial Influences on American Foreign Policy* (New York: Basic, 1970); William Pomeroy, *Apartheid, Imperialism and African Freedom* (New York: International, 1986); Shirley Graham Du Bois, "Nation Building in Ghana," *Freedomways* 2, no. 4 (fall 1962): 371–76; Shirley Graham Du Bois, "After Addis Ababa," *Freedomways* 3, no. 4 (fall 1963): 471–85.

97. Shirley Graham Du Bois to Bernard Jaffe, 21 November 1965.

98. Shirley Graham Du Bois to John Henrik Clarke, 14 June 1964, John Henrik Clarke Papers.

NOTES TO CHAPTER 9

1. Report from William Mahoney to U.S. State Department, 10 January 1964, National Security File, Country File, box 89, Lyndon Baines Johnson Papers.

2. Ibid., Report, 29 March 1964.

3. Reports from U.S. Embassy–Accra, 1 February 1964, 3 February 1964, 4 February 1964, National Security File, Country File, box 89, Lyndon Baines Johnson Papers.

4. Ibid., Report from Embassy, 23 July 1965, LBJ Papers.

5. Ibid., Report from Embassy, 5 February 1964, LBJ Papers.

6. Ibid., Report from Embassy, 13 February 1964, LBJ Papers.

7. Ibid., Report from Embassy, 18 April 1964, LBJ Papers.

8. Ibid., Lyndon Baines Johnson to Adger Player, 5 February 1964.

9. James Engle, interview, 1 August 1988, Foreign Affairs Oral History Program-Georgetown University. See, e.g., Alfred E. Eckes, Jr., *Opening America's Market: U.S. Foreign Trade Policy since 1776* (Chapel Hill: University of North Carolina Press, 1995); Cynthia A. Hody, *The Politics of Trade: American Political Development and Foreign Economic Policy* (Hanover: University Press of New England, 1996); Susan Ariel Aaronson, *Trade and the American Dream: A Social History of Postwar Trade Policy* (Lexington: University Press of Kentucky, 1996).

10. Robert Smith, interview, 28 February 1989, Oral History-Georgetown University. See also U.S. Congress, Senate, Committee on the Judiciary, *Communist Global Subversion and American Security: The Attempted Communist Subversion of Africa through Nkrumah's Ghana*, 92d Cong., 1st sess. (Washington, DC: GPO, 1972). But see the memoir by one of Nkrumah's London advisors, Geoffrey Bing, *Reap the Whirlwind: An Account of Kwame Nkrumah's Ghana from 1950 to 1966* (London: MacGibbon and Kee, 1968), 392: "In so far as Dr. Nkrumah can be accused of favoring any Western country it was the United States and in so far as any of his development projects were of a neo-colonialist nature, the Volta development projects were of a neo-colonialist nature, the Volta Hydro-Electric Scheme best fitted this pattern. It involved . . . 'an extraordinary agreement' with two United States firms, the Kaiser Aluminum and Chemical Corporation and the Reynolds Metal Company."

11. Willard De Pree, interview, 16 February 1994, Oral History-Georgetown University. See also Adama Juldeh Conteh, "Economics and the Politics of Cocoa in the Gold Coast/Ghana: British Politics, United States Response and Gold Coasters' Reactions, 1930–1966" (Ph.D. diss., Howard University, 1993).

12. G. Mennen Williams to U.S. Embassy–Accra, 20 November 1965, reel 5, State Department, G. Mennen Williams Papers.

13. Robert Smith, interview, 28 February 1989, Oral History-Georgetown University.

14. Kwame Nkrumah, *Neo-Colonialism: The Last Stage of Imperialism* (New York: International, 1966), 243.

15. Henry Dunlap, interview, 25 January 1988, Oral History-Georgetown University.

16. Robert Smith, interview, 28 February 1989, foreign Affairs Oral History Program-Georgetown University.

17. *New York Times,* 3 April 1966.

18. *New York Times,* 9 May 1978.

19. *New York Herald Tribune,* 25 February 1966.

20. John Stockwell, *In Search of Enemies: A CIA Story* (New York: Norton, 1978), 201.

21. "How America Toppled Nkrumah," uncertain provenance, undated, box 128-13, folder 302, Dabu Gzinga Papers. See also Okonkwo Nwani, "'. . . and the Fall of Nkrumah': Economics and Politics in Modern Africa," *Negro Digest* 18, no. 7 (May 1969): 35–88; David Apter, "Nkrumah, Charisma and the Coup," *Daedalus* 97, no. 3 (1968): 757–92.

22. Roger Faligot and Remi Kauffer, *The Chinese Secret Service* (London: Headline, 1989), 297, 309. After leaving Ghana, Graham Du Bois's friend Huang Hua became China's ambassador in Cairo. "In June 1965 at the Second Congress of the Afro-Asian conference held in Algiers, Zhou En-lai uttered his famous cry: 'Africa is ripe for revolution!'" This was seen as the beginning of a new Chinese offensive in Africa, launched from Ghana—which caused the United States to become more hostile to Accra. According to Faligot and Kauffer, one U.S. official suggested attacking the Chinese embassy in Ghana during the coup:

> "It's extremely simple, we clean up the 'Chicom' embassy," said Howard Bane with Virginia common sense. "We attack the embassy with rocket launchers, we spray it with machine-gun fire, and sprinkle it with grenades! Once the 'Chicoms' have been liquidated, we take all their archives and blow the whole lot up with dynamite. In the coming chaos, no one will ever [know] that it was us!" Howard Bane, as CIA station chief in Accra, capital of Ghana, had several reasons for wanting to do battle with the "Chicoms." . . . Ten years earlier, he had fought against them in Thailand. Then, having been posted to New Delhi as "political officer," another transparent cover, he had taken great pleasure in helping the Indians to expel Gao Ling for espionage. But the decision of Admiral Raborn, head of the CIA, supported by the director of operations Desmond Fitzgerald, came down like the blade of a guillotine: "Bombing the Chinese is out of the question. Just overthrow Nkrumah!" . . . The CIA agent by cleverly manipulating the army, overthrew [Nkrumah]. . . . Bane pursued a brilliant career in the CIA: in the 1970s he was very appropriately appointed head of the anti-terrorist division.

23. *Daily Graphic* (Ghana), 15 January 1966.

24. Marika Sherwood, *Kwame Nkrumah: The Years Abroad, 1935–1947* (Legon, Ghana: Freedom, 1996), 3.

25. Franklin Williams to Bill Moyers, 25 February 1966; Franklin Williams telegram, 25 February 1966, "Confidential Files," box 8, Lyndon Baines Johnson Papers. Williams had trepidations about why he was sent to Ghana, and wanted Moyers to send him certain items so "that people will think I have influence—which you and I know I don't have." Moyers reassured him that the president "has great confidence in you—and that is the precise reason he personally selected you to represent him in Ghana." Franklin Williams to Bill Moyers, 2 December 1965; Bill Moyers to Franklin Williams, 2 February 1965, "Confidential Files," box 35, Lyndon Baines Johnson Papers. Williams, because he was an Afro-American, may have been placed in Ghana by the White House precisely because it was felt his presence would defuse or distract attention from possible U.S. involvement. Alternatively, his racial heritage may have confirmed a growing perception in Ghana about the nefarious role played by some Afro-Americans.

26. See, e.g., Michael Krenn, ed., *Race and U.S. Foreign Policy from the Colonial Period to the Present: A Collection of Essays* (New York: Garland, 1998).

27. Willard De Pree, interview, 16 February 1994, Oral History-Georgetown University.

28. A. A. Afrifa, *The Ghana Coup: 24th February 1966* (London: Frank Cass, 1966); Peter Barker, *Operation Cold Chop: The Coup That Toppled Nkrumah* (Accra: Ghana Publishing House, 1969). See also Suzanne Cronje, Margaret Ling, and Gillian Croje, *The Lonrho Connections: A Multinational and Its Politics in Africa* (Encino: Bellwether, 1976).

29. Tawia Adamafio, *By Nkrumah's Side: The Labour and the Wounds* (London: Rex Collings, 1982), 82. See also C. L. R. James, *Nkrumah and the Ghana Revolution* (Westport: Lawrence and Hill, 1977).

30. Coups in Africa, 1965–1966, box 72, Lewis Gann–Peter Duignan Papers.

31. Shirley Graham Du Bois to David Du Bois, 2 March 1965.

32. Shirley Graham Du Bois to Michael Myerson, 1 July 1965.

33. Shirley Graham Du Bois to "Visa Authorities, Department of State," 20 December 1965. She shaved ten years from her age in this application.

34. Shirley Graham Du Bois to David Du Bois, 17 September 1965.

35. Kwame Nkrumah to Shirley Graham Du Bois, 12 November 1967.

36. Calendar, 1966, Shirley Graham Du Bois Papers.

37. Shirley Graham Du Bois article on coup, *Essence*, January 1971, Shirley Graham Du Bois Papers; Shirley Graham Du Bois, "What Happened in Ghana? The Inside Story," *Freedomways* 6, no. 2 (spring 1966): 201–23, 220.

38. William Sutherland, interview by author, 1 March 1995.

39. Shirley Graham Du Bois to Charles Howard, 25 June 1966.

40. David Du Bois to Julian Mayfield, 17 March 1966, box 4, Julian Mayfield Papers.

41. Shirley Graham Du Bois to Esther Jackson, 19 June 1966.

42. Shirley Graham Du Bois to Jim Aldridge, 25 June 1966.

43. Julian Mayfield to John Henrik Clarke, 29 March 1966, John Henrik Clarke Papers.

44. Julian Mayfield to John Henrik Clarke, circa 1966, John Henrik Clarke Papers.

45. David Du Bois to Julian Mayfield, 17 March 1966, Shirley Graham Du Bois Papers.

46. Kwame Nkrumah, *Dark Days in Ghana* (New York: International, 1968), ll; Kwame Nkrumah, *Voice from Conakry* (London: Panaf, 1980), 24, 37, 47, 65.

47. Nkrumah, *Dark Days in Ghana*, 28, 43, 46, 73; Nkrumah, *Voice from Conakry*, 2, 7, 23: Major General Barwah "was awakened in the small hours of the morning by some of the rebel army officers and . . . they shot him dead at close range because he flatly and categorically refused to join the plot and hand the army to them." See also Nkrumah, *Dark Days in Ghana*, passim.

48. Sylvia Boone to Julian Mayfield, 29 May 1966, box 4, Julian Mayfield Papers.

49. Shirley Graham to R. Palme Dutt, 19 September 1966, box 154-3, Kwame Nkrumah Papers.

50. Richard Gibson, *African Liberation Movements: Contemporary Struggles against White Minority Rule* (New York: Oxford University Press, 1972).

51. Richard Gibson to Julian Mayfield, 8 March 1967, box 5, Julian Mayfield Papers.

52. Richard Gibson to John Henrik Clarke, 16 April 1966, John Henrik Clarke Papers.

53. David Du Bois to Julian Mayfield, 18 September 1969, box 4, Julian Mayfield Papers.

54. *Daily Gazette* (Ghana), 3 March 1966. Nkrumah had a keen interest in a "'revolutionary solution of the sex problem'" which could involve "extramarital relationships" under "'our circumstances.'" See June Milne, *Kwame Nkrumah: A Biography* (London: Panaf, 1999), 243–44.

55. *Evening News* (Ghana), 6 June 1966; Paul to Bernard Jaffe, 19 June 1966, Shirley Graham Du Bois Papers.

56. Berihun Assfaw, letter to the editor, *New African,* February 1997, 4.

57. Ruth First, *The Barrel of a Gun: Political Power in Africa and the Coup d'Etat* (London: Penguin, 1970), 186–87. See also Bob Fitch and Mary Oppenheimer, *Ghana: End of an Illusion* (New York: Monthly Review Press, 1966), 73: the ruling party "did not work through the trade unions or involve the masses in its battles in any way."

58. Julian Mayfield to John Henrik Clarke, 30 April 1966, John Henrik Clarke Papers. Mayfield wrote to Nkrumah directly, "certain officials have testified that their accounts in Europe are not, in fact, theirs but yours. Your advisor on financial affairs, Mr. Ayeh-Kumi, has testified that you were the proprietor of large enterprises in Ghana. Mr. Krobe Edusei has testified that he personally transferred gold bars for you to be delivered to your wife in Cairo." However, in the manuscript that he wrote on Ghana he cited Nkrumah as saying that his "worldly possessions" are eight thousand pounds in book royalties: see undated questionnaire, box 13, Julian Mayfield Papers. See also Michael E. Williams, "Nkrumahism as an Ideological Embodiment of Leftist Thought within the African World," *Journal of Black Studies* 15, no.1 (September 1984): 117–34; Shirley Graham Du Bois, "Kwame Nkrumah: African Liberator," *Freedomways* 12, no. 3, (third quarter 1972): 197–206; Shirley Graham Du Bois, "Nkrumah's Record Speaks for Itself," *Africa and the World* 4, no. 42 (April 1968): 18–20.

59. Willard De Pree, interview, 16 February 1994, Foreign Affairs Oral History Program-Georgetown University.

60. Erica Powell, *Private Secretary (Female)/Gold Coast* (New York: St. Martin's, 1984).

61. Shirley Graham Du Bois to Kwame Nkrumah, 8 July 1966, box 154-3, Kwame Nkrumah Papers.

62. Kwame Nkrumah to Shirley Graham Du Bois, 26 February 1967, box 154-3, Kwame Nkrumah Papers.

63. Shirley Graham Du Bois to Kwame Nkrumah, 1 June 1967, box 154-3, Kwame Nkrumah Papers.

64. Shirley Graham Du Bois to Julian Mayfield, box 4, Julian Mayfield Papers.

65. Vivian Hallinan to Shirley Graham Du Bois, 6 February 1967.

66. Anna Louise Strong to Shirley Graham Du Bois, 12 December 1968. See also Shirley Graham Du Bois, "Nkrumah's Record Speaks for Itself"; Shirley Graham Du Bois, "Kwame Nkrumah: African Liberator." See also Tracy B. Strong and Helen Keyssar, *Right in Her Soul: The Life of Anna Louise Strong* (New York: Random House, 1983); Anna Louise Strong, *Letters from China* (Peking: New World Press, 1963–65).

67. Shirley Graham Du Bois to Bill, 18 April 1967.

68. Shirley Graham Du Bois to Bernard Jaffe, 15 November 1966.

69. Shirley Graham Du Bois to John Henrik Clarke, 27 March 1966.

70. Shirley Graham Du Bois to Bernard Jaffe, 28 September 1966.

71. Bernard Jaffe to Shirley Graham Du Bois, 24 October 1966.

72. Shirley Graham Du Bois to William Mahoney, 15 October 1966.

73. Ollie Harrington, *Why I Left America and Other Essays* (Jackson: University Press of Mississippi, 1993).

74. Shirley Graham Du Bois to William Gardner Smith, 31 March 1967.

75. Shirley Graham to Gerhart Eisler, 25 January 1967.

76. David Du Bois to Bernard Jaffe, 18 July 1967, David Du Bois Papers.

77. Shirley Graham Du Bois to Kwame Nkrumah, 25 January 1968, box 154-3, Kwame Nkrumah Papers.

78. Shirley Graham Du Bois to Elaine, 8 November 1967.

79. Shirley Graham Du Bois to Herrn. Kerschnek, 14 September 1967.

80. Shirley Graham Du Bois to Bernard Jaffe, 15 October 1966.

81. Shirley Graham Du Bois to Bill, 18 April 1967.

82. Shirley Graham Du Bois to Bernard Jaffe, 28 September 1966.

83. Bernard Jaffe to Shirley Graham Du Bois, 13 November 1964. In 1964 she received $513.84 in royalties for her Carver book, $332.41 for her Washington book, $193.46 for her Wheatley book: Marion Irving to Shirley Graham Du Bois, 4 November 1964.

84. Shirley Graham Du Bois to Bernard Jaffe, 1 January 1974.

85. Shirley Graham to "Dear Friend," 2 June 1966.

86. Shirley Graham Du Bois to Edna, 30 May 1966.

87. Shirley Graham Du Bois to Kwame Nkrumah, 22 September 1966.

88. David Du Bois to Rosey and Isa, 6 September 1969, Shirley Graham Du Bois Papers.

89. Shirley Graham Du Bois to Thelma and Joe, 16 October 1966.

90. Shirley Graham Du Bois to Rosey and Isa, 3 June 1966.

91. Shirley Graham Du Bois to Jimmie and Dina, 3 September 1969.

92. Shirley Graham Du Bois to Bernard Jaffe, 5 December 1968.

93. Shirley Graham Du Bois to Kwame Nkrumah, 28 February 1969, box 154-3, Kwame Nkrumah Papers.

94. Shirley Graham Du Bois to Kwame Nkrumah, 20 October 1966, box 154-3, Kwame Nkrumah Papers.

95. Shirley Graham Du Bois to Ruth, 31 May 1966.

96. Shirley Graham Du Bois, "Return after Ten Years," *Freedomways* 11, no. 2 (second quarter 1971): 158–69; Shirley Graham Du Bois, "Cairo—Six Months after the Blitzkrieg," *Africa and the World* 4, no. 39 (January 1968): 20–24.

97. Shirley Graham Du Bois to Ruth, 31 May 1966.

98. See the useful description of Cairo in Mary Anne Weaver, "Revolution by Stealth," *New Yorker,* 8 June 1998, 38–48.

99. Shirley Graham Du Bois to Esther Jackson, 6 July 1966.

100. Shirley Graham Du Bois, "Cairo—Six Months after the Blitzkrieg"; Shirley Graham Du Bois article, January 1971, *Essence,* Shirley Graham Du Bois Papers; Richard B. Parker, ed., *The Six-Day War: A Retrospective* (Gainesville: University Press of Florida, 1996).

101. Shirley Graham Du Bois to Bernard Jaffe, 8 February 1970.

102. Shirley Graham Du Bois, "The Burning of the Asqa Mosque," *Africa and the World* 6, no. 52 (October 1969): 18–20.

103. Shirley Graham Du Bois, "There Can Be No Peace with Zionism," *Africa and the World* 6, no. 62 (August 1970): 13–15.

104. Shirley Graham Du Bois, *Gamal Abdel Nasser: Son of the Nile* (New York: Third Press, 1972).

105. Shirley Graham Du Bois to David Graham, 15 January 1973.

106. David Du Bois to Julian Mayfield, 7 August 1970, box 4, Julian Mayfield Papers.

107. Shirley Graham Du Bois to Kwame Nkrumah, 1 June 1967.

108. Shirley Graham Du Bois to Herbert and Fay Aptheker, 2 January 1973.

109. Shirley Graham Du Bois to Martha and Alfred, 8 December 1971.

110. Shirley Graham Du Bois to William Allen, 9 February 1972.

111. Shirley Graham Du Bois to Martha and Alfred, 19 January 1971.

112. Shirley Graham Du Bois to Leone Stein, 28 November 1973.

NOTES TO CHAPTER 10

1. Esther Jackson, interview, 2 June 1992, Louis Massiah Papers.

2. Shirley Graham Du Bois to Dr. Lewis Wade Jones, 14 July 1961, Shirley Graham Du Bois Papers, Amistad Research Center.

3. Esther Jackson to Shirley Graham Du Bois, 5 September 1962. Shirley Graham Du Bois to Esther Jackson, 11 May 1963, Esther Jackson Papers: "enclosed is my check for $37.50 representing profit on 50 copies of FREE-DOMWAYS after 25% was paid to the booksellers." Shirley Graham Du Bois to Esther Jackson, 14 June 1963, Esther Jackson Papers: she has secured three new subscriptions from John Elliott, Ghana's ambassador to Moscow, Dr. Robert Lee, and Julian Mayfield.

4. John Henrik Clarke to Shirley Graham Du Bois, 13 August 1962, Shirley Graham Du Bois Papers.

5. Shirley Graham Du Bois to John Henrik Clarke, 24 January 1965, John Henrik Clarke Papers.

6. Shirley Graham Du Bois to Esther Jackson, 31 May 1964. See also Shirley Graham Du Bois, "Centenary of Dr. W. E. B. Du Bois," *Africa and the World* 4, no. 44 (June–July 1968): 27–30.

7. Esther Jackson to Shirley Graham Du Bois, 20 June 1964:

I find your comments on Malcolm X interesting. He is certainly a young man in search of answers at a very trying period in his life. He has much thinking, studying, reading, listening to do in his search for the answers and I think we need to give him time to do without attributing to him a position of leadership which he has yet to earn. I certainly wish him well and believe he has tremendous potential.

Contrary to Aptheker, another witness at the memorial meeting said that

Hansberry read Graham Du Bois's "letter and message magnificently." Charles Howard to Shirley Graham Du Bois, 9 March 1964.

8. Herbert Aptheker to Shirley Graham Du Bois, 22 May 1964.

9. James Aronson to John Henrik Clarke, 9 April 1965, Shirley Graham Du Bois Papers.

10. Esther Jackson to Shirley Graham Du Bois, 28 April 1965.

11. John Henrik Clarke to Shirley Graham Du Bois, 28 January 1965.

12. Shirley Graham Du Bois to John Henrik Clarke, 24 January 1965.

13. John Henrik Clarke to Jean Carey Bond, 7 September 1965, John Henrik Clarke Papers. Jack O'Dell was also a key advisor subsequently to Jesse Jackson. See David J. Garrow, *Bearing the Cross: Martin Luther King, Jr. and the Southern Christian Leadership Conference* (New York: William Morrow, 1986).

14. Calvin Sinette to John and Eugenia, 25 July 1966, John Henrik Clarke Papers.

15. John Henrik Clarke to Julian Mayfield, 21 February 1966, John Henrik Clarke Papers.

16. Hodee Edwards to John Henrik Clarke, 4 April 1966, John Henrik Clarke Papers. This criticism of Graham Du Bois was overly harsh; relative, at least, to those of her African American counterparts, her viewpoints were quite advanced and sophisticated. See, e.g., Ann Gordon et al., *African-American Women and the Vote, 1837–1965* (Amherst: University of Massachusetts Press, 1997); Joyce Ann Joyce, *Ijala: Sonia Sanchez and the African Poetic Tradition* (Chicago: Third World Press, 1997).

17. Shirley Graham Du Bois to Charles Howard, 25 June 1966.

18. Shirley Graham Du Bois to John Henrik Clarke, 19 April 1966, John Henrik Clarke Papers.

19. Shirley Graham Du Bois to Bernard Jaffe, 7 May 1966.

20. Shirley Graham Du Bois to Ruth, 31 May 1966.

21. Shirley Graham Du Bois to John Henrik Clarke, 24 January 1965, John Henrik Clarke Papers.

22. Shirley Graham Du Bois to David Du Bois, 10 August 1967.

23. Shirley Graham Du Bois to David Du Bois, 29 July 1967, David Du Bois Papers.

24. Shirley Graham Du Bois to Kwame Nkrumah, 23 July 1966, box 154-3, Kwame Nkrumah Papers.

25. Shirley Graham Du Bois to Kwame Nkrumah, 4 December 1967.

26. Shirley Graham Du Bois to Bernard Jaffe, 15 November 1966, Bernard Jaffe to Shirley Graham Du Bois, 8 November 1966.

27. Shirley Graham Du Bois to Mary, 1 December 1966.

28. Shirley Graham Du Bois to John Henrik Clarke, 23 February 1967.

29. Richard Gibson to Robert Williams, 18 March 1967, box 1, Robert F. Williams Papers.

30. Shirley Graham Du Bois to Kodwo Addison, 22 May 1965.

31. Shirley Graham Du Bois to Herbert Aptheker, 24 January 1965.

32. James Allen to Shirley Graham Du Bois, 7 October 1966, 24 April 1968.

33. Bernard Jaffe to Shirley Graham Du Bois, 4 October 1968. "He is obviously most anxious to be identified with the publication of the Du Bois correspondence and concerned that you might be induced to let it take place without him. . . . [he] was terribly disappointed to learn that W. E. B.'s will made no mention of his designation as the person to handle the posthumous publication of any of his work." See also Shirley Graham Du Bois to Bernard Jaffe, 7 November 1969, 16 May 1971, 22 May 1971.

34. Jessica Smith to Shirley Graham Du Bois, 28 March 1967; Shirley Graham Du Bois, "Guinea–Sierra Leone Pact Is a Step to African Unity," *Africa and the World* 3, no. 30 (April 1967): 10–11; Shirley Graham Du Bois, "The Little African Summit," *Africa and the World* 3, no. 31 (May 1967): 9–11.

35. Shirley Graham Du Bois to Kwame Nkrumah, 23 April 1967.

36. Shirley Graham Du Bois to *New World Review,* 17 May 1967. See, e.g., Joseph G. Morgan, *The Vietnam Lobby: The American Friends of Vietnam, 1955–1975* (Chapel Hill: University of North Carolina Press, 1997).

37. Shirley Graham Du Bois, review of Anna Louise Strong, *The Stalin Era* (Altadena: Today's Press, 1956), *New World Review* 25, no. 2 (February 1957): 36–38.

38. Gerald Horne, *Black Liberation/Red Scare: Ben Davis and the Communist Party* (Newark: University of Delaware Press, 1994); Gerald Horne, "Gangsters, 'Whiteness,' Reactionary Politics and the U.S.-Rhodesian Connection," *Southern African Political and Economic Monthly* 9, no. 2 (November 1995): 31–34.

39. Shirley Graham Du Bois to Kwame Nkrumah, 18 October 1969.

40. Jessica Smith to Shirley Graham Du Bois, 11 November 1968:

> I am glad to know you are not prepared to join condemnation of the Soviet Union about Czechoslovakia. I myself am in a difficult situation about this. I do not believe, myself, from all the facts that I know—although I realize there are many I do not know—that it has been proved that the intervention was necessary, and it seems to me there were some serious miscalculations involved. I think there was an over-reaction to words as far as the internal situation was concerned, but of the external danger I have no doubt, although I do not believe any immediate attack was imminent.

41. Shirley Graham Du Bois to Mikhail Kotov, Soviet Peace Committee, 3 July 1970: "I am not sure that even here whether all the people really understand what the defense brought by the Russians has meant to us—in spite of President Nasser's repeated declarations. And so, I think that the more of us who speak out—the better."

42. Shirley Graham Du Bois to Lorenz Graham, 7 December 1971.

43. Shirley Graham Du Bois to Bernard Jaffe, 7 November 1969.

44. Eileen Bernal, Women Against War–London, to Shirley Graham Du Bois, 15 November 1963; *New Times,* 18 September 1963.

45. Shirley Graham Du Bois to Cestmir Cuschy, editor in chief, *Solidarity,* Prague, 5 May 1963. Here she thanked this publication for removing the "cartoon serial 'Maiko.' . . . Behind the artist technique is conception of how an African looks . . . a sub-human being. . . . this monstrous conception. . . . the day of distortions is finished."

46. See, e.g., Peter Gran, *Beyond Eurocentrism: A New View of Modern World History* (Syracuse: Syracuse University Press, 1996).

47. Shirley Graham Du Bois to Kwame Nkrumah, 12 October 1962.

48. *People's World,* 4 April 1963, no. 100-99729, FBI.

49. Gordon Chang, *Friends and Enemies: The United States, China and the Soviet Union, 1948–1972* (Stanford: Stanford University Press, 1990); David Allan Mayers, *Cracking the Monolith: U.S. Policy Against the Sino-Soviet Alliance, 1949–1955* (Baton Rouge: Louisiana State University Press, 1986). For an examination of what this U.S. policy has wrought, see, e.g., Ezra Vogel, *Living with China: U.S.-China Relations in the Twenty-first Century* (New York: Norton, 1997).

50. Shirley Graham Du Bois to Kwame Nkrumah, 20 October 1966.

51. Jessica Smith to Shirley Graham Du Bois, 12 July 1968.

52. See, e.g., William Burr, ed., *The Kissinger Transcripts: The Top-Secret Talks with Beijing and Moscow* (New York: New Press, 1999).

53. Anna Louise Strong to Shirley Graham Du Bois, 12 December 1968.

54. Shirley Graham Du Bois to Lorenz and Ruth Graham, 22 July 1974.

55. *Daily World,* 8 August 1968, box 143, Senate Internal Security Subcommittee Papers.

56. Shirley Graham Du Bois to Jessica Smith, 17 March 1973. John Abt with Michael Myerson, *Advocate and Activist: Memoirs of an American Communist Lawyer* (Urbana: University of Illinois Press, 1993).

57. Shirley Graham Du Bois speech, 6 July 1967, Shirley Graham Du Bois Papers. See also Oleg Kalugin with Fen Montaigne, *The First Directorate: My Thirty-two Years in Intelligence and Espionage against the West* (New York: St. Martin's, 1994).

58. David Du Bois, interview by author, 22 June 1996.

59. Shirley Graham to Lin Yutang, 12 September 1943. See also Lucy E. Salyer, *Laws Harsh as Tigers: Chinese Immigrants and the Shaping of Modern Immigration Law* (Chapel Hill: University of North Carolina Press, 1995); Judy Yung, *Unbound Feet: A Social History of Chinese Women in San Francisco* (Berkeley: University of California Press, 1995).

60. Chin Chao to Shirley Graham Du Bois, 15 January 1963.

61. *Muhammad Speaks,* 22 November 1963; Shirley Graham Du Bois, "In

Gratitude of Chairman Mao Tse-Tung," 15 August 1963, Shirley Graham Du Bois Papers. See also Vogel, *Living with China.*

62. Alaba Ogunsanwo, *China's Policy in Africa, 1958–1971* (New York: Cambridge University Press, 1974); Omar Ali Amer, "China and the Afro-Asian Peoples' Solidarity Organization, 1958–1967" (Ph.D. diss., University of Geneva, 1972); Bruce D. Larkin, *China and Africa, 1949–1970: The Foreign Policy of the People's Republic of China* (Berkeley: University of California Press, 1971); *New York Times,* 12 March 1966: hundreds of Chinese technicians leave Ghana after the deposing of Nkrumah.

63. Mrs. Huang Hua to Shirley Graham Du Bois, 31 August 1962, reel 75, no. 900, W. E. B. Du Bois Papers.

64. Bill Sutherland, interview by author, 3 March 1995.

65. T. Christopher Jespersen, *American Images of China, 1931–1949* (Stanford: Stanford University Press, 1996); S. Bernard Thomas, *Season of High Adventure: Edgar Snow in China* (Berkeley: University of California Press, 1996); Robert Ross, *Negotiating Cooperation: The United States and China, 1969–1989* (Stanford: Stanford University Press, 1995); Harriet Dashiell Schwar and Glenn W. La Fantasie, eds., *Foreign Relations of the United States, 1958–1960,* vol. 19, *China* (Washington, DC: GPO, 1996).

66. David Du Bois to Julian Mayfield, 23 February 1967, box 4, Julian Mayfield Papers: his mother "of course is in constant touch with" Huang Hua. "He had been attacked in a wall poster in Peking some months ago." See also Shirley Graham Du Bois, "Minority Peoples in China," *Freedomways* 1, no. 1 (spring 1961): 95–101; Tracy B. Strong and Helene Keyssar, *Right in Her Soul: The Life of Anna Louise Strong* (New York: Random House, 1983).

67. Xinhua Overseas News Agency, 6 March 1979.

68. Sidney Rittenberg to Gerald Horne, 30 April 1997 (in possession of author).

69. Shirley Graham Du Bois to Kwame Nkrumah, 26 November 1967, box 154-3, Kwame Nkrumah Papers.

70. Shirley Graham Du Bois to Elaine, 8 November 1967.

71. Shirley Graham Du Bois to Obi Egbuna, 22 April 1968.

72. Ma Bo, *Blood Red Sunset: A Memoir of the Chinese Cultural Revolution* (New York: Viking, 1995); Ning Kun Wu, *A Single Tear: A Family's Persecution, Love and Endurance in Communist China* (Boston: Little, Brown, 1993); Arif Dirlik et al., eds., *Critical Perspectives on Mao Zedong's Thought* (Atlantic Highlands: Humanities Press, 1997); M. N. Roy, "China: From Confucius to Sun Yat-Sen and Further," undated 472-page manuscript, box 542, Jay Lovestone Papers.

73. Shirley Graham Du Bois to George Murphy, 14 September 1967, George Murphy Papers.

74. Richard Gibson to Julian Mayfield, 8 March 1967, box 5, Julian Mayfield Papers.

75. Shirley Graham Du Bois, "The Great Cultural Revolution," circa 1967, box 154-3, Kwame Nkrumah Papers.

76. Shirley Graham Du Bois to David Du Bois, 15 June 1967, David Du Bois Papers.

77. Shirley Graham Du Bois to Kwame Nkrumah, 6 February 1968, box 154-3, Kwame Nkrumah Papers.

78. Shirley Graham Du Bois to Kwame Nkrumah, 29 February 1968, box 154-3, Kwame Nkrumah Papers.

79. Shirley Graham Du Bois to Kwame Nkrumah, 24 March 1968, box 154-3, Kwame Nkrumah Papers.

80. Shirley Graham Du Bois to David Du Bois, 11 June 1968, David Du Bois Papers.

81. Shirley Graham Du Bois to David Du Bois, 23 April 1968, David Du Bois Papers.

82. Timothy B. Tyson, "Radio Free Dixie: Robert F. Williams and the Roots of Black Power" (Ph.D. diss., Duke University, 1994).

83. Shirley Graham Du Bois, *His Day Is Marching On* (Philadelphia: Lippincott, 1971), 327.

84. Shirley Graham Du Bois to Robert F. Williams, 22 March 1967, box 1, Robert F. Williams Papers.

85. See Gordon Winter, *Inside BOSS: South Africa's Secret Police* (New York: Penguin, 1981), 431–32: Winter, a former intelligence agent for apartheid South Africa, writes that Gibson was a "CIA agent." Gibson had worked for the BBC, CBS in New York, and Agence France Presse in Paris. In 1957 Gibson forged letters in the name of Ollie Harrington, Richard Wright's closest friend in Paris, that purported to condemn French policy in Algeria a sensitive subject that could have forced Paris to deport Harrington back to the United States he had fled as the Red Scare was gaining strength. An outraged Harrington subsequently thrashed Gibson so thoroughly that he had to be carted to the nearest hospital. See, e.g., Michel Fabre, *The Unfinished Quest of Richard Wright* (New York: William Morrow, 1973), 461–62.

86. Akbar Muhammad to Robert F. Williams, 29 April 1967, box 1, Robert F. Williams Papers.

87. Richard Gibson to Robert F. Williams, 19 May 1967, box 1, Robert F. Williams Papers.

88. *Christian Science Monitor*, 20 April 1968; *New York Post*, 9 August 1967.

89. *Baltimore Sun*, 7 April 1968; *New York Times*, 18 April 1968.

90. *Houston Chronicle*, 23 August 1967.

91. *Newsweek*, 22 April 1968.

92. Frank Trager to I-Cheng Loh, 14 June 1968, box 82, Marvin Liebman Papers.

93. Sidney Rittenberg, interview by author, 26 April 1997. See also Sidney Rittenberg, *The Man Who Stayed Behind* (New York: Simon and Schuster, 1993).

94. Sidney Rittenberg to Gerald Horne, 30 April 1997 (in possession of author).

95. Ibid.

96. Reba to Shirley Graham Du Bois, undated.

97. Reba to Shirley Graham Du Bois, 1 November 1971.

98. Shirley Graham Du Bois to Reba, 11 November 1971.

99. Shirley Graham Du Bois to John Oliver Killens, 9 December 1972.

100. Brindley Benn to Shirley Graham Du Bois, 3 October 1974.

101. Shirley Graham Du Bois to Brindley Benn, 18 September 1972.

102. Shirley Graham Du Bois to Bernard Jaffe, 15 September 1972.

103. Shirley Graham Du Bois, "Together We Struggle, Together We Win," *Black Scholar* 6, no. 7 (April 1975): 36–40; Shirley Graham Du Bois, "The Liberation of Africa: Power, Peace and Justice," *Black Scholar* 2, no. 6 (February 1971): 32–37; Shirley Graham Du Bois, "A Ghanaian Questions All-India Radio," *Eastern Horizon* 7, no. 3 (May–June 1968): 49–52; Shirley Graham Du Bois, "Sierra Leone Throws Off Military Dictatorship," *Eastern Horizon* 7, no. 4 (July–August 1968): 53–58.

104. Shirley Graham Du Bois to Kwame Nkrumah, 1 March 1964.

105. Shirley Graham Du Bois to T. Iue, 24 January 1974.

106. K. Funabashi to Shirley Graham Du Bois, 4 July 1966.

107. Shirley Graham Du Bois to K. Funabashi, 9 July 1966.

108. K. Funabashi to Shirley Graham Du Bois, 4 March 1974.

109. Shirley Graham Du Bois to David Du Bois, 15 February 1968, David Du Bois Papers.

110. John Bracey, interview by author, 4 December 1996. See also Nelson Noel Messone, "Japan's Foreign Aid to Africa: International and Domestic Determinants" (Ph.D. diss., University of Kentucky, 1994); Willard H. Elsbree, *Japan's Role in Southeast Asian Nationalist Movements, 1940 to 1945* (Cambridge: Harvard University Press, 1953); Richard Bradshaw, "Japan and European Colonialism in Africa, 1800–1937" (Ph.D. diss., Ohio University, 1992); Musa Adamu, "Japan and Sub-Saharan Africa: A Study of Contemporary Economic and Diplomatic History, 1960–1984" (Ph.D. diss., University of Pennsylvania, 1988); Leonard J. Schoppa, *Bargaining with Japan: What American Pressure Can and Cannot Do* (New York: Columbia University Press, 1997).

111. Shirley Graham Du Bois to Michael Kotov, 10 June 1971.

112. Miriam Makeba to Shirley Graham Du Bois, undated: "I was happy to see Mr. Carmichael even though I did not meet him. I hope it will be possible for me to at least shake his hand. You had said something about President Nkrumah wanting to have us for lunch or dinner one day. I would like to see him again before I leave."

113. *Final Call,* 24 November 1998.

114. Miriam Makeba with James Hall, *Makeba: My Story* (New York: New American Library, 1987), 168.

115. Stokeley Carmichael to Lorna Smith, 23 February 1970, box 4, Stokeley Carmichael Papers.

116. Stokeley Carmichael to Lorna Smith, 26 December 1970, box 4, Stokeley Carmichael Papers.

117. Stokeley Carmichael to Lorna Smith, 19 March 1972, box 4, Stokeley Carmichael Papers. See also Janet G. Vaillant, *Black, French and African: A Life of Leopold Senghor* (Cambridge: Harvard University Press, 1990).

118. Jan Bailey to Lorna Smith, 3 November 1972, box 4, Stokeley Carmichael Papers.

119. Sally Belfrage to Lorna Smith, 19 June 1966, box 4, Stokeley Carmichael Papers. See also Sally Belfrage, *Un-American Activities: A Memoir of the Fifties* (New York: HarperCollins, 1994).

120. Stokeley Carmichael to Lorna Smith, 23 August 1966, box 4, Stokeley Carmichael Papers.

121. Brindley Benn to Shirley Graham Du Bois, 15 May 1970. Subsequently, Nkrumah too criticized sharply Carmichael's view of "Black Power"; he "told him not to visit" him in Guinea, as he was "disappointed by his lack of personal discipline" and "his racialist views." See June Milne, *Kwame Nkrumah: A Biography* (London: Panaf, 1999), 228.

122. Shirley Graham Du Bois to "Dear Friend," 9 June 1970.

123. Shirley Graham Du Bois to Michael Thelwell, 16 April 1974: "Stokeley C. spent several days here with me in February." Stokeley Carmichael to Shirley Graham Du Bois, 5 December 1973: "Dear Grandma." Graham Du Bois's fondness for "Black Power" diverged from Nkrumah's growing alienation with this philosophy: See Kwame Nkrumah, *The Struggle Continues* London: Panaf, 1973; Nkrumah, *Class Struggle in Africa* (London: Panaf, 1970).

124. Alice Childress, "For a Negro Theatre," *Masses & Mainstream* 49, no. 2 (February 1951): 61–64, 61.

125. Shirley Graham Du Bois, "Emergence of the African Personality," *Mainstream* 13, no. 11 (November 1960): 25–31, 27, 29.

126. Shirley Graham Du Bois to Kwame Nkrumah, 30 February 1969, box 154-3, Kwame Nkrumah Papers.

127. Shirley Graham Du Bois to "My Dear Little Brother," 20 February 1967.

128. Shirley Graham Du Bois to Andrew Paschal, 8 October 1972; Jessica Smith to Shirley Graham Du Bois, 13 November 1970: "it seems to me so unfair in what is said about the CPUSA and its attitude toward the Soviet Union and China, and about the SU itself." Increasingly Graham Du Bois was coming to share an idea expressed to her by Robert F. Williams, "Many internationalists

are making the mistake of trying to analyze the Afro-American problem strictly from a class point of view. They want to downgrade its cruel racist aspects in the name of a mythological black and white working class unity. . . . Yours for BLACK POWER." Robert F. Williams to Shirley Graham Du Bois, 14 April 1967. The problem was that this was a caricature of the *Freedomways* position; it was difficult to find any Afro-American Marxist in the 1960s who professed the view articulated by Williams, least of all the Communists, who for the longest time preached the idea of self-determination for the "black nation" in the South. See Horne, *Black Liberation/Red Scare*.

129. Shirley Graham Du Bois to Patricia Romero, 1 October 1973.

130. *Muhammad Speaks*, 24 August 1973. See also John Henrik Clarke to Shirley Graham Du Bois, 29 September 1970:

A Committee of Concerned Black Scholars, including John Killens, Lerone Bennett, Vincent Harding, and myself has been asked by members of the Congress of African Peoples which met in Atlanta recently, to see you relative to their deep concern over the papers of W. E. B. Du Bois which are now in the hands of Herbert Aptheker. It is their opinion that these papers should be in a Black institution such as Atlanta, Fisk or Howard. I concur with this opinion.

131. *Muhammad Speaks*, 11 January 1974; Charles 67X (Moreland) to Shirley Graham Du Bois, 24 January 1974.

132. Zachary Lockman, *Workers and Working Classes in the Middle East: Struggles, Histories, Historiographies* (Albany: State University of New York Press, 1994); Joel Beinin, *Workers on the Nile: Nationalism, Communism, Islam and the Egyptian Working Class, 1882–1954* (Princeton: Princeton University Press, 1987); Zachary Lockman, *Comrades and Enemies: Arab and Jewish Workers in Palestine, 1906–1948* (Berkeley: University of California Press, 1996).

133. Martin A. Lee, *The Beast Reawakens* (Boston: Little, Brown, 1997), 124.

134. Wang Suolao, "Friendship between Nasser and Zhou," *ChinAfrica*, no. 90 (June 1998): 42–44.

135. Africa Company Ltd. to Shirley Graham Du Bois, circa January 1974.

136. Shirley Graham to "Christine," 18 September 1974.

137. Shirley Graham to Gora, 10 October 1972: "I've tried repeatedly to reach anybody at the PAC office." E. L. Makoti to Shirley Graham Du Bois, 7 May 1968: he sends back issues of *Azania News*, a PAC publication, to her office in Beijing. T. Mutizwa to Shirley Graham Du Bois, 3 May 1968: writing from the offices of the Zimbabwe African National Union (ZANU) in Tanzania, he also sends her literature. Tunguru Huaraka to Shirley Graham Du Bois, 29 May 1968: this representative of Namibia's SouthWest African National Union (SWANU) in London referred to "renegade revisionists led by the Soviet Union ruling cabal." Arthur Campos to Shirley Graham Du Bois, 9 March 1969: this Mozam-

bican dissident assailed the "revisionists" working with FRELIMO (Movement for the Liberation of Mozambique), which continues to rule this African nation.

138. Shirley Graham Du Bois to Julius Nyerere, 18 June 1974.

139. Julius Nyerere to Shirley Graham Du Bois, 27 April 1974. See also Colin Legum and Geoffrey Mmari, eds., *Mwalimu: The Influence of Nyerere* (Trenton: Africa World Press, 1995).

140. Shirley Graham Du Bois to Huang Hua, 1 October 1973.

141. Shirley Graham Du Bois, *Julius Nyerere: Teacher of Africa* (New York: Julian Messner, 1975).

NOTES TO CHAPTER 11

1. Shirley Graham Du Bois to Bernard Jaffe, 12 June 1970.

2. Shirley Graham Du Bois to Bernard Jaffe, 1 January 1970.

3. Report, 24 March 1970, no. 100-370965, FBI.

4. Clipping, *Sacramento Observer*, 14–20 November 1974, Shirley Graham Du Bois Papers. He was a native Oregonian; his father owned the first black-owned hotel west of the Mississippi River. He once taught piano at both Howard and Fisk and served as pianist and accompanist to Todd Duncan. He owned real estate in Maui and had lived in San Francisco for two decades.

5. Shirley Graham Du Bois to Ho Li-Liang, 22 February 1970.

6. Shirley Graham Du Bois to "My Dear Brother David," 3 May 1970.

7. Shirley Graham Du Bois to Reba, 8 March 1970.

8. Shirley Graham Du Bois to Kathy, 9 February 1970.

9. John Erlichman to Richard Nixon, circa 1970, box 1, White House Central File, Subject Files, Immigration-Naturalization, 1969–1970, Nixon Presidential Materials Project.

10. Egil Krogh to Ken Cole, 15 June 1970, box 1, White House Central File, Subject Files, Immigration-Naturalization, 1969–1970, Nixon Presidential Materials Project.

11. Raymond Farrell, Immigration and Naturalization Service, to Egil Krogh, 12 June 1970, box 1, White House Central File, Subject Files, Immigration-Naturalization, 1969–1970, Nixon Presidential Materials Project.

12. Congressman Edward Koch to Egil Krogh, 27 May 1970, box 1, White House Central File, Subject Files, Immigration-Naturalization, 1969–1970, Nixon Presidential Materials Project.

13. *Congressional Record*, 4 August 1970, Box 143, Senate Internal Security Subcommittee Papers.

14. *Afro-American*, 13 June 1970.

15. Shirley Graham Du Bois to C. Eric Lincoln, president of Black Academy of Arts and Letters, box 4, Black Academy of Arts and Letters Papers.

16. *New York Times*, 5 May 1970; *New York Amsterdam News*, 9 May 1970.

17. *New York Times,* 12 May 1970; Shirley Graham Du Bois to editor, *New York Times,* 27 July 1970.

18. Shirley Graham Du Bois to Richard Stevens, 29 April 1970.

19. Shirley Graham Du Bois to Bernard Jaffe, 26 August 1970.

20. *Washington Star,* 4 May 1970.

21. *Washington Post,* 26 November 1970.

22. Shirley Graham Du Bois to Nathan Hare, 8 August 1970.

23. Shirley Graham Du Bois to Eva, 14 July 1970.

24. *Washington Post,* 8 November 1970.

25. Shirley Graham Du Bois, "Return after Ten Years," *Freedomways* 11, no. 2 (second quarter 1971): 158–69.

26. See Gerald Horne, *Fire This Time: The Watts Uprising and the 1960s* (Charlottesville: University Press of Virginia, 1995).

27. Appearances, 1970, Shirley Graham Du Bois Papers; *Kansas City Star,* 29 November 1970; *Cornell Daily Sun,* 22 January 1971.

28. Ewart Guinier to Shirley Graham Du Bois, 9 February 1971.

29. *Harvard Crimson,* 22 January 1971; Roger Rosenblatt, "Commission of Inquiry of Faculty Council of Faculty of Arts and Sciences," 1971, box 31, folder 3, Ewart Guinier Papers.

30. Shirley Graham Du Bois, "Return after Ten Years." *New York Times,* 23 January 1971.

31. Sylvia Boone to Shirley Graham Du Bois, 19 February 1971; *New York Times,* 14 December 1970.

32. Nathan Hare to Shirley Graham Du Bois, 20 October 1970.

33. *San Francisco Examiner,* 9 November 1970.

34. *San Francisco Chronicle,* 9 November 1970.

35. *Los Angeles Times,* 15 November 1970.

36. *Jet,* 3 September 1970; Richard Hatcher speech, 2 September 1970, box 4, Black Academy of Arts and Letters Papers.

37. Shirley Graham Du Bois to Elizabeth Moos, undated.

38. *San Francisco Examiner,* 2 August 1971.

39. Shirley Graham Du Bois to Bernard Jaffe, 22 August 1966.

40. *New York Amsterdam News,* 18 May 1974.

41. Shirley Graham Du Bois, *Zulu Heart* (New York: Third Press, 1974), 23, 45, 46, 48, 50, 136, 195.

42. "Shirley Graham Du Bois," *Sepia,* January 1975, Hatch-Billops Collection.

43. Shirley Graham Du Bois, interview, undated (circa 1972), Shirley Graham Du Bois Papers.

44. Maya Angelou to Julian Mayfield, 23 May 1975, box 4, Julian Mayfield Papers; David Du Bois, . . . *And Bid Him Sing: A Novel* (Palo Alto: Ramparts Press, 1975).

45. "Greetings from Shirley Graham Du Bois in Cairo, Egypt to the Pan-African Student Organization of Lincoln University, Celebrating African Freedom Day, May 15, 1970," Louis Massiah Papers: inter alia, she praises the recent revolution in Libya that brought Muammar Qaddafi to power; Shirley Graham Du Bois, article on Palestinians, 1 July 1970, George Murphy Papers.

46. Shirley Graham Du Bois to Vivian Hallinan, 16 October 1973.

47. Shirley Graham Du Bois to David Du Bois, 18 October 1973.

48. Shirley Graham Du Bois, interview, March 1974, *Osagyefo*, Shirley Graham Du Bois Papers.

49. Shirley Graham Du Bois to Sterling Stuckey, 15 March 1974; Sterling Stuckey to Shirley Graham Du Bois, 30 October 1973; Shirley Graham Du Bois to David Du Bois, 2 July 1974.

50. Shirley Graham Du Bois to G. M. Stephens, 26 October 1964.

51. Herbert Aptheker to Shirley Graham Du Bois, 2 June 1964.

52. Shirley Graham Du Bois to C. L. R. James, 22 June 1973.

53. Gerald Horne, *Black and Red: W. E. B. Du Bois and the Afro-American Response to the Cold War, 1944–1963* (Albany: State University of New York Press, 1986).

54. Patricia Romero to Shirley Graham Du Bois, 16 September 1973.

55. Shirley Graham Du Bois to Secretary, Working Peoples Vanguard Party–Guyana, 25 January 1974.

56. Shirley Graham Du Bois to Bill, 22 July 1974.

57. Shirley Graham Du Bois to Howard Fast, 27 June 1972.

58. Shirley Graham Du Bois to Barrie Stavis, 26 June 1972.

59. Shirley Graham Du Bois to Andrew Paschal, 8 October 1972.

60. Shirley Graham Du Bois to David Du Bois, 28 November 1972.

61. Shirley Graham Du Bois to Bertha, 29 August 1974.

62. Martha Dodd to Shirley Graham Du Bois, 27 April 1973.

63. Shirley Graham Du Bois to Martha Dodd, 21 June 1973.

64. Shirley Graham Du Bois to Huang Hua, 1 October 1973; Shirley Graham Du Bois to Bernard Jaffe, 18 June 1974.

65. Shirley Graham Du Bois to Vivian Gornick, 21 November 1973.

66. Shirley Graham Du Bois to Bernard Jaffe, 15 December 1973.

67. The young historian David Levering Lewis met the "vivacious sixty-seven year old widow" in Ghana: "oddly of that meeting with Graham-Du Bois," he recounted years later, "I recall only a pleasing flirtatiousness that was rather surprising in a woman of her years." David Levering Lewis, "Ghana, 1963," *American Scholar* 68, no. 1 (winter 1999): 39–60, 48.

68. Shirley Graham Du Bois to Bernard Jaffe, 17 July 1974.

69. Bernard Jaffe to Shirley Graham Du Bois, 8 February 1974.

70. This same amateur therapist could conclude, as well, that for various

reasons—male supremacy decisively included—she had real difficulty in navigating intergender relations, period.

71. David Du Bois to Julian Mayfield, 22 May 1971, box 4, Julian Mayfield Papers.

72. Shirley Graham Du Bois to Bernard Jaffe, 22 March 1974.

73. Shirley Graham Du Bois to Roger, 5 April 1973.

74. Vivian Hallinan to Shirley Graham Du Bois, 27 February 1967.

75. Shirley Graham Du Bois to Vivian Hallinan, 22 April 1969.

76. Vivian Hallinan to Shirley Graham Du Bois, 1 May 1969.

77. Shirley Graham Du Bois to Dorothy Markinko, 30 April 1974.

78. *Ghanaian Times*, 15 July 1960.

79. *Ghanaian Times*, 12 July 1960, 16 July 1960.

80. See, e.g., Sara Evans, *Personal Politics: The Roots of Women's Liberation in the Civil Rights Movement and the New Left* (New York: Vintage, 1979); Patricia Morton, *Disfigured Images: The Historical Assault on Afro-American Women* (Westport: Praeger, 1991).

81. Takyiwah Manuh, "Women and Their Organizations during the Convention Peoples' Party Period," in Kwame Arhin, ed., *The Life and Work of Kwame Nkrumah: Papers of a Symposium Organized by the Institute of African Studies, University of Ghana–Legon* (Trenton: Africa World Press, 199)3, 101–22, 108. See also Catherine Coquery-Vidrovitch, *African Women: A Modern History* (Boulder: Westview, 1997); Mercy A. Oduyoye, *Daughters of Anowa: African Women and Patriarchy* (New York: Orbis Books, 1995).

82. Shirley Graham Du Bois to Bettina Aptheker, 3 February 1972.

83. Shirley Graham Du Bois to David Du Bois, 25 December 1972: she added, "I do think Angela D. would have done better to have stopped in at [least] one African country when she was travelling rather than to have spent all her time with the white folks! . . . [Tanzania was] frightfully disappointed because she did not accept their invitation."

84. Shirley Graham Du Bois to Irene, 18 July 1974. See, e.g., Christina Kelley Gilmartin, *Engendering the Chinese Revolution: Radical Women, Communist Politics, and Mass Movements in the 1920s* (Berkeley: University of California Press, 1995). The tangled skein of gender politics in China sheds light on Graham Du Bois's own feminist consciousness. Though the Chinese Communist Party employed feminist rhetoric, men monopolized top posts as theoreticians and policy makers. The influence of powerful women like Xiang Jingyu often depended on their relationships to men.

85. Clipping, 6 June 1973, Shirley Graham Du Bois Papers; *New Yorker*, 16 July 1973; Bernard Jaffe to Shirley Graham Du Bois, 23 March 1973: "the total amount being paid is $15,000.00 a year for ten years. If you die before the end of ten years, the balance is reduced by a third. . . . I estimate that with the other

contractual income and royalties to be anticipated that you could average, with the payments under this contract, about $25,000 per year for the next ten years."

86. Shirley Graham Du Bois to Bernard Jaffe, 20 August 1972.

87. Bernard Jaffe to Shirley Graham Du Bois, 13 July 1972.

88. Shirley Graham Du Bois to Herbert Aptheker, 19 August 1972.

89. Shirley Graham Du Bois to Bernard Jaffe, 20 August 1972.

90. Shirley Graham Du Bois to Mr. Kamuma, 24 July 1975.

91. Shirley Graham Du Bois to Martha Dodd and Alfred Stern, 24 July 1975.

92. Bernard Jaffe to Shirley Graham Du Bois, 19 July 1974.

93. Shirley Graham Du Bois to John Bracey, 16 July 1975.

94. Syllabus, 1975 course, John Bracey Papers.

95. John Bracey to Jeremiah Allen, 11 April 1976, John Bracey Papers.

96. *New York Times*, 10 January 1976.

97. *Guardian*, 19 March 1975.

98. *Guardian*, 9 July 1975.

99. *Black Panther*, 5 April 1975, no. 100-370965, FBI. See also Elaine Brown, *A Taste of Power: A Black Woman's Story* (New York: Pantheon, 1992).

100. Shirley Graham Du Bois to Bernard Jaffe, undated.

101. Allison John African (English) Audience Research–BBC, London, to Akpan Udoh (Lagos), 14 June 1973, Shirley Graham Du Bois Papers (Prof. Bracey sent a copy of this letter to her).

102. Shirley Graham Du Bois to Prof. Artz, 4 May 1973.

103. Shirley Graham Du Bois to Accra Health Department, 8 May 1965.

104. Shirley Graham Du Bois to D. A. Graham 18 December 1966.

105. Shirley Graham Du Bois to Bernard Jaffe, 9 April 1967.

106. Shirley Graham Du Bois to David Du Bois, 30 August 1972.

107. Shirley Graham Du Bois to Bernard Jaffe, 15 December 1973.

108. Shirley Graham Du Bois to Bernard Jaffe, 15 February 1974.

109. Shirley Graham Du Bois to Bernard Jaffe, 19 July 1975.

110. John Bracey, interview by author, 4 December 1996.

111. Abstract of medical history, 19 September 1976, Shirley Graham Du Bois Papers.

112. Shirley Graham Du Bois to David Du Bois, 27 July 1976.

113. David Du Bois to Bernard Jaffe, 28 July 1976, David Du Bois Papers.

114. Dorothy Markinko to Shirley Graham Du Bois, 12 April 1976.

115. Shirley Graham Du Bois to Charlotte and Reubie, 20 April 1976.

116. Jacob Aronoff to Shirley Graham Du Bois, 26 May 1977.

117. Shirley Graham Du Bois to Bernard Jaffe, 15 September 1976.

118. Shirley Graham Du Bois to Charlotte Klate, 26 October 1976.

119. Marni Rosner to John Bracey, 2 July 1976, Shirley Graham Du Bois Papers.

120. David Du Bois to Ramona Edelin, 24 March 1977, Shirley Graham Du Bois Papers.

121. Diary, 1977, Shirley Graham Du Bois Papers.

122. Elsa to David Du Bois, 5 April 1977, Shirley Graham Du Bois Papers.

Index

Abrahams, Peter, 219
Abt, John, 228
Adams, Clarence, 234–35
Africa: African Americans and, 27, 59, 165, 168, 191, 248, 275n. 57; in Afro-American theater, 293n. 59; Algeria, 200, 203, 210; Angola, 195, 237, 278n. 67; Burundi, 202; Central African Republic; Chinese offensive in, 326n. 22; Dahomey, 202; decolonization, 30, 34–35; Du Bois on socialism and, 156; in Graham Du Bois's *Tom-Tom,* 62; Guinea, 165, 239, 243; Nigeria, 199, 202; Organization of African Unity, 174, 178, 186; political instability in 1960s, 202; Rhodesia, 195, 202; Robeson on future of, 106; U.S. concern about Communism in, 169; U.S. foreign relations ignoring, 171. *See also* Congo; Egypt; Ghana; South Africa; Tanzania
African Americans: and Africa, 27, 59, 165, 168, 191, 248, 275n. 57; and anticommunism, 109–10, 157; Chinese proclaim solidarity with, 29, 232–34; color privilege, 3; and Communist Party, 32–35, 78, 94, 142–43, 306n. 101; and Democratic Party, 158; in Federal Theater Project, 73–74; at Fort Huachuca, 91–95; and Ghana, 27, 183, 186–87, 191–94, 206; Gilpin Players, 85; Karamu Theater, 59–60, 84–85; at Oberlin College, 63, 64; in Paris, 53; Rosenwald Fund for, 79–80, 81, 126; social interaction with as signifying leftist sympathies, 149; the Talented Tenth, 63, 136, 148; theater of, 56, 74, 293n. 59; unemployment in the 1930s, 55; westward migration during the war, 90–91, 303n. 23. *See also* African American women; black nationalism; civil rights movement; segregation

African American women: avoiding the Left in 1950s, 145; Bennett College, 117; black motherhood and black nationalism, 275n. 51; composers, 57; dramatists, 56; at Fort Huachuca, 91–92; as laundry workers, 64; memorializing famous husbands, 22; patriarchy's effect on, 21; serial identities assumed by, 3; war boom improving economic status of, 90–91
African Methodist Episcopal (AME) Church, 39, 289n. 51
African National Congress, 232
Afrifa, A. A., 202
Afrocentrism, 14, 27, 59, 214, 243, 247, 258, 268n. 27
Alexander, Sadie, 90
Algeria, 200, 203, 210
Ali, Muhammad (Cassius Clay), 192
Allen, William, 244, 340n. 4
American Committee for the Protection of the Foreign Born, 144
American Intercontinental Peace Conference (1952), 145–46
American Labor Party, 114
American Women for Peace, 146
Ampex International, 203
Angelou, Maya, 19, 24, 122, 174, 189
Angola, 195, 237, 278n. 67
Annan, Kofi, 207
anticommunism: African Americans as less influenced by, 109–10, 157; antifascist alliance muting, 13; in black nationalism's development, 29, 191; the Cold War, 24, 29–30, 111, 144, 155; as damaging cause of racial equality, 32; Graham Du Bois resisting, 25; Korean War as escalating, 121; McCarthyism, 148–49, 247, 273n. 39; of Nixon, 236
Appiah, J. E., 171

About the Author

GERALD HORNE is Professor and Director of the Institute of African-American Research at the University of North Carolina, Chapel Hill. He is currently a Fulbright Scholar, University of Hong Kong, and author, most recently, of *Fire This Time: The Watts Uprising and the 1960s.*